The Music and Thought of Michael Tippett

Tippett is often cast as a composer with a strong visionary streak, but what does that mean for a twentieth-century artist? In this multi-faceted study, David Clarke explores Tippett's complex creative imagination – its dialogue between a romantic's aspirations to the ideal and absolute, and a modernist's sceptical realism. He shows how the musical formations of works such as *The Midsummer Marriage*, *King Priam* and *The Vision of Saint Augustine* resonate with the aesthetic and theoretical ideas of key figures in modern Western culture – some known to have been influential on the composer (such as Jung, Wagner and Yeats), others not usually associated with him (such as Kant, Nietzsche and Adorno). These interpretations illuminate the struggle between the rational and irrational in Tippett's music, and suggest that this might ultimately contain an apprehension of an emancipated future society. Analyses of late works such as the Triple Concerto and *Byzantium* also speculate on Tippett's gay sexuality as a (literally) critical element in his creative and political consciousness.

DAVID CLARKE is Senior Lecturer in Music at the University of Newcastle upon Tyne and is one of the leading commentators on the music of Tippett. He is the author of *Language, Form, and Structure in the Music of Michael Tippett* (2 vols., 1989) and the editor of *Tippett Studies* (Cambridge University Press, 1999).

Music in the Twentieth Century

GENERAL EDITOR Arnold Whittall

This series offers a wide perspective on music and musical life in the twentieth century. Books included range from historical and biographical studies concentrating particularly on the context and circumstances in which composers were writing, to analytical and critical studies concerned with the nature of musical language and questions of compositional process. The importance given to context will also be reflected in studies dealing with, for example, the patronage, publishing, and promotion of new music, and in accounts of the musical life of particular countries.

Recent titles

The Music of John Cage
James Pritchett
0 521 56544 8

The Music of Ruth Crawford Seeger
Joseph Straus
0 521 41646 9

The Music of Conlon Nancarrow
Kyle Gann
0 521 46534 6

The Stravinsky Legacy
Jonathan Cross
0 521 56365 8

Experimental Music: Cage and Beyond
Michael Nyman
0 521 65297 9 (hardback) 0 521 65383 5 (paperback)

The BBC and Ultra-Modern Music, 1922–1936
Jennifer Doctor
0 521 66117 X

The Music of Harrison Birtwistle
Robert Adlington
0 521 63082 7

Four Musical Minimalists: La Monte Young, Terry Riley, Steve Reich, Philip Glass
Keith Potter
0 521 48250 X

Fauré and French Musical Aesthetics
Carlo Caballero
0 521 78107 8

The Music of Tōru Takemitsu
Peter Burt
0 521 78220 1

The Music and Thought of Michael Tippett

Modern Times and Metaphysics

David Clarke

CAMBRIDGE
UNIVERSITY PRESS

PUBLISHED BY THE PRESS SYNDICATE OF THE UNIVERSITY OF CAMBRIDGE
The Pitt Building, Trumpington Street, Cambridge, United Kingdom

CAMBRIDGE UNIVERSITY PRESS
The Edinburgh Building, Cambridge CB2 2RU, UK
40 West 20th Street, New York NY 10011–4211, USA
10 Stamford Road, Oakleigh, VIC 3166, Australia
Ruiz de Alarcón 13, 28014 Madrid, Spain
Dock House, The Waterfront, Cape Town 8001, South Africa

http://www.cambridge.org

First published 2001

Printed in the United Kingdom at the University Press, Cambridge

Typeface 10.5/13.5pt Minion in QuarkXPress™ [SE]

A catalogue record for this book is available from the British Library

Library of Congress Cataloguing in Publication Data

Clarke, David (David Ian)
The music and thought of Michael Tippett : modern times and metaphysics / David Clarke.
p.   cm. – (Music in the 20th century)
Includes bibliographical references and index.
ISBN 0 521 58292 X
1. Tippett, Michael, 1905 – Criticism and interpretation.   I. Title.   II. Music in the
twentieth century.
ML410.T467 C62   2001
780.92–dc21   00–052994

ISBN 0 521 58292 X hardback

To my colleagues: Ian, Eric, Agustín, Richard and Magnus

And in memory of my late colleague, Isobel

Last, not least, to Davey

Moral and metaphysical ideas and symbols are as indispensable to Mr Tippett as Celtic mythology or Indian theosophy was to Yeats; even when they are obscure, they convey to the straining, often puzzled, but always moved and at times wholly transported listener a vision of experience about whose authenticity there can be no doubt.

(Isaiah Berlin, in *Michael Tippett: A Symposium on his 60th Birthday*, ed. Ian Kemp (London: Faber and Faber, 1965), 62)

The metaphysical categories live on, secularized . . . What metaphysics has to ponder is the extent to which [subjects] are nonetheless able to see beyond themselves.

(Theodor W. Adorno, *Negative Dialectics*, trans. E. B. Ashton (London: Routledge, 1996), 376)

Contents

Acknowledgements

My thanks go to the numerous individuals, institutions and organizations who have helped in the making of this book.

Jim Samson initially spurred me to consider such a project. Arnold Whittall, as series editor and Tippett specialist, has been magnificently helpful at every stage; I am grateful not least for the valuable comments he offered on draft chapters. Penny Souster of Cambridge University Press has been supportive and patient throughout. Her contribution and the work of the editorial and production team at Cambridge are greatly appreciated. Thanks are also due to Ian Phillips-Kerr for his expert setting of the musical examples.

The Arts and Humanities Research Board and the University of Newcastle upon Tyne funded research leave without which this project would have taken significantly longer to complete. Schott and Co. Ltd kindly gave permission to quote from Tippett's works, and also made various scores and recordings available to me. Boosey and Hawkes Music Publishers Ltd granted permission for the Stravinsky quotation in chapter 7. This book's two epigraphic quotations from Isaiah Berlin and Theodor W. Adorno are cited by permission of (respectively) Faber and Faber Ltd, and Routledge. Chapters 2 and 6 below originally appeared as articles in the *Journal of the Royal Musical Association* (vols. 121/1 and 125/1 respectively), and parts of the text of my article 'Visionary images' published in vol. 136, No. 1823 of *The Musical Times* have been recycled in chapters 1 and 5; I am grateful to the editors and publishers of both the journals concerned for permission to reuse this material. The jacket photograph of Tippett contemplating his portrait by Kokoschka was taken by David Stone and is the property of Morley College; I am indebted to the College for its loan, and to Jane Hartwell of Morley Gallery for her liaison in this matter.

Ron Woodley, Simon Jarvis and Edward Venn kindly let me see typescript versions of articles of theirs prior to publication. Meirion (Bill) Bowen provided information in response to numerous enquiries about Tippett. Max Paddison, Richard Middleton and Ian Biddle gave of their time to read and comment on parts of the typescript in draft (the responsibility for the content of the final text is of course my own). And my research students Rowena Harrison, Richard Pye, Paul Fleet and Iain Stannard have offered much mental stimulus during this book's gestation.

Now to the dedicatees of this book. I am indebted to my present colleagues in the Music Department at Newcastle University – Ian Biddle, Eric Cross, Agustín Fernández, Richard Middleton and Magnus Williamson – for their convivial company, their intellectual dialogue, their continuing interest in this project, and especially their forbearance in its final stages when I might otherwise have spent more time working alongside them. I hope too that my late colleague Isobel Preece might have found some of the values I have expounded in what follows not too remote from her own; in remembering her here I make a belated peace offering. And lastly my thanks and love to David Robinson: the lively dialogue of our different worldviews has, I am sure, subtly affected this book for the better; certainly his presence has done much to assuage the loneliness of the long-distance monograph writer.

References to Tippett's scores and essays

With few exceptions Tippett's scores employ rehearsal figures rather than bar numbers. Accordingly, score references in this volume employ the term 'Fig.', with suffixes where necessary to designate points a given number of bars before or after the rehearsal figure in question. For example, 'Fig. 2^{+4}' means 'four bars after Figure 2', or 'the fourth bar of Figure 2' (taking the first bar to be that in which the figure itself appears); conversely, 'Fig. 7^{-1}' means 'one bar before Figure 7'.

Most of Tippett's essays were originally compiled in the now out-of-print collections *Moving into Aquarius* and *Music of the Angels: Essays and Sketchbooks* (ed. Meirion Bowen). Many, though not all, of these writings are included alongside others (some new) in the more recent *Tippett on Music* (ed. Bowen). When an essay appearing in one of the earlier anthologies as well as in *Tippett on Music* is cited below, references are given to both volumes, though any quoted material is from the earlier version of the text if there is any variation.

1 Tippett and the 'world vision' of modernity

The concept of 'world vision' and the concept of modernity

> On the plane of personal psychology, there are no people more different than
> the poet, who creates particular beings and things, and the philosopher, who
> thinks and expresses himself by means of general concepts . . . [Yet] we must
> accept the existence of a reality which goes beyond them as individuals and
> finds its expression in their work. It is this which I intend to call the *world
> vision*.

At a crucial point in his career Michael Tippett (1905–98) would probably
have read these lines. The book from which they come, Lucien Goldmann's
The Hidden God, is appropriately discussed in the Tippett literature as
being influential on the tragic conception of the composer's second opera
King Priam (1958–62).[1] But Goldmann's text affords other possibilities
too. For one thing it offers me a way round the invidious problem of beginning this book, which – because it deals with a complex of issues where
none takes priority over the others – has no natural starting point. In the
spirit of the present volume I want to use Goldmann as an interpretative
catalyst or intermediary through which to read out certain of Tippett's
own values.

Tippett's growth to artistic maturity is rightly correlated with the technical development of his musical language. Yet his claim to the status of
composer of stature depends on something beyond this: something which
conforms to that characteristic Goldmann terms 'world vision'. The
notion, which he adapts from Wilhelm Dilthey, refers to 'the whole
complex of ideas, aspirations and feelings which links together the
members of a social group'. Goldmann continues:

> A philosophy or work of art can keep its value outside the time and place
> where it first appeared only if, by expressing a particular human situation, it
> transposes this on to the plane of the great human problems created by man's
> relationship with his fellows and with the universe.[2]

No doubt Tippett would have empathized with these sentiments. Indeed
the words themselves appear to find an echo many years later in his
description of *The Mask of Time* (1980–2) as a response to 'the most fundamental matters bearing upon man, his relationship with time, his place
in the world as we know it and in the mysterious universe at large'.[3] No one

could accuse Tippett of humble artistic pretensions! Whatever the hazards of operating on 'the plane of the great human problems', the fact that he risked doing so forms an irrefutable part of his chemistry and significance as a composer. Perhaps the first work where this tendency became evident was *A Child of our Time* (1931–41), and thereafter all his operas and choral–orchestral works were in one way or another concerned with making big statements about the human condition. But the trait is discernible – often as a preoccupation with the 'visionary' – in the instrumental and orchestral works too. It would be remiss, of course, to characterize Tippett's entire *œuvre* in this way, but the engagement with 'grand narratives' (to borrow a term from Lyotard) is certainly a vital stream within it, and it forms a key ingredient of this book's subject matter.

What makes such impossibly grandiose aspirations potentially tractable (for the musicologist as well as the composer) is the mediation of the universal in the particular – a point evident in the preceding quotations from Goldmann, and also in his observation that 'as we move away from the abstract idea of the world vision, so we find that the individual details of each vision are linked to historical situations localised in place and time, and even to the individual personality of the writer or thinker in question'.[4] Concentrating for the moment on the middleground of this panorama, what is the historical situation to which Tippett's world vision relates?

Even here, the scope is anything but modest. What Tippett engages with in many of his major works (even though he does not quite put it this way) is nothing less than the social, epistemological and psychological conditions of Western modernity. This is modernity considered as a historical *longue durée*: the period from around the time of the age of Enlightenment (some would place it earlier) to the present day. To define its conditions in a nutshell is a tall order. But a working basis is found among theoretical accounts which characterize modern consciousness as *divided* following reason's rise in the Enlightenment to the West's dominant paradigm of knowledge. Whereas, so such narratives run, the received dogma of religion had, in pre-modern times, provided men and women with a unified basis for their perception of the world, their moral conduct and their sensuous being, reason's dominion over conceptual knowledge causes a schism between that realm and those of ethics and other, sensory sources of insight. As J. M. Bernstein puts it:

> Modernity is the separation of spheres, the becoming autonomous of truth,
> beauty and goodness from one another, and their developing into self-
> sufficient forms of practice: modern science and technology, private
> morality and modern legal forms, and modern art. This categorial

separation of domains represents the dissolution of the metaphysical
totalities of the pre-modern age.[5]

Tippett was neither an intellectual historian nor a cultural theorist, yet
lying in the background of his *œuvre* are comparable perceptions.
Although he tended to fasten on to the more directly instrumental manifestations of a dominant rationality (science, technology and mass industrialization) and the more overtly catastrophic consequences of its eclipse
of the spiritual (Auschwitz, Hiroshima and the Gulag), it is clear that he
recognized the separation of epistemology, ethics and aesthetics into discrete domains as fundamental to the problematics of our contemporary
condition. (As writer, pacifist and composer Tippett engaged with each of
these spheres, and though the last role came most obviously first, his art
would be of lesser consequence had his path to individuation not also
encompassed moral action and theoretical reflection; only because of this
does the label 'a man of our time' not degenerate into a cliché.) One pertinent example of his awareness of the division of experience into autonomous domains comes in the postscript to his essay 'What I believe'. Here
he posits a dualism familiar in his writings, between the 'outer' world of
empirical reality and the 'inner' world of a reality left uncharted by
rationality:

> I believe in a reality of the physical world outside, experienced through the
> senses and formulated generally by the scientific intelligence.
>   I believe also in a reality of the spiritual world within, experienced, in my
> own case, by some intuitive, introspective apprehension of a kind which, in
> the past, was formulated generally by dogmatic, revelatory, received
> religions.[6]

From this follows the mandate for his own art (in which Tippett effectively
rehearses an agenda set for the domain of the aesthetic by Kant): to hold
open and make palpable the reality of the 'inner world of the imagination'
and perhaps to envision some future situation in which the rift between
different types of knowing might be healed.

While this certainly did not mean Tippett yearned for what Bernstein
terms 'the metaphysical totalities of the pre-modern age' (as a composer
such as John Tavener has arguably done with his turn to the Russian Orthodox church), the kinds of 'introspective apprehension' to which he refers
seem symptomatic of a dogged metaphysical remnant within modern
Western consciousness: a kind of metaphysics despite itself, which while
not rejecting the emancipatory moment offered by reason, suspects that the
way things really are is not reducible to scientific reasoning alone, and
which is alert to possibilities of being that transcend reason's reductive,

subject-eclipsing categories. This situation can be understood dialectically. Reason, in the very demonstration of its remarkable instrumental possibilities for our lifeworld, also makes evident its non-identity with other significant areas of human experience. Hence it becomes imaginable that the kinds of discourse whose vocabulary includes epithets such as 'transcendent', 'visionary' or 'sublime', are not necessarily anachronistic to modern consciousness, but are indeed generated from it.

Tippett as 'post-romantic modernist'

Tippett was alive not only to the problems of modernity but also to the manner in which these had been sounded within the art of his century – in other words to the aesthetics of modernism. Modernism itself was never a single coherent movement; paradoxically, if it is characterized by any single thing this might be the idea of fragmentation. Similarly, Tippett's *œuvre* might be seen as a succession of modernisms, but nowhere are the condition of fragmentation and the knife of an inwardly directed critical scepticism more apparent than in the period ushered in by *King Priam*.[7] The stylistic characteristics of this second style-period are well enough documented within the Tippett literature. As against the lyrical emphasis, largely tonal orientation and developmental forms of his first period there is now a shift towards the rhetorical gesture, a post-tonal – at times atonal – soundworld, and an emphasis on musical discontinuity. On the face of it, this new world of sound and structure might have seemed inimical to the affirmative strain of the earlier works, to their vision of integration and wholeness. Yet just as the music of Tippett's post-*Priam* period did not so much liquidate his earlier stylistic traits as transform them and set them in strange new contexts, so its aesthetic relation to his first period is not one of total repudiation. With the move to a more hard-hitting soundworld Tippett did not abandon his previous visionary aspirations; rather he profoundly problematized them. What makes the discontinuities between the later period and the earlier one so startling is the agon with a value system whose pertinence endures through the very critique to which it is subjected.

Comments by Goldmann are again pertinent here (the 'problems' to which he refers are those 'great human problems created by man's relationship with his fellows and with the universe' indicated in an earlier quotation):

> Now since the number of coherent replies that can be given to these
> problems is limited by the very structure of the human personality, each of

the replies given may correspond to different and even contradictory historical situations. This explains both the successive rebirths of the same idea which we find in the world of history, art and philosophy and the fact that, at different times, the same vision can assume different aspects.[8]

The works of Tippett's second period bespeak a 'different ... historical situation'; they present his world vision in a 'different aspect'. In addition to paying recognition to a more internationalist modernism they reflect, I would argue, the crystallization of a consciousness of the deepening Cold War. This is a consciousness which, threatened by the ominous course of history, is paradoxically also thrown back into its own deepest subjective reaches for something with which to counter the mounting negative forces of the lifeworld. But here is also the point of continuity with the past – both Tippett's and that of European (and Western) culture at large. For the alienation experienced by individual subjects under the threat of the atom bomb – a quintessential product of instrumental reason – is only(!) a more acute version of that felt culturally under the rational paradigm of the Enlightenment. As Julian Johnson puts it, Enlightenment thought, in rendering subjects autonomous, also bequeathed 'a model of man that was cut off from the world around him, from "nature"'. The 'romantic agenda' of Kant, Hegel, Fichte, Schelling, Schlegel and Schleiermacher was 'to create a conceptual framework in which the unity of man and nature, shattered by the mechanistic and atomistic implications of Enlightenment theory, might be restored'.[9]

Within a work such as *The Midsummer Marriage* Tippett deploys a similar romantic agenda – a 'new humanism' of 'The Whole Man' as he puts it.[10] The idea of oneness with nature and its appeal to the fractured post-Enlightenment mind provide an illuminating context for the pastoralism of his first period, whose epitome is the magic wood of *The Midsummer Marriage*. However, in *King Priam* and beyond, particularly in the last three operas, the magic wood is displaced by urban townscapes – a move consistent with an immanent critique on Tippett's part of his 'new humanism'. It is not that this humanism is dispensed with or seen as bankrupt (the later operas also hold on to the idea of some magical 'other' space); but it is tested by a kind of self-inflicted scepticism which allows other voices to speak – among them, I will argue, post-humanist ones. What becomes acute in this period – audible in the music's conflicted, heterogeneous soundworld – is the friction inherent in Tippett's application of a twentieth-century realist and materialist consciousness to the nineteenth century's aspirations to the ideal and the absolute. Arnold Whittall is right to call the composer a 'post-romantic modernist'.[11]

Much of this book explores this characterization. Its emphasis is on Tippett's later works (though I do not confine myself to these exclusively), many of which seem to me to be interesting precisely because their distinctively twentieth-century soundworld brings with it a revitalization of ideas from the nineteenth century – understood here as a 'long' nineteenth century, extending back into the later eighteenth. Hence one strategy I adopt is to interweave analysis of those works with consideration of aesthetic questions from the traditions of philosophical and literary romanticism and idealism – especially in their Germanic incarnations – and their late nineteenth- and twentieth-century successors.[12] (This seems to me one possibly profitable way to engage with the debate about Tippett's later works, and perhaps help to loosen up some of the critical rigidities that have become established there.) And the theme of nature will surface on a number of occasions and in various guises.

Romanticism's attempt to articulate man's position within a nature from which he has become alienated is conformant, Johnson argues, with 'an attempt to define the relation between rationality and irrationality within the human subject, between its linguistic ordering of itself and the world, and its non-linguistic experience'.[13] Even if it is unlikely that Tippett possessed specialist knowledge of the early romantic and idealist philosophical tradition (bar his close acquaintance with the works of Goethe) a form of this consciousness could have been transmitted to him in mediated form. One of the most conspicuous conduits in this regard would have been Jung, whose opposition of the conscious mind and the collective unconscious expressed perfectly for Tippett the dualism between the rational and irrational. As I argue in chapter 2 this is also contained in microcosm in the concept 'image' which is central to Tippett's aesthetic thinking and musical practice, and has its most significant provenance in Jung's psychoanalytic theories. What has also become clear to me, however, is that different incarnations of this dualism between a 'linguistic ordering' and 'non-linguistic experience' surface throughout Tippett's œuvre. In successive chapters, I figure its several metamorphoses in relation to 'successive rebirths of the same idea' (to borrow Goldmann's phrase) within Western modernity – or, less reductively, to different historical–intellectual formations around an abiding philosophical problem: Kant's noumenon and phenomenon in relation to *The Mask of Time* (chapter 5); Schopenhauer's Will and Idea, and Nietzsche's Dionysiac and Apollonian, in relation to *The Midsummer Marriage* and *King Priam* (chapter 3); Adorno's materialist metaphysics in relation to *The Vision of Saint Augustine* (chapter 4); and Kristeva's semiotic and symbolic in relation to *Byzantium* (chapter 7).

Tippett's writings, and writing about Tippett

An invaluable resource in this book's interpretative–aesthetic project – an intermediary between Tippett's musical works and the (linguistic) texts alongside which I contextualize them – are the composer's own writings. His numerous essays and interviews suggest that in his case a considered analysis of the relationship between the artist, the artwork and society was far from peripheral to the activity of composing. Indeed we might consider these writings, reproduced in such collections as *Moving into Aquarius, Music of the Angels* and *Tippett on Music*, as a legitimate part of his *œuvre*.[14] Our opening quotation from Goldmann is again pertinent, in its assertion that, from their different corners, poet – for which, read artist in the general sense – and philosopher might tackle the same realities of their age. It is less the case that Tippett belies the claim that 'there are no people more different than the poet . . . and the philosopher'; more that he demonstrates that it is possible for the same individual to practise both roles and benefit from the interplay of their different modalities of thought.

There is, however, a wrinkle in this convergence which is of key significance for us. While it is true that, as was once said of Tippett, 'whatever this man touches he philosophizes',[15] his very 'maverick' nature (an epithet of which he was fond) and the sheer eclecticism of his reading habits militate against direct alliances with any recognized philosophical corpus. Tippett philosophized without a philosophy. Yet, for all this, I would argue that scattered across and embedded within his writings is evidence of a coherent aesthetic position, even if the vocabulary used to voice it is idiosyncratic, heterogeneous, and at times obscure. For example, Tippett did not use a word like 'dialectic' in any systematic way, but when he describes his own music in terms of 'polarities' he means something closely cognate. Similarly, his talk of 'inner' and 'outer' worlds concerns the philosophical dualism of subject and object; and even his discussion of 'moving into Aquarius' – to an age of 'attempted union of the opposites'[16] – alludes to a dialectical movement of history reminiscent of Hegel, for all that it also indicates a brush with astrology. Just as the individuality of Tippett's music inheres in the idiosyncratic stance it takes towards received historical genres, structural conventions and musical styles, so his intellectual work is distinctive in simultaneously resisting and inviting comparison with canonic Western philosophical ideas.

I have felt this tension quite acutely in writing this book. On the one hand I have been concerned to assemble a profile of Tippett's aesthetic stance (more extensively, I think, than in any previous study); and in so

doing I have tried to represent Tippett's position accurately, and allowed his own words to tell their story. On the other hand, simply to leave matters there would also be to leave unchallenged the notion that Tippett was a composer completely *sui generis*, a maverick pure and simple. While his individuality unquestionably contributed to his significance, it only carries weight – that is, amounts to more than mere eccentricity – because as an individual Tippett also engaged with the wider discourses of modernity (otherwise, once again, 'a man of our time' is nothing more than a publicity slogan). It is therefore incumbent on us to attempt to locate Tippett's thought, both musical and verbal, in the context of those discourses. Accordingly I have attempted to mobilize different facets of Tippett's music, his writings, and the thinking of others into interpretative constellations that I hope will offer new insights into his *œuvre* as well as showing the coherence and richness of his aesthetic position.

This process, then, is a kind of dialogue, though its involvement of a subjective, speculative element carries risks. For it is one thing to explore Tippett's *œuvre* in relation to figures he is known to have read and been influenced by: for example Jung or Yeats (even if my concern with such writers – as with Goldmann in this chapter – soon turns from their influence to the hermeneutic possibilities offered by their writings). But it is arguably more contentious also to line Tippett up with figures with whom he expressed no or little acquaintance or affinity: for example Adorno, Nietzsche, Camille Paglia or Julia Kristeva. On whose authority can such connections be posited?

In one way or another this question has also been addressed by Lawrence Kramer, whose putatively postmodern musicology is centred in a notion of music as constitutive of subjectivity. While acknowledging composition as an aspect of 'the process of musical subject formation', Kramer none the less chooses to privilege reception; his is in effect a species of reader-orientated criticism.[17] Invoking Mikhail Bakhtin, he states that 'in addressing us, [music] is "half-ours and half-someone else's . . . It is not so much interpreted by us as it is further, this is, freely developed, applied to new material, new conditions; it enters into interanimating relationships with new contexts."'[18] Some of the more speculative relationships I have posited below are in this very interest of reinvigorated contextualization. They allow for a 'dissemination' (to borrow a term which Kramer borrows from Derrida)[19] of new, I hope enriched, meanings from the works in question – arguably paying the composer greater homage than merely tautologically retreading known paths of influence.

However, I am less eager than Kramer to put a postmodernist spin on this approach. I want to show where and how Tippett is situated in the

'web of culture' (a metaphor which Gary Tomlinson borrows from Clifford Geertz)[20] – a web which includes such figures as Kant, Hegel, Schopenhauer, Nietzsche, Shelley, T. S. Eliot and Saint Augustine. But my argument is that these connections – even the ones Tippett may not have intended or recognized – are conditioned intrinsically by the sound and formation of his music; its interpretation is not just a matter of the free play of the signifier. This is not to discount the role of the imagination of the listening subject, but it is also to place emphasis on the role of the musical object – as a phenomenon that retains an autonomous substrate – in mediating that subjectivity. Like Kramer, I have ventured to construct an interplay of musical and linguistic meanings; indeed, for whatever reasons, I have tended to prioritize philosophical, critical and literary sources of contextualization over musical ones. However, while I agree wholeheartedly with him that the differences between music and language should not – indeed must not – inhibit the linguistic discussion of music, I feel less easy that this opposition is as deconstructible as he claims.[21] My experience in the following essays is that the passage from formalist discussion of music to other modes of contextual discourse is one of profound discontinuity. It is entirely conceivable that better equipped intellects than mine might handle this problem more adeptly, but my own strategy has been to accept these disjunctures as in some way essential. While I have ventured to find points of mediation between purely musical and conceptual structures, this does not guarantee an easy translation from musical to linguistic signifiers.

Furthermore in pursuing homologies between Tippett's thought and that of other figures, I have tried to remain as sensitive to difference as to similarity. Thus the 'others' with which I have aligned him serve as a kind of ideological litmus, rather than figures of complete identification. It is through both drawing comparisons and locating the points at which comparisons break down that Tippett's individuality – what is non-identical about him – within larger cultural formations of modernity can be established.

All this has also meant accommodating the structure of this book to such discontinuities and disjunctures. At just about every level there is resistance of the part to complete assimilation by the whole. Hence each chapter is intended as a free-standing essay, notwithstanding the fact that it also contributes to a more or less chronological analysis of selected works[22] which reveals discontinuities and discontiguities, as much as continuities, within Tippett's œuvre. Within the longer chapters, numbered sections might almost be read as mini-essays in their own right; and, within these, individually titled subsections also have a measure of autonomy. Although I make no claims to emulate Adorno's antinomic and

quasi-paratactic prose style, I have been open to the notion behind it that the structure of writing might in some way be shaped by the contradictions and problematics of its object of enquiry; and that the most appropriate way to treat such an object might be to build around it a 'constellation' of concepts which interact dialectically upon one another rather than unfold in a logical sequence from some assumed first principle. Hence the character of the present chapter, which is to a degree autonomous, but also functions (heuristically and synoptically) as a simultaneously necessary and dispensable introduction and conclusion to the book as a whole.

The resistance between part and whole is a notion also relevant to the works on which I focus. For, with the exception of *The Midsummer Marriage* (1946–52), they all purvey the fragmented world vision and problematized subjectivities of Tippett's post-*Priam* period. The pieces in question – *The Midsummer Marriage* as mentioned, *King Priam* itself, then *The Vision of Saint Augustine*, *The Mask of Time*, the Triple Concerto and *Byzantium* – individually offer particular perspectives on the general constellation of issues which is the book's concern. I have chosen them because in one way or another they all have a visionary dimension – whether this be metaphysical or social, affirmative or ambivalent. But there is inevitably an element of contingency in their selection; other works – say, the Third Symphony (1970–2), *New Year* (1986–8) or *The Rose Lake* (1991–3) – might equally have taken the limelight (which is not to say that these and yet other pieces are absent from discussion). The point is that the issues in question do not determine *a priori* a necessary and finite set of affected works; moreover, the works one happens to select reciprocally determine the constellation of issues. Again, particulars resist total subsumption into generality. The chosen works are not merely case studies – exemplars of more universal concerns – but are also of interest in their own right, free-standing particulars. And, since I have not ruled out the importance of subjectivity, I may as well add that I have also picked them because they have excited my admiration, and because they afford opportunities to explore issues I believe to be urgent within contemporary culture. (This is also to argue for a more interventionist musicology, not confined to passively commentating on a composer's *œuvre*, but actively engaging with it towards critical, perhaps in the broadest sense political, ends.)

A man of whose time?

I have saved until the end of this chapter a discussion of that part of Goldmann's description of world vision which holds the greatest potential

for critique of Tippett (a facet of the very Marxist epistemology that he wanted to refute with *King Priam*). This is a critique on an ideological level, something which to my knowledge is barely evident in existing critical accounts of the composer. Here is a quotation in full of an excerpt from *The Hidden God* only partly cited above:

> What I have called a 'world vision' is a convenient term for the whole complex of ideas, aspirations and feelings which links together the members of a social group (a group which, in most cases, assumes the existence of a social class) and which opposes them to members of other social groups.[23]

The bits of text over which one might feel uneasy here are terms such as 'social group', 'social class', 'oppos[ition] . . . to members of other social groups'. What's discomfiting is that such phrases do not fit too well with the supposed universality of the issues we have been discussing, and especially of Tippett's humanism. They remind us that humanism, philosophy, autonomous art and indeed the Enlightenment itself are all discourses and/or signifying practices whose roots are bourgeois. The notion of 'a man of our time' begins to look less absolute when we realize that the consciousness of the kinds of people likely to speak the phrase (the subjects behind the 'our') is that of a social group, not that of society as a whole; it is the consciousness of a socially, culturally and historically specific class which by definition excludes others. To polemicize a little: what are the social demographics of those who attend the venues dictated by Tippett's choice of genres – concert hall, opera house, recital room? (Admittedly, the specific demographics in the case of Tippett's own music may not be entirely typical – an important matter for any future reception history of his music.) The critical concern here is not the bourgeois delineation of these venues and practices *per se*, but the fact that within the particular cultural situation of high art Tippett braves statements of would-be universal import.

But now we need to add some nuances. Tippett is unlikely to have been oblivious to such concerns, especially given his earlier left-wing political commitment, and his involvement during the war years with institutions such as Morley College. It would seem that while the materials of high-art music offered him the expressive resources for what he needed to say, he was not unaware of those 'others' who would not be there to hear it. Indeed his *œuvre* shows an increasing responsiveness to the possibilities of stylistic and generic pluralism (a point I develop in chapter 6, below), and even though the bulwarks of a classical practice are never burst, Tippett does much to destabilize its social delineations. The line 'You mother-fucking bastard' from *The Ice Break* may, on the face of it, represent one of those

supposed lapses of taste for which Tippett's librettos are notorious. But I would argue that it could be more profitably seen as an extreme example of a broader strategy of dialogization in his thinking (to borrow a term from Bakhtin[24]): in other words, the articulation of a social polyphony of voices. I argue in the last two chapters of this book that one of the distinctive features of Tippett's late works is that their structural formations can be read as mediated visions of a pluralist society, one indeed in which high art itself may no longer have – or need – its current privileged status. I also argue that such resistance to aesthetic and cultural totality may inhere in insights gained from his own gay sexuality – a level of argument congruent with Goldmann's view that world vision at its least abstract may be linked 'to the individual personality of the writer or thinker in question'. It is perhaps at this level that Tippett comes closest to envisaging a humanism compatible with his democratic sentiments. Certainly such a hope seems to sing out loud and clear in his last major work, *The Rose Lake*, where the image of an enchanted nature retakes centre stage in his repertoire of expressive possibilities.

Even though the technical basis of Tippett's creativity was the recycling, the making new, of materials from the past, he never stopped looking towards the future – from which I take my cue for a little concluding rhetoric. As we enter our new millennium the dialectic of Enlightenment seems only to intensify. In the same week as I write these words the completion of the first draft of the human genome project has been announced; and it seems inevitable that it will only be a short time before we need to face up to the complete demystification of the nature of human consciousness. It may be that our concept of the human will not survive these paradigm shifts. Conversely, such a concept – or some transformed version of it – may become all the more urgent as we search for a basis on which to construct our values in this disenchanted landscape. Following the same logic, we may find that the world vision of Tippett's *œuvre* becomes of historical interest only, no longer of currency in changed times. Conversely we may find it holds in trust an image of values and sensibilities – a 'whole complex of ideas, aspirations and feelings' – which we are not yet ready to lose.

2 The significance of the concept 'image' in Tippett's musical thought: a perspective from Jung

Tippett and images

> I know that my true function within a society which embraces all of us, is to continue an age-old tradition . . . This tradition is to create images from the depths of the imagination and to give them form whether visual, intellectual or musical. For it is only through images that the inner world communicates at all . . . Images of vigour for a decadent period, images of calm for one too violent. Images of reconciliation for worlds torn by division. And in an age of mediocrity and shattered dreams, images of abounding, generous, exuberant beauty.[1]

For anyone seeking a statement epitomizing Tippett's stance as a composer (one only regrets that the promotional copy-writers got there first) the eloquent conclusion to the composer's essay 'Poets in a barren age' could hardly be bettered. It encapsulates his beliefs as to the essence of art and creativity, the role of the artist in society, and, implicitly, the nature of artistic material. The key term, repeated in nearly every sentence and worked into a compelling rhetoric, is 'image'. For Tippett this seemed to be the essential vehicle of artistic communication, mediating between the inscrutable processes of the imagination and an all-too imperfect empirical reality. I propose in the present enquiry to examine this hitherto unscrutinized concept further in relation to two particular aims: first to develop a fuller picture of the aesthetic context of Tippett's compositional practice; second to consider what bearing the concept might throw on the music itself and the way we construe it.

Tippett's extensive writings represent an important – and largely unmined – resource in relation to the first of these aims. However, while his essays display many signs of a cogently formulated aesthetic, they are not theoretical texts in the formal sense: 'image' is just one example of a concept which crops up on numerous occasions but which is not systematically elaborated. To some extent the situation can be ameliorated by tracing ideas across various essays to piece together a larger account. A further strategy is to examine these ideas in the light of particular influences which may have been pertinent. The adoption of such an approach here is intended not as a search for specific origins, but rather as the basis for a hermeneutic framework (implying that the significance of influence

lies beyond a positivistic record of historical facts, albeit grounded in them). 'Image' is certainly a term open to lax application, as Philip N. Furbank demonstrates for literary criticism;[2] but in Tippett's case the usage is self-consistent and has specific resonances with Blake, Yeats and Jung. If in what follows I focus predominantly on the last-mentioned as a significant influence, this is not to belittle the importance of Blake or Yeats (whose voices are discernible in the language of our opening quotation).[3] On this occasion Jung receives the apple, so to speak, because, for all Tippett's literary inclinations, his view of art – at least as it is expressed in certain key writings of the 1950s and 1960s – was a strongly psychoanalytic one. Moreover, Jung offers an extended theoretical system (a quasi-philosophical world view, one might even say) within which Tippett's usage of the term 'image' may be contextualized alongside his own – a practice allowable because of affinities between composer and psychologist, amounting in certain respects to a shared ideology.

The importance of Jung's analytical psychology for Tippett has long been recognized and is well enough documented. His first exposure to Jungian thought came when he was given a copy of *Psychology of the Unconscious* by Evelyn Maude (probably in the late 1920s or early 1930s). He tells of subsequently reading 'more and more Jung', including especially *Psychological Types*. During this same period he was introduced by David Ayerst to the 'maverick' Jungian analyst John Layard,[4] and in the late 1930s Jungian psychology acquired a practical value for Tippett in dealing with his crisis over his sexual orientation. Thereafter, the impact of Jungian ideas on his artistic output is first evidenced in *A Child of our Time* (1939–41) and *The Midsummer Marriage* (1946–52), and in one way or another the Jungian themes of self-knowledge, rebirth and the reconciliation of opposites pervade his later *œuvre* with varying degrees of emphasis. Much of the existing commentary on Jung's influence has tended to concentrate on these aspects, or on identifying archetypal symbols within the works which employ texts. However, as stated above, the intention here is to chart some of the broader philosophical affinities between the two figures, and ultimately to show how these might permeate the immanent substance of Tippett's music.

Images and the unconscious

Unquestionably one of Jung's main attractions for Tippett is the place accorded in the former's theories to the non-rational. This is an issue because of what Tippett saw as the excessive value placed upon the manifestations of rationality – specifically science and technology – in modern

culture. Indeed a recurring theme throughout many of the essays in *Moving into Aquarius* is that of 'the challenge of a world divided unnaturally between technics and the imagination'.[5] For Tippett the value of art is precisely that it offers a corrective to this spiritually injurious imbalance, positing a domain of experience other than that of empirical reality. Art's role is to effect 'a re-animation of the world of the imagination';[6] but more than this, music is in certain cases 'a favoured art for expressing particular intuitions of transcendence'[7] (in referring to a historical tradition including works such as Bach's *St Matthew Passion* and Beethoven's Ninth Symphony Tippett is also implicitly aligning himself with it). And in a further allusion to his concern with the transcendental he mentions 'the possibly strange fact that I have affirmations, though not theologically Christian, which set me in some other place than optimistically or pessimistically bounded by our immanentist world of technics'.[8]

In his perception of modern man as alienated from a world dominated by instrumental reason, and his search for some form of God-term with which to fill the spiritual vacuum (impelled rather than inhibited by his agnosticism), Tippett expressed an outlook uncannily reminiscent of romanticism. Had he been an early nineteenth-century figure, one might conjecture, he would perhaps have attributed his 'intuitions of the transcendent' to the Absolute, the Ideal, or, as in the case of Shelley or Wordsworth, to some hidden Power within the landscape. However, as a modernist ('a man of our time', as we are repeatedly told) Tippett was intuitively aware of the hazards of anachronism which such a metaphysical stance would have entailed. For all his objections to scientific empiricism, he seemed to be implicitly aware that his affirmations of the ineffable must be seen to have some material basis if they were to be perceived as authentic to his times, and not as a retreat into esotericism or mysticism. And here the psychoanalytic movement – and Jung in particular – comes to the rescue, offering the possibility of an epistemological shift from the metaphysical to the psychological. As Jung puts it, in an essay Tippett is known to have read:

> Since the stars have fallen from heaven and our highest symbols have paled, a secret life holds sway in the unconscious. That is why we have a psychology today, and why we speak of the unconscious.[9]

At the root of this outlook, then, is the conception of modern man as psychological man: depth psychology offers an epistemology through which man's relation to the world may be meaningfully articulated and potentially altered; and, crucially for Tippett, art is efficacious because it has an integral place within this scheme.

Attributing the source of the numinous and other non-rational experiences to the unconscious might imply a retreat into a world of profound subjectivity which only sharpens the schism of the individual from the empirical objective world. Yet for Jung the subjectivity of 'inner' experience is commuted back into objectivity in the deeper reaches of the more 'primordial' collective unconscious. This concept is the foundation of his model of the psyche, but also his most ideological construct: ideological because it is presented as a domain in which alienation is assuaged, while making no reference to the associated social and economic conditions which a more politically engaged commentator might see as its ultimate cause. Jung writes for example of 'the healing and redeeming depths of the collective psyche, where man is not lost in the isolation of consciousness and its errors and sufferings, but where all men are caught in a common rhythm'.[10] It would seem that Tippett adopts this ideology when he talks of 'the depths of the imagination' as a source of 'images of reconciliation for worlds torn by division', though the implications of his doing so are complex, requiring an appropriately nuanced critique. Consideration of this will be deferred, however, until the concluding stages of this essay. For the present it will suffice to note that, if for no other reason, the notion of the collective unconscious cannot be dismissed out of hand because it is integral to Tippett's understanding of his own creative processes. He takes from Jung the idea of the collective unconscious as the wellspring of creative activity, a spontaneous drive, an autonomous complex which is liable to exercise an imperious command over the artist.[11] Thus Jung:

> Art is a kind of innate drive that seizes a human being and makes him its instrument . . . As an artist he is 'man' in a higher sense – he is 'collective man,' a vehicle and moulder of the unconscious psychic life of mankind . . . As K. G. Carus says: '. . . he is everywhere hemmed round and prevailed upon by the Unconscious, the mysterious god within him. . . .'[12]

While Tippett writes:

> The drive to create . . . is so intense in its operation that it is difficult for those submitting to it not to feel it as evidence of things beyond the individually personal . . . I believe that the faculty the artist may sometimes have to create images through which these mysterious depths of our being speak to us, is a true fundamental. I believe it is part of what we mean by having knowledge of God.[13]

With this last quotation we have reached the moment where the concept 'image' can be seen to take its place within the larger framework so far outlined. As is clear from the above, images are inextricably bound up with some unfathomable domain (in essence the unconscious) characterized by

depth or inwardness. Indeed, Tippett's writings repeatedly present images as vehicles which make available the otherwise unknowable contents of the 'inner world' – as when the composer states: 'it is only through images that the inner world communicates at all'; and, 'the images which are works of art, are our sole means of expressing the inner world of feelings objectively and immediately'.[14] There are strong resonances here with Jung, who reinforces his definition of image with the epithet 'inner' in order simultaneously to distinguish it from 'sensuous reality' and to underline its true value which is psychological: the image represents 'an inner reality which often far outweighs the importance of external reality'.[15]

Jung also makes a connection with the term's usage in poetry to mean 'a figure of fancy, or *fantasy image*'.[16] And fantasy in turn receives formal definition as an element in his theoretical model; in particular, as 'imaginative activity' it is 'simply the direct expression of psychic life . . . which cannot appear in consciousness except in the form of images or contents . . . Fantasy as imaginative activity is identical with the flow of psychic energy.'[17] Echoes of these remarks would seem to be found in Tippett's description of his personal imaginative activity: 'I feel a need to give an image to an ineffable experience of my inner life. I feel the inner life as something that is essentially fluid in consistency.'[18]

Jung further defines image as a 'constellation' which is 'the result of the spontaneous activity of the unconscious on the one hand and of the momentary conscious situation on the other, which always stimulates the activity of the relevant subliminal material'. The 'inner image', he says, is 'a *condensed expression of the psychic situation as a whole*'.[19] A fusion of elements, a response to a particular moment in consciousness, a resulting interplay between conscious and unconscious domains: these, then, are the image's essential features, and – taking 'outer' and 'inner' to be broadly synonymous with 'conscious' and 'unconscious' respectively – they also resemble the conditions described by Tippett in the following scenario:

> It may only be for a moment, when some quality in the night and the sound of the bird-song combine to make a specially intense image. At such time we respond. It is as though another world had spoken by some trick of correspondence between the outside and the inside. For the 'thing' inside only works if the proper image is offered from outside.[20]

Elaborations: interpreting with Jung

Much of this account of Jung's formulation of image and its related concepts (fantasy, imaginative activity) is drawn from his *Psychological Types*, which we know Tippett to have read in considerable detail in the 1930s[21]

(probably in the English translation by H. G. Baynes, published in 1923). The composer's reading was probably motivated as much by personal need as pure theoretical curiosity, and we can only speculate as to how rigorously he evaluated its content; it is none the less conceivable that the notion of image presented in his own writings reflects an absorption of the spirit if not the precise detail of Jung's work. Thus, although we cannot be sure how fully Tippett studied in particular the eleventh chapter of *Psychological Types*, devoted to definitions, there is some validity in amplifying our understanding of image by relating it to other terms within Jung's system as defined in that chapter. In so doing we move more explicitly from tracing signs of Jungian influence to a reading of Tippett's production through a Jungian hermeneutic framework.

In Jung's scheme image belongs to a network of related concepts, in particular 'primordial image', 'idea' and 'symbol'. Primordial image would seem to be a sub-category of image, and is favoured by Jung, perhaps because its source is the collective unconscious (as opposed to 'personal' image which is relevant only to the personal unconscious). An image is primordial – or 'archetypal' (the term Jung eventually comes to prefer) – 'when it possesses an *archaic* character . . . when the image is in striking accord with familiar mythological motifs'.[22] Given that he attributes a particularly visual character to such an image[23] the possibilities for transferring this notion to music might at first blush appear limited. Nevertheless, it would seem that when Tippett refers to (musical) images he is associating them with a quality which, if not mythological, is in a certain sense primordial or trans-personal – as when he attributes the source of the images described in our opening quotation to a kind of Yeatsian Great Memory: 'that immense reservoir of the human psyche where images age-old and new boil together in some demoniac cauldron'.[24] Just what this sense of 'primordiality' might mean musically is a point to which we shall later return.

It must be admitted that the semantic slippage which Jung sometimes allows between primordial image, idea and symbol can be a cause of obfuscation. Nevertheless it is possible to read his account of the relationship between them as implicitly dialectical, each term representing a stage in a process which brings the various strata of the psyche into meaningful interaction. Thus while the primordial image might be seen as the generating thesis, its antithetical counterpart is the idea. The former is characterized by its 'concretism' – a fusion of 'thinking', 'feeling' and 'sensation' (all formally defined concepts within Jung's system). The latter is arrived at through 'differentiation', specifically the differentiation of thought from the other psychological functions, which coalesce within the image

in its primordial form. The idea 'is nothing other than the primordial image intellectually formulated'; subjecting the primordial image to 'a particularly intense development of thought' brings it 'to the surface'[25] – presumably implying a passage from the (collective) unconscious to consciousness.

Jung then describes a further stage in which the psychological function, feeling, is reinvoked giving rise to the 'symbol', a manifestation of the primordial image which 'embraces the undifferentiated, concretized feeling' and the intellectually abstracted idea. With some justification this could be viewed as a moment of synthesis, in which the final term mediates the first two terms such that they partake of one another. As such the symbol represents for Jung a means of giving form to the unknowable. In his writings he repeatedly stresses (partly in order to distinguish his use of the term from Freud's) a definition of symbol as 'the best possible formulation of an unknown thing'.[26] Significantly this notion also features strongly in his psychoanalytic investigations of art. For example he makes the following reference to the products of a particular creative temperament which seeks to transcend normal limits of comprehension (note too the characteristic semantic osmosis between 'image' and 'symbol' in this passage):

> We would expect a strangeness of form and content, thoughts that can only be apprehended intuitively, a language pregnant with meanings, and images that are true symbols because they are the best possible expressions for something unknown – bridges thrown out towards an unseen shore.[27]

It would perhaps be a little too easy here to suggest parallels with Tippett's musical language (its characteristic tendency to push beyond what the material can apparently accommodate, its strain against accepted categories of musical meaning). What reinforces the argument, however, is that over and above the possible correspondence between the end-product described by Jung and that actually created by Tippett, are also similarities in the accounts of the material's psychological genesis. Tippett portrays musical composition as a staged process, essentially a passage from the inchoate to the articulate – 'the process . . . is one of giving articulation to this fluid experience, and appears in successive stages'.[28] Other statements of his reinforce the notion of his material beginning life in some intuitively apprehended, unformed state – perhaps conceived in terms of its tempo, general shape or timbre – and then being subjected to a process of conscious scrutiny and progressive refinement until, as a final stage, specific notes are articulated.[29] This parallels Jung's depiction of an image first generated from the unconscious – while perhaps not 'primordial' in Tippett's case, nevertheless in a state of undifferentiation – then subjected

to 'a particularly intense development of thought', giving rise to an articulate (musical) 'idea'. The final material construed as a 'symbol' embraces both thought and feeling, capturing both the abstract, intellectually formulated idea and the undifferentiated contents of the unconscious. It is this particularly Jungian conception of the symbol, then, with its quasi-dialectical implications, which Tippett probably has in mind (whether consciously or not) when he speaks of images. The question now arises as to just how this conception affects the material itself; in other words, in what ways does the final product bear traces of its genesis?

Images in music

Passing from a generalized theoretical discussion to one involving specific technicalities of musical language necessitates an inevitable clunking of discursive gears. At least a partial transition between discourses might be suggested by occasional moments in Tippett's writings where he himself talks of images directly in relation to music. Seen in total, however, these remarks also imply an ambiguity as to whether 'image' pertains to the whole work or its individual parts. On the one hand for example Tippett states that the 'pleasure and enrichment' of symphonic music

> arise from the fact that the flow is not merely the flow of the music itself, but a significant image of the inner flow of life. Artifice of all kinds is necessary to the musical composition in order that it shall become such an image.[30]

As important as the further stress on the fluidity of psychic life (a Jungian conceit) is the idea that the musical composition is an image – singular – of this flow: indeed of the flow itself, rather than of particular contents that are subject to it.[31] On the other hand, in the same essay Tippett also talks of images – plural – as if they represented specific resources of musical material: 'Music of course has a tremendous range of images, from the gay (and, if perhaps rarely, the comic) to the serious and the tragic'.[32] And elsewhere he describes the composing subconscious as containing a 'store of images of all kinds, from tiny sounds to enormous sounds'.[33] While in neither of these last quotations does Tippett mention how these materials might be implemented within a specific piece, it seems unlikely that he is assuming a movement or work to consist of only one such image. Image in this context, then, would seem to be synonymous with an element of musical form, rather than an entire form *per se*.

The terminological ambiguity may only be apparent. As individual images presented by the musical parts succeed one another they could be perceived as generating the larger image which is the flow of the musical

whole. But there is perhaps another way of reading this dichotomy, namely in the shift in Tippett's stance towards musical form manifested between his earlier and later works. (It may not be coincidental that a number of essays in which Tippett dwells on the concept image are roughly contemporaneous – dating from the 1950s and early 1960s[34] – with a period of gradual and then abrupt stylistic change within his *œuvre*: as if a concern for the nature and meaning of his musical materials had been driven to the conscious surface of his writings.) For example, an early work such as the Concerto for Double String Orchestra (1938–9) which aspires to an ideal of Beethovenian symphonic continuity could well be said to offer an image 'of the otherwise unperceived unsavoured inner flow of life'[35] – in the energy and organically unfolding structures of the outer movements in particular. By contrast, in certain works post-dating *The Midsummer Marriage* there is a tendency for the constituent parts to become increasingly strongly differentiated – as for example in the *Fantasia Concertante on a Theme of Corelli* (1953) or the Second Symphony (1957–8) – until in *King Priam* (1958–62) the principle of formal progression by immediate succession rather than mediated flow becomes the norm (and continues to be so for much of Tippett's later *œuvre*). Individual sections now take on an increased autonomy in relation to the whole through their distinctive characterization; each is defined by the particular image it projects. Indeed it would not be going too far to conjecture that the image becomes the principal constitutive element of form.

But this is to anticipate a little, since a more concrete examination of how images translate into musical material has still to be offered. This calls for a case study and, given the above comments, an extract from *King Priam* itself would be fitting. Helen of Troy's third-act aria is particularly appropriate since it deals with that most quintessential of fusions between the material and ineffable: sex. The aria follows Andromache's diatribe at Helen's adulterous liaison with Paris.[36] 'Let her rave', replies Helen, indifferent to Andromache's bitter invective, 'she cannot know what I am'. And she then proceeds to tell us, in a striking hymn to sexual love. The dramatic characterization is an excellent example of Tippett's reproduction of an ideology of the 'eternal feminine', probably informed by a reading of Jung's 'Archetypes of the collective unconscious'.[37] But of more immediate concern is the way the music furnishes an image of Helen's apprehension of her transcendent carnality, her semi-divine state of Being, in Eros rather than Logos. This image is manifest from the very opening of the aria (see Ex. 2.1).

To what extent can the musical conditions exemplified here be understood as congruent with the notion 'image' as presented in Jung's analytical psychology? Let us recall that this is a case of the Jungian symbolic

Example 2.1. *King Priam*, Helen's aria (opening), Act III scene 1.

image: a synthesis of feeling and thought; of the undifferentiated contents of the unconscious with the more abstract idea which has sprung from it. The intention is to give articulate form to an 'ineffable' apprehension – 'an expression of an intuitive idea that cannot . . . be formulated in any other or better way', as Jung puts it.[38] In other words, while striving to create an utterance coherent in its own (musical) terms, Tippett is also attempting to evince from his materials a stratum of meaning beyond that of immanent musical signification itself: the musical image, or symbol, contains the musical idea, yet exceeds it. A strategy for understanding the material's properties as a symbolic image might therefore be to isolate the ways in which it functions as an idea, and then look for elements which extend beyond that function.

A brief digression may be fruitfully made at this point to note that the dualism between image and idea is explored by Tippett in his essay 'Air from another planet'. While he attributes the dichotomy to Plato rather than Jung,[39] the terms of his argument would seem to be broader than any particular Platonic debate (that the composer elsewhere interprets a Platonic construct as anticipating notions in Jungian depth psychology is also suggestive[40]). Analogously, while the ostensible subject is Schoenberg's opera *Moses und Aron*, it is soon evident that Tippett has his own artistic concerns at heart:

> Schönberg . . . clearly takes energy from the Image and gives it to the Idea . . . 'Thou shalt not make unto thee any graven image, or any likeness of any thing that is in heaven above, or in the earth beneath.' Such is the second commandment. Naturally, if this commandment is kept literally then art ceases. Where an artist gets fascinated by this commandment, then the psychological struggle is terrible. Such I believe to have been Schönberg's. And when I have clarified things to this temporary abruptness, I feel myself a Greek to Schönberg's Jew. Damned by Jehovah though I may be, rejected even by Plato, on more occasions than I propose to tell you, the Image has been for me divine. Not of course, I hasten to add, an Image of God Himself, but often of his breath.[41]

Tippett's comparison of himself with Schoenberg is illuminating, and may be read as a contrast between the latter's pursuit of (an essentially cerebral) musical logic in the face of a disintegrating tonal language, and Tippett's greater willingness to embrace the irrational and unaccountable, the physical and the exuberantly beautiful.[42] This is far from saying that Tippett abandons the musical idea, but rather points to its occupying a different place in his priorities. That he mentions Schoenberg as one of modernism's key exponents of the idea is apposite for our purposes, since it would in any case be difficult to discuss the term's application to music

without making reference to him (though as we return to a discussion of Helen's aria we should maintain an awareness of some of the ambiguities inherent in Schoenberg's application of the notion).[43]

Pragmatically speaking, the musical idea which underpins Helen's aria in its entirety is first presented in the opening bars. Its salient characteristics are labelled *a*, *b* and *c* in Example 2.1: respectively the oscillating inverted mordent figure of the vocal line, the unmediated descent which follows it, and the quartally based chord elicited in response. Of these it is perhaps the plummet from the top to the bottom of the mezzo-soprano register which remains most strongly characteristic, and indeed reaches an extreme in the aria's final stages, where its compass extends from top A♭ to bottom B – at which point the text reveals the metaphorical meaning of the musical gesture: 'Love such as this stretches up to heaven, / for it reaches down to hell'.[44] This transformation makes it clear that while the idea is initially presented by the opening material it is not identical with it: rather, the idea is synonymous with its evolution – an evolution which generates in particular the primary elements of the formal scheme (the A sections of a design shaped A–B–A^1–B–transition–A^2).

Aspects of this process are shown for section A in Example 2.2. In part I of the analysis the three phrases of the section – the initial presentation of the idea and its two variants – are aligned paradigmatically so as to highlight similarities of shape and rhythmic profile, as well as to show up the differences. Particularly evident is the further development in the second variant (stave iii) of the thematic extension begun in the first (stave ii). As the motivic annotations show, this is engineered through modifications to motif *b*. That these are related by more than a vaguely defined shape is demonstrated in part II of the analysis which abstracts pitch and interval content from *b* and represents them in cellular guise as unordered pitch-class sets (these are described in prime form, but shown in descending order on the stave since this is the motif's typical trajectory). Here we see the subtlety of the transformations. Behind the changes in direction, b^1 is effectively an exact transposition of *b*; while *b′* and b^2 gradually expand the intervals of the original set: [0,1,4] becomes [0,2,5] then [0,2,6]. The latter process is effected by the semitonal 'modulation' of pitches between successive variants, shown with broken lines in Example 2.2: D and B in motif *b* become D♭ and B♭ in motif *b′*; A♭ in motif b^1 becomes A♮ in b^2.

The features outlined here by no means constitute an exhaustive account of the metamorphosis of the aria's musical idea. One might, for example, have included an analysis of harmony and voice leading (traces of the idea's passage through time). Nevertheless this brief discussion allows us to draw certain conclusions and to consider parallels with Jung.

Example 2.2. Helen's aria: the musical idea and its evolution.

I: Paradigmatic analysis

II: Cellular analysis
(notated as pitch-class sets)

As with the latter's formulation for conceptual activity, the musical idea as considered here is characterized by abstraction: it arises (or is cognized) through differentiation from the concrete corpus of the musical material. Detached from the materiality of sound – a form and not a substance, to borrow Saussure's phrase – the idea reflects the action of musical thought. As such it is a facet of consciousness, and available to analysis (whose key metaphor, structure, is likewise an abstraction, emulating that of the idea).

If the above dwells at some length on the idea – relatively familiar territory to music theory – this is partly to establish a basis against which to contrast that aspect of the image which extends beyond it. For the musical image, let us recall, embraces the idea yet exceeds it: while the idea achieves its identity through abstraction from the musical material, the essence of the image resides in the material's very materiality. That material substrate is not itself the image, even though the image is ontologically determined by it. Rather, the image is a synthesis of the abstract idea and its material 'other', in which both domains are emancipated from one another while at the same time being mutually conditioned. That is, the idea's formal configuration may bear traces of an orientation towards sensuous ends, while the material stratum may absorb qualities of the idea and thereby enter into signification. In one sense, of course, all music manifests just such a dichotomy between the formal and the sensuous (suggesting far wider implications to the present discussion than the immediate terms of reference). However, for music to become imagistic as such requires, I would argue, an interactive disposition of these separate elements towards each other, as here described.

Tippett achieves such conditions through various means. One notable channel for imagistic expression is opened by his inclination to push materials to extremes. For example, the extremes of compass in Helen's aria noted earlier are developed further by the instrumental writing. Her prolonged occupation of the upper vocal tessitura in section A¹ sends the violas to the top of their register (Figs. 381–3); while at the opening of the aria (see Ex. 2.1) part of the function of the accompanying chords is to amplify the voice's repeated plunges to the bottom of the mezzo range; the vocal depths are echoed at a register three octaves lower. Thus register ceases to be merely a medium, in which musical material is presented; it itself becomes material – palpable and significant.[45]

A similar transformation is enacted upon timbre. Indeed, Tippett's Second Symphony already marked the completion of a development within his earlier *œuvre* in which the distinction between a musical idea and the instrumental colour which transmits it is progressively blurred (epitomized by the second group of the opening movement). The corollary of this mutation of priorities – whereby the configuration of a musical idea might serve

as much to project a sonority as vice versa – is the potential osmosis between the mental and the sensuous, again suggestive of the fusion between thought and feeling characteristic of Jung's symbolic image. These conditions also obtain for many of the chordal components of Helen's aria, which on the one hand invoke the category of musical syntax known as harmony, and on the other make a claim to be heard as sonorities in their own right – neither position being entirely assimilable to the other. To elaborate: these features are based predominantly on vertical accumulations of fourths or fifths, representing a kind of intensified triad (or 'higher consonance' as Whittall terms it[46]); they aggregate into progressions, governed by a flux between flat and sharp tonal fields and between relative degrees of consonance and dissonance. However, unlike the conventionally functional triadic progression which is their historical prototype, it is not possible here to identify any single higher level governing harmony into which these elements could be subsumed. Each chord contains a degree of resistance to such abstraction – a counter-tendency which demands it be heard concretely in its own terms. Thus, as is also the case with Messiaen, the vertical interval structure of a chord and the instrumental colour with which it is voiced coalesce into an irreducible timbral identity. The in-built resonance – or 'grain', as Barthes might have put it – of these colour-harmonies becomes the source of a subliminal level of apprehension beyond that of their syntactic signification.

Integral to Tippett's imagistic practice is his vivid characterization of material. If this is bound up with the tendency noted above to push materials to extremes, it also relates to his deployment of instrumental resources – *King Priam* is the benchmark in this respect – in which the orchestra is fragmented into a multiplicity of ensembles. (Helen's aria, for example, with only fleeting exceptions expunges all instruments other than violas, piano and harp.[47]) Such a reconsideration of the orchestra amounts to more than an instrumental parallel to the characterization of the opera's *dramatis personae*. It is a means of characterizing the dramatic moment – and indeed moment *per se*. In a condition approaching, though not identical to, that of moment form, time becomes sedimented within the distinctive soundworld of each section; the unique qualitative features of each image mark out an autonomous, unified enclave within the temporal continuum. Certain parallels here are to be found in the Imagist poets of the early twentieth century (although direct influence seems unlikely). Pound, for example, defines an image as that which 'presents an intellectual and emotional complex in an instant of time'.[48] To collapse the temporal sequence which is of the essence of a poem or a piece of music into the appearance of an instant requires no little artifice. These conditions arise in Tippett's music when the features which make for temporal

progression are equalled or even exceeded in importance by other characteristics of the musical material (such as timbre) not ontologically bound
to teleological evolution.

The importance of characterization in Tippett's musical images is explicitly acknowledged when in his later scores conventional expression marks
are supplemented by a sprinkling of epithets or their nominal equivalents –
for example 'singing, rich and golden' (Triple Concerto), 'crystalline',
'ringing' (String Quartet No. 5), 'power', 'lyric grace' (Symphony No. 4).
(The relationship between images and qualities is also implicit when he
writes of 'images of vigour . . . of calm . . . of abounding generous exuberant
beauty'.) These score indications have in at least one case drawn criticism,[49]
and the propriety of Tippett's related tendency to add onomatopoeic annotations to percussive sounds (e.g. 'boom', 'pip, pip, pip', 'clang', 'plop') is
certainly open to question. However, if these practices have about them a
literalness bordering at times on banality, they also point more seriously to
an aspect of the material as symbolic image. In a sense they underline the
way in which the image through its excessive materiality strains away from
a state of musical immanence towards the objective world; the image thus
attracts the epithet, as if drawing it from the empirical world towards itself.
That the epithet is in fact always inadequate to the material highlights the
extent to which the image's mimetic elements are reassumed into the 'inner
world' of subjectivity. But if the epithet itself does not represent a genuine
source of mediation between inner and outer worlds, perhaps this role falls
to the body – a point to which I shall return below.

The significance (and signification) of images

Many analytical observations about music assume a kind of formalism.
Musical signifiers are understood to acquire signifieds from within the
work itself through relationships between their formal properties. To the
extent that Tippett's images encompass a musical idea, they too participate
in such a process. Yet, as we have seen, as symbolic images they also strive
beyond – or even against – a formalist conception of this kind, towards a
different semiotic order.[50] Comprising elements tractable in concepts of
musical structure plus an uncodable (but signifying) residue, these images
simultaneously engage the mind's cognitive faculties and refer it to something beyond conscious cognition. They suggest themselves as a kind of
hyper-sign, whose excessively material signifier would evoke a commensurably unfathomable signified. All this has important implications for
our understanding of Tippett's music, and compels us to return to larger
questions relating to the significance of symbolic images.

The two strata of signification referred to above have their counterpart in Jungian psychology as the dichotomy of 'directed' and 'fantasy thinking' (in turn loosely equivalent to Freud's secondary and primary process[51]). Although, strictly speaking, directed thinking pertains to language and concepts, the manipulation of the musical idea may be argued as a process akin to thought, involving relatively conscious cognition and (as musical 'logic') operating on a level of relative rationality. By contrast, that which exceeds the idea corresponds to fantasy thinking, which Jung held to be 'closer . . . to archetypal layers of the psyche'.[52] On this view, symbolic musical images would be seen to engage the mind on the level not just of the unconscious but of the transpersonal, collective unconscious of which archetypal images are the expression.

With this we return to an issue deferred earlier: whether it is possible to talk meaningfully of archetypes in music, especially in relation to the collective unconscious. Problematic enough when considered purely from the standpoint of analytical psychology, these concepts take on still further complications when considered in relation to music. While an extended discussion would be out of place here, we cannot ignore the fact that Tippett both implicitly and explicitly imputed an archetypal dimension to his images – as in his fourth opera for example, in which he sought to present the 'archetypal sound . . . of the ice breaking on the great northern rivers in the spring'.[53] It remains questionable whether a historically medi-ated product such as music is able to attain the putatively archaic, trans-cultural character which Jung attributes to archetypes. What can be said, however, is that Tippett developed a skill for rhetorically evoking a sense of the primordial which Jung associates with the archetype, through the often strongly somatic properties of his musical images. Exemplary in this respect are the pounding low Cs of the Second Symphony, the generative 'birth' motif of the Fourth (1976–7), and the surging opening figure of *The Ice Break* (1973–6) – the 'archetypal sound' referred to above. This last is quoted in Example 2.3. The material's harmonic and motivic profiles – determinant features of its consciously cognized identity – are subsumed within a gesture whose powerful brass inception and subsequent iterated contractions seem to be apprehended directly in the viscera. Lower-register doublings at several octaves amplified by the elemental timbre of untuned percussion evoke a sublime, abysmal space – apprehended phenomenally as an inner space whose immensity is a translation of the scale of the sound, and the physical resources which generate it, in relation to the perceiving subject's body. That composing was for Tippett a physical as well as a mental act[54] adds further weight to the case for including the corporeal in a consideration of his musical images. Given the variety of discourses around

Example 2.3. *The Ice Break*, Act I scene 1.

the body in the theory of recent decades – as different as the phenomenology of Merleau-Ponty and the post-structuralism of Barthes and Kristeva – further exploration would need to develop a rather more sophisticated epistemology than that so far employed. For our present purposes, however, perhaps the most apposite connection is once again Jung, whose comments on the relation between psyche and body form a regular (if varying) theme within his writings:

> The symbols of the self arise in the depths of the body and they express its materiality every bit as much as the structure of the perceiving consciousness ... The deeper 'layers' of the psyche lose their individual uniqueness as they retreat farther and farther into darkness. 'Lower down' ... they become increasingly collective until they are universalized and extinguished in the body's materiality ... Hence 'at bottom' the psyche is simply 'world' ... The more archaic and 'deeper', that is the more *physiological* the symbol is, the more collective and universal, the more 'material' it is. The more abstract, differentiated, and specific it is, and the more its nature approximates to conscious uniqueness and individuality, the more it sloughs off its universal character.[55]

The content of the Jungian symbolic image as adopted by Tippett is presented, then, as some kind of essence apprehensible only in the 'deeper' layers of the psyche, beyond consciousness. In extreme manifestations such images might be regarded as vehicles of the transcendental – for Tippett a significant preoccupation, as seen in works such as *The Midsummer Marriage*, *The Vision of Saint Augustine* (1963–5) and *The Mask of Time* (1980–2). But positing the unconscious as the origin and ultimate destination of the symbolic image, and the image as a portentous resonance within its 'depths', is not entirely unproblematic. As much as standing for a transpersonal reservoir of timeless knowledge, the unconscious may also represent a kind of black hole of mystification into which tractable meaning disappears: an ideological transmutation of an absence into a presence. It may therefore be worth briefly considering the image from a complementary standpoint: not as the bearer of an immanent, ineffable meaning, but rather as a rhetorical device for disrupting conventional modes of signification, for dislodging signifiers from signifieds, sending the perceiving mind into a state of disorientation in relation to its object. This is the model adopted by Thomas Weiskel (at least in the initial stages of his investigation) in his study of the romantic sublime. Weiskel describes the onset of the sublime moment as follows:

> the habitual relation of mind and object suddenly breaks down. Surprise or astonishment is the affective correlative, and there is an immediate intuition

> of a disconcerting disproportion between inner and outer. Either mind or object is suddenly in excess – and then both are, since their relation has become radically indeterminate. We are reading along and suddenly occurs a text which exceeds comprehension, which seems to contain a residue of signifier which finds no reflected signified in our minds.[56]

Then, in a subsequent phase:

> the mind recovers the balance of outer and inner by constituting a fresh relation between itself and the object such that the very indeterminacy which erupted in [the previous] phase . . . is taken as symbolizing the mind's relation to a transcendent order.[57]

Weiskel, then, locates the sublime at moments when linear, or syntagmatic, structures are disrupted. In Tippett's case this criterion might apply not only to instances of the sublime but to his use of images in general (the difference is in certain respects only a matter of degree). In his more disjunctive later works in particular, the semiotic excess of the image may belong to a tendency countervailing the unfolding of the musical idea. The treatment of harmony in Helen's aria, discussed above, illustrates the point: on the one hand the harmonic succession is partially assumed into the higher-level notion of a progression; on the other hand that which goes beyond the idea resists such assimilation. Such cases, I would argue, represent facets of Tippett's modernist outlook: the internal contradictions of the material function as an immanent critique of received paradigms of musical meaning. In itself, however, this is no guarantee of artistic success, which depends on the individual context and the particular interaction and balance between the idea and its other. At its best, the inner contention of the material offers perceptions of things 'rich and strange' so characteristic of Tippett. Sometimes, however, a reliance on the libidinal immediacy of the image may have more problematic implications. *Byzantium* (1989–90) – a setting of Yeats's poem of the same title, absolutely bound up with the notion of images – is a case in point. Here the succession of opulent, frequently breathtaking images not only dismembers the flow of the Yeats poem which it sets but also dislocates the large-scale musical syntagm to the extent that an overall governing structure is difficult to detect; it remains a moot point whether this is the work's most radical feature or its most serious flaw.[58]

Conclusions

Probably the single most significant corollary of Tippett's imagism is its connotation of a profoundly psychoanalytic epistemology. It suggests

musical material as ultimately emanating from the psychological life of the individual, putatively enmeshed with the psychological life of other individuals through the collective unconscious. As I have mentioned at various points, such a conception (like any model of meaning) constitutes an ideology: it suggests music functioning within an autonomous, 'inner' psychological domain, and implicitly conceals the fact that music's transmission is historical and cultural, operating within a society whose antagonisms are inseparable from issues of economy and class. (It is perhaps noteworthy that Tippett's embrace of Jung in the later 1930s was contemporaneous with his turning away from active, left-wing political engagement, and with his wholesale adoption of an aesthetic of autonomous art.)

To raise this matter, however, is not to dismiss the music produced under such a conception (nor indeed the conception itself) in an unnuanced critique. For one thing, these psychoanalytic factors do not represent the whole story. Whatever Tippett's personal views about musical ontology expressed in his essays, his activity as a composer – indeed as a modernist composer – required him to engage with his material's immanent demands as material: that is, with its intrinsic properties as music, dialectically mediated in its social foundation and historical evolution. But equally, the ideological dimension of the Jungian model Tippett adopted cannot itself be rejected as unequivocally untruthful: in occluding certain perspectives it may well illuminate others; truth and ideology may not be so easily separated. Consider the following passage from Tippett's essay 'Art and anarchy':

> It is obvious enough that whichever way we look at it our social life is being changed and disrupted by tremendous forces. Is it as obvious that modern art is directly responsive to these forces; whether to express them, tame them, or reject them? I do not think so: I believe, because as a creative artist I feel it, that the inner world of man's psyche is in ferment. And that this ferment is forcing up new, and often unwanted, images. But I am not certain at all that the outer ferment or the inner ferment is a cause or effect of the other. It seems to me equally possible that the simultaneity of these two processes is accidental.[59]

Tippett seems to be asserting the absolute autonomy of the inner world – a stance which one imagines might draw opprobrium from a critic such as Theodor Adorno, whose view of modern art was that it should mimetically internalize the antagonisms of society. But Tippett's statement calls for a more subtle reading. What he questions is the directness of the response between inner and outer worlds, the notion of an unmediated causality between them. By stressing the discontinuity between the inner and outer

world he implicitly points to subjectivity's powers of resistance to an objectivity made rigid by rationality. The image thus offers the potential for opposition, and indeed change:

> These spontaneous images which arise from within present often a complementary or even opposed view of things to that of our rational, or conventional conscious mind; and during the process of living with and studying these images as they appear, the inner attitude changes, in such a way that it becomes more attuned to reality than before . . . The new images that first break upon the world through this or that great artist, will only slowly be accepted, as the general attitude changes in their direction.[60]

Thus rather than representing a reactionary indifference to the outer world, the autonomy of the inner world is seen as the source of the possibility for change, for a realignment of inner and outer – hence Tippett's reference to 'images which by their fascination and power will compel us against every intellectual objection to re-order our lives'.[61] This is clearly a different modernism from Adorno's – articulated from a liberal humanist rather than a Marxist standpoint – but it is in its own way radical. Jung understood the image as a medium for apprehending the world, as an expression of 'the unique and unconditioned creative power of the psyche'.[62] The power of the image lies in its mediation of objectivity by subjectivity, and thus its demonstration that objectivity is not an absolute, that the world order posited by rationality is not immutable.

As this essay will have made clear, to trace the various ramifications of the term 'image' for Tippett is effectively to chart a detailed picture of his aesthetic principles. In the process I hope also to have begun to show the importance of his writings. Through the many connections between various essays, and with appropriate interpretation and amplification, there emerges a distinctive and coherent view of the nature of art and its possibilities for articulating humanity's place in relation to society and the world. Jung's place in all of this also calls for comment. His influence in one sense comes as no surprise, given the many references to him in Tippett's essays, and given the symbolic plotlines of the latter's operas. Yet what is possibly unexpected is the full extent to which the composer situates the function of art within a model of Jungian depth psychology. And this holds on more than a general aesthetic level. It actually impinges on the nature of the musical material, such that Tippett's musical images manifest an often productive (though sometimes problematic) tension between the demands of musical syntax and a desire (I think the word is appropriate) to transcend it. For the analyst this has predictable implications, since the material frequently offers resistance to the reductive categories inherent in analytical

models predicated by rational thought. However, rather than signifying defeat for any analytical project, this rather calls upon the analyst to assimilate into his or her own activity the dialectic of the mental and sensuous embedded in the material. The image may exceed the musical idea but it is still related to it (as either amplification or opposition), and there is no rigid line of demarcation at which the point of excess begins. Part of the analyst's task therefore becomes to test these margins, to identify the effects of a different order of meaning upon the music's formalist operation. I am not sure that this can – or even should – entail a cosy homogeneity of aesthetic and analytical enquiry; if anything this study itself highlights possibly unbridgeable differences between them. A more profitable aspiration might be to posit the two modes of discourse as sources of mutual interrogation, so that after repeated exchange each will bear signs of its engagement with the other. What should be evident is the centrality of the image in this encounter. As a term with the potential to mediate discourses, and as a notion at the heart of Tippett's own theoretical observations, it suggests itself as an invaluable conceptual tool with which to explore and register the full significance of his music.

3 Back to Nietzsche? Transformations of the Dionysiac in *The Midsummer Marriage* and *King Priam*

I

The sense of an ending

The way a work ends can tell us much about its stylistic and aesthetic premises. In the case of Tippett's *King Priam* (1958–61) the last forty-five seconds encapsulate in both stage action and sound image the wave of brutality that has coursed through the entire opera. In fulfilment of the augury delivered in the very first scene Priam, the Trojan king, meets his death, run through on the avenging sword of Achilles' son, while around him the once-civilized city of Troy is now a blazing site of carnage. Just seven bars of music drive this last action – a gesture of utter compression. A sequence of colliding ostinati – pounding drum patterns, distorted brass fanfares and stylized shrieks in flutes, clarinets and upper strings – yields a saturation of pitches and intervals which renders every last atom of the musical structure dissonant. (And after: distilled from the silence of no more music, a shift of subjective vantage point: a few eerie sounds which might represent tears, *our* tears, Tippett tells us.)

How strikingly this contrasts with the close of Tippett's previous opera, *The Midsummer Marriage* (1946–52). Its final minute is suffused with the sonority of A major, exploding from a celebrative cymbal clash, like a sunburst, and finally subdued into gentle, blended orchestral hues reminiscent of the close of Wagner's *Tristan*. This sound grounds the dancing energy of all the other figuration and symbolizes the resolution of the oppositions and tensions of the entire opera. Light and shadow, male and female, humanity and nature are reconciled; all is harmoniousness.

There could be no more graphic demonstration of the distance Tippett travelled in the six years between completing his first opera and starting his second than this juxtaposition of their endings; no more striking piece of evidence in support of the view that *King Priam* marks not only a new style period but also a radically different aesthetic disposition. As *A Child of our Time* (1939–41) made plain, Tippett's ruminations on the human lot never excluded an awareness of its darker side – of, we might say, its tragic nature. But whereas in the oratorio's operatic successor the dark, tragic dimension is assumed into a realm of lucent affirmation, in *King*

Priam tragedy is of the essence. The world of the aesthetic now admits the violent reality of the world; and the switch from comedy to tragedy has consequences that will reverberate throughout the rest of Tippett's composing career. Never again will he commit so wholeheartedly to the optimistic vision of *The Midsummer Marriage*, at least not without commensurable injections of acid or irony.

We may never get to the bottom of what motivated this turn in Tippett's *œuvre*.[1] But my interest here is less with finding some kind of causal or deterministic explanation than to develop a hermeneutic reading of its meanings. My thesis will be that what is iconic of the changed 'world vision' of *King Priam* is its altered representation of the Dionysiac (for few theories of tragedy proceed far without reference to the ancient Greek god in whose honour the theatrical genre was originally practised). It should, I hope, be clear that I refer here to Dionysus as myth, or as a metaphor for those drives within the human psyche which lie outside the jurisdiction of Apollonian reason: those aspects (shading off into very dark hues) concerned with the earthly and the bodily; with the experience of abandonment, the liquidation of the individual into the collective. Furthermore, the Dionysiac is also a *discourse* with a rich cultural history, aspects of which it will also be my concern to identify and relate to Tippett's position.

In referring to an *alteration* of the way in which the Dionysiac is represented between *The Midsummer Marriage* and *King Priam* I am of course implying its common presence in both operas – thus that what takes place between them is a metamorphosis rather than an outright schism. This is suggestive of something – or rather someone – else as well. For the notion of a metamorphosis of the Dionysiac contains within it an echo of an analogous paradigm shift in the thought of another, earlier figure closely associated with Dionysus and seminal for our ideas of tragedy: the late nineteenth-century philosopher Friedrich Nietzsche.

If considering Nietzsche potentially helps situate Tippett's aesthetic practices within a greater historical and cultural depth of field, the name is likely to cause consternation among those who would limit contextual discussion of the composer's music to a list of 'official' influences. Opening the door to this possibly troublesome gatecrasher can be justified, however, on three levels. First, we cannot discount Tippett's own acquaintance with Nietzsche's thought. Evidence for this includes not only references in Tippett's essays and lectures, but also the fact that he owned certain of Nietzsche's writings.[2] Secondly, even without such positivistic evidence, aspects of Nietzsche's thought would continue to illuminate aspects of Tippett's. More than coincidental connections, these throw into relief certain shared ideological facets (and I would want

to stress 'certain') arising from the two figures' respective reflections on the conditions of post-Enlightenment culture. Central in this is a common concern with questions of metaphysics, and also an analogous revaluation of those questions between the earlier and later phases of their output.

Such a comparison could be sustained simply on the ground that culturally significant figures represent dense nexus points in the 'web of culture', regardless of their own awareness or ignorance of other figures to whom they are connected. But in fact we can posit a number of intermediary nodes which enrich our picture of the discursive network in which Tippett's work is situated. This, then, provides a third level – arguably the most pertinent one – on which to justify the juxtaposition of Tippett and Nietzsche. Characterized by mediation, this level is concerned with the discursive space between the two figures, a space within which lie such names as Jane Harrison, W. B. Yeats, H. G. Wells, George Bernard Shaw, Richard Wagner, Arthur Schopenhauer and C. G. Jung. A number of these are writers or artists with whose work Tippett was indeed acquainted. Some of the names belong to the Anglophone reception of Nietzsche in the first half of the twentieth century, others to a Germanophone intellectual tradition. Either way, they represent agents of transmission and/or reinforcement of ideas whose philosophical and aesthetic distillation can be found in Nietzsche. 'Nietzsche' on these second and third levels, then, might be understood as a kind of shorthand or synecdoche for an entire constellation of ideas with which Tippett's own thinking in various ways and to various degrees engages.

Nature, myth, Hellenism

Many of Tippett's artistic endeavours were concerned with articulating a view of 'man's place in the world as we know it' – as he would much later put it.[3] (Indeed what is self-evident in the radically different soundworlds of *The Midsummer Marriage* and *King Priam* is that they present commensurably contrasting stances in this regard.) The essentializing terms of such an attitude – 'man', 'the world' – assume a dimension of existence putatively irreducible to any specific cultural, social or historical determination – as if occupying a natural, or indeed mythological, substratum. In *The Midsummer Marriage* especially, nature and myth are convergent ideas, and, analogically, Nietzsche in his first published book, *The Birth of Tragedy* (1872), conflated nature and myth in his portrayal of the Dionysiac as a supra-individual and supra-historical 'ground of being' (which matter we shall pursue in more detail below). Still, Tippett requires the mythological and the historical to rub shoulders,[4] and this partly

explains the dialogue throughout his *œuvre* between the pastoral and the urban: manifested not only within individual works (cf. *The Midsummer Marriage*'s juxtaposition of magic woods and mechanics), but also in the arc that leads from the Concerto for Double String Orchestra (1938–9) to *The Rose Lake* (1991–3), and in between passes through the townscapes of *The Knot Garden* (1966–9), *The Ice Break* (1973–6) and *New Year* (1986–8). Even within Tippett's city limits, however, nature is still present in the guise of myth. The everymen and -women of all his operas act out putatively universal cycles of conflict and resolution in places that are everywhere and nowhere.

In Tippett's thinking, then, the search is on for paradigms of the suprahistorical that are neither Christian nor in any orthodox sense theological: whatever it is that human experience is grounded in must none the less be grounded in human experience. In 1950, in the throes of composing *The Midsummer Marriage*, Tippett wrote to Eric Walter White: 'somewhere at the back of my mind is a dim unformulated notion of some new humanism – or fresh idea of the limits & quality of the human person – The Whole Man, as I call him'.[5] On the other hand, the paradigm of *King Priam* is formulated negatively – as repudiating both Marxism and Christianity. Tippett's message to White regarding this opera was 'no chiliastic philosophy, whether of a classless society or a heavenly reward'.[6] It is into this space that the tragic vision enters: tragedy not as a mere set of generic conventions, but as a worldview or a philosophy of life.

When Tippett stated in connection with *King Priam*, 'I am unrepentantly certain, from some deep intuitive source, that tragedy is both viable and rewarding',[7] he was – unwittingly or otherwise – echoing the affirmation of Greek tragedy made by Nietzsche almost a century earlier in writings such as *The Birth of Tragedy* and 'Richard Wagner in Bayreuth' (1876). While the mediations of Tippett's philhellenism, which deeply informed both *The Midsummer Marriage* and *King Priam*, are quite complex and do not all lead back to the philosopher, this nevertheless represents an obvious point of contact (which also extends to others in the Nietzschean constellation, notably Wagner and Jung). For example, one of the most influential texts on the construction of *King Priam*, Lucien Goldmann's *Le dieu caché*, presents a model of tragedy rooted strongly in, among other things, the neoclassical example of Jean Racine.[8] But what is also pertinent within Tippett's Hellenism is the trope of the *daimonic*:

> I may, like Hölderlin, love the gay Greek Gods (though I must tremble before their dark and terrible natures), yet at the moment of intense creation, when music, if it is to live, must be searched for in those depths of the psyche where the god- and devil-images also hibernate; then how am I so sure, as I am, that I shall take no harm and the music be sane?[9]

(In a slightly earlier essay Tippett states that these 'depths of the psyche constitute a faculty 'nearer to the creation of the mysterious mythological tragedies like *Oedipus Rex*'.[10])

The conceit of possession by a God is what points back to Nietzsche – a connection made by Tippett himself (as discussed below). Also interesting is the route whereby he arrives at it, namely via the classical scholar Jane Harrison, whom he characterizes as similarly overtaken. 'Her books', he writes, 'have the passionate excitement of someone under an influence, of someone, despite all the scholarship, possessed. I doubt if many can read *Themis* without being affected by this sense of possession.'[11] Harrison's *Themis* is documented by Kemp as exerting 'a strong if rather shadowy influence' on *The Midsummer Marriage*,[12] specifically through the figure she calls *Eniautos-Daimon*, the year-spirit invoked in a ritual of death and resurrection which 'was at once the representation of the life of the group and the life of nature', and 'issued in agonistic festivals and in [Attic] drama'.[13] No doubt the collective consciousness which is at the heart of these myths (and a central concern for Harrison) was attractive to Tippett, known for his canonical statement 'I hold for myself that the composition of oratorio and opera is a collective as well as a personal experience'.[14] Indeed *The Midsummer Marriage* could be seen as providing an afterlife for ideas espoused by the so-called Cambridge Ritualists, the group of classicists and anthropologists active in the early twentieth century, who held that the origins of Greek tragedy lay in rituals similar in kind to those of the *Eniautos-Daimon*.[15] Among this group, besides Harrison herself, were Gilbert Murray and F. M. Cornford both of whom contributed chapters to *Themis*.[16] And the god who was central among their scholarly pre-occupations was Dionysus. Nietzsche's presence can be detected among the group as a figure of identification if not overt influence. In the privileging of the 'Dionysus the daimon' in her earlier thought, Harrison admits (in the second edition of *Themis*) to being a 'disciple . . . of Nietzsche',[17] while Cornford was among the early defenders of *The Birth of Tragedy*, which he described as 'a work of profound imaginative insight, which left the scholarship of a generation toiling in the rear'.[18]

As the earlier quotation makes clear, Tippett implies a thin line between creativity and daimonic possession. But equally it is evident that this can involve crossing another boundary: that between irrationality and madness. He asserts his own survival of this risky encounter (and Harrison's too), but Nietzsche himself stands as an example of one who was engulfed:

> Nietzsche was perhaps the first great European to be aware that he had, in his
> own person, experienced the rebirth of an ancient god – of Zarathustra. The
> impact of the experience was so violent that he became eventually clinically
> insane. But it can be shown, I think, that hidden in Zarathustra is an earlier

> meeting of Nietzsche with yet another god – with Dionysus, the god who
> came from the East into Greece to force his way like a wild storm into the
> measured climate of the Olympian system.[19]

That Tippett's few direct references to Nietzsche are usually geared to the question of the philosopher's final insanity may seem unpromising ground for establishing any affinity between them. But there is a profound and signal ambivalence in Tippett's attitude, contained within which is a possible element of empathy. Like Nietzsche, Tippett was driven to open himself up to the full implications of existence in a modern (i.e. post-Enlightenment) world, with all its contradictions, joys and terrors (this is what is connoted when he talks of searching 'in those depths of the psyche where the god- and devil-images also hibernate'). At the same time, Nietzsche stands as a warning against over-identification with the god in whom the distinction between joy and terror dissolves. He serves as a test or limit case for a particular world view, and I shall argue that Tippett's ambivalence towards that view is played out in *King Priam* and the second-period works which follow. At the end, then, we shall need to ascertain both how close the convergence is and where the two part company. Our starting point, however, will be *The Midsummer Marriage*, for it is here that the Dionysiac, as well as the complementary principle of the Apollonian, is particularly clearly represented.

II

Images of the Dionysiac in *The Midsummer Marriage*

Irrespective of whether, or how well, Tippett knew Nietzsche's *The Birth of Tragedy*, its discourse of the Dionysiac and Apollonian has recognizable resonances in *The Midsummer Marriage*. The connections probably obtain because *The Birth of Tragedy* forms an intersection for several other, probably more directly influential, reference points for the opera. Among these are the Cambridge Ritualists, mentioned above; another is Jung, who discusses *The Birth of Tragedy* in his *Psychological Types* – a book which we know Tippett read, probably in the 1930s.[20] A further key figure is Wagner. However problematic Nietzsche's relationship with Wagner subsequently became (both personally and intellectually), *The Birth of Tragedy* was self-admittedly written under the spell of Wagner, as its dedication makes plain. Its conception of tragedy, its figuration of the Dionysiac, its view of man in relation to nature, its promotion of myth, not to mention its Schopenhauerian metaphysics, all served to legitimate Wagner's own pseudo-Hellenic conception of theatre, i.e. Music Drama. And it is this very conception to which Tippett looks for the musical representation of

the marvellous in *The Midsummer Marriage*. His essays 'Drum, flute and zither' and 'The birth of an opera' make both implicit and explicit reference to Wagner's *Oper und Drama* (1851), and we know from Tippett's autobiography that he became familiar with Wagner's operas and operatic writings in his student days.[21] When he writes that 'opera, just because of its music, may be the most suitable medium to hand now to renew the Greek [theatrical] attitude'[22] he seems to be reinvoking a century-old Wagnerian agenda of a collective art ritual based on myth which also held overwhelming significance for Nietzsche.[23]

Despite belonging to the genre of comedy, *The Midsummer Marriage* also has reference points with tragedy. Ian Kemp's analysis argues that the work's dramatic design may well reflect Cornford's thesis that the structure of Aristophanic comedy (on which the opera is modelled) exhibits many points of convergence with that of Attic tragedy. In fact *The Midsummer Marriage* makes far more explicit figurations of Dionysus – as well as Apollo – than is the case with *King Priam*. This is particularly evident in the Act I transfigurations of Mark and Jenifer: Mark returning from the depths in the guise of Dionysus; Jenifer returning from on high in the semblance of Athena, Apollo's female counterpart.[24] Mark's words overtly evoke the tragic god:

> As stallions stamping
> The young men dance
> To the springing sap
> And the leaping life.
>
> We force our feet through the great grass
> And tear the boughs from the bending trees
> That hold the sun from the glorious bed
> Where she, lying fallow through the winter,
> Slept, till pricked awake by our desire.[25]

The exuberant adjectives 'stamping', 'springing', 'leaping' evoke the ritual choric dancing of satyrs, the half-goat, half-human retinue of Dionysus – as, for example, in Sophocles' *Trackers* when the satyrs exclaim 'I'll make the ground ring with my jumps and kicks'.[26] One is also reminded of Nietzsche's description of 'that Dionysiac monster Zarathustra' as 'lover of leaps and tangents' in a passage whose evocation of earthly exuberance (teaching 'the art of terrestrial comfort') is intended as a repudiation of the metaphysics of the earlier *Birth of Tragedy*.[27] (His repeated emphasis on laughter in this passage adds a further gloss to the line 'we are the laughing children' sung by Tippett's chorus at the end of *The Midsummer Marriage*.) Mark's reference to sap is an obvious allusion to fertility – developed in the

final, climactic Ritual Dance of Act III, when he and Jenifer sing of 'the bull / Whose blood and sperm are all fertility'. The fluid elements here are as much symbols of the Dionysiac as the bull: Michael Silk and J. P. Stern write that 'the god, as Plutarch put it in the first century AD, is lord of "the whole wet element in nature": sap and semen, blood and wine'.[28] Finally, the line 'Tear the boughs from the bending trees' is an allusion to the *Thrysus*, the staff carried by Dionysus and his followers – reinforced when shortly afterwards Mark raises 'a golden branch'.[29]

From this celebrative beginning Mark goes on to recount the associated and opposing aspect of the god:

> The ewe is torn by our willing hands
> The child trod by our frenzied feet
> That beat the beat of life inflamed
> By death.

The frenzy which he describes has its more benign counterpart in the Bacchic intoxication of the chorus at the start of Act III – implicitly an invocation to Dionysus as god of vegetation and of the vine in particular. But here Mark is privy to that more extreme form of Dionysiac possession (a kind of madness) that leads to *sparagmos* – the crossing of (in Walter Otto's words) 'the threshold where one step beyond leads to dismemberment and darkness';[30] where life at its most intensely felt is identified with death. It is this erosion of categories – of the articulations of conscious, Apollonian thought – that is at the heart of the Dionysiac: the dissolution of the boundaries between not only life and death, but also mind and body, self and other. Mark's next lines, 'There is no union but in full / Communion, Man with Beast and All in One' would have found a sympathetic ally in Nietzsche, for whom the Dionysiac implies release from the Apollonian principle of individuation (*principium individuationis*[31]) into the 'oneness' of nature:

> Dionysiac stirrings arise either through the influence of those narcotic potions of which all primitive races speak in their hymns, or through the powerful approach of spring, which penetrates with joy the whole frame of nature. So stirred, the individual forgets himself completely . . .
>
> Not only does the bond between man and man come to be forged once more by the magic of the Dionysiac rite, but nature itself, long alienated and subjugated, rises again to celebrate the reconciliation with her prodigal son, man.[32]

This regained consciousness of a primordial state of 'oneness' is for the early Nietzsche the prime achievement of Attic tragedy. It is also a metaphysical notion which in one way or another underpins much of the thinking in the ideological constellation with which we are concerned here.

Looking backwards, its source is in Schopenhauer; looking forwards, it finds a counterpart in Jung's collective unconscious and to Jung-influenced notions of the collective in Tippett, not least his idea of opera as a collective experience.[33] Moreover, the notion achieves a particular currency in *The Midsummer Marriage*, not least in the association between oneness with nature and *enchantment*.

Enchanted nature

The theme of nature in *The Midsummer Marriage* (and for that matter in Tippett's *œuvre* as a whole) has been less than fully explored in the Tippett literature, though some commentators have insightfully touched upon it. David Cairns, for example, writes that 'nature in *The Midsummer Marriage* is an integral part of the opera – both a metaphor of the central argument and an active agent in it. The wood in which the action takes place is at once a naturalistic wood, a symbol of natural energy at its most abundant, and a magic place full of hidden presences from which no one is immune.'[34] Nature in general and the wood in particular are also mentioned by Derrick Puffett:

> The metaphors [of *The Midsummer Marriage*] work because they are firmly embedded in a natural setting: the 'magic wood' . . . which is of course also the wood of *A Midsummer Night's Dream* . . . *Siegfried*, Verdi's *Falstaff* and countless other 'traditional' forest settings. And by metaphors I mean not only the verbal allusions but the musical ones as well, the string figurations that suggest Wagner's 'Forest Murmurs', the celesta that signifies enchantment as surely as it does in Bax or Schreker.[35]

Independently Cairns and Puffett signal the link between nature and magic or enchantment in *The Midsummer Marriage*. For the Nietzsche of *The Birth of Tragedy* enchantment is an essential ingredient whereby aesthetic experience becomes an experience of union with nature: 'In the Dionysiac dithyramb man . . . [feels] the desire . . . to sink back into the original oneness of nature . . . to express the very essence of nature symbolically . . . In the dithyramb we see a community of unconscious actors all of whom see one another as enchanted. Enchantment is the precondition of all of dramatic art.'[36]

But if Dionysiac enchantment makes possible one kind of communion with the totality that is nature, this is only half the story. For in his figuration of the Dionysiac reveller Nietzsche also speaks of a countervailing kind of magic: Apollonian illusion, or appearance (*Schein*). Apollonian art (which Nietzsche relates to Schiller's category of naïve art) represents

'harmony with nature' through 'identification with the beauty of appearance'.[37] As the Dionysiac state is likened to intoxication, so the Apollonian is likened to dream. However, the illusory nature of the latter is seen in anything but negative terms: in it the world appears with the vivid clarity of 'he who is etymologically the "lucent" one, the god of light'.[38] 'Here we enjoy an immediate apprehension of form, all shapes speak to us directly'[39] – which connotes the separation of the perceived world into discrete elements, the principle of individuation.

Thus the Apollonian and Dionysiac represent opposing routes by which to transcend the appearance of empirical waking reality. Corresponding to them are the two exits which Jenifer and Mark take from the stage of *The Midsummer Marriage*: the ladder up to heaven and the gates down into the cave. The Apollonian is a higher appearance, or second reflection; the Dionysiac the amoral, in-different ground of nature which attends the release from appearance. And just as *The Midsummer Marriage* is concerned with the marriage of opposites between the Apollonian and Dionysiac, so too *The Birth of Tragedy* presents Attic tragedy as the child of the 'mysterious marriage' of 'both urges'.[40] Nietzsche's closing exhortation, 'let us sacrifice in the temple of both gods'[41] finds its counterpart in the epigraph to *The Midsummer Marriage*, taken from the Petelia Tablet dating from the fourth century BC: 'You shall say: I am a child of earth and of starry heaven'.[42] In the opera the Dionysiac and Apollonian achieve a balance through their symmetry: for example, Mark's dithyramb discussed above is a counterpart to Jenifer's evocation of Apollonian purity, 'Sweet was the peace'; and presiding over the many expressions of Dionysiac exuberance is the sun, with which Apollo had become associated by the fifth century BC, and to which Tippett attributed such importance in *The Midsummer Marriage* as later to express regret (whimsically, no doubt) at not including it in the list of *dramatis personae*.[43]

For Nietzsche the essential Dionysiac substratum of Greek tragedy is the chorus, which historically had its roots in the comedic satyr play. The chorus is instrumental in a chain of identifications made possible through the enchantment in which 'the Dionysiac reveler sees himself as satyr, and as satyr, in turn, he sees the god'.[44] Through excitation by the dithyrambic chorus the listener was also drawn into the transformed state, and 'would project the shape of the god [Dionysus] . . . onto that masked figure of a man [the tragic protagonist], dissolving the latter's reality into a ghostly unreality. This is the Apollonian dream state . . .'[45] Thus the 'Apollonian dream state' seems to be generated as it were spontaneously from the choric Dionysiac enchantment such that the spectator/listener is held simultaneously in two contradictory states of consciousness.[46]

In *The Midsummer Marriage*, whose principal dramatic conceit is the interaction between 'two worlds of apprehension', the choric role is divided up so that, broadly speaking, the singing chorus of Mark and Jenifer's friends occupies the world of the everyday,[47] while the dancers inhabit the world of the marvellous, and are one with the natural world. In this respect the dancers come close to Nietzsche's depiction of the satyr chorus which is 'the highest expression of nature'. Nietzsche's description of the satyr as 'a compassionate companion re-enacting the sufferings of the god [Dionysus]; . . . a symbol of the sexual omnipotence of nature'[48] is particularly fitting to the character of Strephon in *The Midsummer Marriage*, whose progressively greater symbolic wounding in the first three Ritual Dances, and association with Mark and Jenifer's symbolic rebirth in the fourth, indeed ally him with the Dionysiac myth of death and rebirth.[49] The Ritual Dances, then, are where many of the themes we have discussed so far – Dionysiac union, Apollonian dream-like illusion, magic, enchantment, nature, the Dionysiac role of the chorus – converge.

The Apollonian and Dionysiac in music

It is to the world of the Ritual Dances that I now want to turn in a short case study. My focus will be the music of the 'pre-scene' of Act II of *The Midsummer Marriage* (see Ex. 3.1), which here has a preludial function in relation to the dances, and eventually (in Act III) serves as a climactic post-lude to the deferred final dance. Hence while this music is not strictly speaking part of the dances it is absolutely of their kind: on every occasion it is posited as symbolic of an unchanging numinous state present in nature (exemplified by its abrupt commencement at the start of Act II, suggesting something already under way, always already there).

Self-evidently, if the Dionysiac and Apollonian are important tropes in this operatic work, that importance cannot reside in text or dramaturgy alone: music must play a decisive role in voicing those ideas.[50] Yet these terms are not essences or immanent strata residing within the work waiting to be identified. It would be better to construe them as ideas to think with – ideas that offer various interpretative possibilities. Moreover in their deployment these terms are not so neatly separable. If the Dionysiac is a dimension prior to the Apollonian process of form-making it is difficult to distil this analytically from music (or indeed any other aesthetic practice), which in one sense can only communicate through what is formed. The Dionysiac can only be sensed within its mediation in the Apollonian (Nietzsche saw exactly such mediation as distinctive of Attic tragedy). What transcends technique cannot be wholly divested from technique.

Additionally, the realization of these would-be supra-historical ideas in music cannot be considered apart from the historical and cultural mediations of the musical material in question.

The above suggests, then, that the Dionysiac might be arrived at through consideration of the Apollonian. In the Act II pre-scene the Apollonian is evident in the impulse to aestheticize nature – in that nature's hostile qualities are simultaneously represented and kept at bay through an 'Apollonian dream state, in which the daylight world is veiled and a new world . . . falls upon the eye in ever-changing shapes'.[51] The radiance which Nietzsche associates with the Apollonian state is apparent in the accompanying stage picture, flooded with the light of Midsummer afternoon; moreover, when the preludial music returns before the Ritual Dances proper, Jack and Bella who witness the dances are described in a stage direction as being 'as in a dream'.

Among the musico-rhetorical means Tippett employs to cast a 'veil of enchantment' over the natural world, are the devices of metonymy and mimesis. The metonymic agents are the French horns which initially carry the passage's long harmonized line (see Ex. 3.1), and which through their bucolic associations are semiotically adjacent to the natural world. (Tippett used ensembles of horns to signify closeness to nature several times in his *œuvre*, their deployment in *The Rose Lake*, with their overtones of Wagner's *Das Rheingold*, being perhaps the most pertinent connection.[52]) The horns also signify mimetically through the gentle rocking neighbour-note motion of their muted opening motif (labelled *a* in Ex. 3.1), suggesting cradling, slumber, dreaminess – a sinking back into the maternal principle of nature. But they are mimetic too of natural presences in the landscape – presences such as Strephon and the trees which will eventually come to life.[53] Other voices of the natural are heard in the demisemiquaver sextuplet figuration for flutes and clarinets (and its demisemiquaver duplet counterpart in the harp),[54] which through its own shifting levels of activity and density matches the intensity curve of the horns' line without directly joining it. While this figuration could be heard as stylized birdsong, its qualities are in fact less literal, suggesting at one extreme a kind of anthropomorphic 'creatureliness' (the rather cute movement of the flutes as they enter canonically at Figs. 145f. and 146ff.), and at the other extreme (for example, as the orchestra is in full flood around Fig. 148) a kind of general dance – a celebration of life in the world, touching on the cosmic (a gesture reminiscent of ecstatic figuration in 'Joie du sang des étoiles' from Messiaen's *Turangalîla Symphony*).

With this allusion to oneness in and with nature we begin to move into Dionysiac territory. What would have fallen to the chorus in Greek tragedy

Example 3.1. *The Midsummer Marriage*, Act II pre-scene.

Example 3.1 (*cont.*)

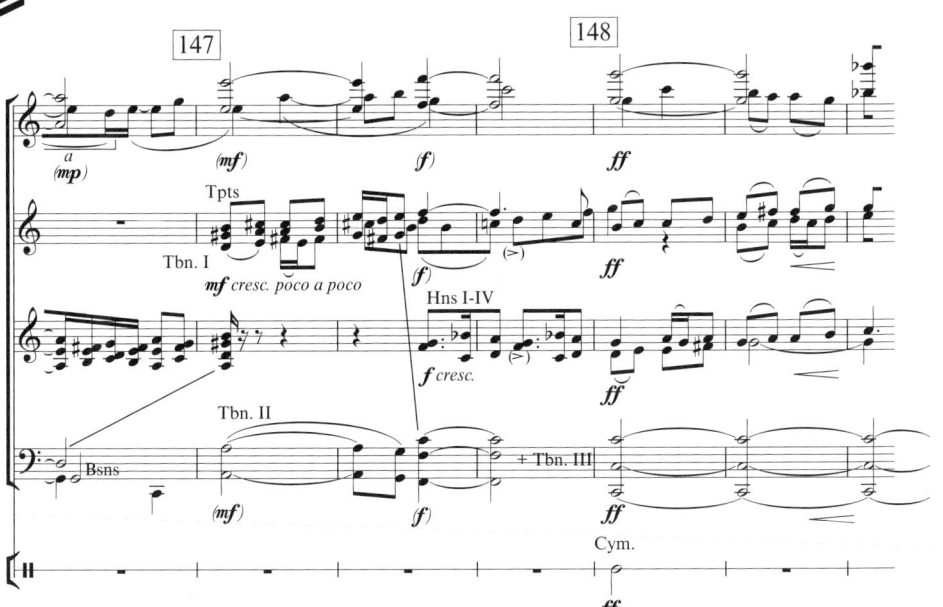

(at least the way Nietzsche saw it) here becomes the task of the orchestra: to engender a sense of universality not only within the depicted world on stage, but also between this world and that of the audience. In other words the Dionysiac aspect of the music resides in its power to compel the listener's full identification with it. It is in this rhetorical requirement that metaphysics and musical technique converge. In the present example the cadential gesture on C (Fig. 148) is central, serving as the focal point towards which the preceding music grows and which it then exceeds: an overwhelming moment of closure into which all musical features, stage

image, and we ourselves are enfolded. The emotional force of this moment – its numinosity – inheres not in the cadence itself but in its structural function as the point of arrival implied and also delayed by the preceding tonal and harmonic process. These several interim deflections enacted on a recognizable harmonic vocabulary foster an increasing emotional invest-ment from the listener and with it increasing identification with the music.

At bottom, then, Tippett's strategy is an old-fashioned one (but sub-jected to a process of renewal, as will presently be discussed): he relies on the affective power of dissonance and resolution, on both the smaller and larger scale. In *The Birth of Tragedy* Nietzsche cites the example of pleasure in musical dissonance (a pleasure predicated on the promise of resolution to consonance) as a metaphor with which to understand the aesthetic delight we feel at the spectacle of suffering found in tragedy.[55] This fact is interesting in the present context not for any direct connection with Tippett, but because just as Nietzsche clearly had the example of Wagner in mind (most quintessentially *Tristan und Isolde*), so Tippett engineers a metaphysical dimension to his music through the Wagnerian example of a prolonged seventh chord – especially clear in the first two phrases of this passage. His practice is Wagnerian not only in that the dominant seventh (as in the prelude to *Tristan*) can function as a point of relative repose (see Figs. 145 and 146 in Ex. 3.1; Tippett also feels confident enough to end Act II on this very same chord: B–D♯–F♯–A), but also in the way that this sonority gains relative stability through being heard as a transformation by semitone and whole-tone part movement of a previously more dissonant seventh chord (not the *Tristan* chord, but the first-inversion major seventh B–G–D–F♯).[56]

The path to the eventual resolution of this sonority, however, is rather more idiosyncratically Tippettian, invoking an amalgam of materials engi-neered by the interaction of tonal polarities. Arnold Whittall has described in some detail the way in which the recapitulation of the passage in the final act, with its triumphant C major cadence, forms part of larger-scale tonal dualism between C and A, especially evident as the opera moves towards ultimate closure in the latter key.[57] As if in a microcosm of these principles, the progression towards the C major cadence of the pre-scene is itself an oscillation between harmonic relatives of that key and those of A major. Hence the motion in the first phrase from V^7 of E to V^7 of A (See Ex. 3.1, Figs. 144^{+3}–145^{+3}) clearly represents activity in the sharper tonal field. However, a hint of what is to come is given after the ascent to the E^7 chord, as its tension is temporarily neutralized by chromatic voice-shifts to the dyad C♮–G♮ – relatively consonant over the A bass (Fig. 145^{+3}). While the tension is then reinstated with a return to the opening sonorities at Fig.

146^{-1}, it is soon clear that what was originally a parenthetical deflection will take a stronger hold: the modified repetition of the initial phrase eventually leads to a much fuller 'white-note' aggregate implying C major once more (Fig. 146^{+3}). But alongside the impending change in tonal priorities comes a change in structural materials and syntax: the white-note vertical is in fact constructed quartally (reading upwards, E–A–D–G); and the subsequent addition to this set of the pitch-classes C and F yields the structural aggregate for much of what follows. In the next bar (Fig. 147^{-2}) the quartal disposition of the interval class 5 is exchanged for a predominantly quintal one, and the entry of the upper strings at this point symmetrically enhances the registral expansion of the bass as it descends through the circle of fifths (D–G–C) in emulation of functional root movement. (All this creates an image of 'opening out' which has a powerful emotional correlative.) It is the continuation of the bass trajectory to F that inaugurates the plagal cadence in C at the passage's climax (Tippett's ability to make this archaic cadence speak again without anachronism is symptomatic of his first-period renewal of diatonicism); but, characteristically, this is made via a final deflection towards A major at Fig. 147, which is assimilated into the plagal cadence as a preparatory prolongation of chord IV to which it descends by step, creating a third-progression in the bass.

This much goes some way to explaining the technical mechanism whereby Tippett sutures his listener into the unfolding music so as to participate in the Dionysiac discharge of its climactic moment. If this resembles an Apollonian mechanism geared towards Dionysiac ends (and if the level of conceptualization required to describe it might have invoked the disparaging epithet 'Socratic' from Nietzsche[58]), the Dionysiac is more univocally suggested by a stratum of the music not yet accounted for: the demisemiquaver sextuplet figures in the woodwind and its simple-time counterpart in the harp.[59] In its emancipation from classical principles of dissonance treatment and voice-leading this stratum represents the historically most 'advanced' element of the musical texture and thereby exerts an influence of renewal over it. While operating within clear diatonic confines, and tapping into the harmonic content and directed flux of the remaining texture, the material nevertheless floats free of the chord progressions it supplements. As if in a state of emancipation from the *principium individuationis*, its horizontal and vertical dimensions seek to evade that 'immediate apprehension of form' that is the hallmark of the Apollonian. For example, the woodwind parts usually comprise some form of tertian, quartal or pandiatonic vertical trichords, while the melodic progress of all four lines is compounded from stepwise, tertian or quartal motion; but Tippett is systematic in avoiding any systematic patterns of distribution of those elements. If any element is

aurally salient, both horizontally and vertically, it is the interval class 5, especially as perfect fourth, and especially around phrase beginnings or phrase endings. But again Tippett countervails the form-defining tendencies through the unpredictability of their precise distribution. The order-resisting function of these dancing sounds seems principally to celebrate their own being as sounds.

Excursus: metaphysical variations

Text, stage imagery and music coalesce in *The Midsummer Marriage* to promote the tropes of the Apollonian and Dionysiac. That these figures, along with that of an enchanted nature, echo patterns of thought in *The Birth of Tragedy* is more than neutrally interesting. It signals a degree of ideological convergence between two historically and geographically distinct co-ordinates in the web of culture – a convergence based around questions of metaphysics. Just as the earlier Nietzsche's metaphysical inclinations are a mark of the influence of Schopenhauer, so Tippett's draw him into alignment with aspects of the nineteenth-century philosophical disposition that followed Kant, the tradition of German early romanticism and idealism. Tippett may not have explicitly used the term 'metaphysical' in his own aesthetic reflections, but the word is most certainly in the air when, for example, he invokes Bach, Beethoven and Wagner as composers of the kind of music which 'expects a desire and willingness on our part to see reflected in it transcendent elements, unprovable and maybe unknowable analytically'.[60]

The desire to know what is 'unknowable analytically' posits exactly the boundary laid down in Kant's critical philosophy between a rational, cognizable world and the world as it exists 'in itself', beyond or prior to any appearance to our senses. This dualism sets the conditions not only of our knowledge but also of our own subjectivity, inseparable from what (or how) we know. Gary Tomlinson encapsulates this elegantly:

> We see reflected . . . an essential ineffability invested in the Kantian subject . . . This new subject incorporates, more fully than earlier models, the framework of its knowledge. The fundamental conditions of knowing no longer lie beyond the mind's borders, as they had in the divine harmonies governing Cartesian thought. Instead they make up the innate, internal equipment necessary for individual knowledge in the first place . . . The system of representation involved in knowing is folded wholly into the soul, and this soul is no longer *transcended* but in itself *transcendental*.[61]

This transcendental dimension to subjectivity, its 'essential ineffability', is assumed in virtually all Tippett's statements regarding the processes of

artistic creation. If the best part of two centuries between Kant's philosophy and Tippett's writings implies this might be a tenuous link, we should bear in mind Tomlinson's comment that 'since the early nineteenth century . . . we witness a growing tendency within Western culture to assimilate all forms of invisibility, all gestures towards metaphysics, to the noumenal limit Kant described'.[62] Between Kant's dualism of noumenon and phenomenon (i.e. the world in itself and the world as appearance) and Tippett's dichotomy of the 'ineffable experience of [the] inner life' and 'the matter-of-factness of the outer world'[63] lie cognate constructions, including Schopenhauer's Will and Idea, and – directly influenced by this – the early Nietzsche's Dionysiac and Apollonian; and if these notions are delivered into the twentieth century (and to the likes of Tippett) via their transmutation into psychoanalytic categories (such as Jung's collective unconscious and conscious), this is not to say that the parties concerned have entirely covered their metaphysical tracks.

Here, then, we gain glimpses of the kinds of cultural discourse in which the Dionysiac and Apollonian assume pivotal status, and with which Tippett continues to engage from his mid-twentieth-century perspective in works such as *The Midsummer Marriage* and *King Priam*. Although to do full justice to these many cultural connections would require a far fuller exegesis than is possible here, it will nevertheless be valuable to explore some of them in a little more detail. A useful starting point will be Schopenhauer, whose explicitly metaphysical conception of the will in *The World as Will and Idea* was decisive for *The Birth of Tragedy*, just as it had been for Wagner in the composition of *Tristan*, and just as it would inform Jung's pursuit of psychological knowledge beyond that offered by rational consciousness. At every stage we will find pre-echoes of ideas in Tippett.

'The world is my idea': Schopenhauer's famous opening of *The World as Will and Idea* echoes Kant's point that we can only know the world phenomenally, that the world conforms to the categories of understanding which we bring to it. However, while Kant held that the noumenal, the world beyond appearances, is unknowable, Schopenhauer believed that there is a source through which we can gain access to this metaphysical realm: our own bodies. On the one hand, I can know my body in the same way I know any phenomenon, through my senses – by looking at it, for example. On the other hand I also have immediate experience of my body, unlike any other phenomenon; I experience it in itself. To give this inner experience a name is of course to bring it back into the realm of ideas, so Schopenhauer's use of the term 'will' is intended as the nearest characterization for something which lies beyond conscious reflection. He chooses this term because all our actions (as distinct from our conscious awareness

or representation of them) are 'motivated', are driven by volition or desire. On this view our bodies and their actions are accordingly objectifications of the will.

Schopenhauer believed that the will underpinned all life, and indeed all phenomena, whether animate or inanimate (it is all a question of higher or lower grades of the will's objectification, he argues). Thus the will is that metaphysical principle of the 'original oneness' of nature which Nietzsche would recast in Hellenized terms as the Dionysiac – an experience of something beyond our individual bodies, but none the less only knowable through the body. From Schopenhauer Nietzsche also borrowed the term *principium individuationis* which he allied with the Apollonian, and which for Schopenhauer meant the many individual objectifications of the will in all their separateness, 'the plurality of things in time and space' – in short, the way we experience the phenomenal world.[64]

Schopenhauer's and then Nietzsche's introduction of the body into metaphysical discourse had radical implications. It deconstructed the sharp distinctions between mind and body found in Cartesian rationalism and put in its place a continuum between the metaphysical (or noumenal), the corporeal and the mental. This notion is significant too for the other figures in our constellation – Wagner, Jung and Tippett – and with the chronological shift from the nineteenth to the twentieth centuries comes a transformation of metaphysical concerns into psychological ones. Mediating between both conceptions is the idea of what I shall term 'registers of consciousness' – already implicit, for example, in Schopenhauer's statement that:

> The will, as the thing in itself, constitutes the inner, true, and indestructible nature of man; yet in itself it is unconscious. For consciousness is conditioned by the intellect, and the intellect is a mere accident of our being, for it is a function of the brain which . . . is merely a fruit, a product, of the rest of the organism.[65]

Also evident here is the challenge to the Enlightenment view of man's rational ego as dominant. In Schopenhauer's account it is the unconscious will ('the substance of man', as he puts it a few sentences later) which takes primacy over the conscious intellect ('the accident'). That his conception is a psychological as well as philosophical one is made explicit in his relation of it to 'the inner life of man' which 'may well yield more knowledge of the inner man than is to be found in many systematic psychologies'.[66] That Tippett also refers repeatedly to 'the inner life' as the privileged ground of human being (and human creativity) shows him to be working, in this respect at least, on similar ideological territory; and Jung if not the sole

agent of transmission of that notion was a key figure in reinforcing it. Jung may not have embraced Schopenhauer's conflicted view of the conscious and unconscious as the natural state of things, preferring instead the idea of a balance within the psyche, but he undoubtedly believed that that balance had to be worked for, and that the conscious ego was, in John J. Clarke's words, 'a function or process which . . . emerges from the interaction between the unconscious and the external environment'.[67]

Most importantly Jung, like Schopenhauer, held a topographic notion of consciousness descending from the particularity of individual self-consciousness through the more somatically determined and increasingly less personal unconscious finally into the common – or indifferent – stuff of the world itself. As he puts it, 'the deeper "layers" of the psyche lose their individual uniqueness as they retreat farther and farther into darkness. "Lower down" . . . they become increasingly collective until they are universalized and extinguished in the body's materiality . . . Hence "at bottom" the psyche is simply "world".'[68] Jung too, then, has a conception of the 'oneness' of humankind, and of humankind's unity with nature, which he at one time expressed with a geological metaphor as a subterranean 'central fire',[69] but which he eventually reformulated more definitively as the collective unconscious.

Thus the metaphysical principles of the will in Schopenhauer and the Dionysiac in the early Nietzsche are now translated into a model for the structure of the psyche which will be influential on twentieth-century culture. It remains moot, however, whether in the transition from philosophy to psychology the foundation of this model has completely shed its metaphysical underpinning. On the one hand, John J. Clarke endorses Jung's refutation of metaphysics, citing, for example, the latter's expressed requirement that 'every statement about the transcendent . . . is to be avoided because it is only a laughable assumption on the part of the human mind unconscious of its limitations', and his assertion that his 'aim as a psychologist is to dismiss without mercy the metaphysical claims of all esoteric teaching'.[70] On the other hand, the reception history of Jung's thought brings with it perceptions not only of a metaphysical determination but also a mystical streak; Richard Noll is just one commentator who has been keen to draw attention to Jung's allegedly 'more metaphysical ideas'.[71] Symptomatic of the ambiguous status of Jung's reasoning is an assertion he makes in connection with Schopenhauer and Nietzsche regarding 'the metaphysical Will': he writes that '"metaphysical" has for us the psychological connotation "unconscious"'.[72] Jung does not spell out how shifting a metaphysical concept into a putatively scientific discourse in itself causes the original metaphysical connotations to be shed.

It is on this ambiguous ground that we find Tippett in his first period. His embrace of Jung's concept of the collective unconscious may be seen as characteristic of a temperament which on the one hand did not deny the rational paradigm of modernity, but which on the other was also open not only to metaphysics, but also to the irrational and to mysticism, albeit, like Jung, from a standpoint that was to some extent anthropological.[73] The collective unconscious was what Tippett had in mind (on another occasion he used the analogous Yeatsian idea of the Great Memory) when he describes himself as belonging to 'an age-old tradition, fundamental to our civilization, which goes back into pre-history': 'to create images from the depths of the imagination and to give them form whether visual, intellectual or musical'.[74] Important in this statement is the notion of 'the depths', which, as in the other accounts we have examined, connotes an ineffable, trans-personal world. Also important is the notion of 'image': the means whereby that world is transmuted into something formed, raised up to consciousness. Again we have the idea of several levels of consciousness, and here 'image' acts as a communicating agency between them. Tippett most probably derived this conceit from (or had it reinforced by) Jung, for whom 'image' and 'primordial image' (also known as 'archetype') were terms of mediation, or communication, between conscious and unconscious strata of the psyche.[75]

Although Jung did not discuss the possibility of music functioning in this way, a precedent can be found in Wagner. The following account is striking in that its figuration of a journey through registers of consciousness, from inner to outer worlds, not only reveals the influence of Schopenhauer's conception of the will, but also anticipates the position of dreams in Jung's theory of the collective unconscious:

> We have seen that in the other arts the will is longing to become pure
> knowledge, but that this is possible only in so far as it stays stock-still in its
> deepest inner chamber . . . As the dream of deepest sleep can be conveyed to
> the waking consciousness only through translation into the language of a
> second, an allegoric dream which immediately precedes our wakening, so for
> the direct vision of its self the will creates a second organ of transmission –
> an organ whose one side faces toward that inner vision whilst the other
> thrusts into the reappearing outer world with the sole direct and sympathetic
> message, that of tone. The will cries out; and in the countercry it knows itself
> once more: thus cry and countercry become for it a comforting, at last an
> entrancing play with its own self.[76]

Wagner here draws a metaphysical-cum-psychological conceit into the realm of the aesthetic: the outcome of the will's emergence into consciousness is tone, and thence, implicitly, music – the art form which

Schopenhauer himself held to be the most direct expression of the will. But if the medium through which the will's progress from a clairvoyant but mute state into the realm of consciousness is analogous to dream, this is a double dream, the first unknowable, the second an allegorizing translation of the first – that is, a translation into *images*.[77] Although Wagner is only using the dream and dream images as analogies for what he considers the 'real' medium of translation – music – this none the less suggests a convergence between the two ideas, and prefigures Tippett's characterization of music as an imagistic medium. 'Cry' and 'countercry' point to a kind of concept-less sound: tone still bears the mark of its source in the inchoate will; and music remains implicated in metaphysics.

Madame Sosostris: voice of the noumenal

Evidence that Tippett contracted-in to these conceits in his actual musical practice as well as his writings is most powerfully provided in the character of Madame Sosostris. Her aria in Act III of *The Midsummer Marriage* is an operatic dramatization of the very passage from inner to outer worlds which Wagner describes: the emergence of the will from its own noumenal domain into consciousness; or in Nietzsche's construction of this dualism, an ascent from the chthonic depths of the Dionysiac world to dream-like Apollonian lucidity (an appropriate enough description given Sosostris's status as Pythian oracle). Reinforcing this alignment, and as most commentators (including Tippett himself) have pointed out, this is also an autobiographic account of the tortured process of artistic creation – from the inchoate to the articulate. Tippett's professed literary models for the aria, T. S. Eliot's *The Waste Land*, and Paul Valéry's *La pythie*, are certainly important reference points, but I would argue that the connections with the more metaphysically orientated discourses I have been examining here are equally if not more pertinent to understanding Sosostris's significance. Symptomatic of this is the fact that, unlike Eliot's ironized fortune teller, Tippett's Madame Sosostris is the genuine oracle (she does not have a cold) – more closely aligned with the numinous earth mother, Erda, from Wagner's *Ring*.[78]

Sosostris, then, might be seen, like the will in Wagner's account, to represent 'that state of clairvoyance . . . beyond the bounds of time and space [which] . . . knows itself the world's one and all',[79] and who translates these apprehensions into images – 'giv[ing] formal clarity to [what is] analytically unknowable', to recall one of Tippett's formulations of the dynamics of creation. At the beginning of her aria Sosostris sings from the depths of some remote primordial world, but by the last part of it the images flow in a 'stream of sound' (to use the language of another Tippettian operatic

messenger, Hermes). The progress from low to high musical registers is something of a topos in Tippett's music for the passage between registers of consciousness – between bodily 'depths' on the one hand, and conscious, cerebral 'heights' on the other.[80] Tippett would no doubt have seen this topography as archetypal: it is certainly presented as such in Mark's descent into the cave, to 'hell', and Jenifer's ascent of the ladder, to 'heaven'. But he is also reproducing here a cultural formation with a clear ideological and historical lineage – back through Jung, Wagner and Nietzsche to Schopenhauer. Schopenhauer talks of 'the deepest tones of harmony, in the bass' as 'the lowest grade of the will's objectification', while 'in the *melody* . . . leading the whole and progressing with unrestrained freedom' is 'the highest grade of the will's objectification'.[81] On the one hand, it would be glib to push for too exact a parallel between this opposition and that between the first and last sections of Sosostris's aria, since the category of melody obtains throughout. On the other hand the opposition obtains here in a more polarized form than Schopenhauer could have imagined. Harmonic activity has strong ascendancy at the opening of the aria, while in the final section (Fig. 387ff.) the orchestral stratum is entirely linearly conceived (one of the more 'advanced' techniques of *The Midsummer Marriage*): superimposed ostinatos eschew functional bass-driven harmony altogether, allowing Sosostris's line indeed to sound like it progresses 'with unrestrained freedom' against its kaleidoscopic background.

These observations are of course meant to imply a homology with, rather than direct influence by, Schopenhauer and others. Indeed, as soon as one looks more closely at the technical details of how Tippett conveys in this aria a sense of the transcendent we move into more idiosyncratic territory: quite clearly the world of an English, post-pastoral neo-tonality. But it is perhaps all the more striking that Tippett is able to capture Sosostris as a figure of the transcendent through culturally shared codes of musical understanding – again a result of his individualization of the principles of common practice tonality. His strategy for invoking the numinous is in fact not so different from that observed in the preceding analysis of the Act II pre-scene: it involves the thoroughly operatic device of the 'big moment'. Sosostris has a number of these, which structurally form major articulations in the tonal scheme, and phenomenologically act as points of orientation in a carefully controlled temporal flux. While harmonic succession is the medium of that flux, there are subtle disjunctions between the implied direction and the eventual goal, and this creates ambiguity as to whether tonal/harmonic centres appear causally or spontaneously generated.

Consider Sosostris's first line, 'Who hopes to conjure with the world of dreams' (Ex. 3.2). While the motion from B♭ minor to D major on the

Example 3.2. Sosostris's aria (opening), Act III scene 5.

word 'dreams' (Fig. 368) is adumbrated in the first two bars by the bassoons' G♭s (which are subsequently reinterpreted as the mediant of D), the D major chord itself opens a new, unexpected harmonic space, in which G♭/F♯, released from its former obligation as a neighbour note to fall to F, finds stability. The D major sonority could be construed as prolonging the tonic B♭: as chord III made very major. However, it also lays claim to an autonomous domain – a sense heightened by the superimposed orchestral colours and glissandi – which is not subsumed under the originating tonic. This sense of disjunction is reinforced and intensified in the aria's second phrase at Fig. 369ff. (not quoted), a variant of this one, in which E♭ minor secedes to A major. The functional principles of the circle of fifths are again invoked as a means to calibrate tonal distance, yet once more a sonority at harmonically remote co-ordinates seeks to emancipate itself from functioning as a prolongation (and subordinate) of the surrounding tonal centre. These emancipation-seeking sonorities, then, become important to Tippett's evocation of 'the world of dreams', or a world beyond appearance.

We need to develop our understanding of the aria's structural conditions a bit further if we are to grasp more fully how Tippett is able to represent the metaphysical through the technical manipulation of sounds. Salient sonorities in the first section of Sosostris's aria – including, but not only the D and A major chords described above – are shown in Example 3.3(b). Played in succession, these sonorities want to carve out a space for themselves, to repel any implied connection with their neighbours; and they function as colourings of the vocal melody, whose skeleton is quoted in Example 3.3(a). What is significant, however, is the supplementary status of these harmonies, for the melody unfolds its own harmonic constituents which (by contrast) do amount to a separate progression in its own right – one which determines Sosostris's overall ascent from lower to upper B♭. In brief, the most structural of the structural tones of Sosostris's line – stemmed in Example 3.3(a), analysed independently in the top stave of Example 3.3(c), and verticalized in Example 3.3(d) – unfold two triadic sonorities: in the first phrase the augmented triad B♭–D–G♭/F♯ (a sonority present in the very foreground of the opening bar and traced out in the bassoons); in the second phrase the diminished triad E♭–A♮–C (or diminished-seventh chord if we include the G♭ which is part of E♭'s prolongation). These two unfolded sonorities effect a motion to the final cadential progression in B♭ with which the section ends. In other words Sosostris's line could be considered as an unaccompanied melody, which takes its coherence from these middleground unfoldings. These are obscured from immediate empirical perception because their elements are

Example 3.3. Sosostris's aria: analysis of melodic and harmonic structures in first section.

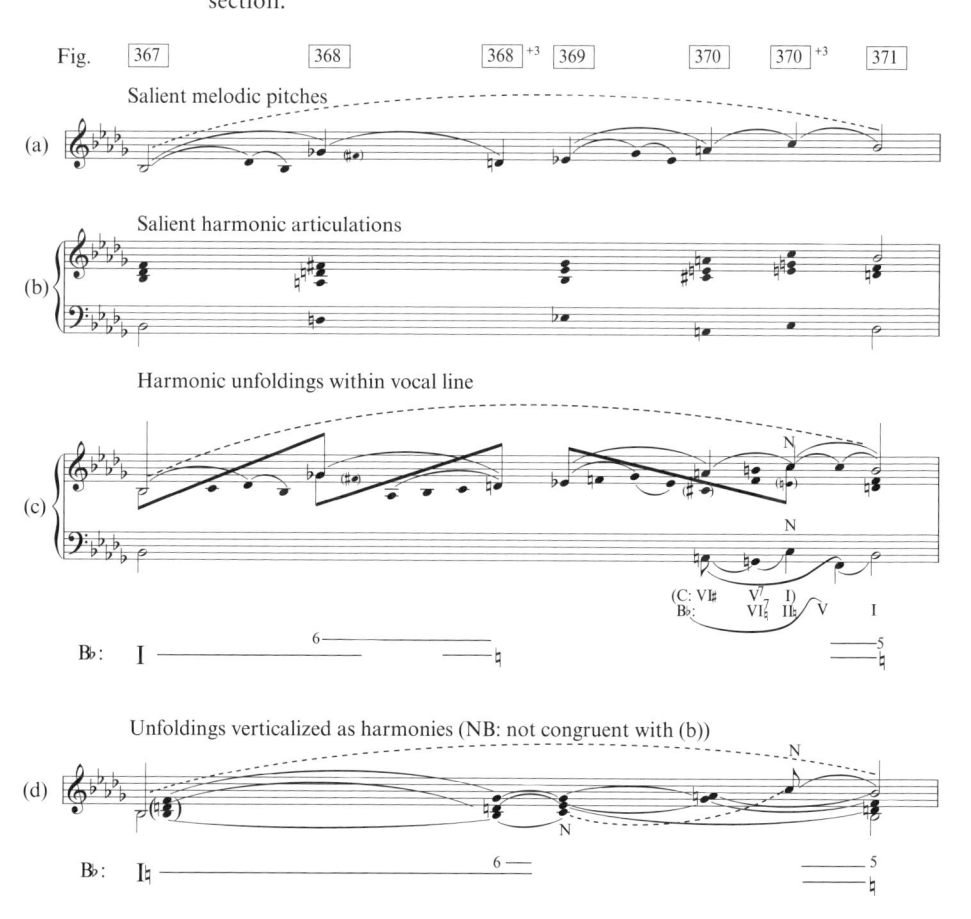

coloured by the major and minor triadic sonorities previously considered in Example 3.3(b). Those triadic colourings are non-functional in that they are not congruent with the augmented and diminished structures of the background;[82] put more strongly, they are dissonant against them.

Such disjunction between strata with conflicting content and organizational principles is also replicated at other levels. Examples would be the quartal sonorities occasionally glimpsed in the foreground (e.g. in the three bars before Fig. 368 – see Ex. 3.2), and voice-leading motions in the inner parts which do not assimilate unproblematically to the triadic sonorities they ostensibly prolong (as at the cadential approach to B♭ in the four bars before Fig. 371). And this disjunction is what enables Tippett both to retain and to renew the expressive potential of triadic tonality. (At this stage in his career, we might say, the relationship of his

musical materials to what is historically received is one of complementation and co-existence rather than antagonistic critique.) It is one of the
means whereby he transfigures the 'everyday' – the *lingua franca* of diatonic tonality – into something of the 'everlasting'. Because the palimpsest of syntactic types inhibits the musical signifiers contained in it from
locking into their accustomed places, the listener's mind is sent looking
(or listening) beyond.

These signifiers accordingly bear a different charge: they cannot be completely mapped by conventional harmonic understanding; hence they must
be understood through feeling rather than through thought. And hence, we
might surmise, the instrument with which we fully register them is the body.
This is an appropriate enough conjecture given the construction of the body
as the noumenal other of the conscious mind in Schopenhauer, Nietzsche
and Jung, and given the corporeality which pertains to Sosostris. Although
at first a disembodied voice offstage (warning against King Fisher's attempt
to break open the cave gates in Act I), Sosostris is revealed in Act III as an
imposing, uncanny physical presence, which occupies centre stage and sus-
pends all other musico-dramatic action. The uncanny, the other, is conveyed at the start of the aria by the deep, hollow vocal timbre, which seems
to emanate directly from the chest, as if by-passing the vocal cords. When, at
the words 'to conjure', Sosostris's hitherto seemingly immovable note rises
to C, the significance of the supporting harmony lies as much in its sheer
feeling of mass (bolstered by additional trombones and lower strings), as it
heaves itself flatwards, as in its precise tonal identity (see Ex. 3.2). Likewise,
at 'dreams' the slow, extended, transparent rising glissando is sensed almost
literally as a gesture – an opening outwards and upwards of the body – of lib-
eration. Academic body-talk may not be without its own share of ideological problems, but it has relevance in this context because it corroborates a
connection with the idea of registers of consciousness found in the his-
torico-cultural matrix of figures with which we are concerned. It reinforces
the notion of the metaphysical grounded in the physical; indeed it even
invites the alternative formulation of the bodily as the 'meta-mental'.[83]

The will to life: optimism vs pessimism

While Sosostris may, for as long as the music lasts, present the 'wholly
other', she does not stand for something alien to humanity. Rather, she
represents an opening on to the full condition of human being – on to 'life'
in an essential sense. She thus reflects a tendency to ontologize life as a kind
of force, which further reinforces Tippett's place in the particular ideological matrix in which I have situated him. For example his statement that

music, and especially symphonic music, is 'a significant image of the inner flow of life' has a number of resonances. One such is Henri Bergson's concept *élan vital*, which George Bernard Shaw (through whom Tippett came to Bergson) translates as 'life force', and which occupies a significant metaphysical place in his *Back to Methuselah* – one of the sources of influence on *The Midsummer Marriage*.[84] Another resonance is again Harrison's *Themis*, whose acknowledgement of Bergson situates his vitalistic ideas alongside an understanding of the Dionysiac that is Nietzschean in character if not influence: 'I saw . . . that Dionysos . . . was an instinctive attempt to express what Professor Bergson calls *durée*, that life which is one, indivisible and yet ceaselessly changing'.[85] And of course the idea of an indivisible life force motivating restless change recalls Schopenhauer's will, also termed the 'will to life' throughout *The World as Will and Idea*. In fact one of Tippett's statements about symphonic music has some striking connections with Schopenhauer's own understanding of the symphony in relation to inner life. Tippett writes:

> Symphonic music . . . fully embodies the otherwise unperceived, unsavoured inner flow of life . . . The miracle is achieved by submitting to the power of its organized flow . . . Artifice of all kinds is necessary to the musical composition in order that it shall become such an image. Yet when the perfect performance and occasion allows us a truly immediate apprehension of the inner flow 'behind' the music, the artifice is momentarily of no consequence; we are no longer aware of it.[86]

And Schopenhauer declares:

> Anyone who surrenders to the impression of a symphony seems to see all the possible events of life and the world pass in procession before him, yet if he reflects, he can cite no similarity between the music and the things that pass before his mind. For music, as we have said, is distinguished from all the other arts by its not being a copy of the phenomenon . . . but is the direct copy of the will itself, and therefore it presents the metaphysical.[87]

Both accounts contrast an aspect of music which may become incidental to the experience of listening (technical 'artifice', the phenomenal quality of events) with an immediate connection between music and the metaphysical correlative which is its authentic ground (the 'flow of life', the will). And the realignment of our selves with that inner or metaphysical domain is possible (only) if we 'submit' or 'surrender' to the autonomous medium that is its copy.

This homology continues in the alliance of a life force with sexuality. Schopenhauer, for example, writes that 'the sexual impulse proves itself the decided and strongest affirmation of life . . . Nature, too, whose essence is the

will to life itself, with all her strength impels both man and animal to propagate.'[88] These notions are explicit at *The Midsummer Marriage*'s exuberantly climactic moment: Mark and Jenifer's transfiguration in the last act as Shiva–Shakti in the pose of eternal copulation. Indeed, their line, 'The world is made by our desire' – suggesting an indivisibility between nature, self and will – has a decidedly Schopenhauerian ring. But rather less Schopenhauerian (and not the only informative difference to emerge from the comparison) is Tippett's take on sexual love. Schopenhauer held that love is simply an appearance, a veil over the 'true' procreative instinct: 'the state of being in love, though it may pose as ethereal, is rooted in the sexual impulse alone . . . [The] future generation is already astir in that wary, specific and capricious choice made to satisfy the sexual impulse – the choice which we call love.'[89] In *The Midsummer Marriage*, on the other hand, sexual love is shown as transformable: 'Carnal love through which the race / Of men is everlastingly renewed / Becomes transfigured as divine / Consuming love whose fires shine / From God's perpetually revealed face'. Could it be that for all the apparent distance from Christian principles Tippett is invoking in his lines, with an imagery of purification by fire that is close to T. S. Eliot, a dualism akin to *Eros* and *agape*? (If so, this only makes its collapse in *King Priam* – of which I shall say more below – all the more telling.)

Another point of contrast arises in the comparison between Tippett's turn to Hindu iconography at this point and Schopenhauer's view of this mythology as prior evidence from the East for an understanding of the will. Schopenhauer relates how Shiva reflects a recognition in Hindu religion that 'birth and death belong in like manner to life, and hold the balance as reciprocal conditions of each other';[90] and in *The Midsummer Marriage* Mark and Jenifer's ritual rebirth is attendant on the ritual death of King Fisher. However, Schopenhauer's view of the will that underpins life is famously pessimistic: it is a negative force, a ceaseless desiring that kicks in again as soon as it has been assuaged; moreover any individual's assertion of it entails its denial in others, hence the conflicted nature of the world. Schopenhauer advocates denial of the will to life and celebrates release from it in death. By contrast, Tippett's ontologizing of life in *The Midsummer Marriage* is celebrative. Of the 'world . . . made by our desire' Mark and Jenifer sing: 'Its splendour, yes, even its pain / Becomes transfigured in the bright / Furious incandescent light / Of love's perpetually renewed fire'. With music to match, the opera's ending is a daringly optimistic declaration that the will to life contains the possibility of a joyous reconciliation of individuals in the totality of nature; provided that this will admits a principle of transformation – which in the discourse we are engaged in here must mean the principle of the Apollonian.

The grand existential statements about life which we have been examining thus seem necessarily toned either optimistically or pessimistically. Nietzsche's relation to this opposition, however, is more complex. When in *The Birth of Tragedy* he dismisses 'the exponents of science, all dyed-in-the-wool optimists like their archetype Socrates',[91] it is to disparage scientific positivism's unqualified belief in progress. Such thinkers are 'the distinguished enemies of tragic views' – which for Nietzsche means not grasping the world as it really is. However, while he follows Schopenhauer in seeing tragedy as 'the high-point of literature . . . the purpose of [which] . . . is to present the terrible side of life',[92] his stance is an emphatic repudiation of the very pessimism which Schopenhauer seeks to legitimate by invoking the genre. As against the latter's turn to the Indian Vedas, Nietzsche promotes his own Hellenic vision in which the Greeks' cultivation of pessimism in their tragic myths is portrayed as a symptom of 'euphoria maybe – sheer exuberance, reckless health and power'.[93] While the Nietzsche of *The Birth of Tragedy* assents to a Schopenhauerian notion of the will, he sees the fact that life exceeds any single objectification of it as an occasion for celebration; or at least, it can be presented as such in a genre such as tragedy through the transformation by Apollonian imagery of the Dionysiac ground of being:

> The metaphysical delight in tragedy is a translation of instinctive Dionysiac wisdom into images. The hero, the highest manifestation of the will, is destroyed, and we assent, since he too is merely a phenomenon, and the eternal life of the will remains unaffected. Tragedy cries, 'We believe that life is eternal!' and music is the direct expression of that life.[94]

This cheerfulness, as well as the principle of synthesis of the Apollonian and Dionysiac, is most closely reflected by the celebration of life in *The Midsummer Marriage*. Of course a crucial difference is that in this comedic genre Tippett's affirmative instincts do not have to face full-on the question of death. So it might be expected that when the time came to attempt his own rebirth of tragedy in *King Priam* a more complete homology with the earlier Nietzsche would be found. This is to some extent the case, though matters are complicated by the fact that *King Priam* to some extent also follows the later Nietzsche in questioning an earlier metaphysics and Wagnerian alignment.[95] That is to say, the opera seeks to create a critical space between itself and *The Midsummer Marriage* in a similar fashion to Nietzsche's repudiation of key aspects of *The Birth of Tragedy*. (The strategy of the latter's 'Critical backward glance' (or 'Attempt at a self-criticism' in other translations) which prefaced the 1886 edition seems to be simultaneously to distance himself from the book and to show how it might

none the less belong to the main body of his work.) That said, *Priam*'s affinities with the later Nietzsche are also in turn equivocal; part of its idiosyncrasy therefore lies in its ambiguous relationship to these contrasting brands of Nietzscheanism, and it is this which I now turn to explore.

III

The turn to tragedy: *King Priam*

The Birth of Tragedy certainly offers an apposite characterization of the situation of the eponymous hero of Tippett's second opera:

> Dionysiac man might be said to resemble Hamlet: both have looked deeply into the true nature of things, they have *understood* and are now loath to act. They realize that no action of theirs can work any change in the eternal condition of things, and they regard the imputation as ludicrous or debasing that they should set right the time which is out of joint. Understanding kills action, for in order to act we require the veil of illusion; such is Hamlet's doctrine . . . Now no comfort any longer avails, desire reaches beyond the transcendental world, beyond the gods themselves, and existence, together with its gulling reflection in the gods and an immortal Beyond, is denied. The truth once seen, man is aware everywhere of the ghastly absurdity of existence, comprehends the symbolism of Ophelia's fate and the wisdom of the wood sprite Silenus [Dionysus's companion]: nausea invades him.[96]

It is Priam's fate, like Hamlet's, to look into the abyss. And through the proxy of his tragic hero, Tippett now presents his audience with a much bleaker version of the order of things. Indeed the evidence suggests that the composer himself only fully grasped the gravity of his second operatic project quite late in the day. In earlier drafts of the libretto Priam's closing words, the last of the opera, were 'I am at peace'[97] – a simple and possibly accurate representation of his feelings (he is certainly calmly prepared for his death), but limp in comparison with what he was eventually given to sing: 'I see mirrors, / Myriad upon myriad moving / The dark forms / Of creation'. From the turning point of the opera (*peripetia* as Aristotle would have termed it) in Act III scene 2, when Priam sings 'I curse this life that has no meaning', his despairing rage is transmuted into a state where there is 'perhaps at the end . . . a residue of meaning' (as the chorus earlier put it). Perhaps. It is of the tragic conceit of the opera that Priam cannot communicate the vision to which he is now privy,[98] but it is clear that he thinks he sees the 'ground of being', and that if there is any meaning, any 'glimmering of sense' to be drawn from this, it is not that life is in itself purposeful or meaningful. The metaphor of

myriad mirrors would seem to suggest the forms of life as ceaseless, non-teleological creation – endless becoming as Nietzsche would have put it, or, in Schopenhauerian parlance, unceasing objectifications of that dark force, the will.

Given that the view of tragedy cited above assumes our identification with the tragic protagonist, it would not be surprising that if we ourselves were fully to grasp the absurdity implicit in this dark vision of nature, we would indeed be invaded by nausea. But in the subsequent paragraph Nietzsche implies a cleavage in this identification:

> Then, in this supreme jeopardy of the will, art, that sorceress expert in healing, approaches him; only she can turn his fits of nausea into imaginations with which it is possible to live. These are on the one hand the spirit of the *sublime*, which subjugates terror by means of art; on the other hand the *comic* spirit, which releases us, through art, from the tedium of absurdity.[99]

While the 'veil of illusion' falls from the eyes of the tragic hero and he is left to his fate, we the audience are redeemed through the intervention of the aesthetic. The apprehension of these insights through the medium of artistic representation makes life bearable, offering 'metaphysical solace'. Yet Nietzsche would soon repudiate metaphysics, and it is arguable that in *King Priam*, Tippett comes close to doing the same. This, I contend, is in large part what the change of musical language between the first and second operas is about. *King Priam* still offers an aesthetic experience, but it is one which problematizes the business of aestheticizing what is appalling in life.

Sex and violence

It is the veil of illusion that *King Priam* problematizes. Not that the veil is torn away from the audience as it is for the protagonist (the unaestheticized presence of the Dionysiac in the opera house would mean literally a battlefield or an orgy); nor – as it might have been if Tippett had been other than selective in what he took from Brecht – is it a case of making us aware of the veil as such, by means of alienation effect or self-referentiality (even the chorus's verbal references to the opera as a story are overtaken by the dramatic immediacy of the music which delivers them). It is rather that the veil itself – the total means of artistic representation – becomes shot through with traces of the complete Dionysiac 'truth' it formerly protected us from. The synthesizing power of the Apollonian is vitiated, and the Dionysiac dynamic now unleashed resembles more 'that witches' brew concocted of lust and cruelty' which Nietzsche in his (historically

questionable) construction of Greek culture imputed to a pre-tragic era.[100] Magic, which animated the representation of nature in *The Midsummer Marriage*, is liquidated. What Tippett confronts us with is a modernist vision of a disenchanted world, in which humankind's relation to nature is represented in its elemental principles of sex and violence.

In another game of elective affinities I shall invoke in my analysis of *King Priam* lines of argument from Camille Paglia's essay 'Sex and violence, or nature and culture'.[101] As a follower of Nietzsche, de Sade and Freud (all 'dark' thinkers of the post-Enlightenment) Paglia also seeks an exposé of what lies beneath the surface of modern civilization – 'the daemonism of chthonian nature [which] is the west's dirty secret', as she feistily puts it[102] (her rhetorical tactics themselves bear witness to Nietzsche's strategy of philosophizing with a hammer). And while she and Tippett may seem odd bedfellows, aspects of her thesis, which includes an account of the Apollonian and Dionysiac, are indeed illuminating of what is (or ought to be) shocking about *Priam*, as well as indicative of key aspects of its ideology. Not the least apposite is her figuration of sexuality and violence as the agency of nature in humankind:

> Aggression comes from nature; it is what Nietzsche is to call the will-to-power. For Sade, getting back to nature . . . would be to give free rein to violence and lust. I agree . . . When social controls weaken, man's innate cruelty bursts forth . . . Feminists, seeking to drive power relations out of sex, have set themselves against nature. Sex *is* power. Identity is power . . .
>
> Sex is the point of contact between man and nature, where morality and good intentions fall to primitive urges . . . It is the place beyond the pale, both cursed and enchanted.[103]

The fall of morality to 'primitive urges' is exactly what Paris experiences at his fateful decision to abduct Helen in the first act of the opera. Priam's decision in the preceding scene to assent to 'the natural life, the father's love' (i.e. his biological parental instincts) and allow Paris to live, and thence to commit Helen's abduction, is also instrumental in the chain of events which will ultimately cause 'man's innate cruelty' to burst forth in the ensuing war between the Trojans and Greeks. Enactments or accounts of bloodlust, vengeance and cruelty abound in the opera: to wit Priam's gruesome end, the mutilation of Hector's body, the celebration of Patroclus's killing (fittingly enacted as a bloody ritual over the corpse in Nicholas Hytner's 1984 Kent Opera production[104]), Achilles' chilling war cry, and Andromache's report that as Troy is sacked, 'Achilles's son is raging through the town swinging my own dead child as club'. As Paglia reminds us, 'The Dionysian is no picnic'.[105]

Sex is no less manifest in *King Priam*, and even if not the opera's ostensible subject, it is a powerful catalyst or agent of explanation in the machinations of the plot. There is Helen and Paris's adulterous liaison, of course, which becomes the pretext for the war that leads to Priam's (and just about all the other male characters') demise; as well as Helen's paean to sex in Act III (I will say a little more about these below). What is more, sex is not allied here, as it was in *The Midsummer Marriage*, with any notion of reproduction or species survival: it is presented as an autonomous, self-serving force – a current of power in the relationships between individuals. Sex, then, is shown as not *a priori* heterosexual. How overtly the relationship between Achilles and Patroclus should be portrayed as gay is to some extent down to the individual producer. (The ambiguous representation of their love compared to the overt eroticism of Helen and Paris could be seen as shilly-shallying – perhaps understandable given the pre-Wolfenden days in which the opera was written – but there is also the point that the rigid hetero/homo binarism of modern Western culture is itself a construction, and earlier times and other cultures, especially ancient Greece, have accepted greater fluidity of erotic sensibility and representation.) At all events the clues are there: the intimacy of the tent, conveyed by the quiet sounds of Achilles' guitar as he sings to Patroclus; and the sheer vehemence of the former's reaction at the latter's death.

Far less ambiguous, but hitherto completely unacknowledged, is the homoerotic attraction which Paris exerts as a boy over (unbeknown to him or them) his own brother and father in the hunt scene (Act I scene 2) – a deftly taboo-breaking moment on Tippett's part. What else could be meant by the bristlingly sensual string figuration which accompanies Paris as Hector (and the audience) first catches sight of him? The description of Paris as 'a beautiful boy' in the stage directions (Fig. 92) leave little doubt; his power of erotic attraction is made audible in the sheer excess of his music: its extreme compass, lush orchestration and ornateness. This stops even Priam in his tracks: as he enters, his own imposing music is abruptly silenced by the restated opening flourish of Paris's (Fig. 101; Ex. 3.4). And during the intervening exchange between Paris and Hector, a version of this string figuration is heard seductively working on Hector as Paris tries to persuade him to take him to Troy; it is arguably this allure as much as anything Paris actually says that makes his attempt successful. We should not of course make an over-literal reading of pederasty here; Tippett's imputation is rather that the erotic is omnipresent, that it operates on many levels, including the subliminal, binding individuals and influencing their decisions, in this case fatefully so.[106] As Paglia rather more bluntly puts it, 'sex *is* power'.

Example 3.4. *King Priam*, Act I scene 2: Priam encounters Paris, 'a beautiful boy'.

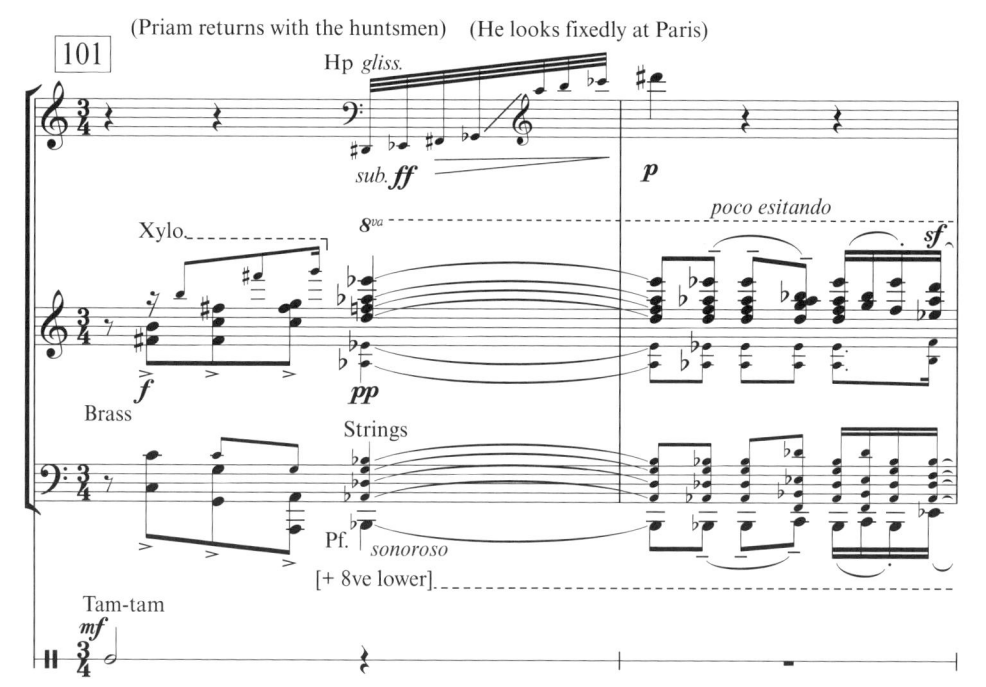

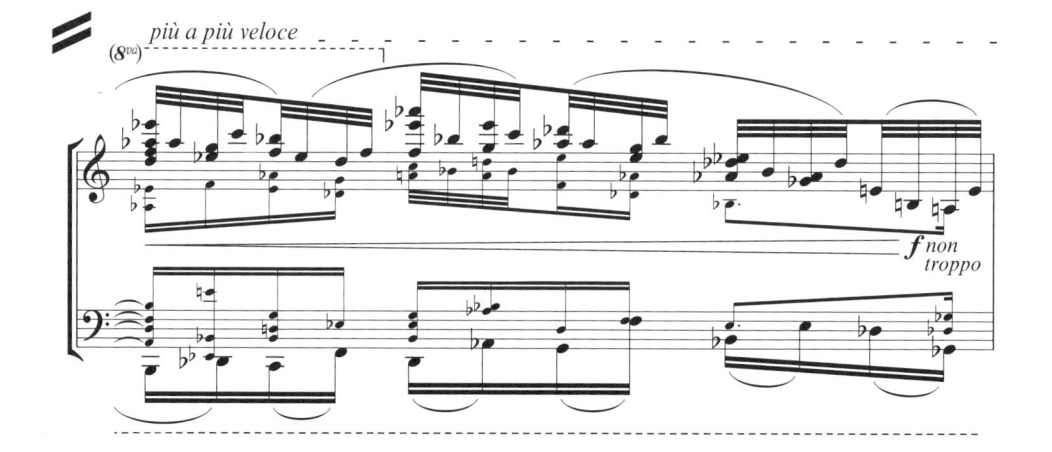

The sound of the Dionysiac

In this context the Dionysiac significance of the association between Paris and the bull he rides (and of which the adult Trojans are in pursuit) needs no spelling out. But what may need underlining is that the figure of the Dionysiac, as well as being represented in the dramatic events and symbols of the opera, is composed into its sound. Of interest in this respect is a reference by Tippett to a comment of Stravinsky's regarding the Apollonian and Dionysiac in music. This comes from the latter's *Poetics of Music* and was cited by Tippett in a radio talk on *Les Noces* first broadcast in 1947:

> What is important for the lucid ordering of the work – for its crystallization – is that all the Dionysian elements which set the imagination of the artist in motion and make the life-sap rise must be properly subjugated before they intoxicate us, and must finally be made to submit to the law: Apollo demands it.[107]

To quote Stravinsky is apposite because he is simultaneously a point of attraction and differentiation in Tippett's new musical style.[108] Stravinsky's influence is manifest in both the radical reconsideration of orchestration and the practice of formal intercutting – transitionless jumps between blocks of musical material – which set in with *King Priam*. But similarities of technique are complemented by differences in aesthetic – at least in relation to neoclassical Stravinsky. Consider the initial, defining string sonority of Paris's music (Ex. 3.4) which could be read, for example, as two superimposed dominant-seventh chords, on B♭ and E♭. Whereas for Stravinsky in his neoclassical period such a conflation would have been intended simultaneously to invoke and atrophy (and thus, in a manner of speaking, ironize[109]) the historically borne functionality of the triadic materials, in Tippett's case this procedure serves to intensify their expressive potential and transpose them on to a different plane of significance: to turn them into complex sonorities with multiple, ambiguous meanings that simultaneously resist and embrace tonality,[110] and to intensify the sensory. This yields an excess of signification, a spillage over boundaries, which summons the unconscious to apprehend what lies beyond the rationally cognizable. In other words, and in contradistinction to Stravinsky's maxim, Apollonian law is subjugated to Dionysiac intoxication.

'Art is the contrary of chaos', Tippett quotes Stravinsky as saying,[111] but the needs of *King Priam* call for a riskier (im)balance between the chaotic and the artefactual – in order to drive home a message about what lies behind the Apollonian 'veil of illusion'. Paglia's words again capture the

Example 3.5. *King Priam*, Act I: prelude.

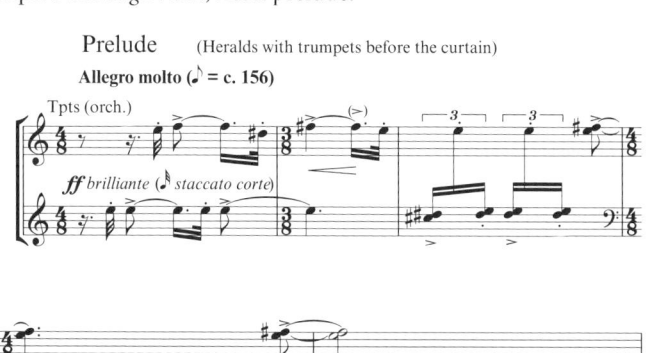

unaestheticized experience of the Dionysiac which Tippett seeks to convey through the aesthetic:

> The great god Dionysus is the barbarism and brutality of mother nature . . . Dionysian orgy ended in mutilation and dismemberment . . . True Dionysian dance is a rupturing extremity of torsion . . . Dionysian nature is cataclysmic . . . When the body's chthonian spasms take over, we are invaded by Dionysus. The uterine contractions of menstruation and childbirth are Dionysus' fist clenching in our bowels.[112]

The prelude to Act I of *King Priam* (Ex. 3.5) captures something of the raw, visceral, agonistic experience invoked in this characterization. Ostensibly a piece of abstract instrumental music, the prelude none the less also has extra-musical connotations: Kemp sees it as indeed a portrayal of child-birth; Bowen sees it as both this – 'an agonized image for the birth of Paris' – and 'a symphony of war'.[113] A double reading is certainly appropriate: the absence of words or stage images places the music in Dionysiac terri-tory, beyond defined categories. In the wordless choral ululations no concept is interposed between the viscera and the outside world: these cries could depict the agony of childbirth, the terror of war, or a general-ized apprehension of barbarity. Similarly, the brass fanfares and pounding

Example 3.5 (*cont.*)

Example 3.5 (*cont.*)

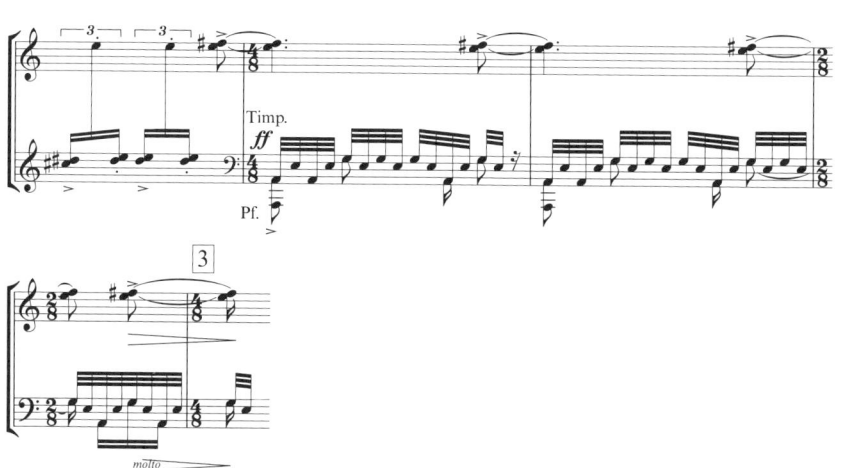

drums might connote militarism or be a more direct evocation of power or force in the abstract.

Tippett's solution to the dilemma of imposing technical control over the inchoate is to promote conflict to a structural principle. In the first part of the prelude (up to Fig. 8) this is manifest in, among other things, the distribution of the performing forces into autonomous stratified layers – trumpets and timpani; female voices; male voices; trombones (reinforced by horns and piano) – each of which asserts itself against the others through an individualized subset of pitch classes. These in turn are determined by two larger diatonic fields, thrown into an unyielding polarity which is most clearly articulated in the oscillation between the tonal centres of E and E♭ in the trumpets (at Fig. 2 – see Ex. 3.5 – and repeated at Fig. 3). The E centre is itself subject to contention: the choral forces together expand the trumpets' source tetrachord, E–F♯–C♯–D♯, by the addition of the pitch classes B, A and G♯ (e.g. at Figs. 1^{+4}–2; see Ex. 3.5), but the arrangement of the material makes E's status as tonal centre more equivocal, suggesting a possible A-Lydian interpretation. A's status as part of a tonal dualism with E is further propounded by the timpani which initially oscillate across the perfect fifth dyad A–E, though later statements (such as that at Fig. 2^{+4}) challenge the purity of the Lydian modality by adding a G♮ to the original dyad. Although in the polarization between E and E♭ in the trumpets it is E which at first exerts the strongest force of attraction, this ascendancy is soon challenged by the weighty assertion of E♭-Lydian at the entry of the trombones, horns and piano (Fig. 5^{+5}; not quoted). It is here that the contention between forces is at its most acute: all the centres so far mentioned

are superimposed. The Apollonian principles which give form to sound now clash in a chaotic orgy of sound in which each element's assertion of its right to existence is simultaneously a struggle against the claim of the others.[114] This is what the Dionysiac has become in *King Priam*: will to life is now shown to mean will to power.

The will to power

Tippett's evocation in his statements about *King Priam* of 'the mysterious nature of human choice' and the paradox of fate and freedom is bland in comparison with the musico-dramatic conception he actually produced. It is not some metaphysical force of destiny meted out under a divine administration that Priam is up against (in any case the gods are de-divinized; Hermes, for example, except on his final appearance, is ironically cast as 'divine go-between'). The world with which the King is compelled to come to terms is closer to that described by the later Nietzsche in works such *The Gay Science* and *The Will to Power*: a world stripped of enchantment, whose 'total character . . . is in all eternity chaos'; a world riven by 'change, becoming, multiplicity, opposition, contradiction, war'.[115] These incarnations of the will to power ('the dark forms of creation'?) seem wholly inimical to Priam's aspirations to a compassionate humanity. And to his creator's – which is to say that within *King Priam* Tippett assails those sentiments, so central to his earlier work.

Power is made audible everywhere. It sounds in the overall 'hard-hitting rhetoric', the 'tough, declamatory style' of the music (Tippett's own descriptions).[116] It is also manifest in the mosaic of musical gestures which is the formal corollary of the new style. Voices no longer 'ride on a river of glowing sound'[117] as they did in *The Midsummer Marriage*. In *King Priam*, with only rare exceptions, for any individual to sing means to displace another individual's music. Characters become isolated expressions of will. The choice over the baby Paris's fate in the opera's first scene is in effect a power struggle between Hecuba and Priam. The furious music to which Hecuba declares she is 'no longer mother to this child' has no potential for unification or integration with the tender material of Priam's monologue 'A father and a King', and is curtailed while he sings. But its rhetorical force renders it still palpable – an absent presence – during Priam's music. And for the time being it is Hecuba's will that prevails. Her music returns to silence Priam's as he acquiesces ('The Queen is right. / Let the child be killed'), and it invades the ensuing fanfare as the couple depart (see Ex. 3.6(b)).

The omnipresence of the will to power as a fact of existence is further expressed in a family of musical figures that issue from the opera's prelude

(aspects of which are quoted in Ex. 3.6). This amounts not so much to a process of musical development as to an array of associations with different aspects of the prelude which resonate throughout the opera. Key players in this respect are the brass, not only because of their martial and regal connotations, but also through their traditional association with the function of herald. (In the prelude to Act I scene 1 the trumpets are actually presented as such before the curtain; though what is heralded is suitably unspecified.) Thus fanfare-like figuration often appears at key moments of decision, rendering them ominously epiphanic – as at Priam's initial resolution to have Paris killed (discussed above). Significantly, there are thematic as well as timbral resonances between this passage (Fig. 50ff.; Ex. 3.6(b)) and the original prelude, especially with the second part of the latter (Fig. 8ff.; Ex. 3.6(a)). These include the iambic rhythms and the middleground chordal motion, which additionally establishes some close harmonic similarities, for example the enhanced first-inversion chord of D♭ (with added G♭) at Fig. 50^{+3} which corresponds to the enharmonically equivalent vertical heard as the curtain rises on the opera at Fig. 8. The fanfare signifies the power which 'the royal pair' (Tippett's designation) exert over their situation, believing – erroneously – that they have gained control of it. That Priam is to lose this agon with life's contingencies is announced by another brass fanfare in Act I scene 2 at the start of his next monologue ('So I'd hoped it might be'), after Paris as a boy, saved through the compassion of the guard who was supposed to kill him, apprises the King of his true identity (Fig. 108; see Ex. 3.6(c)). Portentously, the diatonic resources from which the preceding fanfares drew are now destabilized, and semitones and tritones predominate (technically this involves the set [0,1,5,6], whose subset [0,1,6] acts as a nexus for much of the later 'war' music[118]).

Consistent with this picture is the further sardonic fanfare which frames Paris's deliberations over whether to steal Helen from Menelaus. This is first heard at Fig. 197 (Ex. 3.6(d)) as Hermes summons up the three goddesses who act as allegories for his options, and again at the very end of the act (Fig. 219) as he resolves to take Helen to Troy. As well as its retrospective generic connections with the earlier fanfares, this figure also presages the terrible consequences of Paris's decision, especially in its anticipation of the sound and structure of the music that will accompany Priam's death (Fig. 606ff.; Ex. 3.6(e)). Between these two points, the complex of sounds that issues from the prelude is dramatically expanded in the stylized war music of Acts II and III. Brass, timpani and piano are used in various permutations to signify generalized conflict and individual instances of aggression and enmity. The off-stage wordless (or virtually wordless)

Example 3.6. *King Priam*, fanfare figures.

(a) Prelude: the curtain rises

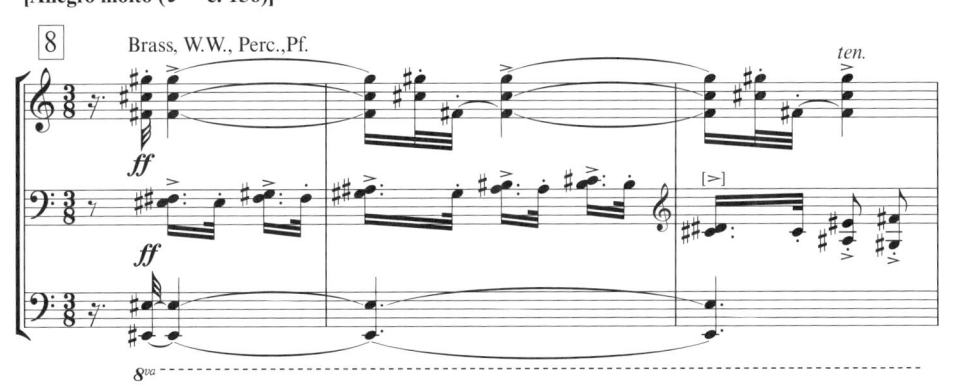

(b) Priam and Hecuba go out as the royal pair

Example 3.6 (*cont.*)

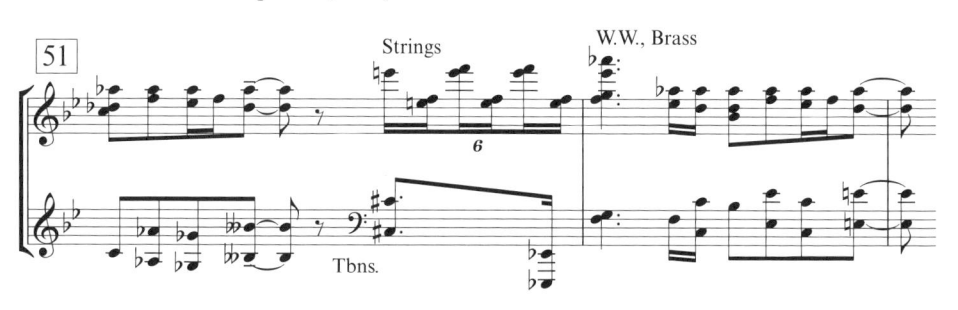

(c) Introduction to Priam's monologue (Act 1 scene 2)

Allegro deciso (♩ = c. 132)

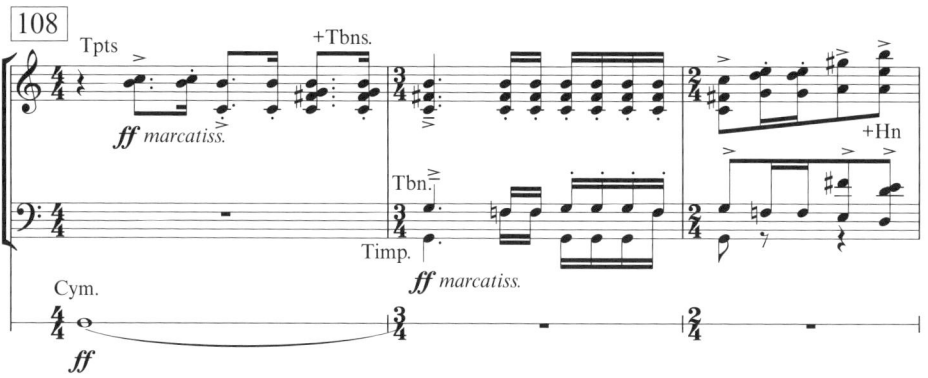

(d) The Goddesses appear [Paris's line omitted]

Allegro

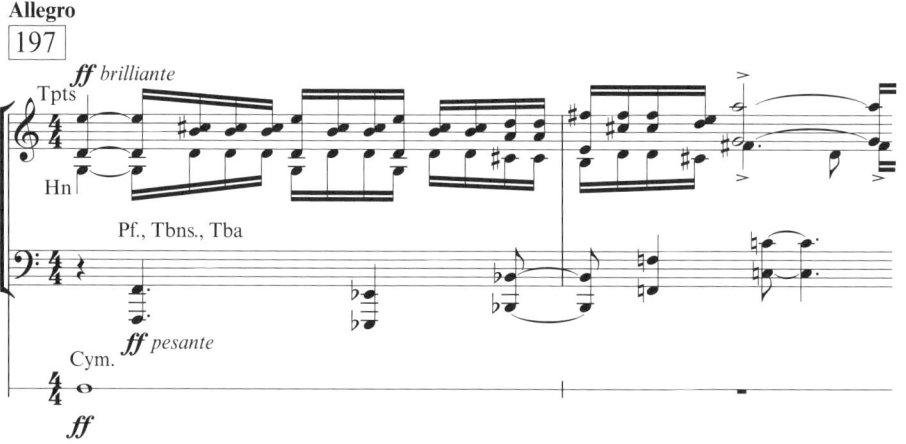

Example 3.6 (*cont.*)

(e) Priam's assassins enter

chorus registers terror and despair, or – in the case of Achilles' war cry – lust for vengeance. And the trajectory of these sounds is back to their origin, the thrilling recapitulation of the prelude as Troy falls and Priam prepares to meet his end.

In total this complex of materials (of which the above is only a sketch) sounds like a musico-dramatic realization of the feelings Tippett reported experiencing on seeing the film *The Four Horsemen of the Apocalypse* in the 1920s: 'all I remember', he writes, 'is the violence and destruction of the war sequences . . . These things combined to give me the sense that there were enormous forces beyond human control which could simply destroy the whole fabric of our civilization.'[119] Tippett the professional composer (as opposed to the left-wing activist of his younger days) is not concerned with a political analysis of this situation (neither in this nor in any other of his writings). His preference is to reify human conflict under the idea of 'forces' which on the one hand are 'out there' – in nature so to speak – and on the other hand are inherent in the relationships between individuals –

in 'human nature'. The Dionysiac sound complex of *King Priam* executes a hypostatization similar to Tippett's verbal account, not only in its musical qualities but also in its spatial representation. For Tippett deploys these musical elements across an imaginary space that extends from the inner, mental world of individual characters to a vanishing point in the outer world beyond the stage set. This horizon is evoked by the amount of material that emanates from off stage: the antiphonal trumpet fanfares of the prelude, for example; or the distant sounds of voices crying 'war', suggesting the encroachment of the forces of destruction into the city. So these forces are presented as an omnipresent feature of the outside world, as something which one might occasionally reach out and harness (as symbolized by the fanfare of 'the royal pair'), but which more often bursts in unbidden (as with the dissonant fanfare preceding Priam's monologue on his rediscovery of Paris). The progress reaches its apogee in the opera's final scene, when the Act I prelude is recapitulated: the forces are heard just outside the door, so to speak, and literally burst through as the cacophonous sounds that usher in Priam's assassins.

Helen

Sounds emanating from the entire diegetical space of *King Priam* metaphorically depict the machinations of will to power in the world at large. But just as Nietzsche believed that will to be omnipresent because vested in the actions of every human individual, so Tippett seeks to portray this Dionysiac force as continuous between the outer world and the inner world of its characters. The archetypal example of this convergence is Helen. She is the figure over whom the external, political conflict is enacted, but that conflict is a consequence of – or is presented as analogically equivalent to – the power she exerts in a more intimate space over Paris, power heard to issue from within herself.

This analogy is especially evident in Act I scene 3, in the musical relationship between the off-stage sounds of Paris and Helen's ecstatic coitus and the opera's prelude. The lovers, like the chorus in the prelude, sing wordlessly (see Ex. 3.7(a)), and although the former tell of a different aspect of Dionysiac experience, semantic contiguity with the more elemental connotations of the prelude is achieved thematically and tonally. Paris's motif, for example, with its Lombardian-rhythm oscillations between A and G♯ recalls the figuration in the female chorus (cf. Ex. 3.5). And his and Helen's lines reinvoke the polarity between the tonal centres of E♭ and E/A that was definitive for the prelude. (While Helen's line is absolutely centred around E♭, Paris's is more ambiguous until the moment where each addresses the

Example 3.7. Helen and Paris, Act I scene 3.

(a) [Choral parts (in first bar) omitted]

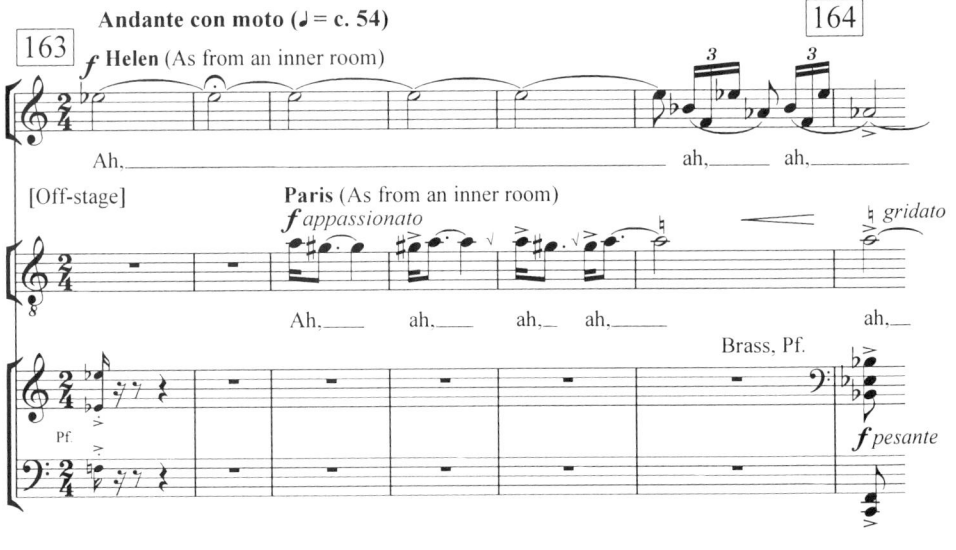

(b) [Orchestral parts omitted]

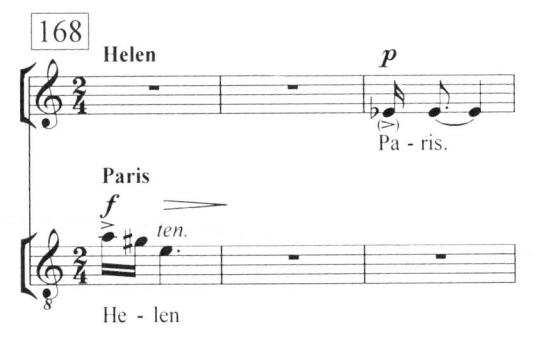

other by name (Fig. 168; Ex. 3.7(b)), at which point his line expands to incorporate the note E.) Brief but emphatic brass interjections (e.g. at Figs. 164, 166, 171) corroborate the association between bodily love and power (which Paris himself will recognize in his ensuing monologue: 'why give us bodies with such power of love, if love's a crime?'). These figures also continue to signify that this power is greater than the individual, and operates externally as well as internally, indifferent to questions of social order; it is, to repeat Paglia, 'the point of contact between man and nature, where morality and good intentions fall to primitive urges'. Hence the brass motif

burgeons (Fig. 178^{-1}) when Helen offers Paris the choice of letting him take her to Troy; its reiteration of the rhythmic topos for death – three short notes, one long – is probably not coincidental.

The fact that Helen is granted an aria (in all but name) in an opera which makes few concessions to lyrical suspensions of action, and that the aria's subject is the erotic itself, is testimony to the centrality of this theme to the work's concerns. There are (one assumes intentional) parallels between the soundworld of this aria and that which shimmers around Paris in his Act I scene 2 encounter as a boy with Hector and Priam (see Ex. 3.4 above). These parallels are especially evident in the third section of Helen's aria (see Ex. 3.8): the extremes of compass in which the piano's role is to add depth and resonance; the ornate figuration for strings, cascading down from the heights. The figuration is of course mimetic of the erotic content of the text, but equally important is the resonance between the text itself and Yeats's 'Leda and the swan'. Helen's line 'For I am Zeus's daughter, conceived when the great wings beat above Leda', beyond affirming her semi-divine parentage explicitly signals Yeats's poem, evoking both its title and its opening lines: 'A sudden blow: the great wings beating still / Above the staggering girl'. (Yeats's text in turn invokes the war that will be fought around the progeny of this congress: 'A shudder in the loins engenders there / The broken wall, the burning roof and tower / And Agamemnon dead.')

Tippett also borrows from Yeats the device of the rhetorical question. Helen's 'What can it be that throbs in every nerve, beats in the blood and bone?' alludes in its tone, for example, to Yeats's 'how can the body, laid in that white rush / But feel the strange heart beating where it lies?' Yeats uses the interrogative to suggest but not (necessarily) assert a degree of assent and ambivalence in the rape his poem describes, as in the lines 'How can those terrified vague fingers push / The feathered glory from her loosening thighs . . .?' Instead of voicing horror at an act of violation, the poem implies in its closing lines an exchange – that the girl might not have left the experience empty handed: 'Did she put on his knowledge with his power / Before the indifferent beak could let her drop?' Tippett's Helen does not sing of exactly this subject, but her aria none the less overlaps with the tenor and tone of Yeats's poem: the suggestion that carnal excess might lead to a kind of knowledge – a knowledge of power; a knowledge which *is* power, and which Helen uses to defend herself against her attackers Hecuba and Andromache, who, lacking it, do not understand their tragic situation.

One way in which the aria captures the ambience of 'Leda' is through the juxtaposition of principles that would conventionally negate one another. Taking the short extract shown in Example 3.8 as an exemplar, we can observe that the viola flourishes which evoke movement are restrained by

Example 3.8. Helen's aria, Act III scene 1.

the static throbbing piano triplets underneath; similarly the chromatic content of the former exists alongside the diatonic content of the latter. At Fig. 381 the piano's pandiatonic collection of C major is pitted against the A♭ implication of the voice and violas (their prolonged pitches in this bar form the aggregate E♭, C and G♯ (=A♭)). Intensifying the polarization between the constituent tonal groups is the semitonal conflict between Helen's prolonged E♭ and the prolonged E♮ in the bass of the piano (that dyad again). Opposed terms (opposition implying a relationship of power) are made to co-exist and hence to be a condition of the experience which the aria describes. That of which Helen is both possessed and possessor is not naïve sensual delight. Her music tells not so much of the pleasure principle, but – like that of most of the opera – of conflict and power as the driving force of human being.

Helen is; she does not act except to assert her own being ('I am Helen') and the being of being. She is the opera's representative of the ontological. Her identification with the Dionysiac ground of existence, that is, with nature, is total. She therefore recognizes the futility of action, and in this sense inhabits the tragic universe (for, to recall Nietzsche, tragic characters 'realize that no action of theirs can work any change in the eternal condition of things'). She represents a construction of the feminine with a long history, one which all but reinscribes a metaphysics into nature – as something mysterious and eternal – in the act of grounding itself in biology. This conception is central to Paglia's thesis regarding the power relations of male and female, culture and nature:

> Nature's burden falls more heavily on one sex . . .
>   Nature's cycles are woman's cycles. Biological femaleness is a sequence of circular returns, beginning and ending at the same point. Woman's centrality gives her a stability of identity. She does not have to become but only to be.[120]

By contrast, the male principle is rooted in action and construction. Indeed for Paglia the entire edifice of Western culture is man's grand Apollonian project intended to achieve mastery over Dionysiac nature: 'Western science and aesthetics are attempts to revise this horror into imaginatively palatable form'.[121] In one sense Paglia's account is a sensationalized rehearsal of Nietzsche's thesis regarding Attic tragedy: that the aesthetic draws a veil over the elemental terror of nature. Significantly, she cites tragedy as a parable of male endeavour to overcome nature:

> Tragedy is a male paradigm of rise and fall, a graph in which dramatic and sexual climax are in shadowy analogy . . . Western dramatic climax was produced by the agon of male will. Through action to identity. Action is the route of escape from nature, but all action circles back to origins, the womb-

tomb of nature. Oedipus, trying to escape his mother, runs straight into her arms.[122]

While Tippett's agenda in *King Priam* is by no means completely synonymous with Paglia's, clearly there are common elements in their representations of gender in relation to an amoral nature. If Helen epitomizes that female principle which 'does not have to become but only to be' then Priam is the male protagonist who at first attempts action in order to find a 'route of escape from nature' only to circle back to origins. This is why 'He will speak only to Helen in the end'; the knowledge he ultimately gains about the human situation is that which Helen has all along. No surprise, then, that their final dialogue takes place against the reprise of the opening prelude – the point at which the musico-dramatic thrust finds its *telos* in its subsumption under the principle of the cyclic.

IV

The aesthetics of violence: Nietzsche, Yeats and Tippett

It will, I trust, be clear that I have been using Nietzsche not only as a historical reference point, but also as a cipher or proxy for an entire constellation of ideas, and to dramatize processes going on across the stylistic divide between Tippett's first two operas and beyond. Nietzsche's construction of Hellenism in *The Birth of Tragedy* throws light on *The Midsummer Marriage* and its Dionysiac substratum at the same time as it draws Wagner and Schopenhauer into the frame; and these connections show some of the specific ways in which the opera rehearses metaphysical concerns current in the nineteenth century. The homology continues in that Nietzsche's subsequent rejection of the metaphysics of *The Birth of Tragedy*, and of Wagner and Schopenhauer, finds a counterpart in Tippett's own critique of the aesthetic world of *The Midsummer Marriage* which came with *King Priam* and the works that followed it.

One of the touchstones for gauging the aesthetic distance between Tippett's first and second periods is the *Ode to Joy* from Beethoven's Ninth Symphony. Nietzsche cites it in *The Birth of Tragedy* as a paradigm of Dionysiac intoxication, and if we subtract his hyperbole it is not difficult to see how his vision of man 'not only reconciled to his fellow but actually at one with him . . . the member of a higher community . . . [who] feels himself to be godlike'[123] finds a correlative in *The Midsummer Marriage*, with its espousal of the collective and its apotheosis of the lovers. Just how uncomfortably such a vision sits with the disenchanted worldview ushered in by *King Priam* is evident from the aggression directed towards the *Ode to Joy* in Tippett's Third Symphony. The composer makes it clear that any

such affirmative sentiment in this work is now conditional upon an uncompromising recognition of what is inimical to affirmation: 'I wanted to come out', he says 'somewhere where the hardness is, and the strengths and the viciousness of all that is involved in a positive act of almost violence'.[124] Given his pacifism, this is an extraordinary statement, even allowing for the qualifier 'almost'; how secure the barrier between an aestheticized violence and an aesthetics of violence?

If the ethos of Tippett's second period – resulting from the absorption of conflict, violence and other manifestations of the will to power into his music – bears Nietzschean overtones, it is likely that this resonance emanates not from Nietzsche directly but through intermediaries with whom Tippett made a more explicit expression of kinship. One of these is Yeats, who referred to Nietzsche as 'that strong enchanter',[125] and whose influence on Helen's aria in *King Priam* has already been examined. The final lines of 'Leda and the swan' with their implied equation between knowledge and power could be seen as a Nietzschean thought-trace, just one example within what Otto Bohlmann terms 'a wealth of like attitudes . . . in [Yeats and Nietzsche's] view of life as the tragic battleground of competing wills to power, of harsh but stimulating conflict in its smallest and greatest parts, and in their approach to art, aesthetics, rationality, to the hero, and to history'.[126] In his mystical opus, *A Vision*, which Tippett probably read,[127] Yeats makes a reference to 'Leda and the swan', going on to say 'I imagine the annunciation that founded Greece as made to Leda, remembering that . . . from one of her eggs came Love and from the other War. But all things are from antithesis.'[128]

For Yeats the way to Nietzsche was prepared by William Blake. He wrote that Nietzsche's 'thought flows always, though with an even more violent current, in the bed Blake's thought has worn'.[129] The strongest Blakean confluence in Nietzsche's, Yeats's and Tippett's outlooks is probably towards *The Marriage of Heaven and Hell* (*c.* 1793) – to which Helen's aria alludes with the line 'Love such as this stretches up to heaven, for it reaches down to hell.'[130] 'Without Contraries is no progression', states Blake; 'Attraction and Repulsion, Reason and Energy, Love and Hate, are necessary to Human existence'. Nietzsche, Yeats and Tippett in their different ways similarly endorsed the necessity of conflict – not as an end in itself, but as a condition for vigour, progress and creativity. For Nietzsche the idea of a stable society, the 'desideratum of former times "peace of the soul", the *Christian* desideratum',[131] was anathema, based, as he perceived it, on an untrue premise and a recipe for decadence. 'One must have chaos in one', he writes in the guise of Zarathustra, 'to give birth to a dancing star'.[132]

'That's me', says Tippett, quoting this aphorism in his autobiography[133] – a unique moment of explicit identification with Nietzsche, whose salience is in inverse proportion to its brevity, as I hope this account will have shown. The authenticity of much of Tippett's music, especially that of his second period, is that it bears the traces of a chaos internalized from the chaos of the world itself, that it shows the scars of, in Tippett's (Nietzsche-like) words, 'that violence of things within you which makes the art come'.[134]

Aesthetics and politics

That Tippett, pacifist and humanist, finds value in violence (albeit in the sphere of the imaginary) ought to be disquieting for our received understanding of the political background to his art. Affinities with Yeats, Nietzsche, Paglia – and we may as well add the name of Tippett's 'spiritual father', Eliot, who led him to Yeats – together begin to draw him towards an alignment with thinkers whose political outlook has at best an attenuated connection with his own liberal humanism. These are figures whose politics challenge democracy and equality as the 'natural' order. Terry Eagleton is just one commentator to have located the likes of Yeats and Eliot within an aesthetic 'right turn',[135] which I take to refer to their espousal of a cultural aristocracy – also at the heart of Nietzsche's philosophy; and to this could be added Paglia's pursuit of the line that nature's drives within us undermine rather than foster our desire for freedom and equality.

Tippett as a modernist of the right? An unthinkable suggestion, perhaps. But then exactly where did he lie on the political landscape? Arguably not unequivocally on the left either – at least not after the late 1930s.[136] (The whole question of what became of his politics after his embrace of pacifism seems barely to have been addressed; there is space here only to raise a few issues that might prompt debate.) Had Tippett wanted to model his aesthetics on thinkers from the left (e.g. Lukács, Gramsci) he would have needed to look no further than Goldmann's *Le dieu caché* which was a decisive text for *King Priam*. But what he took from Goldmann was his reading of Racine's tragedies, not his dialectically informed view of history. Tippett was similarly selective in what he appropriated from Brecht's epic theatre: lessons about dramatic pace and structure rather than left-wing didactics. *King Priam*, as we know, was intended as a repudiation of Marxism – as well as of Christianity – and in that sense we may see it as conditioned by Cold War politics. If Tippett's turn to tragedy represents a kind of 'third way', this is not some bland centrist territory between left and right, but an aesthetic response to a political

climate – which, if for no other reason than its very tragic and aesthetic tenor, resembles a Nietzschean swerve. However, if this move would deconstruct the one-dimensional opposition of left and right, the continued currency of these terms as critical reference points cannot be denied in the more complex discursive space that results.

This is to recognize the need for a reflective analysis of the relationship between political and aesthetic thought while also not allowing critical scrutiny to evaporate in the process. So, for example, queasiness at the potential vicarious connection with fascism through Tippett's ideological overlaps with Nietzsche (and for that matter through the single degree of separation interposed between Tippett and the fascism of Ezra Pound by Yeats and Eliot[137]) can on the one hand be quelled by reminding ourselves that affinity does not mean identity. And there is a second line of defence, in that the historically disseminated associations between Nietzsche and fascism can be traced to the bastardization of his thought by the Nazis which in turn fed into his post-war reception.[138] On the other hand, Nietzsche (in his own words) is dynamite. And J. P. Stern is perhaps right to point out that 'it is absurd to deny that the intellectual superstructure of . . . political movements [such as Italian and French fascism, and German national socialism] is as inconceivable without Nietzsche's ideas as these movements [were] without their superstructure'.[139] For all that Nietzsche's political reputation deserves rehabilitation, for all that many of his less palatable ideas result from courageously envisioning the ultimate consequences and corollaries of a de-divinized, de-metaphysicized world, it is not unthinkable that the realization of a Nietzschean polity – which historically has had its attractions for radical thinkers on both the left and the right[140] – would bring its appropriate measure of terror.

One might also argue that the same requirement for reflective but critical reception ought to go for Marx. Tippett's aversion to Marxism is understandable in the Cold War context under which he wrote *King Priam*. At this time the Gulag was as iconic for perceptions of the Soviet regime as the gas chambers were for Nazism (both feature in Tippett's verses for his Third Symphony – which contain his own attempt to think beyond good and evil). But to dismiss on these grounds the critical insights offered by Marx into the social and economic injustices inherent in capitalism would be as unjust as jettisoning Nietzsche's philosophy because of its (mis)appropriation by German national socialism – albeit that at the same time Marxism, on grounds of its assumption of a dominating, centralizing state, can be no less dissociated from the inhumanities committed in its name.

Tippett can be imagined as caught in the negative cross-currents of these several contradictory tendencies. A concomitant of his resistance to

traditions of critical thought informed by Marx is the absence of any substantial analysis in his mature dramatic works of the social implications of class and capital (no small factors in the sum total of modern human alienation); and this is possibly the biggest lacuna in the *œuvre* of an artist who did not disregard social questions, and who was accredited with the attitude of 'embracing more or less everything sooner or later'.[141] Instead Tippett's analysis of oppression seems to be based on a perception of something eternal in the human psyche, and in the relationships between individuals, which will always undo what humanity builds, and will always seek to remake what humanity destroys – something not unlike Nietzsche's will to power. Yet clearly Tippett would have been chary at following the logic of this concept through to the same conclusions as Nietzsche. It is as hard to imagine the former endorsing the latter's anti-democratic sentiments, or his espousal of war.[142] Likewise, while Nietzsche might have found much to admire in Tippett he would probably have dismissed the latter's pacifism and abiding sense of compassion as a shortfall in spiritual health – though the composer was not beyond problematizing this sentiment, as the dilemmas of his protagonists Priam and Jo Ann make plain. (And one interpretation of Tippett's pacifism – which flowered in the late 1930s, contemporaneously with his abandonment of communism – would be as a turn from party politics to an *individualism* with political consequences – an engagement which in its mode if not its actual content might have found approval from Nietzsche.) If Tippett recognizes himself in certain strains of Nietzsche's thought ('That's me') it is clear that limits are set on this identification. This suggests we might use Nietzsche as a kind of ideological litmus test to ascertain where and why the affinities in Tippett's outlook break down. I will argue that it is at just this limit point that a metaphysics resurfaces in the latter's thinking.

On the uses and disadvantages of Nietzsche for understanding Tippett

Tippett shares with Nietzsche the drive to find a meaningful, indeed affirmative, articulation of the human condition after what the latter termed 'the greatest recent event', that is, the death of God.[143] Both are engaged with a search for an authentic order of values beyond those of scientific positivism that takes full account of the fact that the collective consciousness of Western culture has had its metaphysical lynchpin removed. If Nietzsche's initial turn to metaphysics is more overt and more philosophically grounded than Tippett's, his repudiation is also more complete.

As we have seen, in both *The Birth of Tragedy* and *The Midsummer Marriage* the Apollo–Dionysus dualism is essential to an operatic metaphysics. In Tippett's case this is couched not as a theology, but as a humanism within which the divine still has a role, even if figured as a symbol. His conception of a 'new humanism' based on 'The Whole Man' employs a Jungian conception: the 'God-image' as an archetypal symbol of integration.[144] In their final apotheosis the royal pair Mark and Jenifer are at the centre of a world through which human love radiates, encompassing all of nature. By contrast *King Priam* shows humanity in a far less enchanted, and far less central relation to the scheme of things – expressing an awareness of what Nietzsche terms 'the *hyperbolic naiveté* of man: positing himself as the meaning of all things'.[145] At the end Priam perhaps still finds something in the experience of being human with which to rise to the catastrophic blows which life has dealt him. But his heroism is exactly commensurate with his ability to grasp the full magnitude of 'the dark forms of creation', of humanity's decidedly unprivileged position within an amoral and sublimely indifferent nature.

In his second opera, then, Tippett sets a new agenda, and to my mind this invites comparison with Nietzsche's project of 'the dehumanization of nature' – the confrontation with nature as it really is: shorn of sentimental, picturesque interpretation; voided of any animating metaphysical principle or of any inherent meaning – in a word, disenchanted. This, as Lawrence Lampert points out, is an antihumanist, or at least posthumanist – and certainly post-theistic – mission: the conscientious rejection of the desire to 'elevate the human until it becomes the very meaning of nature and history'.[146] And lest we should be in any doubt as to the magnitude of the implications of this vision, Nietzsche sees it on a cosmic scale:

> In some remote corner of the universe that is poured out in countless flickering solar systems, there once was a star on which clever animals invented knowledge. That was the most arrogant and untruthful moment in 'world history' – yet indeed only a moment. After nature had taken a few breaths, the star froze over and the clever animals had to die.[147]

If this seems a recipe for nihilism, for Nietzsche nihilism is only a 'pathological transition'[148] to a further stage where joy may be predicated of pessimism; and this is possible because we have finally got our position within the universe straight. The dehumanization of nature means not being resentful towards nature when it fails to reflect our anthropocentric image back at us: 'how could we reproach or praise the universe? Let us beware of attributing to it heartlessness or unreason or their opposites: it is neither perfect nor beautiful, nor noble, nor does it wish to become any of these

things; it does not by any means strive to imitate man.'[149] After the dehumanization of nature comes the 'naturalization of the human': 'When will we complete our de-deification of nature? When may we begin to "*naturalize*" humanity in terms of a pure, newly discovered, newly redeemed nature?'[150] Humanity on Nietzsche's view is enhanced not diminished by locating itself in a de-metaphysicized universe, but this means joyfully grasping the terrible truth of our situation.

This situation is literally tragic, and it is tragedy – epitomizing the role of the aesthetic in Nietzsche's scheme – that makes it possible to 'live in accord with nature'.[151] 'The tragic artist is *not* a pessimist – it is precisely he who *affirms* all that is questionable and terrible in existence, he is *Dionysian* . . .'[152] In contradistinction to Aristotle, Nietzsche believes that tragedy exists, '*Not* so as to get rid of pity and terror, not so as to purify oneself of dangerous emotions through its vehement discharge . . . but, beyond pity and terror, *to realize in oneself* the eternal joy of becoming – that joy which also encompasses *joy in destruction*'.[153] It is the ability to find joy in the full economy of life, all the way to destruction, which forms the basis of Nietzsche's polity – a polity in which the aesthetic displaces morality in the accepted sense. In this polity, those who embrace the Dionysiac principle (because they are able to aestheticize terror) constitute an aristocracy. These noble types may assume their place because on the one hand they accept the will to power as necessity, and on the other they place culture above either power politics or any belief in democratic equality.

What can we recognize of the later Tippett in this later Nietzschean landscape? While the notion of an aristocratic individualism may have been alien to him (although in later years he appeared to take no exception to being feted as an individual within his country's cultural elite), his own tragic venture, *King Priam*, is antihumanist insofar as it unflinchingly portrays the reality of human conflict and reveals humanity in a decentred position in relation to the natural order. The opera is moulded by its critique of the earlier humanism epitomized by *The Midsummer Marriage*. And while Tippett's *œuvre* is resistant to generalization it is none the less appropriate to argue that a sense of the tragic (and its correlative posthumanism) is an important ingredient in a number of his post-*Priam* works, and that this is definitive for the modernism we find there. For example the Fourth Symphony (1976–7) projects the individual life as a heroic struggle against the titanic forces of nature, and whatever problems its deployment of breathing sounds poses from the technical standpoint of musical mediation and integration, the last exhalation which is also the work's closing gesture remains a powerful and chilling image of the utter finality of mortality. A de-metaphysicized universe indeed, one might think.

Yet the composer is not able to go all the way down the road of antihumanism. His posthumanism is characterized by ambivalence. If in *King Priam* and after he mounts a critique of his earlier humanism, humanism voices its own critical position from the wings. Notwithstanding its cultivation of a violent exuberance, Symphony No. 3 is ultimately significant for staging a cautious *rapprochement* between modernist and humanist worldviews; and in a late work such as *The Rose Lake* (though this is emphatically not to imply a seamless chronological progression) humanism wants to retake centre stage. One testing ground on which we might imagine this struggle being played out is the will to power. As Stern argues, this became 'the cardinal concept of Nietzsche's only systematic venture . . . the centrepiece of a vast philosophical panorama . . . He presents it as a principle discernible in all nature.'[154] I have argued that the drama and soundworld of *King Priam* make that principle audible. But how unqualified is Tippett's adoption of it, compared with the 100 per cent-proof version Nietzsche espouses in the following?

> And do you know what 'the world' is to me? Shall I show it to you in my mirror? This world: a monster of energy, without beginning, without end; . . . a sea of forces flowing and rushing together, eternally changing, eternally flooding back . . . with an ebb and a flood of its forms . . . : this, my *Dionysian* world of the eternally self-creating, the eternally self-destroying, this mystery world of the twofold voluptuous delight, my 'beyond good and evil', without goal, unless the joy of the circle is itself a goal; . . . – do you want a *name* for this world? A *solution* for all its riddles? . . . *This world is the will to power – and nothing besides!*[155]

Priam's vision of 'mirrors / Myriad upon myriad moving / The dark forms / Of creation' might be a version of what Nietzsche here imagines, but it is that suffix 'and nothing besides' which is the sticking point.[156] While Tippett's later *œuvre* acknowledges the ubiquitous nature of power as a criterion of the human condition, the composer stops short of promoting it to a monism in the way that Nietzsche does – which is to say he draws (or wants to draw) a different moral corollary. 'I have a dream / . . . That my strong arms shall lift the lame' is his affirmation at the end of the Third Symphony (a most un-Nietzschean notion); 'One humanity; one justice' the message pitted against the 'barrage of sound' at the conclusion of *New Year*. And as if making the same point in a more coded way, the representation of 'our inward tears' which follows the final barrage of sounds of *King Priam* contains – as if in mute protest – a distilled, allusive reminiscence of Priam's compassionate monologue 'A father and a King' (see Ex. 3.9). While Nietzsche's tragic artist '*affirms* all that is questionable and

Example 3.9. Ending of *King Priam* – 'our inward tears' – and its allusion to 'A father and a King'.

terrible in existence', Tippett's tragic vision simultaneously embraces *and* remonstrates against those conditions. A justifiable enough modification: Nietzsche did not live to see the genocidal programmes of the twentieth century, in which his philosophy – however speciously – would be implicated. (No art after Auschwitz, as Adorno declared.) Nor did his joyful acceptance of the imagined end of the human species need to be perturbed by the rather less imaginary and more immediate threat of nuclear war.

Tippett's disinclination to follow Nietzsche's logic through to its joyously harsh conclusion, however, means replacing the latter's monism with a dualism, and that brings its own complications. Nietzsche's affirmative position was at least consistent with his antihumanism. In Tippett's case affirmation exists alongside a position which makes tangible a post- or antihumanist world picture; but the former does not issue from the latter. Characteristically, the single moment of light in *King Priam*, Hermes's 'Hymn to Music', is sung, as it were, with a different voice, at one remove. In other words, affirmation emanates from a *transcendental* perspective – as a moment of epiphany bracketed out from the world vision presented by the opera as a whole. And this construction will repeat itself many times in Tippett's later *œuvre*. Words which Tippett quotes from Goethe's *Wilhelm Meister* at the end of *The Ice Break* come to mind: 'Yet you will always be brought forth again, glorious image of God'. For Tippett, then, 'the greatest recent event' seems less than final.

The least metaphysical gloss one could put on the borrowed reference to God here is as a kind of shorthand for a higher-level apprehension of humanity within the human condition. But even if presented as metaphor, these apprehensions are nevertheless posited as having some prior, alteritous existence to the normative struggle of existence. Given that Tippett's position is, like Nietzsche's, post-theistic, and given that at this stage in his career he has come to a view of nature as disenchanted, to what source can these apprehensions be ascribed?

The answer would seem to be art itself – the aesthetic not only as a practice within culture, but also as a faculty of creating images 'through which [the] mysterious depths of our being speak to us', and which 'is part of what we mean by having knowledge of God'.[157] Whereas for Nietzsche, then, the aesthetic came to represent an alternative to metaphysics (in a world in which the Kantian distinction between phenomenon and noumenon, appearance and reality 'in itself' is deconstructed), for Tippett it becomes the locus of metaphysics (so implicitly reconstructing that dualism). 'Music is of itself divine' is how he puts it in *The Mask of Time*; indeed his *œuvre* contains a number of auto-referential claims for music as the paradigm of this higher, or deeper level which is simultaneously outside our plane of existence yet essential to it. Hermes's apostrophe to 'the timeless music' in *King Priam* is a prime example, with its closing appeal, 'O divine music, / Melt our hearts, / Renew our love'. *New Year* also presents within its denouement the conceit of 'a deeper sound: a richer song', which can be known in 'Moments out of time and space' (always the notion of the epiphanic moment) but which nevertheless underpins all being: 'I hear it always' says Pelegrin, the character from 'nowhere and tomorrow'.

One of the most telling disjunctures between Tippett and Nietzsche lies in their figurations of time and history. Nietzsche celebrated history as profoundly unteleological – reflecting a world that is 'eternally self-creating, eternally self-destroying'; a state of endless becoming, with no inherent meaning or ultimate purpose. And from this he derived his idea of eternal return: the will to affirm life exactly as it is, exactly as one has lived it – as if in perpetually repeated cycles. In Tippett's case, however, while the eternal (and therefore eternally unjust) conditions of human conflict are acknowledged, his sights remain fixed on the possibility of a better future. Which implies a notion of historical progress, notwithstanding the absence of any theoretical articulation in his writings of how this might in reality be engineered. In works such as *The Vision of Saint Augustine* (1963–5) and *The Mask of Time* cyclic notions of time are certainly contemplated, but these exist in contention with linear determinations of time; and the image of some timeless otherly domain represents an idealized if inarticulable *telos* which emerges from this struggle. Hence the metaphysical residuum in Tippett's post-*Priam* output might be seen to occupy the space of an absent politics – to which it is nevertheless not unrelated.

On the one hand, then, *King Priam* and its successor works bring a new, critical concept of art into the frame: a faster, more furious, disenchanted picture of the human condition from which the metaphysical is expunged. On the other hand, Tippett's earlier, metaphysically sponsored concept of art, as found in *The Midsummer Marriage*, continues to exert critical tension from its would-be transcendental perspective. In *King Priam* at least, this is not yet a dialectic: the most appropriate description would be – drawing from Bakhtin – dialogical.[158] This is to say that the antihumanist and humanist streams are both given a voice – but there is no synthesis between them. This is why Hermes's Hymn to Music offers an alternative position on the main action; and why a worldview in many respects cognate with that of Nietzsche and Yeats is discernible driving the work, while Aristotelian pity and fear still have their say. But the fact that no final synthetic position is reached means that neither voice is silenced: the Nietzschean/Yeatsian harsh truths are allowed to speak for themselves, while the tender voice of a music that would 'melt our hearts, renew our love' is audible but unable directly to intervene. Tippett, one might surmise, has allowed war to break out within his own psyche.

4 Metaphysics in a cold climate: *The Vision of Saint Augustine*

Reframing the critical debate

The Vision of Saint Augustine (1963–5) is a remarkable work: Tippett's most sustained attempt to convey a human being's experience of what allegedly lies beyond human being. On the face of it, the piece and its attempted subject matter, Augustine's vision of eternity, threaten to set the commentator an equally sublime task: to show how music, the epitome of temporal artforms, reveals through its own essence the essence of time and what lies beyond it. Fortunately, though, the work is not about time in such a pure sense. Its preoccupation with temporality is, I will argue, infused by the temporal concerns of this (material) world, and while exploring those mediations will be tricky enough, this is at least a less terrifying prospect than what might have been had Tippett indeed succeeded in musically mapping time and eternity as absolutes.

There are other ways too in which our investigative business is not quite what it first appears to be. Tippett's own commentary on the work, especially his essay 'Music of the angels', is as significant for what it neglects to discuss as for what it actually says.[1] This is not to suggest deliberate dissimulation; we can certainly detect where the poetic metaphors of the angelic choir have made their mark on the piece. But it is questionable whether these alone point to what the work is 'about', any more than Tippett's references to, say, the vocal device of glossolalia are keys to its musical structure. Another striking lacuna in critical commentary on *The Vision of Saint Augustine* lies in making light of the extremity of its modernist musical language – as if the visionary aspects of *The Midsummer Marriage* (1946–52) could be innocently translated into what just happens to be a more esoteric musical style without any substantial alteration of their significance. True enough, epithets invited by the opera – 'exuberant', 'radiant', 'lyrical' – all obtain here too; but in a highly attenuated sense: problematized, distorted even, by some Other, negative quality. After all, is not the *estatico* coloratura which the female choral voices sing against the Ambrosian hymn 'Deus, creator omnium' also slightly redolent of hysteria?

These observations imply that to grasp what is really going on in this most difficult of Tippett's works we need to alert ourselves fully to the dialectical condition of its musical material, and to the possibility that this condition might be a mimetic response to the strange meetings, contradic-

tions and disquietudes of its informing contexts. One context for the work's discourse of time-transcendence is an entirely timely social anxiety over the direction of history – symptoms of which are present in several of the composer's essays of the period. While the manifest subject matter of *The Vision of Saint Augustine* is not the social and historical *per se*, these dimensions none the less operate in the choices the composer (indeed any composer) makes in his marshalling of musical material. (Something of this is perhaps behind the title 'Too many choices' that Tippett gave to his wide-ranging essay written probably in late 1957,[2] which offers valuable, if elliptical, perspectives on *Augustine* and works of this period.) Tippett's compositional judgement on the musical resources socially and historically bequeathed him was especially evident in the instrumental works that followed *King Priam* (1958–61) – the Sonata No. 2 for Piano (1962) and the Concerto for Orchestra (1962–3) – specifically in their critical reappraisal of fundamental questions of musical continuity and development. That *The Vision of Saint Augustine* takes up these developments (and, as Arnold Whittall declares, advances them[3]) amounts to more than grafting metaphysical content on to a set of formalist musical problems. For the whole stylistic reformulation activated by *King Priam* is already to do with the problematics of the individual subject's integration in the face of an increasingly disenchanted world. So in this sense *The Vision of Saint Augustine* ruminates further on an order already rethought in the mediation of formal and aesthetic domains in preceding works.

This much gives an indication of the critical constellation which surrounds *Augustine*, and of the interrelationships between its elements. Far from detracting from the work's expressed concern for the transcendent, this expanded framework is essential to understanding its urgency. Ultimately, this rearrangement is driven by what is audible in the music's soundworld; for the issues are played out nowhere if not in the work itself. So at the heart of this study is the analysis of musical detail. Before it, however, we shall need to clarify the music's compositional context, which will involve a closer appraisal of Tippett's encounter with Augustine, and the development of a critical vocabulary beyond what that encounter offers as an interpretative resource. Once on the other side of the analytical enquiry we shall be better able to situate the work in the modern context to which it truly belongs.

I

Historicism, history and modernity

Just what was Tippett doing immersing himself so deeply in the world of Augustine of Hippo? We should not lose sight of the strangeness of this

meeting: on one side, the composer – confirmed agnostic, alive to the significance of the Dionysiac in human experience, antithetical to dogma and authority; on the other side, Augustine (354–430) – theologian, eventual ascetic, one of the founding fathers of the Catholic Church. Yet, though a world apart from the saint, Tippett's imagination evidently opened up fully on to his religious experience.

This relationship is encapsulated musically in the 'Deus, creator omnium' episodes of *The Vision of Saint Augustine*, first heard before the second minute of the work is out (Fig. 7^{+3} ff.; see Ex. 4.1). The male voices present the Ambrosian hymn which functions in the work as Augustine's metonymic signature (he sang it to assuage his grief at his mother's death; and in book XI/xxvii of his *Confessions* uses it as an example for how we measure time). Tippett transplants this into a contrapuntal texture of his own making. What we might surmise as the limits of his identification with Augustine is perhaps ultimately a matter of historical distance – the difference between thinking in a theistic and in a secular culture – and this finds its counterpart in the distance between the modal organization of Ambrose's hymn and the full chromatic aggregate in which it is situated. Yet Tippett's added musical strata enfold the quoted chant empathetically, drawing their phrase and cadence structure from it, intensifying the devotional sentiments expressed in it between the singing subject and his God. So while Augustine's and Tippett's worlds are evoked in their separateness, the musical relationship expressed here is not parodic – a somewhat different situation from the near contemporary treatment of historical sacred materials in a work such as Maxwell Davies's *Antechrist* (1967).

Tippett approached his behind-the-scenes theological homework for *Augustine* with an equally non-sardonic attitude. His writings on the work constitute a serious-minded discussion of the secondary literature he read both on Augustine's understanding of time and on biblical descriptions of angel song (a music out of time, and hence a metaphor for eternity). On the one hand those secondary sources impacted on certain aspects of the form the work eventually took, which a brief philological excursus will illustrate. For example, all the characteristics of angelic singing Tippett recounts in his essay are drawn from the account in Reinhold Hammerstein's *Die Musik der Engel*;[4] and one particular image, the antiphonal *alter ad alterum* ('one cried unto another'), is invoked in the so-called 'angel symphony' that concludes Part I of *Augustine*.[5] Hammerstein probably also drew Tippett's attention to the significance of the angels' appearance to the shepherds in the Christmas story: a metaphor for the irruption of eternity into history (in turn an expression of God's relation to humankind)[6] – which sensation is mirrored by the ruptures in the temporal sequence of *Augustine*. And although not

Example 4.1. *The Vision of Saint Augustine*, 'Deus creator omnium' (beginning) (orchestral doublings of vocal parts not indicated).

specifically referenced in Tippett's account, Hammerstein must have been an important source for the former's information on the various kinds of ecstatic wordless ululation – glossolalia, *jubilus*, *alleluia* – which find their place among the vocal techniques adopted in the work.[7] Indeed Tippett's use of Greek vowels from the Gnostic *Pistis Sophia* (ιαω, αωι, ωια) in his own glossolalia is probably directly indebted to Hammerstein's account of this practice.[8]

On the other hand, pinpointing such connections alone – the application of positivist historical method – takes us only so far. One wonders in fact whether the historicist tenor of Tippett's essay is a semi-deliberate red herring to persuade the reader that the difficult soundworld of *The Vision of Saint Augustine* is more traditional than it actually is. However, turning to the historical only drives us back to the modern: the work's historical content functions as a living agency only in relation to its other, the new (and if Tippett is conspicuously silent about that aspect in his prose, it sounds loud and clear from the piece itself). Equally, in his relationship with Augustine, the identifications ultimately carry meaning only if understood against what is non-identical; indeed the extent of our understanding of *The Vision of Saint Augustine* is directly related to extent to which we recognize this tension.

Fortunately, Tippett provides enough pointers towards the modernist concerns in which *The Vision of Saint Augustine* is enmeshed, of which the most crucial is his reference (slightly late in the day, it must be added) to Gilles Quispel's essay 'Time and history in patristic Christianity'.[9] Quispel's paper is important on three counts. First, it seems to have prompted the decision to compose *The Vision of Saint Augustine*, for, as Tippett himself points out, although he had known Augustine's *Confessions* probably since his youth, it was Quispel's essay which brought him back to this figure. An extension to this positive historical fact is the likelihood that Quispel's textual citations acted as sources for aspects of Tippett's libretto.[10] Secondly, 'Time and history' seems to have decisively informed Tippett's understanding of Augustine, and so potentially clarifies for us the points of identification between these two figures. Thirdly, it is clear that Tippett takes from Quispel's reading of Augustine only what suits his aesthetic purposes; therefore this point of departure valuably indicates what is non-identical between Tippett and Augustine/Quispel, and thus provides a gateway into *The Vision of Saint Augustine*'s idiosyncratic territory.

Time and history

Quispel's text must have been exactly what Tippett was looking for in the late 1950s. It provided corroboration of themes in his own thinking, and a

means for developing them. In particular, Quispel wrote of the very dichotomy between linear and cyclic time that Tippett had reflected upon as follows in his essay 'Too many choices':

> There is a sense of Time as unique, from Genesis to World's End. And there is a sense of Time as repetitive, or circular – the myth of the Eternal Return. I am uncertain how objective is my feeling that the movement of these two ideas, one against the other, is another aspect of the new world picture; though others feel with me.[11]

Evidence of the lasting fascination this dualism exerted on Tippett is its recurrence in *The Mask of Time*, over twenty years later (1980–2). But the work on the horizon here is *King Priam*. Tippett's intellectual reflections in the above quotation find their counterpart in the opera's final act, where linear and cyclic conceptions of time dramatically converge: the music both drives towards the final *telos* of the protagonist's destruction and engenders a recapitulation of the Act I prelude under which Priam is all but engulfed. It was the preoccupation with the temporal in this work, not *The Vision of Saint Augustine*, that first set Tippett on the trail of *Man and Time*, the volume in which Quispel's essay was published. An extract from a letter Tippett wrote to Colin Franklin while writing the opera's libretto (not long after the publication of 'Too many choices') makes these various connections clear:

> Priam does not issue like perhaps Harry, in [T. S. Eliot's] Family Reunion, in good works or Jungian wholeness; but in the same rough strength shot through with some other sense of the timeless in Time . . .
>
> And is there then anything in Routledge: Time & Man [*sic*] to help me? I was caught by T. L. S. review of it.[12]

Two points are significant in this extract. First, the reference to *Man and Time* establishes the text as a common denominator in the genesis of *King Priam* and *The Vision of Saint Augustine* – a connection which underlines concerns shared across the works. Secondly (and a possible example of such a shared concern), Tippett suggests that for a protagonist in Priam's situation the Jungian model of the integrated subject may no longer be possible. Explanation as to why invokes a larger complex of ideas. In the opera Priam's integrity as a subject is fissured by the historical events which impinge on him; and his changing relationship with history (from engagement to passivity) is mirrored in his changing relationship to time (from being in it to being out of it). A similar reflexivity between time and history is implied in 'Too many choices' when Tippett surmises that his intuition about time 'is another aspect of the new world picture'.[13]

Quispel reveals the conceptual constellation of time, history and the individual subject also to be at the heart of Augustine's theology. For

Augustine, as for Tippett, history was pertinent as both a force whose nature needed to be understood, and as the background from which his own reflections on such matters as time drew their salience. Quispel describes, for example, how Augustine's arguments about time polemicized against his 'Neoplatonic adversaries' of the day[14] who expressed their antipathy towards Christianity through a Hellenic concept of cyclic time in which the aeons of time are forever and identically replayed: 'As Plato once taught in Athens, so he will teach once again; indeed he will teach innumerable times, in the same city and in the same school'.[15] On this view time and eternity are reduced to the same principle. But Augustine, in providing the philosophical and theological underpinning for the linear model of time instituted by early Christianity, sought to prise these two notions back apart. Eternity would be posited as a realm transcending time; humanity and history would accordingly take their place – become positively meaningful – in the drama of this new existential order.

Quispel's account of time in early Christian thought is worth sketching out because it evidently informed Tippett's own views when he came to write *The Vision of Saint Augustine*. In this consciousness time has a beginning in creation and an end in the apocalypse. This ending also constitutes a goal – a *telos*, an *eschaton* – which imbues time and the cosmos with 'a tension and a meaning . . . because it becomes related to the plan of Salvation'.[16] Moreover, time is also given a centre, 'a divine *ephapax*, a "once and for all"' in the singular event which is 'the life and death of Jesus'.[17] Shaped by this narrative, time becomes synonymous not with eternity (as in the cyclic model) but with history. Eternity, by contrast, is in Augustine's world picture a transcendent domain outside of time, something radically other than it. Since time came into being only with creation, it is nonsense, he says, to ask what God was doing at the time before he created time. In eternity there can be no before and after; one time does not give way to another, but inheres in a state of total presence: 'No element of your word yields place or succeeds to something else . . . you say all that you say in simultaneity and eternity'.[18]

History will end with the *eschaton*, when time gives way to eternity. But Augustine experienced a proleptic vision of that moment. He was able to do so on the one hand through the agency of divine grace, and on the other through the exercise of his own mind. For his solution to the puzzle of time lay in the recognition that we cannot know it (objectively) as an absolute, but only (subjectively) through the mediation of our own mental faculties. The past exists as a memory (*memoria*) of things once present, the future is a mental anticipation (*expectatio*) of things to come; only in the present do we have time in our immediate sight (*contuitus*).[19] However, this potential

centre for our apprehension of time is ceaselessly decentred as the mind's attention oscillates between memory and expectation. This leads to a diaspora of the soul which Augustine calls *distensus*.[20] For the soul to recover this centre requires the concentration of the will he terms *extensus* – an apprehension of the present untainted by anticipation of the future and not allowed to slip into a memory of something past. To sustain this present would be to experience something like the simultaneity of God's eternity (where, as Eliot puts it, and Tippett quotes in his epigraph to the score, 'all is always now'). Such was the vision Augustine shared with his mother at the window embrasure at Ostia.

Augustine and modernity

If the perspicacity of Augustine's reasoning imbues it with relevance for the non-Christian mind, so its theological saturation makes it impossible to rehearse without its Christian world-view (as the above will have made clear). The question of Augustine's relationship to modernity – a vital one for *The Vision of Saint Augustine* – revolves around the problematics of the dual modality of his thought, at once philosophical and theological. It is perhaps unsurprising that Tippett, who recognized polarity as an essential attribute of his own personality and music,[21] would be awake to the psychological conflict inherent in such a dichotomy. Of Augustine's attitude to the truth claims of the Bible he writes:

> All his life he battled with this paradox: that this uncultivated, even at times cruel and improbable book, was word for word *God's* word. It is this battle which made him a religious genius, and stamps him for us as a modern.[22]

On the one hand, we may assume that what Tippett empathized with, and found modern, in Augustine was inner conflict *per se*. The graphic account the latter gives in the *Confessions* of his struggle to master his carnality, and equally to solve purely intellectual problems as the nature of time, shows him in an all-too human state of division against himself. (The sound-world of *The Vision of Saint Augustine* seems shot through with the fallout of this battle.) On the other hand, Tippett's comments imply that Augustine's modernity resides specifically in the agon between reason and revelation, between rationality and its other. If Quispel sharpened Tippett's awareness of these antinomies, the two part company over the diagnosis of modernity. And this difference in emphasis points to what is distinctive about *The Vision of Saint Augustine*.

For Quispel 'St. Augustine was assuredly a theologian . . . he literally believed first, in order to understand afterward: *Credo ut intellegam*'.[23]

Presumably, though, it is Augustine's philosophical bent which explains the tendency in his theology which Quispel recognizes as demythologization:

> Where evil is no longer . . . situated in the cosmos . . . but in the human will; where grace is infused and not forensically imputed; where the criterion for truth is found in an inward and yet not intrapsychic divine master; where Holy Scripture is inwardly inspired by the Holy Ghost; where history is interpreted as the conflict between the love of God and the love of self, and time as subjective; where visions are taken as products of the memory – a long step has been taken toward demythologization.[24]

While modern thought would be keen to claim the demythologizing impulse as its own (because synonymous with the will to rationality), Quispel is prickly about this appropriation and about those who would sequester Augustine for modernity. He seeks instead to reinstall the theologian in his own historical context of late antiquity. This tactic cuts both ways, however. Historicizing Augustine only emphasizes what is untimely about him – most notably his understanding of subjectivity, psychology and inwardness (the most demythologized elements in Quispel's list).

These are the very things Tippett identifies with in Augustine, but, conversely, he cannot have them without the concomitant Christian theology. His acknowledgement of Augustine's theological world in *The Vision of Saint Augustine* and its supporting texts is recognition of this. Yet neither can Tippett (nor we) leave it there: his modernity – the modernity of the post-Enlightenment – must go all the way. We cannot imagine him entertaining the non-rational (or metaphysical) terms on Quispel's list – 'evil', 'grace', 'divine master', 'Holy Scripture', 'Holy Ghost', etc. – as literal realities in the same way as Augustine would have done. Had he done so the significance of *The Vision of Saint Augustine* would lie in its affirmation of the values of a past age, or of a strictly Christian belief system, neither of which would have been acceptable possibilities for Tippett.

Because this point of departure from Augustine and Quispel is crucial for our understanding of *The Vision of Saint Augustine* (however inexplicit in Tippett's own account), I want to rehearse its implications in more detail. On the one hand what is potent for Tippett in Augustine's vision is that, unlike that of his fictional creation, Priam, it really happened: 'There is a plot of earth in Ostia now where he and Monica actually stood'.[25] On the other hand, while this may have been a historical fact, the modern mind would have to put a different interpretation on the visionary experience. For Augustine, his earth-bound yearning for transcendence was directed towards what he believed to be an autonomous, other-worldly (in Quispel's words 'not intrapsychic') domain which, with God's grace, broke

into time to meet him. But for the agnostic or atheist only the worldly half of the equation can be assumed as real.

Yet precisely the problem *The Vision of Saint Augustine* sets itself is to articulate the metaphysical as something *true* while also acknowledging the modern mind's repudiation of any supernatural explanation of the transcendental side of the equation. Augustine's story may be internalized as part of the work's content, but it does not itself cast any necessary spell of truth over it, any more than does a story about mythical Trojan kings. The truth the work seeks can be attributed only to its own material circumstances. There exist only the aesthetic object and its structuring of sound and time, the human subjects responsible for its creation and perception, and the cultural and historical circumstances which mediate these factors. There is nothing more.

Tippett treats the story of Augustine's vision as a parable for an experience which may still be authentically available to modernity – but whose authenticity is dependent on its reference to a modern historical consciousness. This means we should not lose sight of Augustine's world, nor reject what is modern in his vocabulary. But it also means that the theological dimension of his thought must be understood for what it is; and that in its stead we need to talk a language more appropriate to the conditions of post-Enlightenment modernity with which *The Vision of Saint Augustine* is in truth engaged. Finding the right aesthetic language is a prerequisite for an analysis of the work's compositional issues.

II

The aesthetics of inwardness: subjectivity, time and music

Augustine most significantly addresses our own times through his emphasis on mind, which is also the site of the transcendent. His ascent to the visionary moment was a profoundly inward journey: a meditation by the subject on his own psychological experience of time. (He described God as 'more inward than my inwardness and higher than my height'.[26]) Tippett was alerted by Quispel to this 'strong emphasis on inwardness',[27] and no doubt he would have identified with it closely. His own view of the aesthetic was stamped with exactly such an emphasis: witness his comment (in an essay roughly contemporaneous with *The Vision of Saint Augustine*) that 'the one absolute idiosyncrasy of art' is that it presents 'images of *inner* experience'. More especially, music (notably symphonic music, whose paradigm for Tippett was Beethoven) offers 'a significant image of the inner flow of life'. Through the metaphor of 'flow' the conceit also implies that this is a reflection of subjective consciousness *in time*.[28]

For all that Tippett cites Susanne Langer in support of this view,[29] the notion of the ground of the aesthetic as an interior, subjective realm detached from the empirical outer world in fact has a modern pedigree dating back to the late eighteenth and early nineteenth centuries, most notably in philosophical discourse on art in German idealism and early romanticism. Hegel's view of music's aesthetic function for example – that 'What it claims as its own is the depth of a person's inner life as such'[30] – would seem to overlap substantially with Tippett's, and, granted differences due to their different historical situations, suggests a certain continuity of ideology. Moreover, the connection between subjective inwardness, music and the apprehension of time is likewise made by Hegel and other contemporary philosophers and critics.[31]

When the circumstances are right, Tippett tells us, music affords a '*truly immediate* apprehension' of the inner flow of life which lies behind it.[32] Music's inward images, then, are not mere ciphers for subjective consciousness; they are one with it. The flow of one captures the flow of the other; and so, we may infer, each is implicated in the other's temporality, and temporality is implicated in both. Tippett's observation (perhaps unknowingly) connotes an entire theory of the modern subject in relation to time and music, one which contains a conceptual repertory of value to our investigation of *The Vision of Saint Augustine*. These notions are framed by Julian Johnson (in a different context) as follows:

> Time is the constitutive dimension of the subject, and it is for this reason that music stands in a privileged relationship to the subject . . . It possesses the potential for this function because the defining activity of music is also that of the subject – the structuring of time . . . [This] suggests neither that music is 'about' subjectivity nor that its processes are analogous to those of the subject, but rather that its processes *are* those of the subject, and its structuring of time is thereby a structuring of the subject.[33]

On this view, the subject does not exist pre-formed *in* time, but creates and sustains itself *through* its consciousness of time: the subject only comes to know itself as such in its persistence – its identity – from one moment to the next. To elaborate, again with reference to Hegel: each point of time, each 'now', 'proves at once to be its own negation, since, as soon as *this* "now" is, it supersedes itself by passing into another "now"'.[34] Through such negation time constantly strives to become external to itself. And this self-externality is 'the same principle which is active in the self'. The self 'only becomes a self by concentrating its momentary experiences and returning into itself from them'.[35] In other words, for the self to become an object of its own consciousness, it must know itself as other to itself – a

process which might lead to its dissipation were it not for that crucial return into itself which ensures its unity. Self-consciousness is accordingly rooted in a dialectical process *enacted across time.*

For Hegel, music's content is 'the inner life as such'[36] because it charts exactly this process; the act of listening provides the subject with a means for that 'concentration of momentary experience' necessary to its articulation as a self. One such available means is metre or periodicity – *Takt.*[37] Applying this principle of grouping enables the self to synthesize a series of individual moments, that is, to make a unity out of diversity, and through this act to find its own unity (or self-identity) over time. As Hegel puts it: 'In this uniformity self-consciousness finds itself again as a unity, because for one thing it recognises its own equality as the ordering of an arbitrary manifold'.[38] A similar process obtains in the mediation between part and whole, between beginning, middle and end, in a melody: 'Only as this movement, which never runs off into vagueness but is articulated in itself and returns into itself, does melody correspond to that free self-subsistence of subjective life which is its task to express.'[39]

The key notion in all this – and one germane to the current investigation – is 'manifold'. Hegel's use of the term refers back to its application in Kant's *Critique of Pure Reason* where it is similarly linked to the idea of the synthesis of a differentiated series of mentally represented events into a unity. This likewise implies a time-consciousness. In reality the mental states associated with events in the world occur at different times – as discrete 'nows'; however, this series of episodic moments is grasped by the self as a manifold as it creates a unitary awareness through an understanding of their temporal relationships. Although these notions did not percolate with any significant effect into Kant's own understanding of music, their relevance to that temporal art form is none the less great. The cognition of a melody for example could be seen precisely as an example of the self's synthesizing a oneness (German: *Einheit*, unity) out of 'many-ness' (German: *Mannigfaltigkeit*, manifold), in a similar manner to that of Hegel's description quoted above. And writ large the same process obtains in the understanding of an entire movement or work; indeed Kevin Korsyn has argued that Kant's notion of the synthetic unity of the manifold was influential on Schenker's account of synthesis in the 'masterworks of music'.[40]

This last reference is apposite because while it is unlikely that Tippett would have direct familiarity of these issues in the writings of such thinkers as Kant and Hegel, a thinking musician's intuition of them is nevertheless implicit in his comment that 'symphonic music in the hands of great masters truly and fully embodies the otherwise unperceived, unsavoured

inner flow of life'.[41] Also relevant in this respect is the more specific connection between musical and philosophical composition that has often been noted between Hegel and Beethoven. It is a well-rehearsed argument within musicology that the dialectical principles of Hegel's philosophical thought, especially as applied to his understanding of the subject in history, finds its exact aesthetic counterpart in the instrumental, especially the symphonic, music of Beethoven.[42] (This view is invalidated neither by the fact that Hegel's technical knowledge of music was self-admittedly limited,[43] nor by the fact that the homology may not have been based on any direct knowledge of Hegel's philosophy on Beethoven's part.) Developing our earlier point, we might argue that the time-consciousness and associated subjectivity experienced through symphonic and sonata-form principles was very much Tippett's quarry as he fashioned his own versions of the 'Beethoven allegro' in his earlier mature works.

Tippett and the critique of unified subjectivity

But we need to progress a step further, since Tippett, having gained mastery over this aesthetic in his first period, then set about a critique of it in his second. Indeed, what will now be clear is that this would be a critique not only of a formal musical language but of its concomitant construction of subjectivity – of the 'inner life' as an ultimately homogeneous 'flow'. While the image of subjectivity found in Beethoven's music is emancipatory (a bourgeois revolutionary consciousness, as some have argued), it is also true that, in Johnson's words, 'its model of temporal integration helps create the ideology of an integrated subject, one which is never quite realized in every-day life'.[44] To use Augustine's language, such music transforms the *distensus* which is the experience of time and one's self in everyday life into an *extensus* which suggests the possibility of a spiritual wholeness normally unavailable. In Beethoven, of course, this is a different kind of *extensus*, a humanist one predicated on the vision of an associated social wholeness achievable within history, rather than on the subject's translation into a divine realm above time. And while Tippett's earlier music sought to reforge Beethoven's worldly vision in a contemporary language, it is clear that its driving impulse had stalled around the late 1950s – perhaps in the intuitive recognition that *distensus* could not be so readily assuaged, and that history threatened to have the upper hand over the individual subject. Tippett's ensuing strategy was not to dismiss the Beethovenian aesthetic but to subject it to dialectical scrutiny, such that positing it also meant negating it.

   This tactic is most overt in the Sonata No. 2 for Piano and the first movement of the Concerto for Orchestra, both of which court the status

of anti-sonata forms. In the Second Piano Sonata the agency of a synthesizing manifold which would subsume individual musical moments and
their times into the united whole of a single continuous time span is conspicuously resisted. True, certain fragments still emit vestigial suggestions
of formal functionality and structural continuity; but, in general, individual moments incline towards maintaining their autonomy – towards
claiming their allotted time spans for themselves. The temporal conditions which obtain here resemble the category which Jonathan Kramer
describes as 'multiple', 'multiply-directed' or 'gestural time' – in which
'discontinuities segment and reorder linear time'; in which 'gestures are
continually interrupted and transitions frequently do not go where they
seem to be heading'.[45] And all this has ramifications for the experience of
subjectivity. Salient in this respect is Kant's point that 'only in so far as I
can grasp the manifold of the representations in one consciousness, do I
call them one and all *mine*. For otherwise I should have as many-coloured
and diverse a self as I have representations of which I am conscious to
myself.'[46] The discontinuous musics of the Second Piano Sonata, which
generate individualized pockets of consciousness, do not allow themselves fully to be given up into any such larger, single synthesis. If these
anti-holistic tendencies do not quite lead to Kant's quasi-schizophrenic
scenario of a self unable to put the stamp of its own identity on successive
representations in consciousness, they none the less strongly challenge
the sonata's ability to generate an image of integrated subjectivity.

The first movement of the Concerto for Orchestra, with its superimposition of many-coloured and diverse musics, presents an image less of a
single fractured subjectivity than of multiple, colliding consciousnesses.
This is particularly true of the second part of the movement (Fig. 38ff.), a
kind of development section in which musics once discontiguous are now
juxtaposed and superimposed in a dream-like state of free association.
Example 4.2 cites a typical instance, from near the end of the movement
(Figs. 56–8), in which flute and tuba strike up a momentary connection
through the similar contour of their headmotifs. But such relationships
are indeed of the moment; they do not contribute to any sustained higher-
level processes which would serve to synthesize the manifold into unity. It
is not only each element's discreteness of instrumental timbre and
musical content that militates against such a synthesis; it is also their conflicting claims on the phrase structure which might have served it.
Throughout there is 'dissonance' between simultaneously sounding antecedent and consequent phrase elements, which undermines the perceiving subject's ability to reconstruct events into a synthetic order. The tuba
entry of Example 4.2 asserts an antecedent phrase which coincides with

Example 4.2. Concerto for Orchestra, first movement, Figs. 56–8.

and conflicts against the flute's consequent phrase (an answer to its own antecedent element a few bars earlier); and this situation is compounded as the horns enter with a further antecedent phrase shortly afterwards. Each stratum makes, as it were, a claim for the same 'now': the 'now' defined as the moment of inception of a new phrase or section. But this posited 'now' is actually dispersed across three possible locations (or three empirical moments); the listener has no clue as to where exactly to place it in the temporally conditioned manifold – or plot structure – he seeks to construct as he processes the events presented to him. And this kind of equivocation continues as ever new events and new non-congruencies present themselves. If integrated subjectivity arises from forging a manifold out of successive nows, and if this music blurs the very apprehension of 'now', then we can conclude that it fosters an experience of evanescent subjectivity, constantly hovering between formation and dissolution.

III

The Vision of Saint Augustine: general principles of form and structure

And now at last we are where we need to be. The preceding account of the contextual constellation around *The Vision of Saint Augustine* should have made it clear that Tippett's unexpected encounter with Augustine issues from concerns far from antiquarian; rather with matters very much to do with the composer's own day – with his own modernist soul, so to speak. His preoccupation with time is not driven by any academic philosophical – or indeed theological – interest, but is bound up with a typically modernist anxiety over the status of the self: the self in relation to its inner world, whose principal means of articulation is the aesthetic; and the self in relation to the outer world, whose pattern is that of history. *The Vision of Saint Augustine* seems to have been born directly out of a critical reappraisal on Tippett's part of how the temporality of music – its facility to structure time and subjectivity – might express a relationship of mediation between inner and outer domains, given that these both have a temporal foundation. The Second Piano Sonata and Concerto for Orchestra represent experiments in the search for new apprehensions of subjectivity, executed through new formal and structural techniques of composition. Through their critique of historically received materials they mount a critique of the Beethovenian vision of a revolutionary subject – a subject capable of transforming what history has bequeathed him into a new, humanist order. Tippett's project in *The Vision of Saint Augustine*, I want to argue,

was to continue to voice this critique – that is, still to register the duress which the subject suffers under the fractured conditions of modernity – while countering this with a no less intensely inscribed image of the subject striving to transcend the consciousness with which history has endowed it, from within its own historical circumstances. This advance on the preceding instrumental works turns a topic glimpsed in the final minutes of *King Priam* into the subject matter of the entire piece. There should be no underestimating its ambitiousness and the commensurate extent to which Tippett would need to rethink yet again the relationship between form, structure, time-consciousness and subjectivity.

In *The Vision of Saint Augustine* Tippett criticizes his critique of the musical manifold in the Second Piano Sonata and the first movement of the Concerto for Orchestra. On the one hand, he seeks to restore the synthesis of a manifold and its associated construction of subjectivity, while simultaneously representing the fissures of a subject straining against its own limitations for a deeper knowledge of itself. On the other hand, he is also concerned with the imaginative leap into a domain beyond the self. The dynamics of these opposing tendencies are thoroughly mediated. The would-be synthesizing manifold and its associated determination of the subject by a linear construction of time has as its goal the transcendence of subjectivity, while those glimpses of transcendence (for example, the visionary moment at the apogee of Part II), rather than conveying a domain of celestial stillness, are saturated in the intensity of the subjective struggle to attain them.

The Vision of Saint Augustine differs from its two forebears in a further decisive way: it is based on a text. The goal-orientated impulses we find there spring from a musico-dramatic rather than a purely musical structure, and we should therefore not disregard the agency of Augustine's narrative of his vision at Ostia in drawing the manifold events of the work into a unity: that what we are being told is a story provides a strong cue to relate individual moments into a larger whole. Yet while Tippett creates a musical sequence which taps into this teleological tendency, he implants other features – both textual and musical – which make the situation more complex.

The most overt of these is the amplification of Augustine's narrative by related fragments of text, sung by the chorus – whether these be biblical, liturgical or from other writings by Augustine (mostly, but not entirely, from the *Confessions*). So, for example, when the baritone soloist opens the work (see Ex. 4.4(a)) with the first line of book IX/x of the *Confessions* – 'Impendente autem die' ('When the day was approaching on which she [Monica, his mother] was to depart this life') – the word 'die' triggers an interpolated passage in the chorus taken from the next chapter of the

Confessions: 'die nono aegritudinis suae' ('on the 9th day of her illness').[47] In one sense Tippett is emulating, or perhaps illuminating, Augustine's own practice of textual allusion (which we might nowadays term intertextuality). The insinuation into a narrative, which is a performance in the present, of things that have been and things that are to come, exemplifies Augustine's understanding of time as a psychological or subjective phenomenon: the account does not literally take us back into the past or forward to the future but conveys from its standpoint of the present (*contuitus*) 'a present of things past' (*memoria*) and 'a present of things to come' (*expectatio*).[48] Because these textual inserts create a pull between the three modalities of temporal cognition and because they inflate the original narrative to several times its length, we could say that the resulting array engenders the experience of *distensus*. But while such parallels often seem pertinent – the 'hortus conclusus' episode (Figs. 20–28^{-2}) is a case in point, side-stepping, dreamlike, into a remembrance of things past – Tippett on other occasions deploys this counterpoint of texts and musical materials as an image of the concentration of energy Augustine considers necessary to achieve *extensus* – usually cued by the lines from Paul 'et praeterita obliviscentes . . .' ('and forgetting the things that are past . . .') and 'sequor ad palmam supernae vocationis' ('I press towards the crown of my heavenly calling').

These textual glosses dismember Augustine's narrative into an array of discrete moments, each of which becomes a unit of the formal structure. While the high level of self-containment typical of each such unit might seem inimical to its assimilation into any higher synthesis, the piece nevertheless amounts to more than the mere sum of its constituent moments: the musical construction is marked by the same teleological impetus that underpins both the subject and syntax of Augustine's account in language. In part this comes from the judicious juxtaposition of types of musical pace: points of contrast, passages of accumulation, moments of respite prior to still greater cumulative succession – all musico-dramatic techniques which Tippett mastered in *King Priam*. *Augustine*'s scheme of fourteen tempos is integral to this process, and is far more fluid in its effect than its counterpart in the Second Piano Sonata where each tempo was synonymous with a single musical figure. Here, by contrast, tempo functions as a separate agent of musical cohesion, sometimes providing a point of commonality between unrelated ideas (cf. Figs. 43ff. and 60ff. – both Tempo 6), and at other times rendering relatively similar ideas less alike, and thereby enhancing their centrifugal momentum (cf. Figs. 1ff. and 13ff.[49]).

Additionally, possibilities for synthesis into a larger whole stem from a network of relationships spread across the piece. In certain respects these are determined by historically established categories of formal

construction, for example, the cyclic treatment of the 'Deus, creator omnium' passage, and the recapitulatory principles embedded into Part III and also evidenced in the instrumental postlude to Part II. At the same time, though, it would be vain to see these transpiring out of the progress of a musical 'idea' in the Schoenbergian sense of the evolution of a thematic complex. (Let us not forget that ultimately the 'idea' of the piece is in any case a musico-dramatic and notional one.) The most fertile basis for a purely musical connectivity inheres rather in each section's status as a complete musical image – that is, its definition not only through (discretizable) thematic and intervallic properties, but also its total (synthetic) profile, including characteristics of timbre, texture, register, and so on. This last group of properties is perhaps most significant in determining the piece's relational network, which is based on a level of kinship more like that between first or second cousins rather than that of direct progeny, or of siblings. The result is a balance of proximity and distance appropriate to a sequence of musical moments which claim their autonomy as much as they are claimed by the whole.

These resemblances are like sets of *topoi* which on the one hand often have more general musical resonances, and on the other become enfolded into the piece to form its own idiomatic repertory of signs. Tippett defined exactly such a *topos* with his reference to glossolalia, but this is only the tip of a larger topical iceberg. Another *topos* is a type of hymn (albeit rather loosely defined), whose most obvious exemplar is the Ambrosian 'Deus, creator omnium', but under which category we could also include 'O aeterna caritas' in Part II (Fig. 105) and 'Attolite portas' in Part III (technically a psalm). All these emerge from and/or engender moments of particular intensity; which is to say they are related too by an equivalence of function. A further class of figures, again associated with moments of climax, could be termed 'fanfares', often but not exclusively involving the trumpets and brass. The first such example occurs in the trumpets as the chorus sing 'fenestram' (Fig. 19); another would be the antiphonal exchanges in the 'Angel Symphony' concluding Part I (Figs. 70^{-2}ff., 75, 79^{-2}ff., 85); a third would be the full brass fanfares counterpointing the words 'cibus sum grandium' in Part II (Fig. 108ff.), whose association with carnality is reinvoked in Part III at the baritone's lines 'tumultus carnis' (Fig. 155). It virtually goes without saying that the way in which such musical images are defined and related is decidedly mutable; the elements of any given sound image might establish different relationships with elements of more than one other image. The overall picture is therefore one of a veritable network of cross-connections, which in turn overlays the kinesis between successive moments.

The above will have indicated some of the forces at work in the larger-scale structuring of *The Vision of Saint Augustine*. We might summarize these in a sequence of logical moves (which has nothing to do with the actual musical sequence realized out of the process). First Augustine's account of the vision at Ostia provides a manifold which acts as one stratum of the work's temporal organization: a basis for a musico-dramatic rendering and a particular construction of subjectivity. Secondly, that manifold is dissected by the interpolated choral tropes into a mosaic of formal articulations which demands to be resynthesized as a manifold of a different order. Thirdly, this synthesis leaves the individual parts audible as such, but also cultivates their mediation – both contiguously, in terms of the extent to which successive moments foster or resist the sense of cumulative momentum; and discontiguously, in terms of associations between discrete sections, often made through musical parameters traditionally regarded as secondary. That not one of these levels gives itself up completely to the others goes some way to explaining the work's contradictory tensions: a mimesis of the modern soul trying to get beyond itself. We now need to examine the realization of these tensions and their associated images of subjectivity in the detail of the piece.

Vision II

Because the formal, temporal and subjective constructions of *The Vision of Saint Augustine* involve subtle degrees of mediation, we might usefully first look at one of the extreme moments, where the principles are in one sense simpler, if less typical.[50] Hence I want to proceed directly to the pivotal point of Part II, and indeed of the work itself, which depicts Augustine's vision of eternity (hereafter 'Vision II'; Figs. 131– 6; the music is recapitulated – or 'remembered' – at Figs. 193–8). This moment articulates a climax at the same time as it nullifies the linear conception of time on which the idea of climax is based. Indeed it brings about a decisive change of temporality to one close to that of Karlheinz Stockhausen's 'moment form', and is thus a moment in a highly specific sense. In this conception (incidentally, also formulated in the 1960s to address certain of the compositional concerns of the avant garde of the day) a moment equals a 'cut' through the linearity of time, eschewing any causal connections with what preceded and what follows. It is thus a 'now' freed from teleology, a slice of eternity.[51] Tippett achieves this state by negating any internal division of the moment into parts that could take their identity in terms of before and after. As Kemp puts it, 'the vision of eternity has a form only in as far as it sounds and then ceases to sound'[52] (which chimes in with Stockhausen's

view that moments do not begin and end, but simply start and stop, as if cuts from a phenomenon always already there[53]). Not that the musical organization is form*less*. It is structured along lines that are as prosaic as that which it signifies is metaphysical. The material comprises eight superimposed ostinati, quoted in Example 4.3; their differing lengths are so calculated that a vast number of repetitions would be required to return to the initial alignment and so mark a formal repetition of the entire text.[54] This produces a music which is always different yet always the same; thus even the relatively brief period in which we hear it is enough to convey the sense of a quasi-infinite duration.

But it would be mistaken to see this moment as simply an incarnation of number. Whittall's point that eternity is represented here 'not as something which is empty of life, but as something full of spirit' is well made.[55] My (admittedly less elegant) gloss on 'full of spirit' might be 'saturated by the universal'; for what Tippett gives us is a moment of subjectivity mediated by a sense of totality. Totality emanates from the music's sheer polyphonic density – which includes its assemblage of diverse rhythms and metres, and its twelve-note aggregate of discrete types and sizes of pitch-class collections (many of which are diatonic, in contrasting tonal fields). Subjectivity inheres in the different types of vocal glossolalia (sung either to 'alleluia' or vowels taken from the *Pistis Sophia*): expressions of the innermost self whose instrumental extension is found in related *topoi*, for example fanfares and peals of bells (or their equivalent in further instrumental extensions – piano, xylophone etc.). This passage, then, represents a manifold of a different order: a many-ness presented through simultaneity rather than succession – a possible metaphor for Augustine's understanding of God's view of time from his position in eternity, in which all events, past, present and future, are simultaneously available.

That the moment includes all performers except the baritone soloist should not be taken to imply that the individual subject is excluded from the picture, rather that for this moment this subject is assumed into the totality. For most of the work the chorus and orchestra function as extensions of the subjectivity, or the subjective situation, conveyed by the baritone soloist: they are not separate 'accompaniments'. And, in a similar complication of extremes, most episodes are not 'moments' in this pure sense, even though the concept retains a certain relevance.

'Impendente autem die …'

The very opening section of *The Vision of Saint Augustine* displays just such hybridity in its expression of temporality. On the one hand, the section is

Example 4.3. *The Vision of Saint Augustine*, 'Vision II': constituent strata (orchestral doublings of choral parts not indicated).

implicated in linear time in that it is orientated towards the future: its opening words – 'Impendente autem die . . .' ('When the day was approaching . . .') – are portentous of not only Augustine's mother's death, but also his own momentary, proleptic entry into eternity. Apart from its long-range trajectory towards Vision II, this passage also contains processual characteristics orientated towards its own final seconds (which I will outline presently). That is, the internal events of the section reveal a necessary temporal ordering which promotes a synthesis of the manifold. On the other hand the section as a whole resists an analogous synthesis at a higher level. It is not repeated anywhere else in the same guise; nor does its musical content directly specify what follows. In this sense, then, it still partakes of some of those qualities which Stockhausen defines for moment time.

A similar hybridity obtains in this passage's construction of subjectivity. The presence of Augustine the narrator is both focused in the baritone solo line and also dispersed across the entire texture. Like Vision II the 'Impendente' passage presents a 'vertical manifold' of quasi-discrete, simultaneously sounding layers. But unlike Vision II the strata here display stronger functional distinctions, while at the same time contributing functionally to the texture as a whole. In other words they are partially mediated (in fact in a hierarchy of degrees): each stratum is neither wholly independent nor completely subsumed into the whole. The image is not that of a convergence of separate consciousnesses, as in the Concerto for Orchestra I, but that of several facets of single consciousness working in parallel.

Example 4.4(a) modifies the layout of the score to highlight this stratification. Each of the four strata so revealed is defined through its register and instrumental/vocal deployment, as well as through the specific organization of its material. Any description of these particulars needs to consider not only elements of mediation between layers, but also the differing extent to which each layer succumbs to or resists principles of form. For the stance towards form – here I mean the word in its most comprehensive sense of 'formation', musical construction in general – is another means, alongside the structuring of time, whereby subjectivity renders itself apparent, and is a matter I shall increasingly pursue below.

By way of example, let us consider the baritone soloist's line in stratum iii. Its mediation with the harmonic stratum below it is evident from its first two notes, C and B♭, which are distilled from the diatonic vertical of the latter: C–F–B♭ (the points of connection are encircled in Ex. 4.4(a)). As the line unfolds, however, it shows itself to be the element of the texture most emancipated from the dictates of purely musical formation, conceived as it is throughout the work as a kind of highly individualized

endless melody. It 'subjectivizes' Augustine's text (Tippett is a long way from the hieratic, de-individualized setting of Latin Stravinsky favoured in his Mass) by translating the rhythms and intonations of its language into the qualities of song, and by simultaneously using that linguistic determination to ward off assimilation into objectifying categories of musical form. For example, it resists the diatonic implications of the quartal set from which it is generated by lacing its opening line with tritones as well as fourths – which are then reflected back into stratum i as inflections of its original quartal purity. The baritone's second phrase then develops the whole-tone implications which emerge from this process (see Ex. 4.4(b)). But, importantly, as soon as such structures look like becoming identifiable as such they are subverted. The embedded whole-tone collection D–E–F♯–A♭–B♭–C in the passage after Fig. 4 is negated by impurities (other, non-whole-tone elements) which confound complete identification with any prefabricated archetype of structure. This simultaneous invocation and side-stepping of identifiable (and identifying) concepts of musical organization – a dialectic found, incidentally, in much of Tippett's music – is as much a trace of the agency of authorial subjectivity as it is responsible for incarnating individual subjectivity into the vocal line.

The choral stratum, ii, again takes the dyad B♭–C as the point of mediation with the strata below it. However, whereas the baritone's line sought to countervail the initial diatonic implications of stratum iv, the chorus elaborates upon them. Its material, which has something of the soloist's lyricism, is far more susceptible to historically passed-down principles of formation – particularly in its tonal, or neo-tonal, organization. The first phrase prolongs the generative B♭–C dyad through a set of melodic diminutions which draw almost exclusively from a diatonic set identical to the Aeolian scale of B♭. (This way of putting things avoids claiming that we are actually 'in' the 'key' of B♭ minor, and thus draws attention to the separation Tippett puts between himself and the traditional materials of tonality: again a way of asserting his subjectivity over objective resources.) B♭'s privileged status in this collection is highly individualized, since its strongest relative is not the dominant, but the supertonic, into whose identity it merges – a relationship which in turn establishes the diatonic second as a characteristic colouristic feature of this stratum, and eventually of later sections.

Like the choral stratum below it, stratum i (also emanating from the pitch B♭) is characterized by its thematic profile. Only this is a much more saturated thematicism, an almost all-motivic treatment, based on the celesta's permutation of embedded [0,1,4], [0,1,5] and [0,1,6] trichords (echoed by piano and harp), as indicated above the musical notation in

Example 4.4. At (a): 'Impendente autem die' opening, showing constituent strata. At (b): second baritone phrase (vocal line only, with scale-form analysis).

(a)

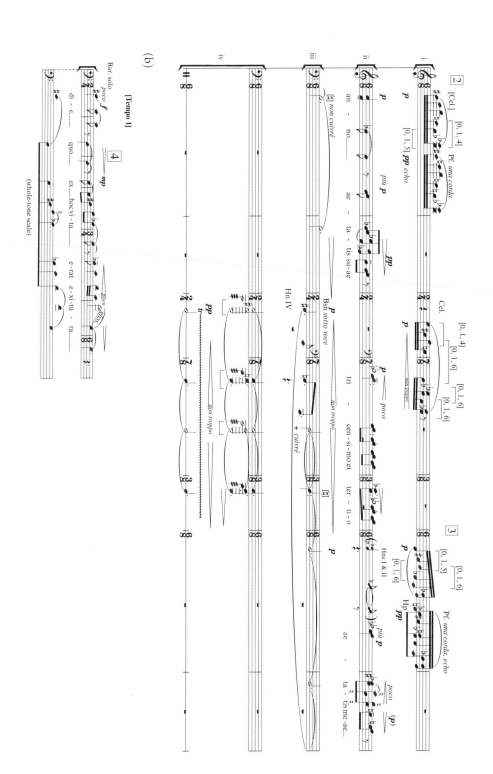

Example 4.5. 'corpore soluta est': mutation of celesta motif into flute motif.

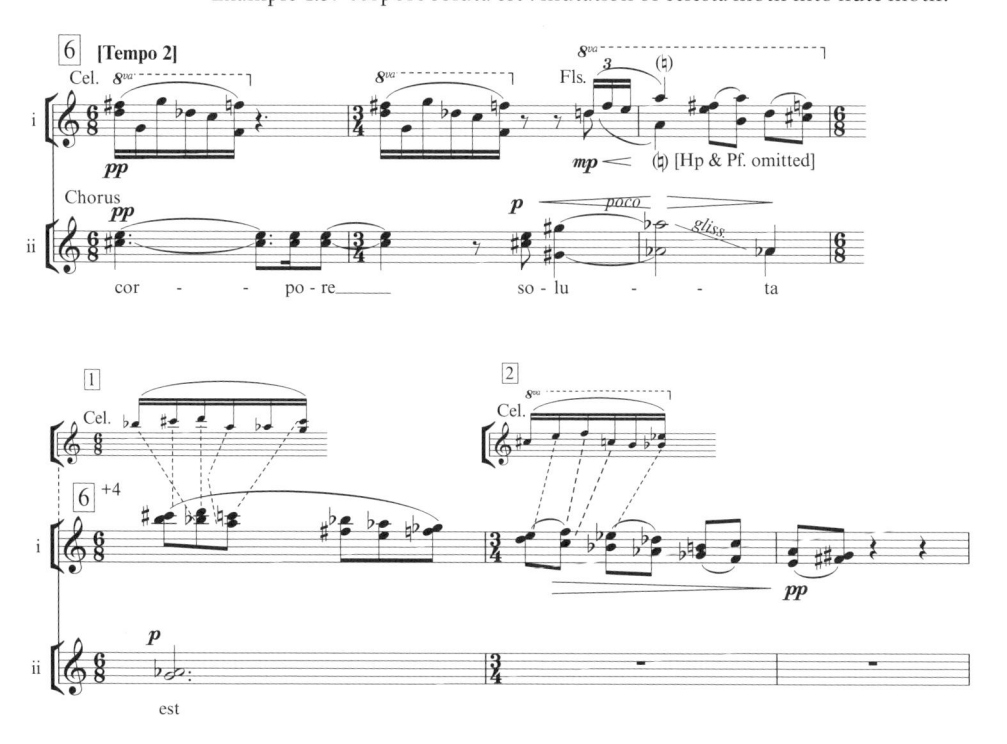

Example 4.4(a). Again, this principle is subjectively inflected before these characteristics become too clearly identifiable; but its *telos* is the metamorphosis of the celesta motif into that of the flute duet which ends the section (Fig. 6^{+2} onwards). Some of the details of this process, which includes a degree of pitch invariance, are shown in Example 4.5.

Metaphorical and structural functions intertwine at this point. The translation of one version of the material into another symbolizes the release of Augustine's mother's soul at her death – the event signified by the text ('corpore soluta est', 'was released from the body'). This moment within a moment confirms the teleological nature of the music's temporality, which is marshalled not by stratum i alone but by a co-ordination of processes between strata. One such processual feature is the gradual encroachment of ever more significant pitches from the complement set of the B♭ Aeolian collection governing stratum ii. This leads a path out of this flat tonal field towards the implications of A major in the chorus at Fig. 6. The complement of B♭ Aeolian is the pentatonic set B–D–E–G–A, whose first element becomes salient as the final pitch of the baritone's first phrase, prolonged by the horn and then bassoon (Figs. 1^{-1}–4; see Ex. 4.4(a),

stratum iii) and polarized against the originating B♭–C dyad of the choral and bass strata. The remaining complementary pitches, E–B–G–A, are most saliently presented as aggregates of the last two dyads of the male chorus entry just after Fig. 3 ('aetatis meae'; Ex. 4.4(a), stratum ii). The final major-second dyad, G–A, escaping from both the immediate A♭ Dorian and the larger B♭ Aeolian context, is like a chink of light shining from a dark background, which although occluded at the start of the next phrase, fulfils its work at 'corpore soluta est'. (The dyad E–C♯(=D♭) in the voices at 'corpore' represents a sensitive point of mediation between B♭ Aeolian and its pentatonic complement, and also acts as a springboard to the focus on A at the beginning and end of the ensuing duet for flutes.)

The 'Impendente' section is typically individual. The configuration of materials and structures described here is peculiar to itself, and the moment ends as soon as their processes have been achieved. The description of any subsequent section would need just as detailed an account of its own defining features. So, for example, the next section ('quem diem'/'Deus, creator') cancels the characteristics of the first, assigning the latter to the past at the same time as setting up its own structuring of past, present and future. The syntagmatic axis of the piece as a whole is, generally speaking, an accumulation of such short bursts of linear temporality. However, as we have already asserted, these parcels of forward movement amount to more than a medley of unconnected events. The point is that connections are elliptical, like those between the 'Impendente' passage and the third episode of the work ('ut ego et ipsa'; Fig. 13ff.) – established by the common prevalence of whole-tone dyads (as found in the chorus of the first section), bell and bell-like sonorities (a transformation of the initial celesta and piano sounds), and the orientation towards a pivotal moment to do with Augustine's mother (the chorus's acclamation 'Monicae' at Fig. 15). This new episode, then, remains *sui generis*, but nevertheless creates a relationship at one remove from the first by reincarnating its materials in new guise.

'Fenestram!' (Strategies for the transcendent)

If the manifold that transpires from the interaction of synthesis-promoting and synthesis-resisting forces outlined here is already complex, things are complicated further by another set of features which both establish a complementary line of continuity and – necessarily – disrupt the work's linear sequence. These are moments which seek to break free of the music's syntagmatic axis, such as the choral exclamation 'Fenestram!' at Fig. 19. The sheer illocutionary force of this gesture – compounded from the explosive

fortissimo entry of chorus and orchestra; the charged 'higher consonance' of fused C, G and A major triads (further powered by the majestic trumpet descent through A♭ Lydian/Ionian); and the turbulent percussion interjections – is evidence enough of the significance Tippett ascribes to it. (The case is further supported by the fact that *Fenestra* was the originally intended title for the piece, signifying the actual window at which Augustine and his mother stood and the metaphorical window through which they glimpsed eternity.)

Through their excess of content such gestures spill over the formal boundaries established by what precedes them, and thereby militate against the synthesis between successive moments necessary for a sense of integrated subjectivity. And so the subject is confronted with an image of something beyond its grasp – or at least beyond the temporal standpoint which it makes for itself. This strategy, which corresponds to Thomas Weiskel's description of the subject's experience of the sublime,[56] is less a guaranteed formula for conjuring up the transcendent, and more a stroke of rhetoric in which is held the potential for, or a promise of, such experience. That promise is a gloss – a translation into musical terms of reference – on the conditional clause with which Augustine concludes his reflection on his vision (which text forms Part III of the work): if such moments, and their attendant musical techniques, could be sufficiently intensified and sustained, would this not be an image so consuming as to be equivalent to apprehending eternity?

Such is Tippett's goal, and if his eventual conclusion is 'not to have apprehended', his tactic of progressively intensifying this syntagmatic disruption is none the less single-mindedly pursued. Indeed this progress manifests a thread of associations which implies a line of continuity complementing that of the linear sequence they disjoint. This is perhaps clearest in Part I of the piece, which presses with increasing urgency to its concluding 'angel symphony' (Vision I). All the moments in question are in some way epiphanic or premonitory, and most are based on higher consonance.[57] These sonorities, some of which have already been mentioned, are abstracted in Example 4.6 which highlights the connections between them. For example, the dyad E–C♯ at the 'corpore saluta est' moment, together with its A major implication, is projected into the chord to which the chorus sing 'Monicae', at Fig. 15, as the latter's treble and bass notes (see Ex. 4.6(a) and (b)). The quartal component embedded in this chord, E–B–F♯, is taken up in the next higher consonance, at 'Fenestram!' (Fig. 19; Ex. 4.6(c)), as is its A major content, this time polarized against the C major element in the lower reaches of the chord. C is in turn taken up as the implied centre of the next higher consonance in the chain, at

Example 4.6. Higher consonances and their connections.

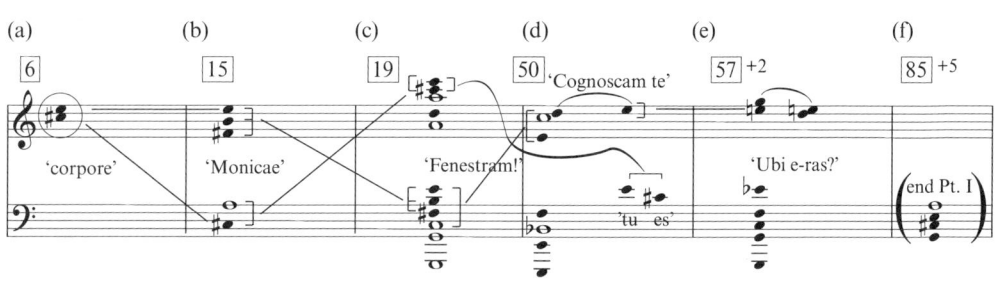

'Cognoscam te' (Fig. 50; Ex. 4.6(d)). This sonority's 'other' (negating) components are the dyad E–C♯ sung to 'tu es' in the baritone – a retention of earlier versions of itself and its A major implication – and the pitches F and B♭ – signifying a complementary, flatward orientation through the circle of fifths. This tendency is continued in the next sonority, at 'Ubi eras?' (Fig. 57^{+2}; Ex. 4.6(e)) which incorporates the collection G–C–F–[B♭]–E♭, against the continuing C major in the upper voices. Finally, the closing sonority of the angel symphony (and of Part I) returns to an A major focus.

Not all these sonorities carry equal force. The first two (Ex. 4.6(a) and (b)) operate within, indeed co-ordinate, the temporal parameters of their respective sections (in the manner described earlier). It is really the moments signified by parts (c), (d) and (e) of Example 4.6 which seize the 'now' with such intensity as to create a breach from the immediate past. As I have asserted above, this is engineered through an apparent excess of content over form, through a rhetoric which asserts that what the composer is trying to 'say' far surpasses the means available to say it. But this observation needs qualification, for ultimately an artwork can only communicate its content through the manner of its formation. In Adorno's words 'form in artworks is everything on which the hand has left its trace, everything over which it has passed'.[58] Thus form renders subjectivity objective; but the subjective element in this mediation is only tangible if the creating subject asserts himself over the habitual usages his materials have acquired historically. 'Form converges with critique', as Adorno puts it. Tippett's own theorization of this historical dialectic used the terms 'historical archetype' and 'notional archetype' in which the latter acts as a subjectively centred critique of the former.[59] And while he himself applies this dualism to the macroscopic domain of genres, it can also be seen to obtain with a far finer degree of resolution, down to individual details of musical construction.[60]

Romanticism turns to modernism as this dialectic changes its construction. Indeed *The Vision of Saint Augustine* shows Tippett utterly caught up in a tide whose movement can be charted in the shift between the aesthetics of Hegel and Adorno. In a backward glance towards Hegel, let us consider his comments on harmony – apposite enough, given our current discussion of that feature. Characteristically, Hegel relates consonance and dissonance as terms of a dialectic. Dissonance functions as a negation of consonance, but is bound (under the laws of harmony of his day) to return to it. This is a *positive* dialectic, because the negation of the preceding negation embodies 'the return of identity to itself': it is a *resolution*, and as such confirms the identifying power of the initial sonority over what is other to it. The composing subject may, for aesthetic purposes, attempt to interpose his individual will into this temporal progression: 'more profound music not only *may* push its movements up to the very limits of immediate consonance ... it *must* tear apart the simple first harmony into dissonances'.[61] This enacts 'a battle between freedom and necessity', which is also how Hegel couches the emancipation of *Geist* (mind/spirit) in history. However, even the most extreme exploration of dissonance eventually finds resolution in consonance, just as the dialectical progress of history finds its resolution in the full realization of *Geist*.

For Adorno, any such envisaged resolution is premature. Seeking to foreground the extreme antagonisms of history, his dialectic is a profoundly negative one, in which antithetical terms are presented as unresolved; there is no resting point in synthesis. It is this negative dialectic which gives his aesthetics its modernist tenor. That *The Vision of Saint Augustine* lives on the modernist side of this turn is evident in its treatment of consonance and dissonance. For example, the category of higher consonance which marks the 'Fenestram!' moment, and those like it, could be seen to embody a negative dialectic: it is simultaneously consonant and dissonant, referring to both terms but conforming to no obligation to resolve the latter into the former within a temporal process. These highly subjectivized harmonies go a step beyond the order implied in Hegel's 'battle between freedom and necessity'. They express the priority of the subject over blind historical necessity. And this agon is writ large over the encounter between the composing subject and the historical dictates of form. The stakes become acute in *The Vision of Saint Augustine*, whose concern is the most inward reaches of subjectivity. In order to assert subjective inwardness and what lies beyond, Tippett must create a music whose every detail contains a critique of the medium in which it posits itself. It is for this reason that the work in which he most relentlessly pursues the transcendental is also his most uncompromisingly modernist statement.

'Quaerebamus...'

By way of closer examination, let us consider the section in Part I of *Augustine* which begins at Fig. 48 with the lines 'Quaerebamus inter nos apud praesentem veritatem, quod tu es' ('we were discussing in the presence of truth, which you are'), and leads to the choral interjection 'Cognoscam te' ('Let me know you') at Fig. 50 – signified in shorthand in Example 4.6(d). The beginning of the episode is quoted as Example 4.7. There are, it is true, continuities between its first part and the episode which precedes it – 'sequor ad palmam supernae vocationis' ('I press towards the crown of my heavenly calling') – one aspect of which are the chordal dotted rhythms in the trombones. However, in most other respects the new passage is a gesture of profound displacement, due among other things to its immediate shift to a broader tempo coupled with an altered harmonic rhythm, and to fuller instrumentation coupled with a louder dynamic. The abruptness of this cut makes synonymous the composing subject's assertion of itself over form and the portrayed subject's attempt to transcend itself. 'Forgetting the things that are past' (and forgetting, as it were, the musical formation of a moment ago) the subject makes a momentous effort to hold in the now – in *this* now – the fullness of his apprehension of his own temporal being. This inward 'concentration of energy' (*intentio*) is projected not only by the baritone's prolonged C$\sharp$ but also through the metrical intensification of the harmonic stratum which complements it: at Fig. 49^{+1-2} three changes of harmony which previously took three bars are now compressed into two; then, at Fig. 49^{+3}, two changes are compressed into a single bar. The forward momentum latent in this harmonic acceleration is made manifest through the rising linear motion of the bass; and all is orientated towards the inception of the 'Cognoscam te' moment in the female chorus at Fig. 50.

Tippett's rhetoric for the transcendent permeates the micro-world of the music's formation. For example, the linear progressions and the hemiola rhythms already discussed, together with the triplet figurations in the violins, all have identifiable historical counterparts. Yet Tippett does more than individualize them; even this individualization is not allowed to rigidify into formality. The quaver triplet phrase in the violins, for example, sets out at the first bar of Fig. 48 in parallel minor sevenths and ends with a minor ninth. It thus negates the diatonic possibilities it contains, including the more lush kind of parallel triadic motion found in the triplets which accompany the similarly epiphanic *Sanctus* of Bach's B Minor Mass – a possible historical archetype for this idea. Through the combination of their own qualities and the associations they evoke and

Example 4.7. 'Quaerebamus inter nos'/'cognoscam te'.

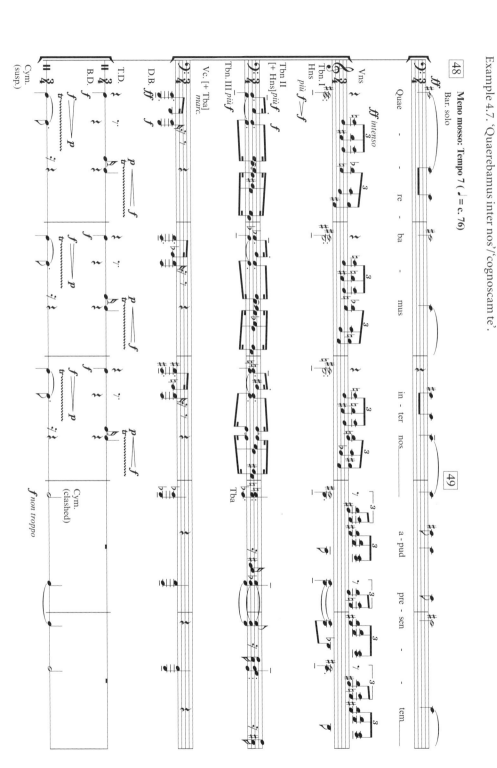

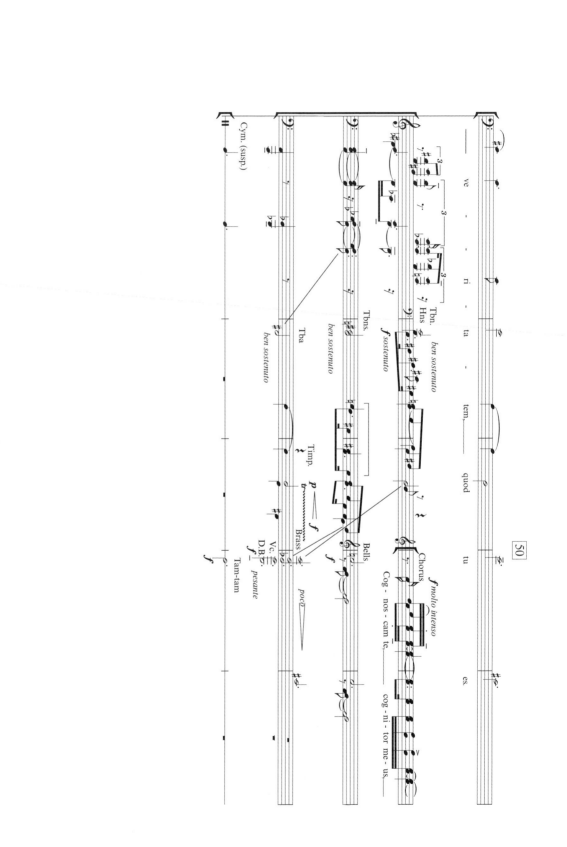

cancel, the triplets are simultaneously rebarbative and celebrative. However, Tippett does not leave it there. Each repetition of this idea (and, for that matter, all the other figuration) is varied in a less than predictable – that is, in a non-rational – way. In subsequent versions of the triplets the intervallic distance between the violins mutates (first incorporating other types of dissonance, such as tritones and major sevenths, then more consonant intervals), and the tendency towards parallelism is eroded. The effect is not to change the meaning of the material but rather the very opposite: to prolong it while repelling identification with the technical means used to articulate it. In order not to reduce what he desires to say to the form through which he says it, the composer must continually exert his critical, subjective will over the already formed.

The wilful dislocation of what is signified from what signifies it is of the essence. As a strategy it binds such parochial decisions as which intervallic alignment should follow which to the fundamental aporia of attempting to give expression to the transcendent. If what is to be apprehended is by its nature inapprehensible, it cannot be identical with any set of signifiers summoned up in the attempt. Yet the inapprehensible cannot even be invoked without the signifier – whose basis is something material, something made. However much the artwork might aspire to the status of God's word as described by Augustine – heard 'not through any mortal tongue or voice of angel or sound of thunder or riddle of resemblance, but . . . without the mediation of these things'[62] – the possibility of a signified transcendent of a signifier is not available to it. The signifiers which the composer manufactures must accordingly bear the mark that they are not the thing they signify, that what is signified inheres in what is other to them. Hence the radical instability of signifiers in *The Vision of Saint Augustine*; they bear the stigmata of the unsignifiability of the signified they attempt to grasp.

The result of this process on the material is the all-pervasive obstinacy of a sound whose constituents will not resolve into pre-formed conceptual categories – a sonic graininess which bears an affinity for the non-conceptual. This is perhaps why untuned percussion features so prominently. In the 'Quaerebamus' episode it adds a kind of visceral turbulence (in fact the texture is like an energized version of the 'Impendente' section – cf. Ex. 4.4(a)). For all that the work is preoccupied with the spiritual, it is entirely appropriate that the body might be invoked as an instrument with which to register the non-conceptual empathetically. Yet, for all that the orchestration is distinctive, and far from merely functional, it abjures hedonism (especially as compared, say, with the later *Byzantium*). While tuned percussion does feature, the greater emphasis on untuned instruments reflects an

element of self-denial – just as Tippett could have used more than two lines in the *intenso* violin triplets of the 'Quaerebamus' section, but chose not to. The admittance of tubular bells at the 'Cognoscam te' moment, and a corresponding release on the diatonic third of C major in the female voices thus become all the more powerful. But even this relaxation is negated at the corresponding moment in the equivalent episode shortly afterwards – 'Ubi eras?' (Fig. 57ff.: Ex. 4.8). Here, as the dissonance quotient rises, the resonance of the bells is replaced by the utterly resonance-less whip (an act of self-discipline?), and the corresponding figuration in the female chorus prolongs a diatonic second rather than third. Rising ecstasy seems to elicit increased austerity.

'Et . . . transcendimus eas'

Ecstasy, a state beyond reason, finds mounting expression in Part II of *The Vision of Saint Augustine*. Its climax is most obviously Vision II, but in fact this is prefigured from different perspectives, just as Augustine's text is filled with the anticipation of the moment. So in fact the path which Part II ascends finds its first plateau at Fig. 100ff. (Ex. 4.9) – as the baritone sings 'et venimus in mentes nostras et transcendimus eas' ('and so we came to our own souls and went beyond them'), and the chorus complement with words from *Confessions* VII/x: 'intravi in intima mea; et vidi lucem incommutabilem' ('I went into myself and saw the unchangeable light').

The conceit of subject's progress to a point of utter inwardness finds its musical realization here. Although the soundworld contrasts strongly with that of previously discussed extracts – in that it withdraws from the previous dramatic ambience into a world of intense calm – its concerns are no less aporetic: the subject's apprehension of what lies beyond itself; the knowledge of what it is to be out of one's mind ('transcendimus *mentes nostras*'). These extremities are evoked in the singers' response to demands that are almost literally unreasonable. The choral voices (here and in the preceding section) are required to navigate a sea of dissonance, to enter *pianissimo* at the top of their register, to sing in clusters, and in all this to remain in tune. Tippett must have known that the likelihood of even the most accomplished professional choir singing this material cleanly would be extremely small. Yet this of course is the point. The whole ethos of the section is breathtakingly on the edge, hovering between worlds: potentially both alienatingly ugly and captivatingly, uncannily beautiful. The challenge for the listener – as significant in its own way as that for the performer – is to aestheticize that sound, to transform it into something meaningful.

Example 4.8. 'Ubi eras?'

Example 4.9. 'et venimus in mentes nostras'/'intravi in intima mea'.

(*continues*)

Yet form as a vehicle for meaning is no more abandoned here than any-where else in the piece; rather it raises to a more acute level the simultane-ous positing and negating of itself. The material of this section, for example, is itself an audible transformation of what has gone before, and the lead in at Fig. 99[+3] is crucial in engineering this. Here the three-part *pulsando* diatonic clusters are transferred from male to female voices, and out of this emerges a new motif in the piccolo trumpet which will accom-pany each choral phrase in the forthcoming section. This figure sym-bolizes the soul's release[63] a further aspect of which is its emancipation from tonal constraints. (Although on paper the pitch-class sets generated by this motif and its variants could just about sustain a diatonic interpreta-tion, the freely disjunct melodic motion makes a stronger claim for atonal-ity.) Each phrase of the 'et venimus in mentes nostras' section is a different variant on itself, aspects of which process include the temporary exchange of female voices for male at Fig. 103, the substitution of oboe then cor

Example 4.9 (*cont.*)

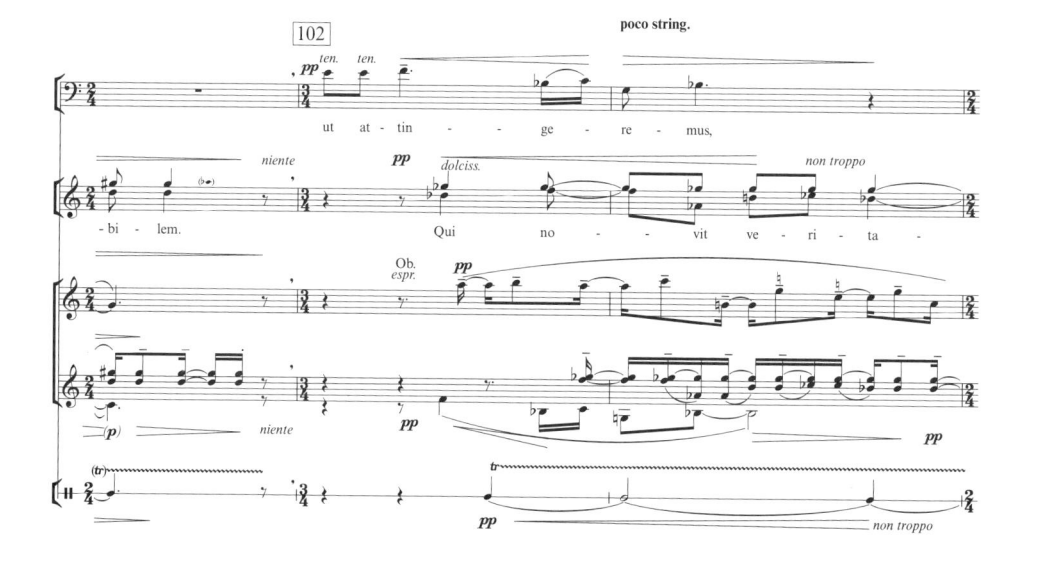

Example 4.9 (*cont.*)

anglais for piccolo trumpet after Fig. 102, and the shift from a diatonic second to perfect fourth as the predominant vertical interval in the two-part choral writing in the time between the first and the last phrase.[64] Each phrase ends cadentially – albeit in atonal terms; and although the cadential sonority does not escape variation, it usually incorporates at least one tritone and semitone.

While these form-defining features serve as points of orientation for the listener, they also present their own negation and indeed negate one another. Form must contend against amorphousness – a principle evident in the avoidance of any point of metrical coincidence between the three main strata of the texture (baritone, chorus and solo wind instrument obbligato). (The string figuration which mediates between the chorus and wind soloist by combining the pitch content of the former with the rhythmic content of the latter serves only to make this quality more integral to the texture, rather than offering clarification or resolution.) The dissolution implicit in this conjunction of mutually negating rhythmic profiles is further promoted by antinomies of pitch organization. For example, the choral stratum has putatively strong diatonic affiliations, drawing at first (Figs. 100–2) from a pitch-class set identical to the scale of A major, and then (Figs. 102–5) largely from one resembling an extended D♭ major (admitting the inflections D♮ and E♮). Yet this potential diatonic substance disperses under the influence of the instrumental obbligato placed against it: both are subsumed within the (nearly or actually) full chromatic collection which they aggregate.

Furthermore, in the first two phrases the negation of the diatonic can also be seen to come from within. The female voices' linear motion in parallel seconds dissolves the separate elements into an aggregate of clusters – with an associated meltdown of any residual diatonic functionality these elements might have. Whereas the conventional tonal counterpart of this figure might have yielded such formal features as a voice-leading motion or a harmonic progression, what we in fact get is a trail of sound, at once anxious and serene, intense yet calm: a sound on the verge of falling back into the white noise of the suspended cymbal (later, tam-tam) rolls which lie behind it. This is the sound of a negative aesthetic space, projected as the antinomic other of what remains recognizable as form. It is a space beyond any meaning describable in positive terms, yet it is not meaningless either. In it we hear movement, singing, human presences – which none the less are by no means its entire content: an image, then, of human subjectivity in a state beyond (or other than) itself, but generated from itself.

Evaluation

This last episode may be considered an extreme case of what is going on in the work as a whole; and we should wake ourselves up to what Tippett has achieved in both. My gloss on this is cognate with Kemp's and Whittall's summary comments, yet, in the work's own spirit, wants to push further. As I have drawn attention to how every radical aspect of *The Vision of Saint Augustine* springs from a critical relationship to historically received categories of musical form and meaning, so both these writers have stressed the work's relationship with 'tradition'. Kemp looks down both ends of the telescope, stating first that 'if the new predominates it is still held in place by the traditional', and then that '*The Vision of Saint Augustine* is one of those very special works that alter existing conceptions of a tradition and demand its reformulation'.[65] Whittall also stresses both the challenge to tradition and Tippett's continuity with it in his assertion that 'it can be said of few other modern composers that they have achieved so complete a departure from tradition and yet remained so close to the essential dynamic forces of that tonal music which still seems to many the most natural, as well as the most appealing, which man is ever likely to devise'.[66] I concur fully with the notion of a dialogue with the past; yet I would want to present this as a far more agonistic relationship – in a way that seems to me more commensurable with the sound of the piece. Everything hangs on the words we choose. To establish a relationship with something called tradition – a word which has strong intertextual overtones with Eliot (and which, admittedly, Tippett himself liked to invoke) – ultimately serves to highlight what is conservative (as given away by the conciliatory, commonsensical tenor of Whittall's statement that 'Tippett seems to have the best of both worlds'[67]). Yet of all Tippett's works *The Vision of Saint Augustine* is the one that least warrants that epithet; and for all that it bears conspicuously Eliotic hallmarks it is the one in which Tippett also distances himself from his spiritual mentor (just as in 'Too many choices' he assails Eliot – not for the first time – for his own cultural and theological centrism). With this work Tippett moves definitively away from his English roots into international modernist territory; and this calls for a different, if more alien, critical language.

In the music analysed above, especially the 'et venimus in mentes nostras' episode, I hope to have shown how Tippett finally comes to breathe – and encourage us to breathe – 'air from another planet'. He has, for the time being at least, let go his old preoccupations with the archetypes of the collective unconscious. Instead his business is with the most

fundamental scrutiny of what he calls historical archetypes, but which I have thematized here as the critique of form – or what Adorno calls the rupture between self and forms. Form, I would argue, is music's version – or semblance – of the conceptual: a set of categories, whether of genre or structural device, to which individual musical features might conform as representatives. Yet, as we have seen, throughout *The Vision of Saint Augustine* individual musical elements put up the strongest resistance to being considered as examples of a class; they rebel against identification with the merely conceptual, and thus point to what is beyond any existent conceptual framework. Tippett's achievement, then, is precisely this: to have opened up a space between the already existent and the not-yet existent. In other words, *The Vision of Saint Augustine* points – through its own musical material, rather than through recourse to myth or the theological world-view which is only ostensibly the world it inhabits – to the renewed possibility of metaphysics.

IV

Metaphysics: a perspective from Adorno

While Tippett's purported subject matter in *The Vision of Saint Augustine* is the metaphysical experience of a theologian of the late classical world, his endpoint is a work which – in an implicit critique of both sacred and secular – distils a metaphysics for his own time: nothing less than a metaphysics of modernity. Augustine's metaphysics is certainly no less reliant on negation than Tippett's – witness his description of God's word in terms of what it is not; or his account of eternity as a silencing of all that is existent. But the crucial difference is that while for Augustine the negation of the material by the metaphysical is a relationship of complementation, in Tippett's case this negation is part of a dialectic: the metaphysical is posited not as an evacuation of the material, but as anchored in it, at the same time as being non-identical with it. And it is for this reason that the antinomic model applied by Adorno in such texts as his *Negative Dialectics* and *Aesthetic Theory* offers a valuable, if strenuous, critical language for a work such as *The Vision of Saint Augustine*. In what follows, I will make a short digression to examine some of these ideas before considering their relevance to the work.

'I went into myself and saw the unchangeable light': Augustine finds his metaphysical domain in a search that begins in the self and ends in some other place which he chooses to define positively with a metaphor (light). Tippett again follows Augustine by making a journey in his work into the deepest reaches of subjectivity (a process into which the listening subject is

also drawn through his/her engagement with the temporal processes of the music), but where we end up is somewhere which can only be defined negatively, as the non- (or not yet-) existent, though this is still rooted in the materiality of the work itself. This is perhaps an extreme case of what Adorno sees as being 'precisely . . . art's spirit', namely that 'every act of making in art is a singular effort to say what the artifact itself is not and what it does not know'.[68] While Tippett's quotation of Paul, 'I count not myself to have apprehended', resonates out of Augustine's world, its significance is transmuted in its present-day context: 'I count not myself to have apprehended' could be the composer's confession that he has made a work which attempts to say 'what [it] itself is not and what it does not know'.[69]

For Adorno, 'what the artifact itself is not' is its 'truth content' – to which it stands 'in the most extreme tension'. On the one hand 'truth content cannot be something made', but on the other hand, 'conceptless, [it] appears nowhere else than in what is made'.[70] This is another way of saying that artworks, even though they are nothing if not aesthetic objects, are more than aesthetic objects: they point beyond themselves; indeed they demand philosophical interpretation.[71] It is in the notion of an art whose truth resides in what is made yet is not identical with what is made, that art converges with a philosophy – notably Adorno's – whose principles are materialist yet which considers that precisely within this materialism the possibility of metaphysics cannot be eliminated.[72]

It might have been expected that the atheism of Adorno's worldview would have ruled out any concern with the transcendent. Yet, like Kant before him, the idea is in some way necessary to his critical project because of an ethical imperative within it to find a position from which to postulate the possibility of change in the present existential order of the world. Kant distinguished between the materially existent, 'sensible' world, the necessary ground on which the concepts of our understanding are validated, and an 'intelligible world' whose content is purely intellectual – made up of ideas only, with no reference to any actual cognizable objects. In *Negative Dialectics* Adorno speaks of the 'grandiose ambiguity' of this latter concept.[73] On the one hand Kant is critical of the metaphysics inherent in it (because its concepts of the absolute – such as freedom, God and immortality – are rationally unverifiable).[74] On the other hand this sphere is necessary if he is to demonstrate that morality, the question of what ought to be rather than what is, has a necessary philosophical basis for effecting change in the world.[75]

Adorno draws attention to the contradiction implicit in the *mundus intelligibilis*. If this sphere has no empirical component, it cannot be envisaged (or visualized): it cannot be thought in positive terms, as Kant would have us believe.[76] Nevertheless, Adorno empathizes with Kant's 'rescuing

urge' with regard to this sphere, for he too remonstrates against the reduction of experience to the merely empirically known. He thus posits a different conception of the intelligible world, based on fundamentally *negative* premises:

> The concept of the intelligible is the self-negation of the finite mind . . .
>   To be a mind at all, it must know that what it touches upon does not exhaust it, that the finiteness that is its like does not exhaust it. The mind thinks what would be beyond it.[77]

Thus Adorno agrees with Kant that the mind is not limited by what it knows through the concepts of understanding. But its transcendence of these limitations comes not from some realm of the ideal or absolute, but through the finite mind's apprehension of something beyond itself that is the concomitant of recognizing its own finitude.[78] 'The question of whether metaphysics is still possible at all', Adorno continues, 'must reflect the negation of the finite which finiteness requires'. Here, then, he suggests the possible ineliminability of metaphysics from experience (which would seem also to presuppose a deconstruction of the Kantian distinction between sensible and intelligible worlds). This is a metaphysics rooted in the mind's (ceaseless) negation of the limits of its own conception of a material world – a process activated 'as soon [as the mind recognizes that] all there is does not evaporate in things of the mind. The mind, for all its indirectness, shares in existence, the substitute for its alleged transcendental purity.'[79]

The 'solidarity between such thinking and metaphysics at the time of its fall' resides, then, in its rigorous negativity: in thoughts such as: 'The concept of the intelligible realm would be the concept of something which is not, and yet it is not a pure nonbeing'.[80] To think antinomies is no small challenge; Adorno's siting of metaphysics in such an arcane non-space seems an almost desperate long shot against empiricist or positivist fundamentalism. But he has things to say about despair,[81] just as he does not seem oblivious to the possibility that his requirements may be impossible. His response is characteristically dialectical, setting up the possible and the impossible as yet another antinomy. And, crucially, he finds a paradigm for the thinkability of the unthinkable in art: 'the fact that artworks exist signals the possibility of the nonexisting. The reality of artworks testifies to the possibility of the possible.'[82] Artworks may not be any more empowered than philosophy to express the intelligible realm in positive terms, as it actually is; but they may be able to say what this domain is *like* in terms other than the literally conceptual. That is, art may function as a *semblance* of this realm, or of the dynamics of envisioning it. As Adorno puts it, in a

formulation closely analogous to that in which he negatively framed the intelligible realm: 'Aesthetic experience is that of something that spirit may find neither in the world nor in itself; it is possibility promised by its impossibility'.[83] The convergence of art and philosophy thus lies in the conformance between the notion of truth content in relation to the art work, and metaphysics in relation to epistemology.

Although the pairing of Adorno and Tippett (as strange a meeting as that between Tippett and Augustine) might have been anticipated as one of non-identity, on the evidence of *The Vision of Saint Augustine* (or at least the way I have figured it) there is a case for construing some kind of homology between the two figures' respective domains of thought. Whereas for Augustine it may have been desirable that the transcendent was achievable only by an exit from philosophical thought into theology and dogma, for Tippett transcendence of the immanence of his own medium of thought can only truthfully take place through immanence. This is to say that he seems to sense something of Adorno's anguished understanding that the only opening on to the metaphysical in a material world – the only way to think beyond thought – is to think against thought.[84] This is borne out analogically in *The Vision of Saint Augustine* in that it approaches the transcendent not by trying to seize it out of the air but through an intense dialectical struggle with the categories of musical meaning made available by history, and then with its own reformulation of them within the work's own context. The work's receptivity to metaphysics is reflected in the construction of its temporal axis. It takes to heart Adorno's aphorism regarding metaphysics: 'only if "that which is" can be changed[,] is "that which is" not *all* there is'.[85] Its mosaic-like structure is an unceasing attempt to move away from each given state towards something beyond itself. While every section still bears second-order relationships with others, and while repetition and recontextualization of material is permitted, the resistance of each section to synthesis is a measure of the extent to which it offers itself to the transcendental; and so too is its problematizing of closure. For complete synthesis and complete closure would have laid emphasis on the artefactuality of the artefact itself, rather than on what lies beyond its principles of immanence. The ultimate aporia of the work is that it cannot achieve what it sets out to achieve (which presumably Tippett foresaw in the words he selected to end it); for to have done so would be to clothe what is beyond articulation in the articulate. The element of despair which is a concomitant of this situation (and whose own concomitant is none the less its opposite) is audible in a soundworld which must torture itself in order to attain its freedom of thought.

Time and history revisited

> An artist can – maybe sometimes he must – involve himself in the political
> and social ferment of his time. He can also detach himself completely. There
> exists a whole genre of twentieth-century creative work ... which seems to
> stand proudly and eloquently alone, independent of external turmoil and
> internal neurosis, granite-like in its aesthetic objectivity.[86]

Tippett's mature *œuvre* unquestionably rests on an aesthetic of autonomous art; and he delivers the verdict that – at least at the time he was
writing the above (around 1980) – *The Vision of Saint Augustine* represents
the pinnacle of his achievement in that aesthetic. We have seen, however,
that the truth about such an artwork is that, in its immanence, it points to a
truth whose locus is beyond the artwork. Tippett is both right and wrong in
his judgement, on several counts. 'Aesthetic objectivity' correctly signifies
the artefactual nature of the work, yet it belies the intervention of subjectivity as a counteractive agency against the demands of the objectivity of form.
And while 'granite-like' connotes a Stravinskian aesthetic of absolute music
(for Tippett an archetype within a dualism that always preoccupied him),[87]
The Vision of Saint Augustine perhaps comes closer to Busoni's conception
of absolute music: the notion that the 'Absolute in music' is engendered
through the dissolution of form.[88] Furthermore, if a discourse of the absolute provides one context for the piece, at the other extreme its qualities are
inseparable from historical and social contingencies.

  The latter dichotomy is in effect tackled by Tippett in the essay 'Too
many choices', where his questions regarding the ontology of time – for-
mative in the genesis of *The Vision of Saint Augustine* – are made in a
context absolutely of the historical moment. The essay's subject is precisely, in the composer's own words, 'the feel of the times' – meaning, I
think, both the general conditions of twentieth-century modernity, and
the specific anxieties that were their manifestation in the late 1950s. A
symbol for several of these concerns is Sputnik, the first man-made satel-
lite to be successfully launched into space. Given that Tippett talks of this
event just a few months after it took place (the launch was in October 1957;
'Too many choices' was broadcast by the BBC in January 1958) he is surely
registering the shock waves sent round the world as Soviet Russia appeared
to gain the technological upper hand in the Cold War, including the potential for long-range missile warfare. It is perhaps only since the ending of
the Cold War in 1991 that we have been in a position to begin adequately to
evaluate its impact on the consciousness of those times – both social consciousness and that of individuals such as Tippett. It is worth recalling for
example, that the Kruschev era (Nikita Kruschev was elected first secretary

of the Communist party after Stalin's death in 1953, and was removed in 1964) was near-contemporaneous with the period in Tippett's *œuvre* between the completion of *The Midsummer Marriage* and *The Vision of Saint Augustine*. Among the events which fed the deepening political instability of this time were the Hungarian revolution of 1956, the Suez Crisis (also 1956), the beginning of the erection of the Berlin Wall (1961), and the Bay of Pigs invasion (1961). With the Cuban missile crisis which ensued from this last event in 1962 the end of history began to look like more than a speculative theological possibility.

But in our understanding of *The Vision of Saint Augustine* how are we to bridge the gap between the transcendental concerns of its aesthetic world and 'real world' events such as the Polish uprising of 1956? Tippett supplies a possible answer when he considers how such events may generate a consciousness of history which is allied to a consciousness of time:

> If there is only one meaning of Time – historical time in a straight line – then it is an anguished matter if one's society is like Poland continuously and absolutely in the Path of History . . . Can Poland never be free? The Polish intellectual often despairs, as he does now. But I can imagine the Polish peasant may survive with his dumb vitality unimpaired because his sense of Time is not of this historical kind, but of an eternal renewal in which every spring is the miraculously pristine sprouting of the new corn. If through our deepening sense of relativity and insecurity within, and our nuclear armaments without, we all, English and Polish alike, stand equally in the Path of History, what then? Shall we like the peasant find Time as a straight line inadequate, because too frightening, and will the other sense of Time, of an eternal return, sustain us better? Or are these two senses of Time really complementary, and in some unexplained way both necessary, even though superficially and intellectually they seem contradictory?[89]

The historical consciousness of the day is shot through with anxiety. If historical time is indeed teleological its *telos* may be too ghastly to contemplate in the light of actual events. And Tippett sees the situation not only as that of the overt drama of impending nuclear catastrophe. More than the harbinger of enhanced weaponry, Sputnik also symbolizes another leap in the supremacy of technology, whose principles of rationality are associated with the drive to industrialization, and with it the sacrifice of the local to the global, and of the individual subject to social domination.[90] But a mythological construction of time offered in lieu of a historical one may bring no comfort. Eternal return merely means a repetition of the same unredeemed time, as Augustine understood. Tippett does not name the principle on which his two types of time offer complementary perspectives, but he may be alluding to the fact that, in their different ways, each

time offers all that there is: that both assume a principle of immanence. Tippett acknowledged this notion (with regard to historical time at least) when he spoke on another occasion of a post-Christian 'non-transcenden-tal world of absolute immanence, or . . . a world of technics'.[91]

The bricolage of Tippett's theoretical writings may not have approached Adorno's sustained antinomic *tour de force*, but it is possible to surmise from a reconstruction of the pieces that by the late 1950s the composer had arrived at a view of metaphysics as aporetic in its own terms as the philoso-pher's. On the one hand Tippett rejects a 'non-transcendental world of absolute immanence': this much is clear when in 'Too many choices' he declares his openness to 'the further sense of moments which are out of Time altogether'.[92] On the other hand both orthodox religion and Marxism are unsuitable ground for these seeds of a metaphysics. Marxism's answer to the anxieties of historical immanence – their resolu-tion through revolution – remains an immanent one, and for Tippett was terminally tainted by the unfolding of real historical events in Soviet society; while Christianity's (supra-immanent) answer – the transcen-dence of history altogether as time gives way to eternity at the last judge-ment – would, for Tippett the agnostic, be tainted by its basis in dogma. While this of course is the very eschatology which underpins the subject of *The Vision of Saint Augustine*, the point is that the work is a trope on that eschatology through which Tippett delivers a different construction of metaphysics. In his disbelief Tippett honours Augustine's belief system by treating it not as mythological but historical. Whereas in *The Midsummer Marriage* the composer used myth to enable a pseudo-immediate celebra-tion of transcendence, he now employs a different, arguably more testing criterion against which transcendence is measured as true: the escape from immanence is now possible only through its immanent critique. *The Vision of Saint Augustine* is true to this notion in that it seeks to get beyond itself through the relentless internal critique of the historically handed-down formal devices that enable it to function as an autonomous artwork.

'Truth content is not external to history but rather its crystallization in the works', states Adorno. On this understanding metaphysics is not a supra-historical phenomenon but is entirely dependent on its engagement with history. He goes on to state that the emergence of the non-existing from the existing is driven by *longing*: the longing which is the concomi-tant of historical consciousness:

> That by which [artworks] transcend longing . . . is the neediness inscribed as a figure in the historically existing. By retracing this figure, they are not only more than what simply exists but participate in objective truth to the extent that what is in need summons its fulfillment and change. Not for-itself, with

regard to consciousness, but in-itself, what is wants the other; the artwork is the language of this wanting and the artwork's content [*Gehalt*] is as substantial as this wanting. The elements of this other are present in reality and they require only the most minute displacement into a new constellation to find their right position.[93]

The Vision of Saint Augustine is a dramatic particularization of this principle of the desire of what is for the other, a desire for a consciousness which would be the negation of that currently determined by history. Tippett may not have expressed this in the kind of Adornian language which declares 'the nonexisting in artworks is a constellation of the existing', but he recognizes a similar sentiment in lines from Goethe which are quoted on two separate occasions in *Moving into Aquarius*: '*Und umzuschaffen das Geschaffene, / Daß sich's nicht zum Starren waffne, / Wirkt ewiges lebendiges Thun*' ('*And refashioning the fashioned, / Lest it stiffen into iron, / Is work of an endless vital activity*').[94] Significantly, the second time Tippett quotes this is in illustration of a point that links transformation with longing: 'my art might form a tiny fragment of the great mirror, in which we see our unconscious longings reflected as images that have power to changes us whither we must go'.[95] And this is preceded by a further statement that the artist has 'the inescapable duty to make conscious the repressed longing locked up in the inner violence and psychic disarray'. These comments together suggest the musical image, the currency of Tippett's creative thought, as a materially existent vehicle for metaphysics; as the nexus of the subject, the historical, and the negation of the historical through desire, which strives to bring about historical change from within by releasing what history represses.

Coda

Tippett's own account of time and history – as revealed in his theoretical writings but especially in *The Vision of Saint Augustine* itself – makes a 'minute [but crucial] displacement into a new constellation' of those terms as found in Quispel's reading of Augustine – one which brings the composer closer to a negative dialectics. The transcendent now appears within the historical through the socially constituted subject's negative stance towards the limitations of what society and history make thinkable (that is, the limitations of immanence). The appearance of the unknown through the negation of the known inevitably risks the inchoate, since we do not have the schemata through which to cognize what appears to cognition. In the name of truth, beauty, the subject's happy reconciliation with the known, must unflinchingly embrace its other, and the subject must

experience what is inimical to its integrity in the sublime struggle to voice the unknown. In taking up this struggle within its own construction and soundworld *The Vision of Saint Augustine* presents itself as both not affirmative and affirmative. It is not affirmative because its truth depends on sounding the agonies and antagonisms immanent in the historical moment it seeks to transcend. These sentiments were pinpointed by Tippett in a quotation from another essay in the volume *Man and Time*:

> Anyone whose ears do not burn, whose eyes do not cloud over at the thought of the concentration camps, the crematoriums, the atomic explosions which make up our reality – at the dissonances of our music, the broken tattered forms of our painting, the lament of Dr. Faustus – is free to crawl into the shelter of the safe old methods and rot.[96]

Against such a background the idea of humanity cannot be blindly affirmed, cannot be merely posited. On the other hand, *The Vision of Saint Augustine* is affirmative in that its crystallization of this background into its own immanent principles means that the glimpses of transcendence distilled from it ring true. If the work declares the possibility of metaphysical knowledge in the material world it also declares experience in the existent world as the source of its legitimacy.

5 'Shall we . . . ? Affirm!' The ironic and the sublime in *The Mask of Time*

I

The sublime and the ridiculous

Of all Tippett's works *The Mask of Time* (1980–2) seems to have provoked the most polarized critical reception. This is not just a matter of quibbling over nuances. When one commentator esteems the piece for its 'extraordinarily heterogeneous coherence' while another assigns it to the category of 'eclectic lead balloons'; when summary evaluations have rated it on the one hand as 'the climax and crown of Tippett's output' and on the other as 'an almost complete disaster on aesthetic grounds', we may surmise instability as something essential to its makeup – an objective property, perhaps, to which the cleavage in the pattern of subjective judgement may not be unrelated.[1]

One source of that instability could be the disparity between the grandeur of the work's ambition and the means the composer uses to realize it. '*The Mask of Time*', he declares,

> is explicitly concerned with the transcendental. It deals with those
> fundamental matters that bear on man, his relationship with Time, his place
> in the world as we know it and in the mysterious universe at large. But it
> subscribes to no particular liturgy or standard theory, Biblical or otherwise,
> about the creation of the world and the creation of mankind.

'Inescapably', then, Tippett

> had to accommodate a plurality of co-existing viewpoints. At best, [the]
> composition offers fragments or scenes from a possible 'epiphany' for today.
> The forces used in each scene or fragment are heterogeneous: hence [the]
> description 'for voices and instruments'.[2]

While the embrace of pluralism follows logically enough from the wish to avoid any single, pre-established ideology or epistemology,[3] Tippett here also lays bare the key compositional problem this entails: to articulate a grand narrative of humanity's relation to life, the universe and everything, on the basis of fragments. If I am less convinced than Whittall that Tippett fully musters coherence from his heterocosmic creation, I would nevertheless want to argue, *pace* Puffett, that its achievement lies precisely in the

musico-dramatic force with which it engages key aesthetic questions of modernity.

On this level too, instability makes it mark. It would not be going too far to claim that the work plays out the struggle to find a stable aesthetic and epistemological standpoint. Epigrammatically, Tippett conveys this point in lines from the libretto's second movement which read, 'Shall we . . . ? / Affirm!' Here, thanks to the eccentric punctuation (further complicated by the vocal distribution in the musical setting itself), even the intention to present affirmation as a question – as just a possibility – stalls midstream. Such instability is writ large over the work: the transcendental might be affirmed in one voice, but there are others which would tell a tale of scepticism, not only on epistemological grounds, but also on the empirical evidence of humanity's track record so far. In other words, any given authorial position in *The Mask of Time* is vulnerable to irony. But such instability can veer in more than one direction: the awareness that the sublime might at any time collapse into the ridiculous has its counterpart in moments where banality is transmuted into something lofty. Bathos and sublimation belong equally to this work troubled by the world's abysmal discrepancy between what ought to be and what is. Perhaps it is not surprising, then, if what transpires from this chemistry is critical disorientation.

The third movement, 'Jungle', illustrates these points. Its opening animal-noise onomatopoeia ('Clatter-chatter, clatter-chatter, Monkee') could be censured as a typically embarrassing lapse in Tippett's libretto-writing. A less po-faced attitude, however, might acknowledge the comedy behind this treatment of nature's absurdities. In any case, where we begin is not where we will end up; it might almost be said that the movement forfeits progression in purely musical terms for a progression of musico-narrative positions. Having established a comic backdrop, Tippett quotes from Annie Dillard's novel *Pilgrim at Tinker Creek* a passage which graphically illustrates nature's morally indifferent economy of life and death. With this the initial pseudo-naïve humour turns sardonic. 'Well, Lord God . . . what's it all about?', asks the hungry lacewing, eating the eggs it has just laid[4] – to which question the composer adds an additional barb: his 'somewhat grandiose' harmonization of Saint Ambrose's 'Deus, creator omnium' (Figs. 82–4). The ironic deployment of this hymn to God the creator of all things marks a radical break from its empathetic treatment in *The Vision of Saint Augustine* (1963–5). Now Tippett wants to add his voice to Dillard's point about a *deus absconditus*.[5] But then comes a further, still more decisive change of register: a spontaneous moment of epiphany from which banality is expunged and in which nature is apprehended as the source of a transcendent order: 'occasionally the mountains part. The tree

with the lights in it appears, the mockingbird falls, and time unfurls across space like an oriflamme.'[6] The rhetorical effectiveness of this moment resides in the affective power with which higher consonances infuse the now; those here are borrowed from earlier Tippett works: the Triple Concerto (1978–9), the Fourth Symphony (1976–7), and *The Ice Break* (1973–6).[7]

Humanity and nature

'Jungle' concentrates on a question which in one form or another underlies much of *The Mask of Time*: that of humanity's place in the natural world. The way a culture couches this relationship says much about its estimation of the purposefulness (or otherwise) of its own existence, indeed existence in general. Consider, for example, the anthropocentricity of Kant's position in that key work of the European Enlightenment, *The Critique of Judgement*:

> All the manifold forms of life, co-ordinated though they may be with the greatest art and concatenated with the utmost variety of final adaptations . . . would all exist for nothing, if man, or rational beings of some sort, were not to be found in their midst. Without man, in other words, the whole of creation would be a mere wilderness, a thing in vain, and have no final end.[8]

On this view, then, Man's emergence as a rational, moral being is what gives nature its ultimate purpose (its 'final end') – which argument requires Kant's elaborate, philosophical critique in which the aesthetic, the sublime and the divine are systemically essential. Patently Kant's view is not Tippett's. None the less, Tippett seeks, like Kant, to assert human nature as something not reducible to nature, however strongly grounded in it; and to present that affirmation as if it were a transcendental principle, something resembling an *a priori* truth.

But it will take the entire course of *The Mask of Time* to reach this point, and before this Tippett countenances various other perspectives on the question, establishing an ironic framework within which to situate it. Hence his attraction to Dillard's worldview, for example, which learns to live with the equivocation in nature far more pragmatically. Unlike Kant's anxious yearning to reconcile the contradictions of nature into a unified philosophical system, Dillard is willing to accept nature as potentially a source of both mockery and wonder: as something whose extravagant fecundity ridicules the attempt to find any rational purpose behind it, and yet which none the less perversely holds a meaning:

> Sometimes I ride a bucking faith while one hand grips and the other flails the air . . .

> The universe was not made in jest but in solemn incomprehensible
> earnest. By a power that is unfathomably secret, and holy, and fleet. There is
> nothing to be done about it, but ignore it, or see.[9]

Her stance is essentially dialogical – a term which I shall explore at greater length below. Given that Tippett himself once spoke of finding 'an acceptance of this *and* of that as a reality' his sympathies are understandable.[10] 'Jungle' presents both the possibilities described by Dillard, and similarly recognizes the schism between them. In this episteme both views must be lived in their mutual contention.

Briefly, let us consider some of the subsequent takes on the nature–humanity question explored in *The Mask of Time*. Movement 4, 'The ice-cap moves South-North', invokes a mythological consciousness of the natural, whose dark side is a communion with nature in its Dionysiac aspect. References to sacred cave paintings ('Images of bison running') and the annual harvest (whose cyclic pattern connotes immortality)[11] lead finally to the depiction of violent rituals atop ancient pyramids – 'where priest unsheathes th'obsidian knife / tears out a human beating heart / an offering to the sun'. Movement 5, 'Dream of the paradise garden', also portrays humankind in a state of oneness with nature, but now 'a perfect communion of the numinous, animals, and man'. As Tippett points out, though, this state of affairs is 'dream-like' – or, one could say, a kind of *participation mystique*.[12] And his version of the Fall could be interpreted as a depiction of the turn from mythological to modern consciousness: the natural and the divine evacuate to realms of alterity or infinite remoteness, and men and women are left alienated from both.

This is arguably a parable for what modern Western culture has inflicted on itself in the name of reason: the spiritualization of the divine into abstraction or ideality, and the construction of nature as other to ourselves, an object for our rational scrutiny and exploitation.[13] The lines which Tippett gives to his Man and Woman characters – 'What piercing sense of loss! / What aching unstaunchable wound!' – and the situation to which they are a response recall John Dewey's words of 1891: 'Nature, in ceasing to be divine, ceases to be human . . . We must heal the unnatural wound.' J. M. Bernstein's commentary on Dewey's pronouncement is also apposite:

> This wound is unnatural, or contrary to nature, because the human is a part
> of the natural world. In raising ourselves above it, in making the world an
> object of representational knowing in which, ideally, even the perspective of
> the knower would disappear . . . all subjective response to the world, and thus

the world as it *appears* to human subjects, disappears. By this route, which is the path of enlightenment, the knife of a proclaimed self-sufficient methodological rationality slices into the flesh of the one who wields it.[14]

Tippett's fragmented narratives in *The Mask of Time* are cognate with the conditions Bernstein describes. The syndrome whereby nature is treated as 'an object of representational knowing' is addressed in movement 7, 'Mirror of whitening light', where three short paragraphs describe the historical arc from the Pythagorean realization that 'nature is number' (a gloss on an earlier movement's quotation from Yeats, 'Measurement began our might') to the most darkly sublime product (so far) of modern mathematics' and physics' exploitation of that fact: the nuclear bomb.

Bernstein links Adorno's injunction that 'although art and science became separate in the course of history, the opposition between them should not be hypostatized' with Dewey's exhortation, 'We must bridge the gap of poetry from science'.[15] And embedded in the kaleidoscopic movement of *The Mask of Time* is, I would argue, the same desire to heal the wound of the separation of spheres – not by an ideological return to a mythological consciousness, but through some posited future reinscription of humanity's subjective experience of itself into its representation of the world (which points to a partial convergence with Kant). The image of this possibility is embryonic in the numinous higher consonances which surface, often spontaneously, throughout the work – not only those mentioned, at the end of 'Jungle' (which include the sonorous 'space' chord quoted from the beginning of Tippett's Fourth Symphony), but also those which pulse and shimmer through the words 'sound' and 'resounding'. These sonorities, which are linked to depictions of nature not only in its natural-historical sense, but also on its most cosmic scale (including, in the opening movement, an image of the inception of the universe, and also an imagined sphere of pre-creation), already bear a strong insinuation of subjectivity through their very individuality of construction and colouration. But it is only in the final movement that this latent subjective presence becomes emphatic.

From Shelley's vision . . .

I will eventually argue that implicated in *The Mask of Time*'s final affirmation of humanity's 'place in the world as we know it and in the universe at large' is a notion of the sublime. The term is prompted by the gesture's order of magnitude ('the name given to what is *absolutely great*', as Kant put it) as well as its emotional correlative (the sublime 'is productive of the strongest

emotion which the mind is capable of feeling', in Edmund Burke's words).[16] But it is also apposite because, as the preceding parenthetical quotations have indicated, it reveals an aesthetic tradition whose roots are in the Enlightenment, and whose tendrils extend into early romanticism.

As Angela Leighton points out, many of the terms of reference of the eighteenth-century sublime were already in circulation by the end of the seventeenth century, even if the word itself was not used. She cites Thomas Burnet's *The Sacred Theory of the Earth* of 1690 as arguing that 'natural grandeur . . . becomes an image of divine presence. It is the vast in nature which points to and approximates the incomprehensible vastness of God.'[17] After the mid-eighteenth century the focus began to shift from sublime objects to human subjects as a source of the sublime, and with this comes a concern for the psychology of creativity – the notion of original genius. These various aspects might be seen to converge in the English romantic poets of the early nineteenth century, for whom the notion of genius is related to the ability to transmute the natural in the inner vision of the imagination to reveal apprehensions of some hidden Power within the landscape. But whereas for the likes of William Wordsworth the sublimity of nature could be used as corroboration for pantheism, for an atheist such as Percy Bysshe Shelley the sublime held an altogether more equivocal prospect. On Leighton's view, the Shelleyan sublime is characterized by 'its unbelief, and its recognition, therefore, that what the human imagination confronts in its creative aspiration may be only a vacancy'.[18]

The sublime was always an aesthetic predicated on ambivalence; this much is evident in Burke who formulated a sublime of terror, and in Kant who construed the sublime as an oscillation or vibration between unpleasure and delight. In Shelley's case, ambivalence becomes a conflict at the heart of a poetry which on the one hand 'refuses to concede any epistemological evidence for the existence of a God', and on the other 'is drawn to an aesthetic which idealises the immaterial and numinous properties of the landscape'.[19] It is not difficult to see why Tippett, who professed 'an endless agnosticism' and yet still sought a metaphysics within 'the human mind's imaginings', might have found empathy with such a position – and thus why a fragment from Shelley's final poem, 'The triumph of Life' (1822), should have entered the fragmented array of *The Mask of Time*.[20]

Tippett was perhaps first and foremost attracted by the power of the 'marvellous metaphor' at the heart of this uncompleted poem: the chariot of Life driven by a blindfolded figure, from which some are thrown and to which some are chained, and around which swarms a 'mighty torrent' of individuals 'Numerous as gnats'. But as much as the phantasmagoric imagery, it is also the ironic tone of the poem which he seemed to want to

capture:[21] its vision in which Life triumphs as an unstoppable force, indifferent to humanist attempts to find meaning in it, hostile to those who would attain dominion over it, and confounding those around it who seek fulfilment in what is vain and ephemeral. Yet, as Michael O'Neill points out, 'the poem has as little time for pessimism as for optimism as a fixed stance'; its vision is remarkable for its constant collapsing of categories of judgement[22] – just as the ironic and the sublime are mingled in it. And this matches the tenor of, especially, the second part of *The Mask of Time*, where the desire to affirm and the acute awareness of the precariousness of doing so permeate one another deeply.

Affirmation and irony had already converged in Tippett's modernist practice by the time of the Third Symphony (1970–2). There, as in *The Mask of Time*, the composer seemed to be establishing an axis between modernist and early romantic aesthetics – with the references to Beethoven and Schiller, as well as mentions of Hölderlin in the composer's own commentary on the symphony.[23] Tippett's ironic consciousness, then, has resonances not only with the English romantic poets, but also the German early romantics. Friedrich Schlegel's romantic irony, for example, as summarized by D. C. Muecke, has many resonances with Tippett's aims in *The Mask of Time*:

> For Schlegel the basic metaphysically ironic situation of man is that he is a finite being striving to comprehend an infinite hence incomprehensible reality . . . Nature is not a being but a becoming, an 'infinitely teeming chaos', a dialectic process of continual creation and de-creation. Man, as but one of these created, soon to be de-created, forms must acknowledge that he can acquire no permanent intellectual or experiential leverage over the whole . . .
>
> [However,] just as a personified Nature might be said to play with or ironize its created forms . . . so man too, or more specifically the artist, being himself a part of nature, has both a creative and a de-creative energy, both an unreflecting, enthusiastic inventiveness and a self-conscious, ironic restlessness that cannot be satisfied with the finiteness of achievement but must endlessly transcend even what his imagination and inspiration has created . . .
>
> Artistic creation, Schlegel argued, has two contrary but complementary phases. In the expansive phase the artist is naïve, enthusiastic, inspired, imaginative; but this thoughtless ardour is blind and so unfree. In the contractive phase he is reflective, conscious, critical, ironic . . . Both phases are . . . necessary if the artist is to be urbanely enthusiastic and imaginatively critical.[24]

The idea of *reversal* which Tippett thematizes in *The Mask of Time* has affinities with the dialectic of 'creation and de-creation' which Muecke

identifies in Schlegel. ('Lord Shiva dancing with informing feet' in 'Creation of the world by music', for example, turns into 'Shiva dancing our destruction' in 'Mirror of whitening light'.) Moreover, Tippett's tactic for dealing aesthetically with what is ironic in nature (and, for that matter, culture) is, similarly, to adapt to it creatively – a kind of mimesis. Thus he seeks to transmute affirmation from a state of mere naïve enthusiasm by taking up other positions within his 'plurality of viewpoints' and so relativizing as he affirms. I will presently show how his treatment of Shelley's 'The triumph of Life' exemplifies exactly such a process of compounded artistic self-scrutiny.

...to television

First, though, there is another ingredient to throw into the critical pot. For all that Tippett fixes the moment of early romanticism within *The Mask of Time*'s discursive horizon, the work does not seek to perpetrate pastiche. The romantic elements are themselves fragments within a plural text, ironized from the perspective of the later twentieth century. Hiroshima, Auschwitz and the Gulag, as events of the utmost material consequences (real bodies of actual individuals exposed to brutality and annihilation that is anything but imaginary), do not sit easily with romantic aspirations to the infinite and the absolute (though longing for something other is perhaps the common denominator of both consciousnesses). This is one source of inhibition of romantic lyricism. Another lies in the means of construction of *The Mask of Time* which similarly reflects the consciousness of a later, emphatically post-romantic age, conditioned by forms of cultural consumption founded on technology. And I would argue (taking it as read that the observation is over-schematized) that the emblem of this is the technology which Tippett confessed to enjoying in later life: television. For while the composer may have liked to wander the landscape like the romantic poets, his view of the natural world probably owed more to David Attenborough than to Wordsworth.

What I want to suggest here is that television may have had more than anecdotal significance for Tippett, and that its working extends beyond such factual connections as that between Jacob Bronowski's classic 1970s series *The Ascent of Man* and *The Mask of Time*'s libretto (that is, beyond usual commonplaces about Tippett's TV-watching habits mentioned in the biographical and autobiographical literature).[25] So, for example, just as the biblical epic stands behind certain of Handel's oratorios, so, I would argue, aspects of the aesthetics of television inform *The Mask of Time*. And this includes the possibility that Tippett may not have avoided (indeed

may not have wanted to avoid) the bathos that goes with the passage from Shelley to the telly.

I should reiterate that in this discussion I am using the notion of television in more an emblematic than a literal sense: as a kind of shorthand for a larger group of informing factors. Among other things, I am allowing for a degree of conceptual spillage between technical features shared by television and cinema. This has a bearing, for example, on the fact that Tippett's turn to form-building in blocks in his second period owes much to Stravinsky's quasi-cinematic techniques of transitionless formal intercutting: it is probably not worth arguing the toss over whether in *The Mask of Time* the application is more closely filmic or televisual. However, one feature distinctive to television which may be relevant is the way it relays constructions of the world into a space which is domestic. And those constructions are less than ideologically neutral. They both determine and are determined by the social mediations embodied in the very space which is their destination. Although in our own times the experience of interior space is not confined to any single class, Walter Benjamin's comments about the origins and cultivation of such space in nineteenth-century bourgeois culture are worth noting:

> For the first time the living space became distinguished from the place of work ... The private citizen who in the office took reality into account, required of the interior that it should support him in his illusions ... From this sprang the phantasmagorias of the interior. This represented the universe for the private citizen. In it he assembled the distant in space and time. His drawing room was a box in the world theatre.[26]

Since the later twentieth century television seems to have become the perfect and near universal instrument for 'the phantasmagorias of the interior'. It is through this mass medium that private citizens (composers included) obtain many of their principal 'representations of the universe' – meaning not just nature and cosmos, but also society and world. Even the most sublime and terrible images can be tamed for (and in) domestic consumption.

It is plausible that aspects of the modes and ideologies of representation of the 'box in the corner' rubbed off on *The Mask of Time*, and survive as traces in this work for the concert hall. This thesis calls for careful interpretation of course. But the gap between private interior and public concert hall is no greater than that between concert hall and royal court in which space was performed the theatrical genre which the title of Tippett's work invokes: the Renaissance masque. *The Mask of Time*, we might argue, is in part a mediation of these two, historically and socially different, media. In

Tippett's own words, the masque 'was a theatrical form with a great diversity of ingredients, a mixture of formality and flexibility, and an ultimately lofty message'; 'It is a pageant of sorts'.[27] That mixture of elements and registers was clearly attractive to the composer as a way of resolving the scope and pretensions of his work into manageable material form. But for audiences of *The Mask of Time* their cultural reference point is unlikely to be the masque itself, given not only the genre's archaism but also its social situation as an entertainment for royalty and nobility. The event in which most modern-day listeners are likely to recognize the experience of 'a diversity of ingredients', a mixture of forms and *niveaux*, an assemblage of 'the distant in space and time', is an evening's television viewing.[28]

    We are talking here about cultural forms of the heterogeneous, and as Raymond Williams pointed out in the 1970s (the period in which Tippett developed the televisual predilections which informed *The Mask of Time*) the experience of television programming 'is one of sequence or flow'; and this is 'perhaps the defining characteristic of broadcasting, simultaneously as a technology and as a cultural form'.[29] Williams continues, 'It is evident that what is now called "an evening's viewing" is in some ways planned, by providers and then by viewers, *as a whole*; that it is in any event planned in discernible sequences which in this sense override particular programme units.'[30] *The Mask of Time*, similarly devised as an evening's entertainment, has just such a mix of discrete elements (movements) which are none the less intended as a sequence. Many of these are of course 'indigenously' musical, and certain of them – madrigal, sarabande, the 'Three songs' (which include quotation from a Dowland lute song) – indeed invoke the era and milieu of the masque. But these take their place alongside other principles more reminiscent of television.

    Particularly televisual is the treatment of pace and place. This includes a similarity to television's editorial principles and production values in the parcelling up of complexes of ideas into bite-size chunks – Tippett's editing of 'The triumph of Life' for his own purposes, let us note, pays its own dues to three-minute culture. On a related tack, *The Mask of Time* also emulates television's propensity to telescope represented time and to juxtapose locations remote in reality (a feature particularly endemic to science and natural history documentaries). Among the most dramatic examples of this is the compressed cosmological narrative of 'Creation of the world by music', which crunches the time frame of its counterpart in Haydn's *The Creation* into just a few minutes. The same treatment is applied to the agrarian history of humankind depicted in 'The ice-cap moves South-North' – modelled in fact on scenes from Bronowski's *The Ascent of Man*. Here Tippett additionally condenses disparate scenes: from

Table 5.1 *The Mask of Time, 'Presence': constituent sections and their durations*

Gesture	Fig.	Text	Duration (sec.) subsection	section
A	[0]	'Sound'	20	
A^1	2	" "	19	39
B	4^{-1}	'All metaphor ...'		9
A′	5	'Sound'	9	
C	6	'Song'	12	
D	7	'Resounding'	12	
D^1	8	" "	12	45
E	9	'A barnacle goose ...	19	
F	11^{-1}	dawn breaks loose'	4	23
G	11	'Exploring,	22	
H	13	exploding, into	15	
I	14	Time into	15	
J	15	Space'	15	67
		'I through the terrible novelty of light,		
K	16^{+3}	Stalk on'		7
L	17	'Turning, returning,	21	
M	19	eternal re-[versal]' [*segue* No. 2]	8	29

ice-flows, to caves, to open fields, to Mexican pyramids, all in a single narrative span. What these constructions also share with television is the expurgation of specific historical and social contexts as fragments are mobilized to serve the homogenizing purposes of a different narrative. A similar essentializing tendency is apparent in the stylized oriental musical gesture in 'Jungle' at the words 'Allah asks', which reappears later in the work to signal the context of China. Music is here being used for its connotative power, as in film and television; on its second appearance especially it acts as a synecdoche for 'the East', just as it might on the soundtrack of an establishing shot.

As a more detailed example of televisual construction in *The Mask of Time*, Table 5.1 makes a simple analysis of the sequence of musico-narrative events in the first movement, 'Presence'. Materials are labelled in the first column according to the order in which they appear, and are

identified by their associated text; the approximate duration of each element is listed in the right-hand column.[31] Although successive gestures often aggregate into short sections (which resolve into a pattern of episodes for the solo tenor against the shifting background presented by the chorus), these gestures are distinctive enough to be heard as discrete, relatively autonomous entities (so much so that Tippett is able to relocate various of them into new contexts later in the work with virtually no adjustment). Especially noteworthy is the brevity of the units and the sheer rapidity of change between them: sixteen gestures (A–M, with variants) in three and a half minutes. The basic principle of formal construction is that of a concatenation of 'shots', an array of almost freestanding images.

While this is one of the more extreme examples of formal telescoping in *The Mask of Time*, it is by no means atypical. The procedure is a recipe for ambivalence – a contributing factor to the instability of the work's critical reception. In some ways Puffett has a point in his critique of Tippett's collage technique:

> It is as if Tippett thinks that the allusions will do the work for him, that it is enough simply to put the quotations together: 'All metaphor, Malachi, stilts and all' . . . The problem is not so much that we need to know who Malachi is, or what his stilts are for, as the facile assumption that metaphor will do all the work . . . Image (or gesture, or allusion) replaces substance, because there is no substance, no mythological substratum, for it to rest on.[32]

Undeniably *The Mask of Time* is over-reliant on the instantaneous impact of the musical image. However, I do not agree with Puffett that the problem is the absence of a 'mythological substratum' (myth is itself hardly problem- or ideology-free). Rather, what threatens aesthetic substance is exactly the editing out of such facts as who Malachi is; or, to use another example, what 'the tree with the lights in it' refers to.[33] These are indeed 'marvellous metaphors', but they are often bound up with telegraphic tendencies which inhibit the extension of ideas and the development of musical thought.

The slick succession of moving images – for which television acts as a suggestive metaphor – is the principal manifestation of Tippett's cultivation of the fragment in *The Mask of Time*. But if this is a problematic feature it also brings a positive side. It is not just that the constant influx of new stimuli ensures that the piece is never less than interesting. It is, as mentioned above, that this acts as a potential corrective to any anachronistic expression of romanticism; in other words it fosters an other style of representation with which the romantic traces must negotiate in order to make their mark. Simplifying slightly crudely, one might characterize this

as a tension between televisual and poetic functions, or between low-brow and high-brow media. On the one hand television represents a cultural form whose mode and place of consumption is that of entertainment within domestic space, and whose distinctive aesthetic medium is an often rapid sequence of visual images of a predominantly referential content. On the other hand, the poetic medium offers greater opportunities for subjective discursive reflection, and by definition involves a degree of self-reflexivity in its deployment of language. In musical terms such self-reflexive discursivity is recognizable in the developmental processes most evident in genres such as sonata and symphony, the latter having a strongly public (as opposed to domestic) dimension.

If in *The Mask of Time* the interplay between these different registers creates a process of mutual ironization, the ultimate motive behind such irony is its own overcoming. This is not so much – as Ronald Woodley has put it with reference to a different composer – 'a desire for cathartic release into some supremely positive state of being, where meaning – musical and supra-musical – is transparent and unironisable'.[34] Rather, it is the quest for some stabilization of irony's restless critique of what is posited by enthusiasm, through the sublime's homeostatic ordering of positive and negative forces – terror and delight. In *The Mask of Time* these two different configurations of ambivalence never entirely work free from one another. However, I want to argue that the most developed, and most potent, realizations of the ironic and the sublime are found, respectively, in the sixth and tenth movements, 'The triumph of Life' and 'The singing will never be done'. I intend to treat these as case studies – in which process I will also be concerned to examine some of their technical means of construction, partly for its own sake, but not least because ultimately Tippett's communication of his aesthetic concerns inheres in the way he has formed his material. While these two separate movements with their different aesthetic goals call for comparably discrete treatment – amounting in effect to two separate essays – I nevertheless hope that these different accounts will mirror the progression of ideas between them. One important point of continuity – a topic also present in much of the prefatory exegesis above – is the theme of nature.

II

'The triumph of Life': from Shelley to Tippett

The most overt irony of Shelley's fragment 'The triumph of Life' lies in the twist which it brings to its title. The depicted triumph is not a celebration of life, but a vision of life's enslavement of those who attempt dominion

over it. Embodying this state of thraldom is the character Rousseau, who
acts as the poem's second narrator. Indeed the tale of 'the failure of . . . the
great spokesman for the new age of Liberty, Equality and Fraternity'[35]
accounts for more than two-thirds of the extant text. At its heart, then, is a
scepticism towards the ideals of the Enlightenment (and the depiction of
Napoleon as principal among those chained to the chariot is, further,
Shelley's disillusioned comment on the failure of the ideals of the revolution[36]). Yet the tenor of 'The triumph of Life' is not so much despair or
nihilism as ambivalence[37] – as adumbrated in the poet's opening description of dawn, where idyllic tones are countered by a sense of dis-ease:

> But I, whom thoughts which must remain untold
>   Had kept as wakeful as the stars that gem
> The cone of night

As Alan Weinberg puts it, 'These qualities represent, for the narrator-poet,
that period of adulthood when there is a disruption of the self and nature,
perceiver and perceived, and it is no longer possible to live in complete
innocence'.[38] There is also an intimation here of the polarity between the
'naïve, enthusiastic, inspired, imaginative' and the 'reflective, conscious,
critical, ironic' phases of the artist, which Muecke identifies in Schlegel's
account of romantic irony (as quoted earlier).

Tippett's 'Triumph of Life' is pivotal in *The Mask of Time* in its similarly
ambivalent stance towards life. Here the artistic tactics both resemble and
are different from those of Shelley's poem. Only a fraction (in fact less than
one-tenth) of the original fragment is employed. Tippett chooses lines
mostly from the early part of the poem, in which the protagonist, who has
spent the night sleeplessly musing from his hilltop perspective, describes
the dawn, from which ensues his waking dream of the chariot of Life and
its tragic procession. (Further excisions from within the text of these episodes complete the dissolution of Shelley's *terza rima* structure; but in this
Tippett is merely being consistent with his own view that setting poetry to
music 'destroys the verbal music of a poem utterly', and that the composer
responds 'to the poetic *situation*, rather than to the verbal music of
poem'.[39]) As a result of this selectivity, the original poem's extended narration by Rousseau is omitted. However, the composer presents a version of
the idea of a double narrative by following the Shelley text with a parallel
episode recounting the story of the historical poet's death by drowning in a
storm at sea.

Tippett's own switch to a second narrative position is also driven by
ironic intent, in this case a meditation on the artist who for all his visionary
imaginings is impotent to exercise any influence over the empirical world

– indeed over nature itself. His characterization of the 'moral navigator on the sea of life' as 'less skilful on the sea itself' sounds like the kind of sarcastic jibe which commonsensical everyday folk might level against the dreamy romantic artist. However, the matter is a little more subtle. For one thing, the composer alludes to a critical tradition which has drawn attention to the parallels between Shelley's biographical circumstances and their mediation in 'The triumph of Life' – not only the resemblances between the landscapes evoked in the poem and those of the Bay of Lerici where Shelley and his entourage had set up home at the time, but also the fact that the question 'Then, what is Life?', posed near the end of the fragment, was left pregnantly unanswered at the author's demise. Moreover, Tippett's shifting narrative position makes a point about the mutability or relativity of authorial authority. For Richard Rorty, an ironist is someone self-consciously aware that the truth claims of any writer (including especially his/her own) are always unstable, because always open to being 'redescribed' from the standpoint of another.[40] Tippett's libretto implements just such a redescription as the lyrical (i.e. first-person) visionary musings of the poet are displaced by a more detached, third-person account (in Tippett's suitably bathetic prose) of the historical Shelley putting out to sea and with heroic folly attempting to defy the mounting storm that will crush him.

Ultimately, one assumes, the composer's portrayal of Shelley here is as a proxy for the fragility of his own artistic aspirations. Even so, he does not quite leave it there. We finally cut (in televisual fashion) to a further scene which reflects, from a still more detached narrative perspective, on the story (and its attendant metaphorical implications) of Shelley's cremation, according to which the poet's heart would not burn.[41] In this last turn Tippett ends on a note of equivocation as to what meaning is to be drawn, and where the boundaries between art and empirical reality lie: 'Real the time, / the place? / . . . / Real the drama that we do? / . . . / Real? / Or unreal? / The trance . . . / wherein we visioned / that the human beating heart / can never be burnt up / utterly.'

Excursus: irony, dialogism and heteroglossia in Tippett

If an ironic consciousness is one aware its utterances invite redescription by another subject – a second voice – then to speak ironically is itself to speak with a double voice, and so to decentre one's own subjectivity. In music, with all its polyphonic possibilities, this figurative description can be made literal, as *The Mask of Time* makes plain. In 'Dream of the paradise garden' (movement 5) the parting line of the divine 'Ancestor' figure as he

evacuates to a realm 'far, far beyond the stars' is ironized by its simultane-
ous presentation in two voices. The hollowness of his would-be consola-
tory words, 'but you may pray to me' (Fig. 202), is exposed by the
rhythmically displaced duplication of his line an octave higher, sung in a
ridiculous falsetto (or by voices of the opposite gender).[42] A more metaphorical example comes later in the same scene, when it is the virtual voice
of the composer which becomes unstable. As the bereft 'Man' and
'Woman' characters sing 'let's go' (Fig. 218), their ornate melisma (which
itself sounds like an ironic gloss on the prosaic text) effects an abrupt men-
sural shift in which the underlying crotchet pulse is compressed to two-
thirds of its former length. The metre is in effect 'redescribed': uttered by a
different 'voice' from outside the norms established by the existing pattern
of musical discourse – and not for the first time in the work.[43]

    In exploring these techniques further we can usefully draw upon
Mikhail Bakhtin's dialogical conception of language (a reverse perspective,
as it were, on a theoretical conception which in its use of conceits such as
the 'polyphonic novel' acknowledges insights gained from music).
Bakhtin included irony among his categories of 'double-voiced discourse',
all of which are 'internally dialogized'. That is, 'A potential dialogue is
embedded in them, one as yet unfolded, a concentrated dialogue of two
voices, two world views, two languages.'[44] Bakhtin, then, sought to counter
unitary views of language; indeed he believed all linguistic utterances to be
heteroglot – enmeshed in a conflicted encounter between speech types
which are differently culturally situated. The last example from 'Dream of
the paradise garden' discussed above is a case in point: the everyday words
'let's go', sung by the disenfranchised 'Man' and 'Woman' characters, inter-
rupt a madrigalian setting of lines borrowed from Milton's *Paradise Lost*
('This was the everlasting place of dreams'). And looking beyond *The Mask
of Time* itself, we might posit much of Tippett's *œuvre* as ripe for analysis in
terms of such heteroglossia. Consider, for example, the incorporation of
(variously) Negro spirituals, blues, electric guitars (with their connotations of rock music) into musical textures otherwise structurally determined by a high-art aesthetic.[45] (Indeed this notion holds potential for a
more interesting critical reading of Tippett's librettos than the usual, all
too unreflective digs about their self-evident infelicities.)

    Bakhtin makes a distinction between poetic and prosaic double-
voicedness. Whereas in the former case double-voicing 'remain[s] within
the boundaries of a single hermetic and unitary language system, without
any underlying fundamental socio-linguistic orchestration', in the latter
case (whose epitome is novelistic discourse) 'double-voicedness sinks its
roots deep into a fundamental, socio-linguistic speech diversity and

multi-languagedness'.[46] Tippett's *œuvre* moves along a continuum between the musical equivalents of these poles: at one extreme the Concerto for Double String Orchestra (1938–9), in which Beethoven and folk-song serve a mutually critical purpose, but nevertheless find a strong measure of synthesis;[47] at the other extreme, *The Mask of Time* and other late pieces such as the Triple Concerto, in which different subjectivities remain audibly distinct against each other, are resistant to forces within these works that would pull all towards a unifying centre.[48] This is consistent with Bakhtin's notion of the tension between centripetal and centrifugal forces at work within heteroglossia[49] (and in *The Mask of Time* is broadly speaking homologous with the dualism posited above between televisual and poetic functions).

It remains a moot point how extensively Tippett 'orchestrates' heteroglossia along social lines – that is, to what extent the centrifugal tendencies within his musical structures mobilize the kind of critique of a dominant, centripetal socio-linguistic ideology which Bakhtin identifies and esteems, for example, in the novels of Dostoevsky. For in the last analysis Tippett's allegiance is to a high-art aesthetic and to the notion of transcendence which goes hand in hand with it. His deployment of heteroglossia certainly connotes a plurality of cultural and historical contexts, but ultimately this inclines towards articulating a self-ironizing bourgeois ego (again, the double-voiced 'Shall we . . . ? / Affirm!' encapsulates the matter) through which rhetoric it seeks to legitimate its visionary apprehensions.[50] *The Mask of Time* teeters between the twin desires of universalizing and relativizing this aesthetic imperative; and this instability is probably the root of all others associated with the work.

For all that investigation of *The Mask of Time* calls for a different emphasis from that found in Bakhtin, concepts of 'the dialogical imagination' none the less remain valuable, helping us to map the unstable polyphony of voices in a movement such as 'The triumph of Life'. Of course, in the culture of the new musicology this application from literary theory is hardly new. Most famously, the Bakhtinian notion of 'voice' has been adapted by Carolyn Abbate, in her *Unsung Voices*, to signify 'a presence or resonating intelligence' operating discretely within a musical continuum.[51] Her use of the term also engages critically with Edward T. Cone's notion of 'the composer's voice' (espoused in his book of the same name[52]). For whereas Cone's identification of, for example, 'vocal persona' and 'instrumental persona' within a song-plus-accompaniment texture is ultimately grounded in a synthetic 'complete musical persona', Abbate rebels against such a monological conception. She eschews this 'centering and hegemonic authorial image of "the Composer"' in favour of 'an aural

vision of music animated by multiple, decentered voices localized in several invisible bodies'[53] – a dialogical conception, in which elements of the musical work can be considered as distinctly not in the service of an all-controlling authorial subject. However, neither conception is exclusively relevant to 'The triumph of Life', since it involves an interplay of both centripetal and centrifugal agencies.

'Voices' and their deployment in Tippett's 'The triumph of Life'

The decentring agency of multiple voices becomes a crucial determinant of irony in 'The triumph of Life'; and the analysis made earlier of the several narrative positions articulated in its libretto (the lyric ego speaking within the poem, the third-person account of Shelley's demise etc.) offers a starting point for investigating this in more detail. Table 5.2 graphs the distribution across the movement's formal structure of the 'voices' identified in the preceding analysis, separating them out vertically (usually only the beginning of each relevant fragment of text is given for each formal section or subsection). The top stratum indicates the framing (third-person) narrative with which Tippett surrounds his selections from Shelley's poem. Reading down, the second stratum delineates Shelley's text itself, whose voice is the lyrical ego of the poet-protagonist. The third stratum belongs to the 'reflective' voice, which even if considered an extension of the first, framing narrative voice none the less represents it in a different subjective disposition – as evidenced by the more poetic construction of its text (for example, its principle of equivalence between interrogative clauses based on the repetitions of 'real?'). Finally, the irruption of the numinous 'resounding' music into the last section constitutes a fourth voice. Strictly speaking, however, it does not belong to the movement as such, being part of a set of sound images that are the property of the work as a whole, and I will treat it as extraneous to the scheme of textual voices.

The formal design itself also calls for comment. The centre of gravity is unquestionably the three sections I have labelled D, E and F, each lasting around three minutes, and together accounting for about three-quarters of the movement's duration. By contrast, the prefatory material of sections A, B and C presents an altogether more fragmented structure. If one takes into account the subdivisions of section A (the hierarchic division between section and subsection in any case has an ambiguous status), then what is rendered is a chain of 'shots' each lasting between about a quarter and three-quarters of a minute.[54] Here, then, we have two contrasting approaches to formal construction: one based on the concatenation of numerous short ideas (sections A–C), the other on the development of a

Table 5.2 *'The triumph of Life': formal structure (NB not to scale) and disposition of 'voices'*

Section:	A (Introduction)				B (Recit.)	C	D (Chariot scene)	E (Storm scene)	A'	F (Cremation scene)				
Subsection:	a	b	c	d					a					
Fig.:	222–6	223+3	225	227	229	230	236	252	279	280	289	290	293	294
VOICE: *Framing*	'At dawn…'	'that insomniac poet…'												
Poetic ego			'Before me fled the night…' [+ choral jubilus] …'	'when a strange trance…'	'As in that wond'rous trance…'	'A crowd numerous as gnats …'	'And whilst the sleeping tempest…'	'Out from the harbour speeds a yacht' [reprise]	[instru-mental reprise]	'The trance which was not slumber …'				
Reflective											'Real, the time…?'	'Flames feasting on flesh…'	'wherein we visioned …'	
Numinous														'Resound-ing'
Duration:	0′29″	0′16″	0′22″	0′30″	0′18″	0′44″	3′32″	2′54″	0′12″	2′52″				

limited number of ideas (sections D–F). And this is symptomatic of the pull within the movement between centrifugal and centripetal tendencies (to use Bakhtinian parlance). One subtlety we need to observe, however, is that these opposing principles are mediated throughout: the shorter sections still evidence a kind of flow, while the longer ones still resist complete synthesis into a single larger unit of form. I will explore these matters in more detail below.

What concerns us now is the way the three textual voices discernible within the libretto are 'orchestrated' within the musico-dramatic scheme. Here complications begin to arise, for just as the textual scheme is not entirely congruent with the formal design (as Table 5.2 makes plain), so neither is there a clean one-to-one mapping of the notional subjectivities which inhere in the libretto and the actual (singing) voices which deliver the text. For example, while the chorus is exclusively responsible for the framing narrative voice in section A, this role passes to the four vocal soloists in section E, albeit that they are also joined by the chorus. The projection of the poetic 'I' is similarly blurred. Initially this emanates principally from the tenor soloist – entirely appropriate to the romantic tradition of the tenor as heroic protagonist, and especially clear in the recitative of section B. However, it soon becomes clear that what Cone terms the 'vocal persona' is to be dispersed between tenor and chorus.[55] The chorus begins to assert its importance in delivering the poetic narrative in section C's account of the appearance of the crowd, 'numerous as gnats' (with an appropriate ironic nod back to the onomatopoeic devices of the earlier 'Jungle' movement).

However, if these complexities serve to cloud the deployment of the voices implied by the libretto (paradoxically making more evident the distinction between sung and 'unsung' – i.e. musically manifest and textually latent – voices), matters are brought into sharper focus in the three principal sections, D, E and F. For, as Table 5.2 shows, these respectively project the three principal voices of the libretto. This much stronger isomorphism comes about through an unambiguous alignment between textual voice, thematic material and orchestral colour: in section D the tuba's grotesque ground-bass figure in uneven beats, depicting the monstrous progress of the chariot (quoted in Ex. 5.2(a), below); in section E the whistling glissandi and gyrating clarinet runs (Ex. 5.5, below), representing the flight of the historical Shelley's yacht among the elements; and in section F the dissonant tolling bells and gentle repeated Lombardian rhythms in the double-reeds, as if uttering a distorted litany for the dead poet[56] (Ex. 5.8(a/i), below). Through their association with these instrumental figures, then, the textual voices are here indeed almost literally 'orchestrated'.

The 'instrumental voice' enters

So far we have examined two large-scale principles of organization in 'The triumph of Life', the first the overall formal design, the second the agency of discrete voices within the libretto. The convergence of these principles (represented by the horizontal and vertical axes of Table 5.2) in sections D–F would suggest that area as articulating particularly clearly a decentred or peripatetic subjectivity – one disinclined to fix on any single position as its authentic voice. (Intentionally or not, this complements the situation in Shelley's 'The triumph of Life': whereas successive episodes in the poem, especially the long narrative of Rousseau, chart a passage into ever deeper levels of forgetful oblivion,[57] the several narrative voices of Tippett's movement successively haul us towards the shore of sceptical realism.) However, beneath these principles lies the trace of another 'voice', another 'resonating intelligence'. And while this compounds the impression of the movement as a palimpsest of organizational forces (and subjectivities), its particular corollary is a countervailing, centring tendency.

This additional voice is the expression of a presence seeking to sustain itself through purely musical structures. I have alluded to such structures above as corresponding to the poetic function of language, whose principle is the temporal extension of an utterance through the elaboration of equivalences out of its own substance.[58] To avoid confusion – for, as I will shortly show, the contrast *against* language is also paramount – I shall now drop the term 'poetic function' to refer to this musical stratum, and instead use the term 'instrumental voice'. This nomenclature draws attention to the fact that the principle of autonomous musical organization which it connotes takes place primarily in the orchestral texture. I would argue that this stratum has a further, symphonic connotation – something which becomes unequivocally manifest at the dramatic core of the movement (the climax of section E) which quotes music from an actual symphony: Tippett's Fourth (see Ex. 5.6(b), below).[59]

What makes this autonomous musical stratum audible precisely as a 'voice', and not just – as in the Fourth Symphony itself – a norm of the musical environment, is that it sounds against its other: language.[60] While 'The triumph of Life' has a stronger impulse than most movements of *The Mask of Time* towards autonomy of musical structure, the meaning system of verbal language itself resists complete assimilation into it. To adapt a metaphor which Abbate associates with 'unsung voices', it is as if a membrane had been interposed between these two domains of signification.[61] In the prefatory sections of 'The triumph of Life' (sections A–C) the instrumental voice has little chance to speak against the mosaic of fragments

Example 5.1. 'The triumph of Life'. At (a): tenor recitative (section B); salient
thirds shown with brace. At (b): related thirds from introduction (section A)
(some orchestral parts omitted).

(a)

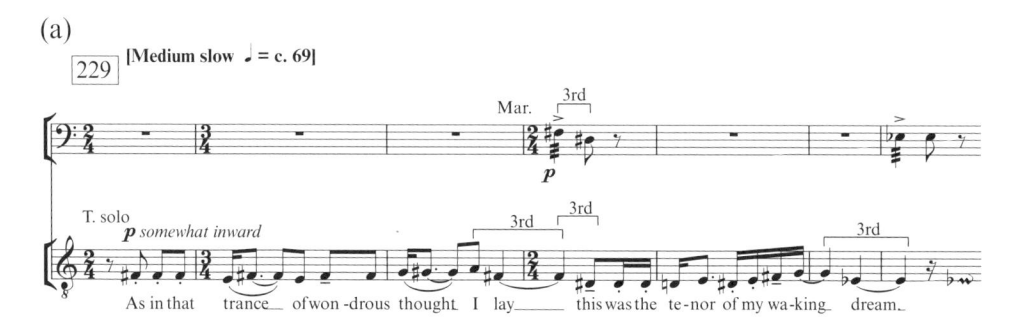

(b)

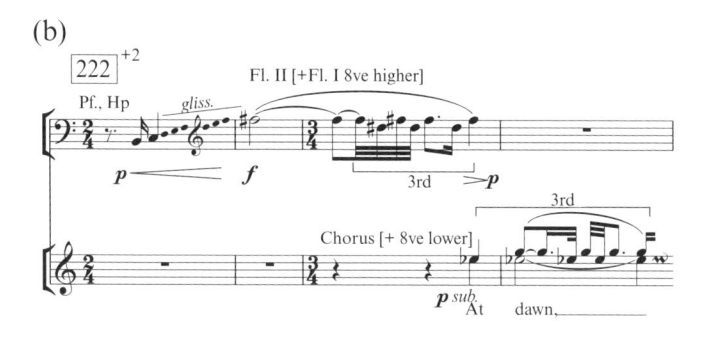

whose sequence and content are dictated by the text and what it depicts.
And language achieves greatest ascendancy in the recitative for the solo
tenor at Fig. 229 (section B), where Shelley's words ('As in that trance of
wondrous thought I lay') are allowed maximum influence over the musical
configuration, and for the moment need not contend against other musical
strata – see Ex. 5.1(a). Even here, though, autonomous musical forces exert
a subtle competing influence, evidenced by equivalences perceptible
between third-based dyads underlying the vocal melody (a feature highlighted by the fleeting doublings in the marimba and xylophone). The last
two dyads, F♯–D♯ and G–E♭, refer back to an identical configuration near
the beginning of the movement (cf. Ex. 5.1(a) and (b)); moreover the first
dyad, F♯–A, will become structural in the next section. The membrane
between music and language, then, is partly permeable, permitting a degree
of mediation between the principles it separates. An example of such mediation in its complementary guise can be found in choral passages like that
at the beginning of the chariot scene (section D). Even though this is where

Example 5.2. 'The triumph of Life', chariot scene. At (a): basic motif (*a*) of ground-bass figure, prolonging C♯. At (b): analysis of sequence of prolongations resulting from transpositions of motif *a*.

autonomous musical principles begin to set in in earnest, the choral texture, which contributes significantly to the forward musical drive, remains decisively shaped by the sound and morphology of the words it delivers ('And whilst the sleeping tempest gathers might / so came a chariot on the silent storm / of its own rushing splendour'[62]).

It is in the chariot scene that the instrumental voice makes itself unequivocally heard for the first time. The inception of that voice, the entry of the lurching $\frac{8}{8}$ ground-bass figure in the tuba (Fig. 236; see Ex. 5.2(a)), is arguably also where the movement proper begins – a moment rendered all the more dramatic by the plunge to the hitherto unoccupied extreme bass register. The instrumental voice achieves its autonomous status largely through developing repetition, on a variety of levels. On the shortest time-scale, the basic motif, *a*, is repeated in practically every bar, and is occasionally extended to two bars' duration through the repetition of its anacrustic component, *ii*. The headmotif, *i*, holds fast to the initial C♯ during the first four bars, and thus determines prolongation over a time-span of between

two and four bars as a higher-level principle of organization. Subsequent repetitions on this two-to-four bar level involve the transposition of the prolonged initial pitch of the headmotif, and this yields the sequence of prolonged pitches shown in Example 5.2(b). The resulting pattern, which establishes a still higher organizational time-span, reveals a degree of pre-compositional planning. The prolonged tones are grouped in pairs of ascending minor thirds (beamed upwards), whose precise identity is determined through the interaction with a second process (whose elements are beamed downwards). Under this process every fourth prolonged pitch is a major third higher than its successor – generating the set C♯–F–A – and each of these elements is immediately followed by an intervening motion of a rising minor third (indicated by a slur).[63] These two interlocking processes steer the pitch content gradually higher until the original generative pitch class, C♯, is reached, prompting a return to the initial register and the beginning of a further macro-cycle at Fig. 242. A third cycle begins at Fig. 248, but is not completed.

The instrumental voice also begins to sound in other strata of the musical texture – an event subtly prefigured in the chorus. The first such prefiguration is at Fig. 238, where the chorus reaches the end, and climax, of its first statement ('so came a chariot on the silent storm / of its own rushing splendour, and a Shape'[64]). On the final word, 'Shape', the membrane which separates linguistic from purely musical determinations of structure is breached: the choral voices break out into a melisma, and change from two parts doubled at the octave to three (similarly doubled) – see Ex. 5.3(a/i). This breach may be momentary, but it is decisive, and seized upon by the trumpets and trombones, who echo the figure and thereby stake a claim on the material on behalf of the instrumental voice. Two comparable gestures follow in the course of the next fifteen bars: at the words 'so ill was the car guided' and 'majestically on' (Figs. 241 and 241^{+4}; quoted in Ex. 5.3(a/ii, iii)). Trumpets and trombones again repeat the gestures, this time *fortissimo*, and, having asserted their presence, immediately launch a reiterated, sardonic fanfare figure of their own: motif *b* (Ex. 5.3(a/iv)). This moment (Fig. 242) crucially marks the onset of a continuous, immanently structured instrumental stratum in the upper register which counterpoints that of the unfolding ground-bass figure (no accident therefore that this coincides with the beginning of the second ground-bass cycle).

Elaborations

One of the generic characteristics of symphonic composition (which a modernist critique evokes even in the act of contesting it) is the elaboration

Example 5.3. Chariot scene: emergence of 'instrumental voice' in upper register.
At (a): salient moments from choral and higher orchestral stratum. At (b):
analysis of linear, set-class and interval-class connections.

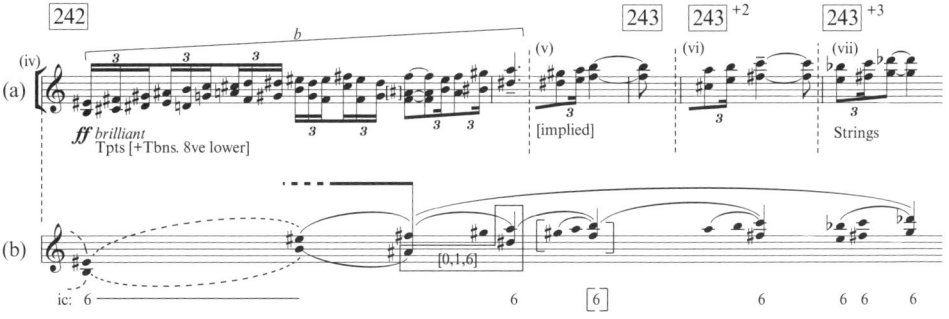

of a musical idea across time and its attendant synthesis of the diverse particulars of a temporal manifold into some form of unity. The action of such
structural tendencies in 'The triumph of Life' is significant in that it exerts a
monological gravitation over the movement's other, dialogical energies. It
will repay us to spend a little time examining how this works in practice.

Processes of intra-musical elaboration can already be heard at work
across the fragments quoted from the upper stratum of the chariot scene in
Ex. 5.3(a). Part (b) of the same example analyses those connections which
promote musical unity. Of primary importance is the link between the
structural F♯s of segments (i) and (iv) – clinched not only by the similarity
of rhythmic profile between the former and the tail of the latter, but also by
the association in both cases between F♯ and the A a third higher. (The salience of this third-relationship was adumbrated, it will be recalled, in the
recitative section, discussed above (see Ex. 5.1(a)). While this association
gives a minor-mode colouring to F♯'s operation as a melodic centre, A is also
heard in both cases as an inflection against a closely juxtaposed inner-voice

Example 5.4. Chariot scene: horn counterstatement.

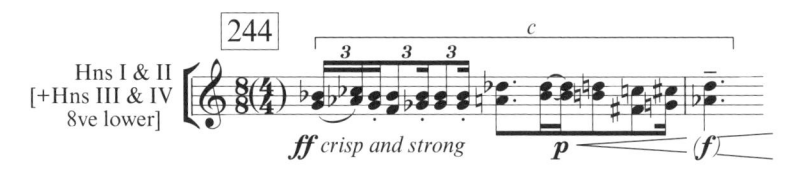

A♯. Equally pertinent is D♯, whose proximity to the other pitches so far mentioned creates a further array of associations within the overall collection. In particular D♯ is interposed vertically between the upper A and inner-voice A♯. On the one hand this is experienced as a further inflection of the overall modal colouring, while on the other it establishes a network of intervallic relations based on the combination of the perfect fourth (or fifth) and tritone – more succinctly described as the set class [0,1,6]. As is especially clear in Example 5.3(b) this set harmonically defines the intervening segments, (ii) and (iii), thereby acting as a force for cohesion. The analysis also graphs the function of these segments within the larger-scale prolongation of F♯. E♭ in the treble acts as a middle-term prolongation, initially manifesting a disjunction from F♯ at the beginning of segment (ii), but then returning to it via a chromatic linear ascent in segment (iii) and a temporary register transfer in segment (iv) – all coloured by associated [0,1,6] verticals.

As stated above, from Fig. 242 the instrumental voice establishes a continuous presence in the upper orchestral register. Initially this is achieved through the modified sequential repetition of the trumpet fanfare (motif *b*), which yields the ascending linear motion graphed in the latter part of Example 5.3(b).[65] The predominant sonority in all of this is the tritone – drawn from the [0,1,6] collection – which rings out at the end of every fanfare. A further means of extension is thematic complementation, executed by a new motif, *c*, which is always played by the horns, and first appears at Fig. 244 – see Example 5.4. Among this motif's contrastive features (in addition to the change of timbre) are its lower register, different additive rhythmic distribution (3+2+3+3/8, rather than motif *b*'s 5+3+3/8) and syncopated tail-motif, which furthermore is at times extended – a licence not granted to its forebear.

This counterstatement also retains certain general characteristics in common with motif *b*: triplet figuration; an ascending profile; and, above all, the prominent tritone sonority at the end of the figure. The various modified sequential repetitions of *c* similarly manifest an ascending middleground voice-leading progression harmonized in tritones, and once *c* approaches the characteristic register of *b*, *b* itself is reinstated. The

two figures alternate this way several times, generating a simple verse/refrain form which acts as a counterpoint to the section's two other simultaneously unfolding strata: the through-composed setting of the text, and the cyclic principle of the ground bass. The climax of section D arises at Fig. 250, as the tenor soloist/poet-protagonist asks 'And what is this? / Whose shape is that within the car? And why ? . . . Is all here amiss?',[66] to which comes the emphatic choral response, 'life!' Thereafter the texture dissipates in response to the protagonist's question 'Then what is Life?' – an eloquent parallel to the almost exact same moment at which Shelley's poetic fragment breaks off.[67]

The storm scene: the instrumental voice resumed

The next section, E, depicting the demise of the historical Shelley, has a delicately ambiguous relationship with its precursor. Just as the text makes no direct attempt to broach the poet's final, unanswered question yet at the same time demands to be read in the light of it, so the music of this section breaks decisively from what precedes yet also smuggles through features which maintain connections. This enables the instrumental voice to retain its identity between sections D and E, notwithstanding the rupture necessary to establish an ironizing distance between these sections. The music is caught in the cross-currents of the movement's centripetal and centrifugal delineations of subjectivity.

In the opening stages of section E, which depicts the poet putting out to sea, discontinuity is certainly in the ascendant. The bass register, from which section D was primarily driven, is now vacated, the lurching tuba ground and thudding bass drum replaced by sprite-like glissandos in piccolos and high violins and whirling semiquavers in the clarinet (motifs *e* and *f*, both quoted in Ex. 5.5). What these opposing extremes of register and timbre conceivably have in common is their ironic tone: grotesque in the first instance, mercurial in the second. Yet while section E's material is, like the ground-bass figure of section D, extended through transposition, this time there is no evidence of any systematized approach to the process (the general contour of a double arc can be extrapolated from successive transpositions of motif *e*, but even this is blurred by various deviations from the overall trajectory). On the whole, then, the first part of section E seems more informally structured, indicating a symphonic presence suspended.

But if Tippett at first silences the instrumental voice, this is only to dramatize its eventual reappearance – in the guise of the brass episode transplanted from the Fourth Symphony (see Ex. 5.6(b)). Summoning up this

Example 5.5. 'The triumph of Life', storm scene: 'Out from the harbour speeds a yacht'.

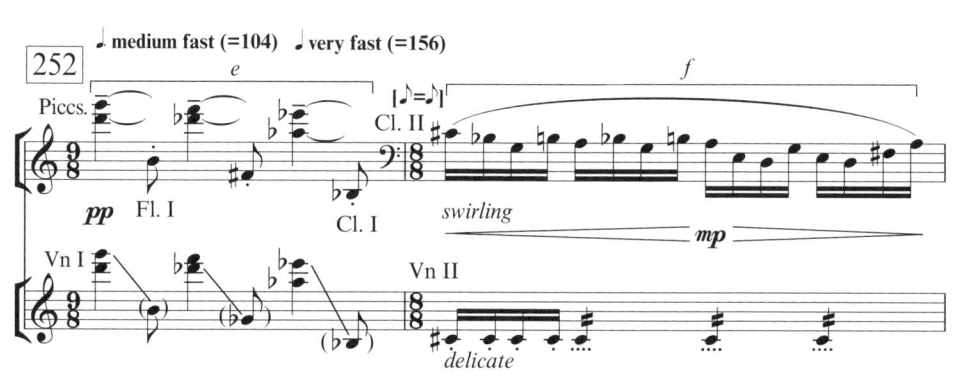

music (which in its original context bore the annotation 'power') to depict the might of the storm fuses what is dramatically and structurally apposite. In a darkly sublime moment we are invited both to 'feel the terror' of the poet as he confronts the forces that will engulf him, and to register the structural dominance of the new material which analogically eclipses the other strata. That dominance arises from, among other things, the breadth of the brass music's phrase structure (and associated middleground harmonic rhythm) which swallows up the faster-moving, more paratactically organized statements of motifs *e* and *f* sounding against it (cf. Ex. 5.5), relegating them to apparent surface activity. In a display of its symphonic credentials, the new layer strongly projects the evolution of a musical idea. Initially presented in the form of motif *g* (Ex. 5.6(b)), the idea mutates with each successive brass phrase, as does the harmonic sonority which it prolongs, generating the progression extrapolated in Example 5.7(a).

As stated above, this material, while self-evidently new, also establishes subterranean connections with ideas from the previous section. Not only is the timbre of brass important to this end, the paradigmatic alignment of Example 5.6 (cf. parts (a) and (b)) shows an essential similarity of contour between the trumpet fanfare, *b*, from section D and the germinal motif, *g*, from section E – in both cases a scalic ascent (incorporating at least one deflection) leading to a prolonged chord. Comparison between Examples 5.3(b) and 5.7(a) also reveals the common feature of a middleground ascent – only in the latter case the compass (from chords A to H) is greatly expanded. Conductor Colin Davis's anecdotal remark about the material from the Fourth Symphony finding its home in its new setting is borne out by this analysis, but also points to a relationship beyond that of passive resemblances of shape. The new idea energizes the

Example 5.6. At (b): storm scene: beginning of Symphony 4 quotation in brass
(= motif *g*; other parts omitted). At (a): paradigmatic comparison with motif *b*
from chariot scene.

structural potential latent in its forebears, and in that sense functions
developmentally – expanding and diversifying not only thematic but also
harmonic content.

Decisive in the latter domain is the more complex flux of relative consonance and dissonance which remain crucial signifying categories in the
movement's harmonic language. In section D the stratification of different
sections of the brass also articulated an interplay between the interval of
the consonant perfect fifth (motif *a*/i of the ground-bass idea, played by
tuba and other bass instruments), and a tritone (at the end of motifs *b* and
c, played by trumpets and horns), presented as a 'soured' equivalent; while
the [0,1,6] trichord represented the conflicted conjunction of both elements. In the Symphony 4 quotation of section E these features are now
compounded *and* synthesized, intensifying the factors which make for
tension and stability.

The crucial harmonic elements of the Symphony 4 quotation, extrapolated in Example 5.7(a), are predominantly higher consonances, the function of whose elements 'is mediation rather than resolution', under
Whittall's definition.[68] Nevertheless, consonance and dissonance here are
not uniformly or equally mediated on each occasion, and what is needed
is some way of analysing the empirically sensed interrelation of these elements (just as Tippett himself composed very much through evaluating
properties latent in empirically presented sounds). While ultimately this
might require quite an elaborate account of theoretical premises, for our

Example 5.7. Analysis of Symphony 4 chord sequence. At (a): voice-leading reduction. At (b): consonant and dissonant subsets of principal harmonies.

Fig.: [263] [264] [267] [270] [271] [272] [273] [274] [275] [276] J [278]

(a)

A [266]   B   (A) [264] [267]   C   (A) [270]   D [271]   E   F [272]   (D) [273]   G   H [274]   J

(b)

A

| A-E |

B

| A-E-(G♯)-B |

C

| C-G-D-A-(C♯)-E |
| *C-G----------C♯ |
| *G-D----------C♯ |
| +C----D-----C♯ |

D

| ⟨D-(F♯)-A-E⟩ |
| G♭-D♭-(F)-[A♭] |
| *D----------G♯ |
| *D----A-----G♯ |
| +E-G♭----F |

E

| ⟨A-E⟩ |
| [A♭]-E♭-[B♭] |
| *A----B♭-A♯ |
| *A--G♯-E♭ |
| *E---B♭-A♯ |
| +A--G♯----A♯ |

F

| C-G-(B)-D |
| B-(D)-F♯ |
| *C-G-------F♯ |
| *C----B---F♯ |

G

| A-E-----B-[D♯]-F♯ |
| E-(G)-B |
| (*)A---------E♭ |
| (+)G--------F♯ |
| (+)E------E♭ |

H

| ⟨D-A⟩ |
| D♭-A♭ |
| *D---D♭-A♭ |
| *D-A---A♭ |
| +A----A♭-B♭ |

J

| G-D |

present purposes we may proceed using a more informal set of criteria – whose application can be examined in part (b) of Example 5.7, beneath the harmonic reduction. Here the salient chords of the overall progression, enclosed in boxes, are represented using note names (which has greater immediacy than the 'Fortean' practice of describing absolute pitch classes with integers; occasionally, therefore, I have needed to show enharmonic equivalences with square brackets). Each chord is analysed into subsets, whose classification as consonant or dissonant is reflected by their position respectively above or below the broken line which bisects each box.

Consonance is clearly understood here in an extended sense, and is based on the notion that the interval class 5 (e.g. the perfect fifth and its inversional equivalent the perfect fourth) continues as a signifier of stability when compounded within a diatonic context. A clear example of this is chord B which adds a further fifth to the dyad A–E of chord A to yield the ic5 chain A–E–B. Moreover, the G♯ inserted into this chord is also interpreted as consonant because it is assimilated within the diatonic-major framework suggested by the A root, and, more specifically, creates a triadic identity for the fifth E–B (such thirds are shown parenthetically in Ex. 5.7(b)). Together these four pitches yield one of Tippett's favourite sonorities, which I have elsewhere designated Z', and which may be considered (within the present context) as fully consonant and stable.[69] (All instances of this chord are shown with a horizontal brace.)

Conversely, the tritone and diatonically foreign semitone (which are combined in the sonority [0,1,6]) are judged as forces of dissonance, which again may be compounded.[70] Such configurations are shown below the bisecting line in Example 5.7(b), and what is clear is that these are often reinterpretations of their consonant reading above the line[71] – as in the case of chord C. This reinforces the point that these sonorities are indeed *mediations* of consonance and dissonance, of stability and instability. More speculatively, the cognition of these features would seem to entail in microcosm exactly that indeterminacy, or oscillation, between pleasure and unpleasure which characterizes the sublime (of which I shall say more below). Although the dissonant elements of these chords could be represented in a number of ways, I have elected to restrict their representation to [0,1,6] trichords (indicated with an asterisk) – which have a particular significance in this movement – or as [0,1,2] trichords (shown with a cross) – which pinpoint particularly dissonant clusters of pitch classes. Only chord G resists interpretation in terms of these dissonant markers (and is thus enclosed by broken lines in Ex. 5.7(b)), though it none the less

presents tritone- and semitone-based dyads (represented, respectively, by parenthetical crosses and asterisks).[72]

Even this fairly informal demarcation facilitates an analysis which effectively tracks the flux of relative consonance and dissonance across the passage. Chord B changes the consonant dyad of chord A into a 'pure' higher consonance of a Z′ type; then in chord C the preceding pitch content is further embedded within a more dissonant collection, which admits several examples of the dissonant markers [0,1,6] and [0,1,2] (shown below the bisector). The next chordal progression, D–F, takes this process further. Collection D contains a similar array of dissonant markers, and added to this is the greater complexity of its consonance-promoting elements, which comprise two Z′-type subsets that are nevertheless dissonantly polarized against one another (shown by the angled brace in the analysis). Chord E, while only part of a passing motion to F, none the less further intensifies the tendency towards dissonance through its sheer preponderance of dissonant markers, and through its eschewal of any stability-promoting Z′ subset; like D, its consonant elements themselves embrace a semitonal polarization. The goal of this motion, chord F, represents a moment of regained equilibrium, with its balance of a Z′-based consonant array and [0,1,6]-based dissonance content; but the ensuing variant of this progression, the succession D–G–H, again rejects Z′ constructions in favour of an astringent array of dissonant elements. The thrice presented final dyad, G–D (collection J), posits a more stable sonority, and suggests a possible symmetry with the initial generative dyad A–E. However the absence of any mediating harmonic linkage with the preceding cumulative dissonance only makes evident the gap between collection J's aspirations towards resolution and its actual achievement – a gap entirely appropriate to the dramatic and ironic situation being portrayed at this point.

This detailed account provides evidence of the continuing, indeed dominating, presence of the instrumental voice in the second part of section E; yet that voice is again muted as the section comes to a close. And again this silencing is both dramatically and aesthetically apposite: dramatically apposite because the music is curtailed at exactly the point where the poet disappears from the scene ('The yacht . . . / heels over – and is gone'); aesthetically apposite because it prevents the mounting monological tendencies from becoming normative – which would have diminished the significance of the movement's ironizing vein. With the inception of the next section (A′) we are jolted out of that universe of discourse, and from this extraneous standpoint grasp the instrumental voice as just that: one voice within a larger signifying polyphony.

The cremation scene

'Jolt' describes fairly accurately the manner in which section E is quitted. With section A′ (Fig. 279) Tippett presents a restatement of the movement's opening material. But far from being a recapitulatory gesture – which would have cohesively drawn the preceding music into its orbit – its effect is paradoxically one of dislocation, as if summoned up from the outside to erase the intervening quasi-symphonic discourse from the memory – a kind of cancellation without *Aufhebung*. This gesture of negation, however, soon cedes to several further shifts of perspective in section F, where the instrumental voice is not so much resumed as reinvoked.

Textually speaking, the narrative standpoint of section F is certainly one of detachment. As observed earlier, the vocal soloists contemplate the significance of what has been recounted ('Real the time / the place?' etc.): the question of what is story and what is reality; the question, implicitly, of whether lifeworld and aesthetic world are best considered immanent and entirely separate domains, or whether the latter might indeed have some meaningful bearing on the former. Musically too, this section establishes a separate discursive space through material previously unheard, including the new timbre of tolling bells and double reeds (Ex. 5.8(a/i)). Yet just as section E re-entered the symphonic discourse abandoned at the end of D, so too section F establishes elliptical links with these predecessors while maintaining its particular autonomy; once again the instrumental voice is discernible beneath a metamorphosis of identity.

These connections are made on several levels: often through structural details (which will be examined presently), but also through the section's global formal function. For if section E represented a development of preceding material, then F functions as a kind of coda, grounding much of the previous dramatic momentum, and emitting strong closural signals (even if the eventual ending adds yet a further twist). Technically these things are achieved by the slower pace, and by the refrain (Ex. 5.8(a/i)) which creates unprecedented tonal stability. This is established in a progression through three sonorities, labelled K, L and M in Example 5.8(b): a pandiatonic B major hexachord with shades of D♯ minor, leading to an 'other' hexachord (more closely aligned to B♭ major, less overtly diatonic, and hence less stable), and returning to a slightly differently formulated B major/D♯ minor hexachord.[73] (The progression as a whole could be heard as functionally analogous[74] to a tonic–dominant–tonic progression in classical tonality.) Closer analysis of these sonorities reveals connections with those of the Symphony 4 quotation from the preceding section (cf. Ex. 5.7). For example, the first hexachord, K, contains two interlocking Z′ sonorities,

Example 5.8. Significant harmonic configurations in *The Mask of Time*. At (a/i): refrain progression from section F of 'The triumph of Life'. At (a/ii): final chord of 'The triumph of Life'. At (a/iii): final moments of 'The singing will never be done'. At (b): set-class analysis of chords and their interrelations.

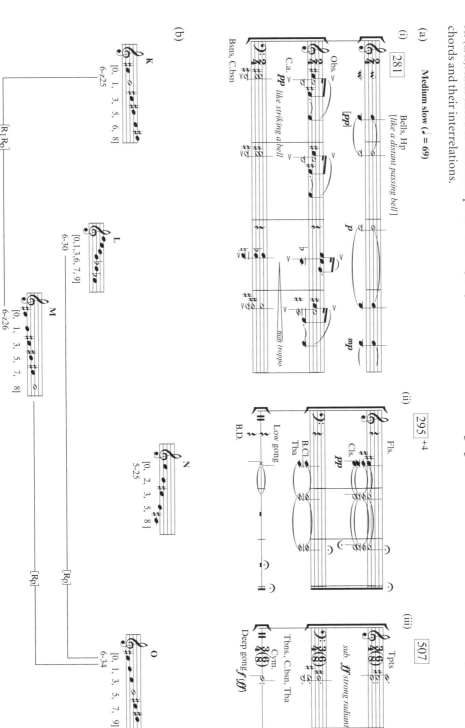

B–F♯–A♯–C♯ and E–B–D♯–F♯, and may therefore be seen as a developed form of chord B. Its total interval content is also identical to that of chord C,[75] but at the same time its pandiatonic pitch content exercises a strong assimilative power over the dissonant intervallic elements; so, for example, the tritone A♯–E is synthesized within the B major context.

This chordal refrain also marks the resolution of a further line of continuity. The dyad F♯–A – first pertinent in the tenor recitative (Ex. 5.1(a)), and then brought into conflicted association with the pitches D♯ and A♯ in section D (Ex. 5.3(a/i)) – now resolves those tensions by 'modulating' to the dyad F♯–A♯ within the collection K (Ex. 5.8(a/i), (b)), thus rendering itself consonant with D♯ and the surrounding diatonic B major context.

These salient autonomous musical connections, then, suggest the continuing presence of that trace of centring subjectivity we have dubbed the instrumental voice. The importance of this stratum, let us recall, is that it counters the opposite tendency in *The Mask of Time* towards a plurality of voices, and towards the rapid heterogeneity of imagery whose archetype might be found in the markedly less transcendentally aspirant medium of television. It is in 'The triumph of Life' that these centripetal and centrifugal tendencies find their most effective equilibrium in the piece as a whole (with the former most strongly in evidence in sections D–F, the latter in sections A–C, but each tendency always to some degree mediated by the other); and for this reason that I have sought to detail the process at some length in the foregoing. The stratum of autonomous musical signification extends beyond the movement itself; I will presently argue that the instrumental voice resumes in its most potent guise in the final movement, 'The singing will never be done', thus identifying itself with, and becoming integral to, the work's peroration.

But meanwhile the ending of 'The triumph of Life' is altogether more ambiguous. Its own final chord, N (see Ex. 5.8(a/ii)), on the one hand suggests a measure of relatedness to other sonorities associated with the instrumental voice. Its treble and bass pitches, F♯ and A, evoke a dyad whose autonomous musical significance we have already detailed; moreover, the three pitches, F♯, C♯ and E, are also present in chord K, so definitive for this closing section. Additionally, the bass elements of the chord, A and E, are also those in the bass of chord A which generates the sequence of the Symphony 4 quotation (Figs. 263, 264, 266, 267, and 270; cf. Ex. 5.7). On the other hand, chord N sounds new, its synthesis of timbre, pitch, dynamics and articulation, distancing it radically from what has gone before. The mysterious presence it evokes comes as close as anything in the movement (indeed the entire work) to a 'narrating voice' as defined by

Abbate.[76] From its detached position outside the rest of the proceedings, this sonority seems to be an enigmatic comment on the movement. Sphinx-like, it suggests knowledge gained from the assimilation of previous elements – perhaps a clue to Shelley's unanswered question 'What is Life?' Yet, disengaged from the previous struggles, it seems resolutely disinclined to speak.

III

Human values and the separation of spheres

'What *can* we now praise, what can we affirm?'[77] While the tactics of heteroglossia in *The Mask of Time* (and in 'The triumph of Life' in particular) imply that Tippett is chary about proffering any unequivocal, or unironized, answer to his own question, the developing autonomous musical stratum (and the model of unified subjectivity it connotes) suggests the intention to attempt some form of resolution to these questions from a univocal standpoint. This matter at the heart of *The Mask of Time* is also a central problem of Western modernity, and on a related tack Tippett states that 'throughout the work . . . we are confronted in varying degrees with the polarity between knowledge of the kind obtained through intellectual processes (the knowledge of scientists) and that obtained from deep inner sensibilities (the knowledge of creative artists)'.[78] Thus the question of what, in our own time, we might affirm – of what values we might hold, and how we might come to hold them – articulates a third sphere of enquiry in addition to these other two.

By common critical consensus the condition of modernity is defined by exactly this partitioning of our understanding of the rational, moral and sensual into autonomous – and thus separated – realms.[79] It is this situation and its corollaries that *The Mask of Time* addresses, and in this Tippett places himself in a discursive enterprise that goes back to the late eighteenth century, the moment of the critical philosophical project of Kant. The achievement of Kant's three critiques – *The Critique of Pure Reason* (1781, 2nd edn 1787), *The Critique of Practical Reason* (1788) and *The Critique of Judgement* (1790) – was to have attempted to marry these three separate spheres into a single, systematic body of philosophical enquiry, while none the less acknowledging their different theoretical presuppositions and requirements. That Kant's attempt to find a resolution to the situation brings with it an even more acute awareness of its irresolvability only underlines what is of continuing relevance in his account.[80] And I argue here that even though Tippett may have only had passing or informal knowledge of Kant's philosophy,[81] it offers a pattern of thought

through which to draw out more fully the implications of *The Mask of Time*. This is emphatically not to say that Tippett draws (or intuits) the same conclusions as Kant, but that he addresses the same problem with just as strong a sense of its acuteness; moreover, like Kant, he desires to ascribe to ethical values some kind of transcendent, universal status – 'One humanity; one justice', as he would later put it in *New Year* (1986–8).

My eventual concern will be to investigate the tenth and final movement of *The Mask of Time*, in the light of Kant's account of the sublime. What prompts this cross-interrogation is the music's intimation of infinity (eternity is implicit in its title, 'The singing will never be done') and terrible immensity (its final gesture suggests an image of what is 'absolutely great'). But to grasp the full implications of this connection – which will, I hope, show just how meaningful are the resonances of a few sounds – we need to get a fuller sense of how and why the sublime belongs in Kant's philosophical enterprise.

Excursus: Kant, Tippett, and the aporia of reason

In the cosmic magnitude of 'The singing will never be done' (and indeed of *The Mask of Time* as a whole) and in its image of humanity at the intersection of empirical being and transcendent values, Tippett envisions a situation not so far from one of Kant's most famous pronouncements, from *The Critique of Practical Reason*:

> Two things fill the mind with ever new and increasing admiration and awe . . .: *the starry heaven above me and the moral law within me* . . . The first begins at the place which I occupy in the external world of sense, and broadens the connection in which I stand into the unsurveyable magnitude of worlds beyond worlds . . . The second begins at my invisible self, my personality, and depicts me in a world which has true infinity.[82]

While what Tippett affirms is something less specifically defined than Kant's 'moral law', what is nevertheless germane (indeed sublime) in this passage is the implication of an alignment between 'the external world of sense' (that is, the empirical world) and the world of an 'invisible' (and, Kant implies, inner) self which is above the sensible. This corresponds to a dualism running through Kant's critical philosophy as a whole: between the world as phenomenon – given to us as appearance, through the senses – and the world as noumenon – the world as it is 'in itself', a supersensible, empirically unknowable domain, to which we nevertheless belong, as beings in the world, as much as we do to empirical reality. Tippett's view of the totality of things bears striking similarities. He too posits a dualism between the 'outer' reality of the empirical world, and an 'inner' reality

resting on something ultimately ineffable (though in his case not necessarily extending beyond the mind itself). But also significant is the fact that Kant implies that an alignment between the phenomenal and noumenal can be brought about through a contemplation of the former through a mode whose character is *aesthetic* (his attitude towards the stars in this context is not that of the astronomer). On a parallel tack, Tippett places at the centre of his artistic practice the aesthetic notion of the *image* (in his case musical), which serves as a mediating vehicle between 'outer' and 'inner' worlds. For Kant, as for Tippett, the aesthetic holds out the possibility of bridging the gap between the empirical and the transcendent, the phenomenal and noumenal. But the success of the prospect is not guaranteed, precisely because of the profoundly problematic nature of the gap. To grasp this fully we need to take a few steps back.

For Kant morality has its source not in divine revelation or in the negotiation of what is socially desirable but in pure reason itself (that is, it exists *a priori* – as something logically necessary, not merely something empirically observed in the world). This is because, according to the categorical imperative, one should 'act only on that maxim through which [one] can at the same time will that it should become a universal law'.[83] To act immorally is irrational because if such action were to become a universal law its purpose would become self-contradictory. If we follow it, the moral law, because it has a supersensible, *a priori* basis, places us above subjection to empirical nature and therefore underwrites our freedom. However, this same supersensible status means that pure practical reason (morality) cannot empirically legislate for happiness.

In his 'canon of pure reason' Kant asserts that everyone may reasonably 'hope for happiness in the measure in which he has rendered himself by his conduct worthy of it'.[84] And the 'ideal of the highest good' is that whereby the worthiness to be happy and actual happiness coincide. However, the principles of practical reason 'cannot give rise to laws of nature': they assert only what *can* or *ought* to be; they cannot causally bring it about. 'Owing to . . . all the special difficulties to which morality is exposed (weakness or depravity of human nature), this [moral] world is so far thought as an intelligible world only . . . a mere idea'.[85] We are thus once again brought up against the experience of diremption: there is a gap between things as they ought to be (the intelligible world), and things as they actually are (the sensible, i.e. empirical, world).

'The alleged *necessary connection* of the hope of happiness with the necessary endeavour to render the self worthy of happiness cannot therefore be known through reason':[86] Kant's sober tone belies his having grasped the utter poignancy of this, our human predicament. It is not simply an

empirical misfortune – a sad fact that things just do not happen to work out the way they should – but a philosophical aporia. Reason, the very structure which requires worthiness to be happy, cannot through the same structure deliver actual happiness. This is what is really at stake in the question 'what *can* we now praise, what can we affirm?' The recognition that values can have no necessary connection with the empirical world risks instituting despair as a philosophical principle. Despair is the nemesis which silently stalks Kant's attempt to posit transcendent values.[87] Despair is given voice in *The Mask of Time*'s threnody, 'Hiroshima, mon amour'. Despair is projected phantasmagorically in the imagery of 'The triumph of Life'. Affirmation and despair are dialectically locked together.

It is within just such a dialectical sphere that Tippett's post-*Priam* period moves. Its poles correspond to positions also identified by Kant in terms of theology and atheism – a discourse which is far from absent in Tippett's *œuvre*, even if the conclusions are not identical. Moreover, for both figures this issue is co-ordinated with a debate about nature – albeit again with different outcomes.

The theological turn is Kant's own striking response to the aporia of the separation of spheres. On his own account this is far from an irrational appeal to a *deus ex machina* to bail him out of a tricky situation. On the contrary, God is a logically necessary postulate of that very intelligible world which is the rational pattern for our moral action in the sensible world:

> Morality, by itself, constitutes a system. Happiness, however, does not do so, save in so far as it is distributed in exact proportion to morality. But this is possible only in the intelligible world, under a wise Author and Ruler. Such a Ruler, together with life in such a world, which we must regard as a future world, reason finds itself constrained to assume; otherwise it would have to regard the moral laws as empty figments of the brain, since without this postulate the necessary consequence which it itself connects with these laws could not follow.[88]

Kant's postulation of the divine here, let us repeat, is not a positive act of faith. It is the negation of a negative: it is projected out of the need to refute the claim of 'moral laws as empty figments of the brain' – a claim whose vindication would imperil his entire critical edifice. Having deduced this divine, unifying piece of the jigsaw, then, Kant draws several corollaries. Among them is the deferral of the actualization of the morally intelligible world into the future – on which basis he postulates the immortality of the soul.[89] Additionally, nature may now be posited as 'the purposive unity of all things'.[90] But this is nature understood not as we encounter it in the phenomenal world, but as a noumenal nature, 'a nature-in-itself (which

exists in the idea of reason)',[91] through which the amoral wilderness of empirical nature can be reconceived as purposive, and therefore meaning-ful – because contained within it are beings whose moral actions can now be grounded as entirely rational.

As we have observed earlier, *The Mask of Time* wrestles with both these figurations of nature, and in 'Jungle' Tippett leaves us – as does Dillard – with a sense of undecidability between them. At this stage in the proceed-ings, then, he is, as it were, agnostic on Kant. But in 'Dream of the paradise garden' the ironizing stance towards 'the pure inviolate deity', 'far, far beyond the stars' suggests a less than sympathetic disposition towards Kant's kind of transcendental theology. Justifiably enough, perhaps: for Kant's institution of the divine does not solve the problem of the separa-tion of spheres; it only intensifies it. As he himself admits, these things remain 'ideas of reason', that is, *a priori* constructs with no necessary con-nection with the empirical world.[92] The persuasiveness of his argument is ultimately staked on its formal perfection; but the move that was meant to foreshorten the gap between material and ideal domains in fact only pushes them further apart. The last pages of Kant's third critique relent-lessly pursue the possibility that the divine might be something cognizable within empirical nature, and repeatedly return to the conclusion that it pertains to the supersensible world of practical reason only.[93] The unified logic promised by theism threatens to split into the dialogics of agnosti-cism. *Sotto voce*, despair still speaks behind the voice of theological affir-mation intended to eradicate it.

By contrast, the atheistic construction of the dialectic of affirmation and despair looks unflinchingly into the abyss between the (only intelligible) moral world and the (actually sensible) empirical world. Stoically, it affirms virtue, but has no expectation of a necessary justice – in this world or any other; it declines to construct a theology out of the aporia. Kant's model for such a position is Spinoza, whose case he describes in Part II of *The Critique of Judgement*:

> A righteous man, such, say, as Spinoza, who considers himself firmly persuaded that there is no God . . . may, it is true, expect to find a chance concurrence [between the moral law he reveres and the establishment of good] now and again, but he can never expect to find in nature a uniform agreement . . . Deceit, violence, and envy will always be rife around him, although he himself is honest, peaceable, and benevolent; and the other righteous men that he meets in the world, no matter how deserving they may be of happiness, will be subjected by nature, which takes no heed of such deserts, to all the evils of want, disease, and untimely death . . . And so it will continue to be until one wide grave engulfs them all – just and unjust, there

is no distinction in the grave – and hurls them back into the abyss of the aimless chaos of matter from which they were taken.[94]

Here, then, supersensible and sensible worlds are held as resolutely auton-omous, desperately separate. Kant finds such a stance untenable – irra-tional; but perhaps because it only makes explicit the aporia which is still unreconciled in his own argument.

What also contrasts significantly in the atheistic account is its vision of nature: phenomenal only, emphatically unharmonized with any human virtues posited against it; barbaric, amoral. This view comes very close to what the later Nietzsche meant by 'the naturalization of the human' and 'the humanization of nature': the positing of humanity as part of a de-metaphysicized nature.[95] It is not difficult to see why Nietzsche, who saw such a disenchanted world as potentially liberating, distanced himself so aggressively from Kant, just as Kant could not identify with the Spinozan scenario he outlines. What this scenario seems inadvertently to describe – something very close to Nietzsche's heart – is the aesthetic of tragedy. As George Steiner puts it, 'tragic drama tells us that the spheres of reason, order, and justice are terribly limited . . . Call it what you will: a hidden or malevolent God, blind fate, the solicitations of hell, or the brute fury of our animal blood. It waits for us in ambush at the crossroads. It mocks us and destroys us . . . It is a terrible, stark insight into human life.'[96]

It is to this darker pole that Tippett migrates in his second period. Whereas in the comedy of *The Midsummer Marriage* (1946–52) human wholeness is mirrored in an enchanted nature – in a manner not totally unrelated to Kant's vision – so now in the tragedy of *King Priam* (1958–61) the human protagonist's attempt to act morally is shown to have no con-nection with the natural order of things – in a manner close to Kant's account of Spinoza. Tippett's post-*Priam* period contains a greater, more consistent readiness to contemplate despair, as the next two operas, *The Knot Garden* (1966–9) and *The Ice Break*, testify; and it is little wonder that his formerly cohesive language now becomes 'a music / Compounded of our groans and shrieks'.

And yet, for all that Tippett (on our behalf) faces up to despair this is not his final position. Nor can it be. For just as despair is the unsung counter-point to Kant's would-be affirmative position,[97] so affirmation lies dormant in the stoic's attempt to deny it. This is the inconsistency which Kant sensed in Spinoza. To sustain some notion of moral worth in the face of an indifferent nature is to posit some thing, some generalizable princi-ple extrapolable from human experience, not itself inherent in nature, supersensible. What remains dialectical here – indeed negatively so – is the

intimation that it is those forces external and inimical to humanity that draw out this awareness from within human consciousness. As Adorno puts it in his *Negative Dialectics*, 'Grayness could not fill us with despair if our minds did not harbor the concept of different colors, scattered traces of which are not absent from the negative whole'.[98] Tippett grants Priam, at the point where all is lost, some visionary moment against the negative whole that is the opera's final situation. In *The Knot Garden* Thea and Faber resolve to 'submit to love' after the unrelenting exploration of their antagonisms. And at the end of *The Ice Break* the re-nascence of humanity is presented as a possible metaphysical principle emerging from a conflicted and bloody materiality – as captured in the final quotation from Goethe's *Wilhelm Meister*: 'Yet you will always be brought forth again, glorious image of God, and likewise be maimed, wounded afresh, from within or without'.

Tippett's position in relation to the Kantian aporia can now begin to be discerned; the issue is not only how the composer defines that position, but also the fact that in formulating it he enters a discourse that is key to the cultural history of Western modernity. His stance implicitly contains a critique both of Kant and of Spinoza as criticized by Kant. He spurns the notions of the sensible and supersensible as absolutely autonomous principles that have no bearing on each other, but at the same time suggests that the convergence or interaction between them will not necessarily be concordant. The 'glorious image of God' is not synonymous, then, with a supreme principle of reason that reveals the entire order of nature as harmoniously purposive.

The sublime in Kant and Tippett

In Tippett's second period the hard-won ground for transcendent values is envisioned in encounters with the sensible world that are simultaneously abrasive and sublime. These twin epithets describe the point of divergence from and convergence with Kant. The sublime is key for Kant (as is the domain of the aesthetic, of which it forms a part) because it demonstrates analogically how our supersensible ideas of morality can be grounded in the sensible world. (Analogues are not proofs, of course, but this strategy is as close as Kant is able to get; again the harmoniousness between all the parts of his system is crucial to his rhetoric.) The Kantian sublime contains radical potential. Its notion of a heightened awareness of pure, supersensible reason triggered by what is overwhelming or threatening in nature implies a metaphysics founded on something material. To adapt a remark made by Adorno in another (by no means

unrelated) context, these elements 'require only the most minute displacement into a new constellation to find their right position'.[99] I will
argue that Tippett, especially in the closing minutes of *The Mask of Time*,
makes just such a displacement, refiguring the Kantian model into a
vision of sublimity congruent with a modernist world view. In exploring
these matters I will first sketch out the sublime as it is discussed by Kant,
then consider how the last movement of *The Mask of Time* presents a
version of these ideas, and finally examine how in doing so it achieves a
meaningful realignment of them.

For Kant the sublime is a state of delight which arises under particular
conditions of duress in our relationship with nature. (Although nature
holds the privileged position he also recognizes human artefacts as a possible source of the sublime; his examples include St Peter's in Rome, the
pyramids and, significantly, 'the well-known inscription on the Temple of
Isis (Mother *Nature*): "I am all that is, and that was, and that shall be, and
no mortal hath raised the veil from before my face"' – a version of which is
also sung by the character Sosostris at a climactic moment of her aria in
Tippett's *The Midsummer Marriage*.[100]) Kant portrays this ambivalent
emotional interplay as a drama played out between the discrete parts of
our mental apparatus (or 'faculties', to use his eighteenth-century notion).
He identifies two versions of the sublime, the mathematical and the
dynamical, and I shall briefly discuss these in turn, given that both are relevant to *The Mask of Time*.

The mathematical sublime, 'the name given to what is *absolutely
great*',[101] comes about when an object is so vast that we cannot comprehend it aesthetically in a single intuition. To be sure, measuring a moun-
tain or distances to the stars in mathematical units makes magnitude
tractable through numerical concepts (through the faculty which Kant
terms 'understanding'), but this does not help our imagination to make a
mental representation of that greatness as it is given to us sensorily. And
while the imagination can represent individual parts of the phenomenon
(as 'apprehensions'), it cannot grasp the phenomenon as one totality (as a
'comprehension'). But then comes the paradoxical turn, the sublime
moment. The very defeat we suffer in our attempt to comprehend an
object of the sensible world makes us aware of the higher faculty which
drives that attempt, our faculty of reason; we are made 'alive to the feeling
of this supersensible side of our being'.[102]

This is a mind-stretching thought. Kant seems to be saying that in our
failure to get our minds around the total magnitude of an object being presented to us in the sensory here and now we are nevertheless woken up to
the fact that somewhere else in our minds is an idea (an 'idea of reason' in

the strict Kantian sense) of what it is we haven't grasped. And so we grasp infinity as a pure, negative idea. The (phenomenal) 'nature beyond our reach' elicits a feeling of a (noumenal) dimension in ourselves which is non-sensory and non-temporal, a dimension which is above nature.

The role that Kant assigns to the sublime in his critical system now becomes clear. The sublime is analogical evidence of a connection between the sensible world and the intelligible (or supersensible) world. The experience of the supersensible to which it gives rise is of the same order as other ideas of reason, especially, morality. As he puts it, 'a feeling for the sublime in nature is hardly thinkable unless in association with an attitude of the mind resembling the moral'.[103] Each of the terms of this parallel speaks as it were for the necessary place of the other in the Kantian scheme.

The same parallel between aesthetic and moral ideas is invoked by dynamical sublime, which is engendered when we are confronted with what is threatening in nature (e.g. 'thunderclouds piled up the vault of heaven, borne along with flashes and peals, volcanoes in all their violence of destruction'[104]) but from a position of safety. This allows us to contemplate the irresistible might of nature, and 'forces upon us the recognition of our physical helplessness as beings of nature, but at the same time reveals a faculty of estimating ourselves as independent of nature, and discovers a pre-eminence above nature that is the foundation of a self-preservation of quite another kind'.[105] In other words, under the imagined threat of nature we are also able to imagine ourselves positing against it some quality that is of ourselves but not of the empirical world, and this again reminds us of a supersensible, moral dimension to ourselves which is not subject to nature's dominion.

Although Tippett's own writings about art and discussions of his own music do not name the sublime, it certainly features in his œuvre, even if, as implied above, the moral to be drawn from it is by no means identical to that found in Kant. The dynamical sublime is figured for example in Priam's darkly visionary glimpse of the abyss, in the monstrous cracking of the ice that heralds Spring in *The Ice Break* (see Ex. 2.3, above), and in Jo Ann's final resolve to face the socially intractable 'Terror Town' in *New Year*. And similarly, adumbrations of the final sublime moment of *The Mask of Time* are discernible within earlier stages of the work itself. Some of these have already been mentioned, for example the images of the infinite projected through the higher consonances associated with the words 'sound', 'resounding' and 'space'. Perhaps the most dramatic connection comes in 'The triumph of Life', where the sublime is the tenor not only of the chariot scene, but also of the encounter between the poet and nature that follows in the storm scene. In his image of the poet, 'the tall black

figure at the prow', Tippett invokes a topos of 'the artist in the storm' which has a history extending back through the nineteenth and later eighteenth centuries – for example, the legendary story of the marine painter Joseph Vernet (1714–89) who had himself tied to a ship's mast during a storm so as better to study its sublime effect; which scene was itself the subject of a painting of 1822 by his son, Horace.[106] Steven Levine traces the cultural lineage of this topos through Kant and Schopenhauer to the Freudian death instinct, or *Thanatos*: 'In Diderot's self-annihilation, Kant's self-consciousness, and Schopenhauer's contemplation; in Vernet's *ravissement* and Monet's *jouissance*, we find the sea offering the opportunity for displacement and discharge of the desire to return from the tremors of life to the inviting tranquillity of death'.[107]

The path from philosophical to aesthetic to psychoanalytical formations of the sublime is important here, given the role played by Jung (for whom Kant, Schopenhauer and Freud were seminal) in the shaping of Tippett's aesthetic views. However, while Tippett certainly does not shy from linking the sublime with death (as his Shelleyan parable makes plain), the message he presents is not that of the Nirvana principle. Albeit less ambiguously than the poet's narrative in 'The triumph of Life', Tippett's depiction of Shelley in the storm scene seeks not to figure death as a source of 'inviting tranquillity' – a release from the will or our unconscious drives – but rather to present it as inflaming our instinctual desire for life in the face of what threatens to extinguish it. In this sense at least, Tippett is closer to the Kantian sublime. But of course the various layers of irony in this movement also infuse this would-be affirmative sublime with a measure of the darker ambiguity of Shelley's poem. The elusive final chord is in effect a question mark over the attempt to posit something meaningful in the encounter with the violent forces of nature. In this final equivocation lurks the atheistic suspicion of any imputed connection between the inner and outer spheres of our existence. In other words, Tippett's stance towards the sublime in this movement is double-voiced. However, his aim in the work's climactic final movement, I would argue, is to bring these voices closer to speaking in unison: simultaneously to affirm some form of epiphany, while maintaining that necessary principle of doubt that prevents the swerve into the realm of theological idealism.

'The singing will never be done'

As if to make it clear where he stands on transcendental theology, Tippett prefaces his peroration – in the last of the preceding 'Three songs' – with a quotation from Mary Renault's *The Mask of Apollo*: 'O man, make peace

with your mortality, for this too is God'. These words borrowed from a less than high-brow novel are made to work much harder in this new context, with its far more ambitious aesthetic and philosophical aspirations. The words are apposite because, on the one hand, they are implicated in the sublime – the lines which precede the text describe a young actor gaping in contemplation of a giant statue of the god Zeus ('my eye, / travelling upward, / met the face of power'); and because, on the other hand, the message from 'the face of power' is an exhortation to reconcile ourselves, in our search for the divine, to our own existential finitude.

At this stage, then, Tippett continues to sing an ambivalent song. Its affirmative strain is captured in the sustained, diatonically ordered melodic line to which he sets Renault's epigraph, and the full singing style it dictates (Ex. 5.9(b)). As bit by bit the whole text is revealed (Tippett's way of boosting its impact and import) the final sound of each instalment is echoed, and, so to speak, contemplated by the semi-chorus. (The braces beneath Ex. 5.9 show the extent of the melodic line given on each successive statement; the echoed sonorities are enclosed.) It is here that the ambivalences literally sing out. While eventually these captured sounds – savoured precisely for their sonic properties – present diatonically stable thirds, the interval initially favoured is a diatonically inimical semitone. Reinforcing this resistance to monological affirmation is the dancing counterpoint of the trumpets and trombones (Ex. 5.9(a)). Although the anhemitonic basis of this ostinato-style figuration (which draws exclusively from the whole-tone scale starting on B♭/A♯) is partly mirrored in the vocal lines, its staccato articulation doggedly refuses to assimilate to the collectivity represented by the sustained choral sound.

For all that a dissenting, ironizing voice can still be heard amidst the would-be affirmative sentiments, the latter still achieve relatively greater ascendancy than in 'The triumph of Life'. Indeed, this might have been where the barometer had been left set had Tippett gone through with his original plan to end the work with Renault's words. As we now know, however, Tippett was urged by Meirion Bowen to add a further movement,[108] and the unenvisaged outcome certainly takes the work on to another plane. In a wordless chorus Tippett now carries through many of the implications from earlier in the work – a vision of the infinite over which Renault's words hover like an after-image. As Bowen points out, this passage has a harmonic connection with the 'Sound' chord from the beginning of the work,[109] but it is also a fulfilment of all the previous intimations of the sublime, bringing these to a moment recognizable as transcendent. This is to say that the movement recognizably *enacts* the sublime, even if it can be left to the individual to decide whether he/she

Example 5.9. 'Three songs', iii: 'O man make peace with your mortality' (Fig. 491ff.): vocal line and trumpet–trombone countermelody (dynamics omitted; orchestral doublings not indicated).

chooses to apply the epithet to their experience. And just as Kant describes the sublime as comprising more than one moment, so Tippett's performance of it is a process involving more than one phase.

The first and longest part of the movement invokes the mathematical sublime in that it presents an object (in sound) whose temporal extension cannot be comprehended in a single intuition. Careful measurement is responsible for this image of the measureless. The musical texture is built

Example 5.10. 'The singing will never be done' (Fig. 498ff.): component strata (dynamics, articulation and phrase marks omitted; material rebarred); analysis of pitch and interval content.

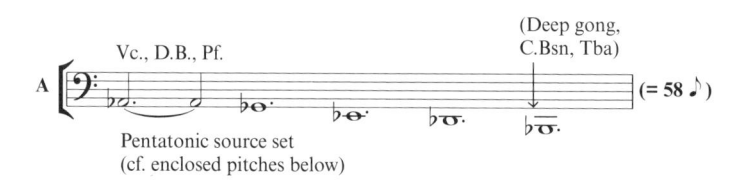

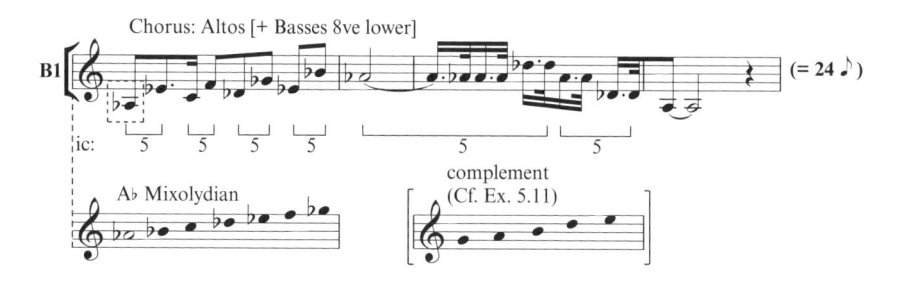

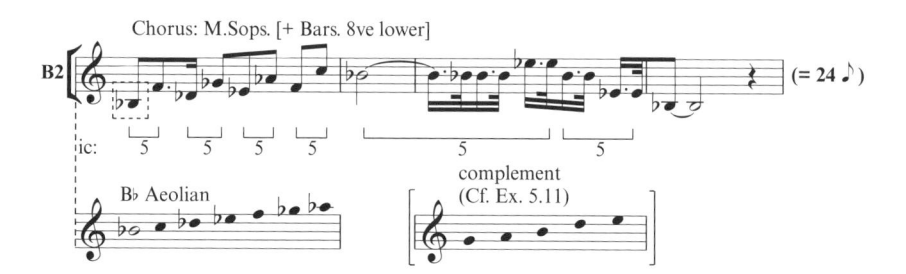

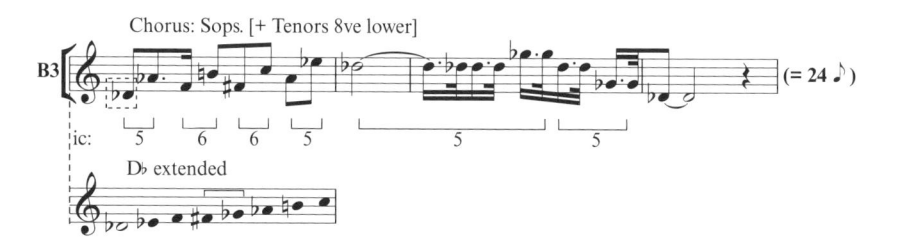

Example 5.10 (*cont.*)

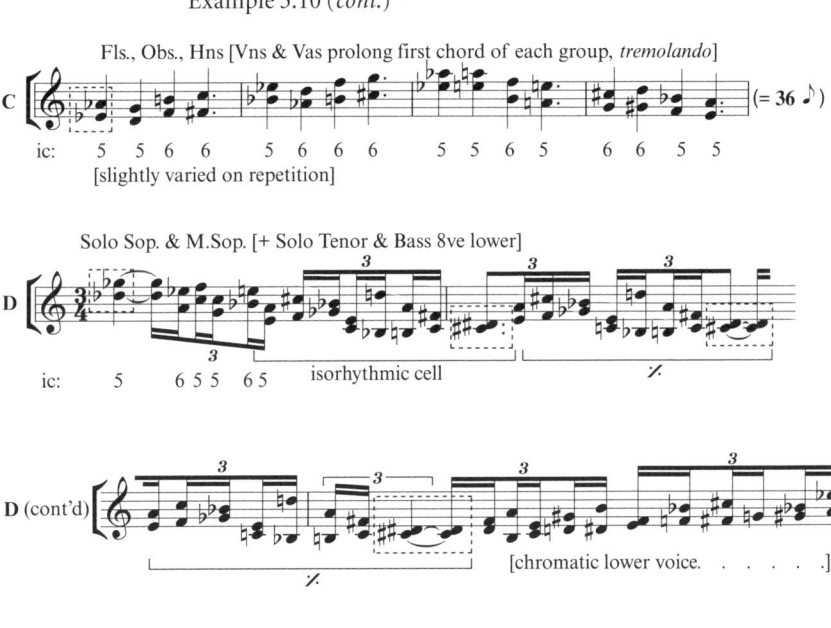

from ostinati (quoted discretely in Ex. 5.10) fixed at differing lengths (namely 58, 24, 36 and 30 quavers), whose superimposition is such that it would take an inordinately long time for any given alignment to be repeated. Thus we are offered a phenomenon whose scale, though not literally infinite, may as well be, rhetorically speaking. And beyond this durational metric the content of the material is itself structured in such a way as to prompt an experience of the sublime. This too involves a dialectic between what can and cannot be measured, between what is and is not rationally tractable. At one extreme lies the ostinato in the bass instruments – stratum A of Example 5.10 – whose structural premise is quite clearly identifiable and leaves no remainder; this is the anhemitonic pentatonic scale, formed from the pitch classes Ab–Gb–Eb–Db–Bb. At the other extreme, the ecstatic *jubilus* in the solo voices – stratum D of Example 5.10 – betrays no such singular principle of organization, nor can all the elements be rationally accounted for. On the one hand there are discernible paradigms at work: for example the predilection for interval classes 5 and 6 at the beginning and end of the figure, the references back to the pentatonic

set of stratum A made by the notes of longer duration (enclosed), the iso-rhythmic treatment in the middle of the figure, and the chromatic ascent in the lower voice which follows it. On the other hand these principles are beset by indeterminacy (for example, the free handling of the upper voice's counterpoint to the ascending chromatic element); moreover there is no larger principle into which they are all subsumed; they remain a motley set of devices. The extremes of susceptibility and resistance to rational order found respectively in strata A and D means they ought to sound strongly differentiated; but in fact the remaining layers interposed between them registrally also serve to mediate their differences, thereby encouraging the listener to perceive the texture as a totality. These are likewise shown in Example 5.10, and crucial in the process is the subdivision of stratum B (for the choral voices) into three, allowing for a very gradual shading of one set of structural premises into the next. Hence stratum B1 (for altos and basses) embraces the pentatonic content of stratum A, but adds the pitch classes C and F to form a diatonic set readable as A♭ Mixolydian. Each successive pair of pitch classes within the phrase yields the interval class 5 (the perfect fifth or its inversional equivalent, the perfect fourth) – shown by braces beneath the example. And both this feature and the aggregated pitches are carried up to the next stratum, B2 (for mezzo-sopranos and baritones) – only now the latter are arranged so as to suggest B♭ Aeolian. (In passing we should note that the initial pitches of each stratum draw from the generative pentatonic collection of stratum A, and can indeed be seen as a projection of it vertically.) Stratum B3 (for sopranos and tenors) uses a closely related melodic form to its progenitors, but now beginning on D♭, and inflecting the original diatonic set to include B♮, which causes interval class 6 (the tritone) to be admitted into the sequence of pairs of melody notes (again see the braces beneath the example). This mixture of interval classes 5 and 6 then becomes the essential principle of stratum C (wind), which eschews tonal and diatonic aspirations altogether (it is in fact an extension, encompassing all twelve pitch classes, of one of the ostinati accompanying the work's recurring 'Sound' chord – just as the pentatonic set of stratum A is an expansion of the unchanging quartal set underpinning the same sonority). Finally we reach stratum D, which begins and ends with an unstructured pattern of dyads based on interval classes 5 and 6, but otherwise releases itself from such constraints to draw from the full set of chromatic and intervallic possibilities. Thus it is clear that each stratum belongs to the totality through the mediation of its most closely related neighbours – a metaphor perhaps for a universe in which everything relates to everything else. Nor is this judgement undermined by the fact that what is discernible analytically (through concepts of the understanding, in

Kantian parlance) is unavailable to us aesthetically, that is, in perception (for our cognition of this texture as a sensuous object is unlikely to be in terms of the quanta and data of its rationalized aspects). As Kant points out, numerical concepts do not feature in the experience of sublime; what matters is our attempt to comprehend the object in terms of its sensory appearance. We must approach it 'as the poets do, according to what the impression upon the eye reveals'; 'if we call the sight of the starry heaven *sublime*, we must not found our estimate of it upon any concepts of worlds inhabited by rational beings, with the bright spots . . . as their suns moving in orbits prescribed for them with the wisest regard to ends [i.e. in Newtonian fashion]. But we must take it, just as it strikes the eye, as a broad and all-embracing canopy.'[110] By analogy, then, what strikes the ear in 'The singing will never be done' is the sound of manifold voices – no longer Shelley's multitude 'numerous as gnats', but voices whose diversity is assumed in solidarity, whose celebrative enthusiasm is no longer destabilized by bathos or irony, but is measured in recognition of the environment in which they sing, namely an unbounded world in which dissonance has its place as much as consonance; in which movement is perpetual; in which a seemingly endless process of ascent takes place against a background of latent, morally unconditioned power.

   Like an irruption the latent bursts forth, and an image of the sublime moment presents itself – an image whose emotional correlative is an entirely appropriate mix of terror and elation (see Ex. 5.11(a)). To describe the temporal (dis)connection between this moment and the previous passage with the adverb 'then' would be fundamentally misleading. More accurately the new gesture both displaces and assumes what precedes – on the one hand by reversing the polarity of prominent pitches, and on the other by compressing the material. The reversal of pitch prominence is effected by the collection E–B–G–A aggregated from the choral and vocal parts at the beginning of the new figure (enclosed in Ex. 5.11(a)) – which is part of the complement of the A♭ Mixolydian/B♭ Dorian collection that governed strata B1 and B2 in the previous material (only the D is missing from that collection's 'other', and this will soon make its presence felt). Compression comes about through concentration on particular aspects of the vocal material. The choral stratum, B, now presented in only one guise (B′: see Ex. 5.11(a)) rather than three, confines itself to the headmotif of its former version; while the soloists' stratum D (now D′) is determined exclusively by the semiquaver triplet element from the previous figuration. Moreover, the instrumental strata against which the vocalists previously sang are now condensed into a 'strong, radiant' higher consonance (labelled O in Ex. 5.11) in which brass predominate. This sonority alternates with a second version of

Example 5.11. At (a): 'The singing will never be done': final gesture. At (b): analysis of chords O and P.

itself (chord P, Ex. 5.11) which additionally absorbs a layer of astringent dissonance (including the 'missing' pitch class D from the complementation process described previously), and which momentarily displaces the chorus. The two sonorities could oscillate infinitely, one feels, though in fact the pattern is soon broken off abruptly – or rather, supplanted by silence.

These sonorities can be analysed a number of ways. Example 5.11(b/ii) shows, for example, the strong whole-tone colouring of chord O. On the other hand, part (b/iii) of this example shows how the same chord can be understood as a notional chain of thirds (two major alternating with two minor), whose extension yields chord P (except for the pitch class D

belonging to the complementation process). This can also be seen to contain all four triadic forms – major, minor, diminished and augmented – which can be empirically sensed as the welter of quasi-triadic sound that constitutes chord O, and which is also mirrored in the linear construction of stratum B′ in the chorus (see Ex. 5.11(b/i)). Further significance accrues to chord O through its relation to sonorities essential to the refrain of the final section of 'The triumph of Life'. Perhaps the most obvious connection here is that of B major, expressed by the root and lower elements of O and by the pandiatonic chords K and M of the refrain progression – cf. Example 5.8(i) and (iii). Further relationships come to light when the sonorities are analysed as pitch-class sets (see Ex. 5.8(b)). Chord O, set class 6-34 ($[0,1,3,5,7,9]$), bears maximum similarity (the relationship R_1 in Forte's nomenclature) to both chords L and M of the refrain progression: set classes 6-30 ($[0,1,3,6,7,9]$) and 6-z26 ($[0,1,3,5,7,8]$).

Whatever the minutiae of the cross-relationships, the larger point conveyed in the final moments of *The Mask of Time* has to do with the apotheosis of the ironic conditions found in previous movements such as 'The triumph of Life'. Irony is still given its due, as the dissonant accretions of chord P make clear; but the sublime, previously only glimpsed, is now seized and is momentarily all-present. In voicing the sublime these final sounds tap into a key discourse of modernity just as Kant's account did two hundred years before. It is these factors which give them their emotional charge. But, as I have implied above, this is a sublime which offers a critique of Kant's formulation even though it must resemble it sufficiently to invoke it as an object for critique. So to close, I will explore both sides of this dialectic.

From mind to body

Sublimation is the name given in chemistry to the passage of a chemical directly from a solid to a vapour state. By analogy, in the Kantian sublime there is no intermediary state between the overwhelming of the imagination by the object of its attention, and the intervention of the faculty of reason. The latter state is not deduced from the former; rather our awareness of the supersensible kicks in – quasi-spontaneously – at the point where our attempt to grasp the sensible fails. Which is consistent at least with Kant's view of the supersensible: a noumenal realm that exists out of time, and therefore always already there; not something which follows 'then' in a logical sequence. The performance of the sublime in 'The singing will never be done' is faithful to this scheme. In its first stage no outcome can be logically predicated from the endlessly cycling ostinati. At the sublime moment the new sonorities simply burst in. They are presented

(that is, made present), but they are not arrived at 'then'.[111] Tippett mimics Kant's narration of the sublime as a leap across the aporia between the sensible and supersensible, into the timeless domain of the latter.

Except that what Tippett gives us seems anything but supersensible. This is not just because, working in an aesthetic (i.e. sensible) medium, it is difficult to do otherwise. At the inception of the sublime moment the sensory is absolutely played up, and as if to make the point, Tippett even annotates the accompanying *forte* stroke on the deep gong with the word 'boom'. It is as if he intuitively fastens on to the most unstable point in Kant's account – which is also potentially its most radical.

For what is most problematic in Kant's formulation of the sublime is the status he ascribes to the supersensible. What is it that we think at the moment where we fail to comprehend sublimely great objects? Kant says this is an 'idea of reason': the infinite couched not as a number, not even the mathematical term infinity (which is a mere 'concept of understanding'), but something else – which is *not* material, but not a conventional concept either. A what, then? Kant is explicit that this 'can never be anything more than a negative presentation'.[112] Hence, under the sublime we are compelled 'subjectively to *think* nature itself in its totality as a presentation of something supersensible, without our being able to effectuate this presentation *objectively*'; 'we cannot *cognize* nature as its presentation, but only *think* it as such'.[113] These are breathtaking assertions. Kant seems to be saying that the sublime makes it possible to think without concepts, subjectively to know what is nevertheless unsignifiable. (This is a thought that itself seems unthinkable, though perhaps the act of attempting it amounts to a performance that gives us a kind of experiential knowledge of what thinking without concepts is like.) At the limits of what is rationally tractable, reason teeters on the verge of incoherence, yet in doing so gains a squinting vision of what is outside its horizon. Little wonder that the sublime and the ironic are linked.

That Kant posits this experience as utterly subjective, something we cannot 'effectuate . . . *objectively*', does not mean a retreat into a realm of solipsistic, idealistic fantasy. What is noteworthy is exactly the way in which the subjective is anchored in the objective, the supersensible in the sensible. Each term is dependent on the other, but negatively. The presentation of the infinite 'is altogether negative as to what is sensuous . . . As such it can never be more than a negative presentation – but still it expands the soul.'[114] Thus the sublime heightens to an acute pitch our awareness of the polarity that is nevertheless also a co-dependence – between subject and object, ideal and material, noumenal and phenomenal, intelligible and sensible, what ought to be and what is.

When Kant contrasts the sublime experience of seeing 'as the poets do, according to what the impression upon the eye reveals' (i.e. as a 'pure aesthetic judgement'), with the non-sublime experience of founding our estimate of an object on concepts, or being 'wont to represent it in *thought*',[115] he is alluding to just such a polarization. But this is also the chink in his armour; for this acute separation of spheres seems impossible to maintain. His examples of the pure aesthetic judgement of the 'starry heaven' as 'a broad and all-embracing canopy', or of the sublime ocean as 'a clear mirror of water bounded only by the heavens', may well be intended to emphasize sensory (material) rather than teleological properties, but in their use of metaphor they could hardly be considered conceptless.[116] And if it is unthinkable to make an aesthetic judgement on the material without thought, so, conversely, the attempt to think unthinkability (i.e. to think the noumenal) is impossible without the sensory. For if the supersensible is non-identical with thought and yet knowable as thought's other, then the only instrument of knowing left to us that is not mental must be the body. This is not to suggest the identity of mind and body, for these need each other as the other of themselves; but it is to contest their relationship as one of absolute apartness; it is to posit their necessary mediation.

This, then, is the slight but crucial displacement necessary to the Kantian order – one which obviates that order's theological underpinning while drawing out the humanist or anthropomorphic constellation latent in it. And there is no doubt that the sublime in Kant is bound up with an affirmation of humanity as such. He says, for example, that it is 'in human nature that [the sublime's] foundations are laid'; and the sublime is allied (unlike 'Romances, maudlin dramas [and] shallow homilies' with which it is contrasted) with 'respect for the worth of humanity in our own person and the rights of men'.[117] On Kant's view, what elevates humanity above nature is our capacity for a supersensible reason, notably practical (moral) reason, which is necessarily removed from the empirical, sensible world. But, as subsequent critiques – notably Adorno's – have argued, this is where the Enlightenment project has worked against its own ends. For, as Bernstein has put it (glossing Adorno), the sovereignty of reason has led to the disenchantment of the world, to the expulsion of human subjectivity:

> What began with the critique of myth and religion continues with the elimination of values and secondary qualities until only the mind's own forms (method, logic, and mathematics) remain . . .
>
> In eliminating, for example, secondary qualities as objective features of the natural world, what is eliminated simultaneously are those features through which humans respond to the world. But without the somatic features of perception (images, sounds, smells, tastes, feelings), all that

remains of the subject are its mental powers for abstraction, analysis, and synthesis: the rational, autonomous subject, in eliminating its own natural capacities for response, simultaneously eliminates subjectivity, which, a fortiori, can be seen to reside in its somatic stratum.[118]

The aesthetic becomes a crucial paradigm for healing the rift between the spheres of knowledge and experience. For it represents a kind of conceptualization that is nevertheless rooted in the sensory; and a kind of materiality that is neither reducible to nor exhaustible by the conceptual. And the version of the sublime which Tippett presents so potently at the end of *The Mask of Time* is a vivid rendering of the displacement of the Kantian order called for in Adornian and post-Adornian critical theory. The work's closing gesture, as we have observed, is certainly not devoid of mediation by the conceptual (or quasi-conceptual), placed as it is in a network of relationships with other parts of the work. But this is exceeded by the gesture's sheer somatic force – so violent as to root the preceding passage's sensation of boundlessness to the earth, to ground its timelessness in the here and now. The passionate, ecstatic voices – whose wordless song signifies no concept, only the subjective being of the beings from which they emanate – imbue this moment with all those qualities of the human Kant ascribes to the sublime. Only the ground of that humanity – while still as undefined as Kant's noumenon – is found in the finite somatic sphere.

Tippett's gesture takes on critical force in another respect too. For the somatic does not give *a priori* grounds for celebration (recognition of which is given in the critical distance the composer puts between the works of his second period and the unproblematized Bacchanal of *The Midsummer Marriage*). The somatic has as ambivalent (or dialectical) a significance for men and women as rationality. As Adorno points out, if the bodily represents a potential source of emancipation that is because the body is also the only domain in which we can make intelligible the horrors of which Auschwitz stands as the archetype:

> A new categorical imperative has been imposed by Hitler on unfree mankind: to arrange their thoughts and actions so that Auschwitz will not repeat itself, so that nothing similar will happen. When we want to find reasons for it, this imperative is as refractory as the given one of Kant was once upon a time. Dealing discursively with it would be an outrage, for the new imperative gives us a bodily sensation of the moral addendum – bodily, because it is now the practical abhorrence of the unbearable physical agony to which individuals are exposed even with individuality about to vanish as a form of mental reflection. It is in the unvarnished materialistic motif only that morality survives.
>
> The course of history forces materialism upon metaphysics, traditionally the direct antithesis of materialism.[119]

Tippett signalled his own understanding that such suffering is not discursively (that is, rationally) tractable in lines from *A Child of our Time*: 'Is evil then good? / Is reason untrue? / Reason is true to itself; / But pity breaks open the heart.' The pity and particularity of the sensible world rebukes the autonomous, subject-liquidating order of reason. In 'Hiroshima mon amour', movement 8 of *The Mask of Time*, Tippett offers his own threnody to those who have suffered under human hands on a scale made possible only by modernity. How is it possible to affirm anything in the wake of such an acknowledgement? If 'The singing will never be done' expresses such a possibility it does so only because its particular somatic qualities acknowledge the presence of negative experience in positing a transcendent humanity.

Speaking of the dynamical sublime, Kant says that 'this saves humanity in our own person from humiliation, even though as mortal men we have to submit to external violence'.[120] Tippett's final sublime gesture is terrifying and exhilarating – and perhaps also ultimately moral – because it registers violence, power and human dignity in an abrasive admixture. He, like Kant, wants to assert that the human condition is not reducible to raw natural causality; that human beings are able to find something peculiar in their humanity that enables them to practise moral choice freely. But unlike Kant he cannot accept that this lies in the appeal to some utterly ideal world beyond. To make peace with our mortality means not to spurn metaphysics, but also not to locate it where it is unavailable. Tippett's final sounds rail against the separation of spheres that is the condition of modernity, but at the same time they acknowledge that present diremption. Their higher consonances – a welter of triadic forms – argue for resolution, but absorb contradictory forces as an ontological necessity. They present an image of human subjectivity restored in the world, but not yet in harmony with it. They endorse the idea of humanity as transcendent over nature but not at the price of its removal from nature.

So much from a single gesture. Not merely from the gesture itself of course, but also from those larger discourses which drive it: on the one hand that of the work itself in its entirety; and on the other the discourse of modernity into which it pitches. This moment, if no other, attests to Tippett's achievement in investing fragments with massive rhetorical power. For, whatever else one makes of *The Mask of Time*, it is difficult to deny the compelling force of its final moments – arguably one of the most striking passages in twentieth-century music. This does not, of course, blot out what is problematic about the work, but it does suggest that its would-be detractors need to measure their criticisms against its contribution to the most crucial of philosophical and aesthetic concerns.

Coda

After this stunning moment, Tippett leaves us with a couple of further twists. For the work's true final gesture is not the blazing sound of voices and instruments itself, but the silence which follows. In this moment Tippett achieves in 'real' terms the 'sound where no airs blow' which he represented metaphorically at the beginning of the work and elsewhere. Now we have a silence that is none the less full of the sound that preceded it – as if, having pulled the noumenal into the phenomenal world, Tippett now dispatches the phenomenal into the noumenal. Or into nothingness. Could it be, then, that this final gesture is an image in (non-)sound of the agnosticism implicit in Kant?

And finally, as Tippett was fond of saying, 'we go out into the street'. That is, we return to the mundane empirical world – the ultimate ironization of our aspirations to the sublime. This is also a reminder that the artwork is not a substitute for reality, nor a vehicle for intervening directly in it. What it presents no more guarantees the harmonization of what is and what ought to be than does Kant's 'ideal of the highest good'. In Adorno's words, the artwork is a 'necessary semblance'. It offers a 'promise of happiness' which it itself is not in a position to keep.[121] At the same time, the power of the artwork is that for all its illusory nature it is also real. It is an occurrent autonomous object of the empirical world – in the here and now. While the music lasts, we are offered a rhetorically powerful sign that things could be other than they are.

Here the sublime is again directly relevant, and two utopian aspects of Kant's thinking might survive the journey to a materially based sublime. First, Kant touches on the sublime's subversive potential, in the fact that the knowledge it gives us can only be represented negatively, not in relation to any known object or concept. For this reason he applauds the ban on objective representation in Judaism and Mohammedanism; and, conversely, he points out the political consequences of encouraging the opposite practice:

> Governments have gladly let religion[s which use representation] be fully equipped with these accessories, seeking in this way to relieve their subjects of the exertion, but to deprive them, at the same time, of the ability, required for expanding their spiritual powers beyond the limits arbitrarily laid down for them, and which facilitate their being treated as though they were merely passive.[122]

By implication, then, the sublime, by displacing what is thinkable in our known lifeworld, tells us that what we experience is not all that there is to

be experienced – a thought that again carries political potential. Secondly, for Kant, the 'ideal of the highest good', which the sublime underwrites, is achievable, but only in a future world – in his case the world of the immortal soul. The rearranged sublime which Tippett posits is also orientated to the future. But it presents the diremption between what ought to be and what is by sounding both simultaneously – by combining the qualities of dissonance and consonance into a densely material sound whose future resolution is posited in a domain no less material. Here, then, the sublime signifies not an escape into a different world, but a challenge to the existing one.

6 The meaning of 'lateness': mediations of work, self and society in Tippett's Triple Concerto

Prospects

If periodization is an inveterate musicological habit, Tippett's *œuvre* is certainly among those which provoke it. Putting it this way is a reminder that the practice involves two elements not necessarily pre-disposed to mesh (and this gears us up for a little dialectical thinking). On the one hand, the division of a composer's body of work into style periods may seem to be dictated by its formation as an object. On the other hand, periodization is the practice of an investigating subject who applies the conceptual schemata of a particular discursive culture (musicology). And since concepts by their very nature come preformed, they are less than completely customized to the particulars they map (and less than unmarked by the ideology of their previous applications). 'Lateness' is exactly such a concept – one that Tippett's *œuvre* attracts at the same time as laying open the problematics of its usage. Those problematics surface as soon as we begin to ask the most basic questions regarding a possible late period – such as, when did it begin? what are its characteristics? But if we want to construe an *œuvre* as more than just a list of works, we can neither ignore such problematics nor expect to find a tidy resolution of them.

While the ascription of a late period to Tippett is beset by equivocation and contradiction, the earlier stylistic juncture marked by his second opera, *King Priam* (1958–61), is much more clear cut. (The present book is obviously predicated on this assumption.) *Priam*'s post-tonal soundworld, formal fragmentation, textural stratification and melodic disjunction created such a radical rupture from the dominant stylistic premises of most of the composer's preceding works as to clearly signal a new period. What Robert F. Jones has termed 'the great divide' in Tippett's style around *King Priam* is effectively endorsed by most commentators even when periodization is not their explicit concern.[1] And given that from this work onwards (perhaps even from the earlier Second Symphony of 1956–7) Tippett never completely let go the principle of composing with discontinuous formal blocks of material, it would be eminently plausible to claim that his output falls essentially into two periods. However, this quite tenable model has to coexist with the possibility that developments in the latter part of Tippett's composing career might be read as markers of a 'late' style.

Part of the ambiguity surrounding Tippett's 'lateness' lies in exactly the fact that this is often a matter of inference or implication; added to which there is a markedly lower level of critical consensus as to which works would qualify for the epithet 'late'. Ian Kemp, for example, is exceptional in explicitly identifying a late period in Tippett's *œuvre*, seeing its inception in the Fourth Symphony (1976–7), and citing as the period's hallmark a mood of resignation and/or acceptance.[2] Meirion Bowen on the other hand identifies a late period by allusion, and in more upbeat language, when he talks of the 'Indian Summer of Tippett's late 70s and 80s', whose chief characteristics are 'a gradual resurgence of the lyricism that flooded out in [Tippett's] earlier music' and 'a considerable refinement of texture so that often the entire weight of the musical expression is carried by one or two lines'.[3] The incompatibility of these accounts is by no means resolved by the commonsensical observation that Bowen had the 'benefit of hindsight' – that his observations date from a time when Tippett had completed works such as *The Mask of Time* (1980–2), *New Year* (1985–8), *Byzantium* (1989–90) and the Fifth String Quartet (1990–1), while Kemp's position was made at an earlier time when Tippett's most recently published works were the Fourth String Quartet (1977–8) and Triple Concerto (1978–9). True enough, late works are, pragmatically speaking, those which come last; and on this view the jury remains out until the composer dies. But lateness is also a notion invested in works as part of their reception, and thus becomes part of their historical baggage – problematized, no doubt, by changes of perspective arising from what follows them, but not simply subtractable as if a factual error of judgement. This is an example of the dichotomy formulated above, that periodization is as much a function of its own discourse as it is of the *œuvre* under scrutiny, and this can lead to contradictory perspectives for which it would be quite misguided to seek a positivistic resolution. (Tippett himself seemed to have got caught up in exactly this paradox. The neat teleological narrative which *The Mask of Time* looked like offering at the time of its composition and première – as the consummation of his *œuvre*, the pinnacle of a series of late works beginning with the Fourth Symphony – was subsequently negated by the accident of his remaining alive, and creatively active, for more than a decade longer. Starting work on *New Year*, Tippett had to recant his earlier declaration that *The Ice Break* (1973–6) was to be his last opera; and in the new stage work and its successor pieces he subtly reinvented his own lateness through further stylistic and aesthetic developments.)

As if the antinomic fallout of trying to apply conceptual order to disorderly particulars were not enough, matters are complicated further by the plurality of approaches dictated by the task at hand. For if we want not

only to discuss technical aspects of an alleged late style – which entails getting our analytical sleeves rolled up – but also to consider what *meanings* are attached to the imputed new strain of music, we shall need to take into account the social and cultural context of Tippett's compositional practice. This is a corollary of acknowledging that Tippett's musical material contains its own 'world vision'. Since *King Priam* that vision had darkened in acknowledgement of a more conflicted view of the human condition, and thus taken on the mantle of a particular kind of modernism. The question therefore arises as to how the stylistic mutations of an alleged late period might embody an altered view of social relationships and might resonate with the 'latening' (or 'post-ening') of modernist discourses across our culture at large.

Behind this project is the idea that musical material and social relationships are in some way *mediated* – which of course is a notion from Adorno. But, further, I want to consider how these mediations might have been mediated in turn by Tippett's biographical particulars. Specifically, I shall argue that his sexual orientation may have been salient among the personal contingencies that informed his creative production. This may be an unanticipated tack – contentious given the ultimate unverifiability of what will be posited – but its vindication lies in the less than parochial fact that sexuality (of whatever persuasion) is one of the key forces through which individuals live out the not necessarily benevolent dynamics of social mediation. That is, while sexuality is experienced as something individual, it is at the same time filtered through, indeed ordered by, the values and representations delivered by society at any given moment of its historical and cultural development. What can be (and I argue in Tippett's case was) universalized from gay experience is the particular inescapability of that dissonant remainder of one's self which cannot assimilate to its social mediation. One of the principal compositional challenges Tippett set himself in his late works was still to register that field of dissonance while sowing a greater harmoniousness into it.

All this promises, or maybe threatens, an array of terms and modes of enquiry (formalist analysis at one extreme, discourse on sexuality at the other) which will not smooth out into a homogeneous narrative. However, if the ensuing attempt to capture something of the complexity of the mediations of work, self and society in late Tippett leads to a structure in which individual parts of the discussion resist complete synthesis into the whole, then I console myself with the observation that, coincidentally or otherwise, this mimes my subject of investigation. Moreover, I see this as preferable to some of the alternatives (to invoke debates current within musicology): either a rigorously formalist investigation that evades questions of meaning

beyond the immanent musical text; or a hermeneutic reading that finds it acceptable to treat music as if it were in essence literature.

The model of late Beethoven

Lateness, it will by now be clear, is a musicological trope. Carl Dahlhaus reminds us that the concept is 'derived essentially from the *œuvres* of Bach, Beethoven, and Liszt'.[4] Given the towering significance of Beethoven for Tippett, it would come as no surprise to find that the model of the former's late works – which Tippett would have termed a 'historical archetype' – exerted a powerful allurement over the latter as he contemplated the possibility of a late style of his own. His description of the Sonata No. 3 for Piano (1972–3) as his 'late Beethoven sonata' is suggestive in this respect (following on as it does from the critical engagement with the *Ode to Joy* in his Third Symphony (1970–2)). While at that point Tippett seemed not necessarily to be implying with this reference to a historical archetype a late period of his own, by the end of his composing career he was dropping subtle hints that a parallel might indeed be appropriate. In a radio interview about *The Rose Lake* (1991–3), semi-officially declared Tippett's final work[5] by the time of its première in 1995, the composer stated: 'I have moved bit by bit into another soundworld, if that's the proper term. You can begin, if you want, to put it into periods like it's done with Beethoven – you know, late Beethoven and all the rest of it.'[6]

But Tippett's most signal reference to late Beethoven came in the later 1970s, at a time when he was showing signs of an incipient mutation in his aesthetic priorities. This was in the E. William Doty Lectures which the composer gave at the University of Texas at Austin in 1976.[7] The three 'lectures' were in fact delivered – typically by this stage in his life – as informal question–answer sessions. If this lends a touch of chaos to the proceedings, recurring themes within them nevertheless reveal the composer marshalling an agenda for what we may retrospectively consider a late period. For this reason, if no other, the Doty Lectures merit far greater scrutiny than they have received up to now, and I will make substantial reference to them below.[8]

The date of the lectures is apposite. Tippett had recently finished his fourth opera, *The Ice Break*, and had just begun work on the Fourth Symphony.[9] Perhaps the most sensational sign of some kind of impending aesthetic reorientation comes with his exclamation at the end of the second lecture that 'all the "knot gardens" and the howlings and the screams and shrieks have altered your ears, they've ruined your style . . . you're lost . . . To be found again –? Well, we'll try.'[10] Taken in isolation,

these comments might seem symptomatic of an acute compositional crisis;[11] but they are more properly read in their context as a counterpole to another matter, raised earlier in the lecture – Tippett's serendipitous encounter with one of Beethoven's late string quartets. He recounts with particular vividness how he was caught unawares by the use of this work as incidental music to a television documentary on portraiture:

> A sound came, which was a string quartet, the purest of sounds, intensely compassionate.
>
> Suddenly I realized that it was the beginning of one of the greatest slow movements of the late Beethoven quartets. I could not see. I literally couldn't see for a while because the emotion was so extreme . . .
>
> Of course, the moment that it happened . . . I turned it into my own subjective problems. I said 'Oh, I must, I must before I die, find that sound in our own time!' But I can't find that sound in our time, because it depends upon a purity of structure and harmony, and in my acid world of harmony, I can't find it.[12]

Tippett appears to be describing here a moment of illumination, or *Einfall*, of the kind he elsewhere portrayed as germinal to longer-term creative projects.[13] Clearly at this particular juncture of his composing career, the late-Beethovenian soundworld exerts a potent hold: he fixes on its 'purity', 'intimacy' and 'compassion' – 'so immediate that . . . all the humanity is inside'.[14] Yet equally forceful is his realization of the seeming unviability of these qualities 'in our time' – that is, in a modern context – because these depend on 'what will always appear now as the naivete of a harmonic sound which had this purity'.[15] What has seized him, then, is a compositional problem centred on a contradiction: how to reconcile the desire for what is in effect a diatonic vocabulary, and (implicitly) its potential for a serene lyricism, with the harsh reality of a modernist soundworld whose extremes are 'howlings . . . and shrieks'.

If any single thing could be said to define a late period for Tippett it is this problem. Moreover, the composer universalizes it when he calls it 'an ache . . . which is a part of our time'.[16] In other words he implies a cultural dimension to these personal, conflicted sentiments, which might include the notion that this private compositional conundrum reflects the need for a reassessment of modernism among composers at large – a point I shall consider later. One corollary for Tippett of engaging with these contradictions was to revisit certain technical and expressive features of his first-period style: notably the tonal language and lyricism of works such as the Concerto for Double String Orchestra (1938–9), *The Midsummer Marriage* (1946–52), and the Piano Concerto (1953–5). This was of course not the same thing as returning to the style of that period (which would

have been a kind of self-pastiche), but instead entailed the readmission of certain of its features into the aesthetic world of the second (post-*Priam*) period. Given that the latter was itself defined by its critique of the former, this amounts to a further dialectical turn, in which that critique is now itself criticized.[17] We might hypothesize, then, that Tippett's late works neither constitute a discrete, third period of their own, nor are accommodated as a subset of the second period; instead they distance themselves from the second period by mounting a critique of it from within.

Tippett's Triple Concerto and its late status

The full measure of the creative inner disunity which Tippett was experiencing at the time of the Doty Lectures is found in the disparity between his protestation that 'I can't be Beethoven in any sense whatsoever. I can't produce that now', and the counter-assertion 'I don't believe it's impossible, don't misunderstand me. I think it's going to come again.'[18] But if Tippett's positive prognosis was correct, when did the anticipated stylistic shift materialize? Not immediately, I would hazard: the Fourth Symphony, in progress at the time, undoubtedly inhabits less conflicted territory than the Third Symphony or *The Ice Break*, but for all its moments of stillness it retains a predominantly dark-hued, dynamic undercurrent; similarly its successor, the Fourth Quartet, is one of Tippett's most sustained atonal creations, unflinchingly rebarbative when necessary, so that even the radiance of its final lyrical vision is a sublimation rather than a repudiation of those qualities. The moment of epiphany which we might conjecture as the compositional counterpart to (perhaps indeed the first outcome of)[19] the moment of *Einfall* of Tippett's late-Beethoven quartet encounter is found, I would argue, precisely at the beginning of the slow movement of the Triple Concerto for violin, viola, cello and orchestra.[20] The work as a whole is permeated by, as Bowen puts it, 'the ardent lyricism that had become secondary in importance in [Tippett's] works since *King Priam*';[21] and its exotic orchestral palette (based on an instrumental line-up that includes tuned gongs, alto flute, bass oboe, and a choir of clarinets) also suggests a transformation into a new world of apprehension. But it is the rhetorical impact of the unashamed romanticism of the opening of the slow movement (see Ex. 6.1), with its naked F major melody, that suggests a symbolic moment of stylistic sea-change.

The condition of positing the starting point for a late style so explicitly is simultaneously to register the features which would negate such an assertion. The Triple Concerto quite definitively marks the start of a new compositional agenda at the same time as continuing earlier ones. On the one

Example 6.1. Triple Concerto for violin, viola, cello and orchestra; beginning of 'slow movement': introduction and first phrase of principal theme (dynamics omitted).

hand, for example, its lush soundworld anticipates the opulence of *Byzantium*; and in quoting music from *The Midsummer Marriage* before its last movement the concerto stages a *rapprochement* with Tippett's past – both of which connections support the case for its status as late. On the other hand, the concerto also aligns itself with its two sister works, the Fourth Symphony and Fourth Quartet, in that it adopts like them a quasi single-movement form that incorporates a cyclic element (specifically, the Triple Concerto sets two interludes into the interstices of the traditional three-movement concerto conception to produce a larger formal mosaic of five sections played without any major break). These features do not constitute markers of lateness in my formulation (since they also belong variously to such second-period works as the Second Symphony, *King Priam* and the Second and Third Sonatas for Piano), and this therefore renders the concerto's status as a late work ambivalent.[22] All this is a reminder that Tippett's late works remain attached to the second period in the process of establishing critical distance from it. It is also a reminder of the self-identity of individual works, of their resistance to being considered merely as a slice of the continuum implied by the concept of a style period. Thus, in taking the Triple Concerto (specifically its central, slow movement) as a case study we need to be careful about considering it as 'representative' of a single, homogeneous period, and to remain alert to the specificity with which it configures certain 'late' characteristics.

Essential in this process will be to delineate the technical realization and resolution of the compositional problem from which Tippett's late style issued: the problem, namely of continuing to embrace modernist principles while also seeking to recover something from the past – not only Tippett's own past (his first period) but also the past of Western tonality. The overtly diatonic principal melody of the Triple Concerto's slow movement, which appears on three occasions as the main strophe of what is basically a refrain structure, accordingly makes an ideal focal point for analysis. How is F major presented here, and how is Tippett able to tap into the expressive resources that diatonicism offers without sounding anachronistic or nostalgic?

Example 6.1 quotes the beginning of the first statement of the melody (Fig. 80), on this occasion played by the three soloists in octaves, along with its three-bar introduction. Among the cues for rendering F major unambiguous is the tonic pedal against which the diatonic function of each note of the melody, including its status as structural or ornamental, is readily identifiable. (The third and fourth horns confirm membership of the diatonic in a slightly different way in the second and third bars of the melody by doubling adjacent conjunct pitches from the soloists' line, to form dyads

Example 6.2. At (a) and (b): analysis of principal theme of Triple Concerto 'slow movement' (cf. Ex. 6.1). At (c): analysis of troped material on restated principal theme (cf. Ex. 6.3). At (d): pitch mediations between principal theme and troped material.

Example 6.2 (*cont.*)

based on the interval of a second.) This general level of diatonic transparency makes possible the voice-leading analysis shown in part (a) of Example 6.2, and from this a number of features emerge as salient. Among these is the generative role played by the pitch A in the principal theme, made all the more prominent through being withheld from what is primarily an anhemitonic pentatonic set in the introduction. It is from this pitch that each phrase of the melody issues and to which it returns an octave lower – a motion interpreted in Example 6.2(a) as a prolongation of the primary tone $\hat{3}$ through a downward coupling. Importantly, this descending register transfer is made via the pitch E♭ (flagged in Ex. 6.2(a)), which will also assume considerable structural significance. This much is insinuated by the orchestral violins which sustain this note as the soloists quit it on their continuing path to the lower A; as a consequence, in this latter part of the phrase the prolongation of chord I of F becomes supplemented by its flattened seventh. Because this sonority is heard as stable (it signals no impending modulation) it calls for a reading of the diatonic structure as modal – a situation adumbrated by the oscillation between tonic and flattened leading note in the bass of the introduction.

Alongside this formalist reading, the E♭ also has other signifying functions. The flattened-seventh sonority which it creates connotes the natural overtone series – as if Tippett had synthesized a less abbreviated version of what Schenker termed 'der Klang in der Natur'. And the linear intervallic

context in which E♭ appears has to do with a related connotation, this time an ethnic one: as Tippett himself reports, the theme is modelled on a 'serenely flowing' melody he heard played by a Javanese gamelan while on a tour of the Far East in 1978.[23] The idiosyncratic re-creation of an Eastern soundworld in the slow movement has a counterpart with another, more lively 'gamelan' episode in the first movement – this time using a Balinese model – which returns and is developed in the finale of the concerto. While Tippett anecdotally recounts that in the case of the former (Javanese) element he noted down the melody on the back of a laundry card, Bowen states that for the latter element the composer drew on an example from Colin McPhee's *Music in Bali* (1966).[24] (Significantly, Britten's emulation of the gamelan – with which we shall later make a comparison – also owed much to McPhee, whom he met in the course of his American sojourn during the Second World War.[25]) Tippett not only mimics more than one gamelan style in the Triple Concerto, but also appears in the slow movement to conflate orientalisms (in a time-honoured if ideologically tainted Western tradition): the pedal, or drone, over which the melody sounds is reminiscent of classical Indian rather than traditional Indonesian music – and this is borne out further by the indication for the pizzicatos in the orchestral violas to be played 'sitar-like' (see Ex. 6.1).

The 'gamelan' episodes form a focal point for two contradictory tendencies within the Triple Concerto, also more broadly significant within Tippett's later output. On the one hand, these episodes are allied with a tendency towards unity – in this case thematic unity. Motivic elements prominent in both passages, and drawn from the Javanese scale *pelog* or its Balinese equivalent *saih pitu* (annotated as motifs *x*, *x'* and *y* in Examples 6.1 and 6.2),[26] also permeate much other thematic material within the work, in both the original ethnic profiles and in intervallically modified form. This integrative tendency has been usefully charted by Stephen Collisson, and is argued by him as a distinguishing feature of the Triple Concerto, setting it apart from its precursors, the Fourth Symphony and Fourth Quartet.[27] On the other hand, the gamelan episodes can be construed as symptomatic of an opposing tendency within the concerto, towards diversification, towards *heterogeneity*; and while recognizing the pertinence of the connections outlined by Collisson, I want here to examine the case for this countervailing aspect.

One powerful example of heterogeneity is the gong-determined sonority that clouds the tonic prolongation of F at the end of each phrase of the slow movement's principal melody – for example at Fig. 81^{-1} (see Ex. 6.1). By the very last quaver of the phrase these new accretions of timbre and pitch content become clarified as a D♭ major triad, which on the face of it

can be interpreted as chord ♭VI of the prevailing tonic. Yet both this reading and Whittall's, which fastens on to the major–minor conflict engendered by the A♭ of the new collection ('a welcome dash of acid'),[28] are too localized and misconstrue the superimposed sonority as bearing a functional relationship to the F major prolongation. As my bracketing out of the D♭-rooted sonority in Example 6.2(a) implies, it should not be considered *harmonically* as part of a prolongation of F; rather, operating outside F's sphere of influence, the D♭ sonority is generated *intervallically* as part of an accumulation of pitches based on the perfect fifth or its inversion – that is, on interval class 5 (ic5). This process is graphed in part (b) of Example 6.2. Working backwards, the bass D♭ falls out of the low A♭ that is pitted against the A♮ of the soloists' melody; and this A♭ is generated from the all-important E♭ of the melody itself, which acts as a crucial point of mediation between the harmonic and intervallic principles. Working back still further (again see Ex. 6.2(b)), the series E♭–A♭–D♭ is in turn an extension of another ic5 series, C–F–B♭, embedded in the quasi-pentatonic ostinato of the introduction.

To summarize so far: here are two systems of organization, one based on more traditional patterns of harmonic construction and linear voice-leading (albeit modally inflected), the other based on a principle of interval invariance. Although these two principles are not without contact and convergence, they are to a large extent kept structurally discrete: each construct is governed by a different law. This context of structural heterogeneity is paramount; indeed I would argue that it is not only a further key characteristic of Tippett's late style, it is also nothing less than the necessary condition for the reflowering of diatonic lyricism that is its other hallmark. Tippett voiced something similar in the film documentary *Songs of Experience*, of which he was the subject. In a voice-over to footage to a rehearsal of the Triple Concerto (indeed of the very passage under discussion here) under his own directorship, he comments:

> If . . . I want a melody that sings, I know that for that melody to be heart-easing it will have to be placed against music that is hard-headed and possibly violent; the fundamental difficulty of our time is to be able to write the heart-easing tune which isn't a cliché.[29]

This is of course another formulation of the dichotomy experienced in his late-Beethoven encounter described earlier, but significantly Tippett now comments from the retrospective standpoint of the problem's solution. The epithets 'hard-headed' and 'violent' might not best suit this particular example, but the principle none the less obtains: the 'heart-easing tune' is aesthetically viable provided it represents a music set apart from others

Example 6.3. Restated principal theme with troped countermelody (first phrase; remaining parts omitted).

juxtaposed against it; provided, in other words, that the heart-easing tune and the larger surrounding structure (ultimately the whole that is the entire work) resist assimilation into one another.

Tippett intensifies this process in its application to the slow movement's refrain on its next appearance. In this second statement the principal melody, still in F major, is transferred to the piccolo, oboe and bassoon (thus preserving the statement at three different octaves); but now the three soloists trope on to it a countertheme of an altogether different nature: more rhythmically active, more ornate and altogether removed from the main tune's neo-romantic vein of expression. Example 6.3 shows the troped material in relation to the first phrase of the principal melody (other aspects of the original texture, as quoted in Example 6.1, reappear, but are omitted from the present example); a fuller picture of this material's place

within the overall pitch organization of the passage can be determined from Example 6.2(c), which aligns it with the analysis of the original melody given in part (a). As Example 6.2(c) in particular makes clear, the troped material is governed by a number of structural principles. First, the pitch prolonged at the beginning of each phrase rises a semitone on each occasion, thus creating a middleground motion from D♯ to E to F (at Figs. 91, 92 and 94 respectively). Secondly, alongside various chromatic foreground diminutions and other deviations, broken-chord figuration is strongly in evidence, especially that drawing from triads of B and E major; these might be seen as analogues of dominant–tonic motion in E – analogues because, in the absence of appropriate supporting counterpoint, the configurations in question allude to those functions formalistically, rather than making them subjectively palpable.[30] Thirdly, the countertheme incorporates numerous motivic references to the *pelog/saih pitu* scale form, labelled *x* in Examples 6.2(a) and 6.3 – which relates it to the main theme even as other features radically differentiate it.

Precise description of the relationship between the F major melody and the added stratum is instructive. On the one hand, the overwhelming overall impression of the passage is of the resistance between the tonal implications of the troped material and those of the original melody; the former seem almost to act as a kind of wilful interference against the latter. On the other hand, there are subtle points of mediation, as detailed in Example 6.2(d). Most notable among these is the convergence between the pitch class D♯, to which the soloists frequently return, and its enharmonic equivalent, E♭, so salient in the F major melody; and a similar relationship obtains between A♭ and G♯ in the last part of each phrase. In the same vein, there is an elegant enharmonic symmetry between the ascending ic5 series C♯–G♯–D♯ at Fig. 90 (see the beginning of Ex. 6.2(c)) which ends the preceding solo cello episode, and the descending ic5 series, E♭–A♭–D♭, originally used to blur the melody (Ex. 6.2(b)). One could cite other mediating features too, such as the coincidence of phrase boundaries and congruence of phrase construction between the layers – notwithstanding considerable independence between the interior phrase dynamics of the two strata.

The tension between related and different features outlined here should be construed dialectically, the troped material occupying an antithetical position to the material originally posited as a thesis. What is significant, however, is that the points of mediation described above none the less constitute only a very partial synthesis: while there are some features of which the two strata mutually partake, their differences in general remain unresolved. In other words, identity and non-identity need each other in order to establish themselves as principles of meaning, but it is the non-identical

which is in the ascendant. Heterogeneity in Tippett's late style – of which the preceding examples are an index – connotes something radically different from either a pot-pourri of musical ideas or the presence of contrast within a smoothly synthesized whole. What is ultimately significant about each element and principle of organization within this state of affairs is that it restricts the extent of absorption of the others into any organic continuum.[31]

The mediation of lyricism and fragmentation

While the juxtaposition and superimposition of the structurally heterogeneous is a key factor in Tippett's late style, it would be mistaken – too undialectical – to consider it the style's only criterion or exclusive property. The principle is no less distinctive of Tippett's second period, appearing in developed form as early as the Second Symphony (1956–7).[32] But this only bears out the point that the late style is marked not by a rupture from the post-*Priam* period but by a critique from within of that period's more alienated features. We can gain a more precise picture of what that means by comparing the previously analysed passages from the Triple Concerto's slow movement with an excerpt from the 'Night Sky Music' – part of what is in effect the slow movement – of Tippett's (earlier) Third Symphony.

While the two movements are somewhat differently formed, the 'Night Sky Music' is nevertheless founded on a strophic technique not completely unlike the refrain principle of the concerto. Successive statements of the form-building strophe manifest an accretion of musical strata, as illustrated in Example 6.4, which quotes an extract from the third strophe, beginning at Fig. 113. In a manner reminiscent of passages from the Triple Concerto slow movement, the strophe presents several simultaneously operative layers of material in which each layer takes its identity from a distinctive timbre and structural premise. For example, the layers for solo violas, solo violins and oboes which constitute the lyrical foundation of each strophe (comparable with the principal melody in the Triple Concerto) are mainly diatonically tonal; the harp and tubular bells meanwhile aggregate a pentatonic subset in a contrasting, flat tonal field; while the phrase ending is blurred as in the Triple Concerto, this time through the superimposition of a vibraphone tag drawing from the whole-tone scale, and through anti-expressive demisemiquaver figuration in the piano (a similar device to that troped on to the second refrain of the Triple Concerto) drawing from the full chromatic set.

That these comparisons suggest the 'Night Sky Music' as a prototype for the Triple Concerto slow movement could be taken to undermine any

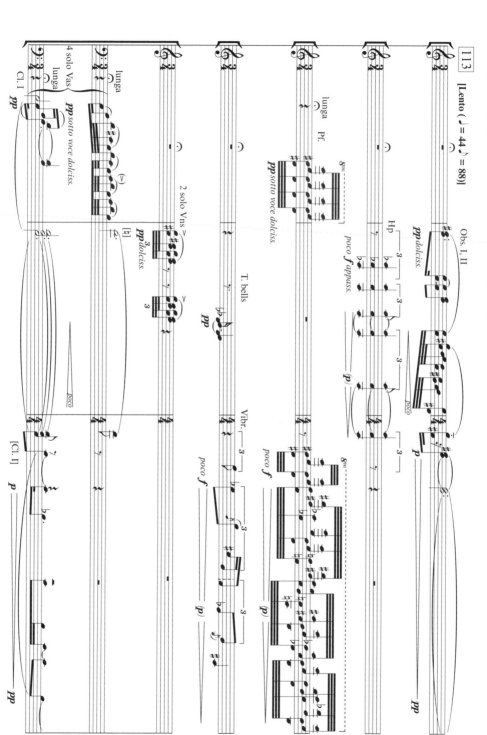

Example 6.4. Symphony No. 3: extract from 'Night Sky Music'.

argument for the latter's place on the other side of a stylistic divide. But what marks these two works as stylistically discrete is not a positively defined set of features exclusive to each, but their different mediations of style-defining elements. Heterogeneity, a characteristic of both pieces, is a principle particularly strongly married in the Third Symphony to high levels of fragmentation. As a consequence, diatonic lyricism – an opposing tendency – exists only as a possibility within the surrounding kaleidoscope of fractured ideas, not as a fully fledged actuality; and pitch centres merely provide momentary points of focus, rather than generating the more sustained tonal environment found in the Triple Concerto. The concerto, it might be said, unlocks the lyrical potential latent in the symphony, transforming what were pieces in a mosaic into the more fully grown limbs of a musical form, and – because this affords each constituent greater opportunity to assert what is unique to it – intensifying the experience of heterogeneity. But what has to be stressed is that lyricism is still mediated by fragmentation, rather than displacing it. The songful moments of the concerto, despite their expansion, still bear a dislocated relation to what surrounds them, and hence retain the status of fragments. Emblematic in this respect is the fact that the primary tone of the slow movement's refrain, identified as $\hat{3}$ in Example 6.2(a), never makes the descent to $\hat{1}$ which would have indicated a role for this material in articulating formal cohesion and closure. This is part of a strategy for preventing a lapse into nostalgia: for making possible 'the heart-easing tune which isn't a cliché'. Fragmentation, which served to repress lyricism in the Third Symphony, becomes lyricism's enabling other in the Triple Concerto.

After modernism

Tippett's concern to avoid cliché, and equally his anxieties about the 'purity' and 'naivete of a [diatonic] harmonic sound', point to an awareness of musical material as being implicated in history. Writing 'the heart-easing tune' presumably constitutes a 'fundamental difficulty of our time' because the kinds of material implied by such a gesture have become worn out over time, their associated sensibilities questionable to a modern(ist) consciousness alive to the antagonisms and ironies of the age. Apposite here is the Homeric story of Odysseus and the Sirens as recounted by Adorno and Horkheimer in their *Dialectic of Enlightenment*. On this reading, '[the Sirens'] allurement is that of losing oneself in the past';[33] Odysseus, tied to the mast of the Argos so as to be able to hear but not succumb to the Sirens' song, symbolizes a state in which 'pleasure is simultaneously yearned for

and denied' (to use Alastair Williams's paraphrase).[34] It is this very ambivalence which Tippett seems to register in his late-Beethoven quartet encounter, reflecting on his own second-period style, in which his resistance to the allure of the past is staunchest. That resistance is built into, i.e. immanent in, such works as the Third Symphony – in the way, for example, that the diatonic elements of the 'Night Sky Music' suppress their own potential for expressive lyrical expansion through their preoccupation with tiny ostinato patterns. However, in the Triple Concerto that which must be resisted and that which resists are more decisively separated into distinct principles; the lyrical impulse is now unfettered. And the presence, rather than mere implication, of the purely diatonic takes an ever greater hold in Tippett's later works, in contexts that are subject to ever greater degrees of structural, formal and textural simplification – for example in *Byzantium* and especially *The Rose Lake*. So for all that Tippett chose to stay bound to the mast of modernism, it is undeniable that from the Triple Concerto onwards he loosened his bonds more than a little. Stamped on to these works is a sense of coming *after* the period of his most unequivocal embrace of a modernist aesthetic.

This way of putting things contains a distinct and perhaps unexpected insinuation: could it be that Tippett's late style might invite the designation 'postmodern'? The question causes a double jolt. First, it suggests that the ostensibly private matter of Tippett's stylistic development may in some way also relate to recent discourses within culture at large. Secondly, it embodies a shocking incongruity of terms. Can an idea which connotes the rejection of 'grand narratives' (to use Jean-François Lyotard's phrase)[35] really be applied to a figure who has held so tenaciously to the emancipatory ideals of liberal humanism? Or, considered even from a strictly musical point of view, can a composer so consistently concerned with the big musical statement, through genres such as symphony, string quartet and opera, be equated with the likes of Michael Nyman, Gavin Bryars, John Tavener, Steve Martland or Graham Fitkin (to name only his compatriots), who through their music, and in some cases their own pronouncements, have consciously and conspicuously distanced themselves from the premises of a modernist aesthetic – from the grand narrative of the historical dialectic of musical material (this time to use an Adornian notion) and its associated discourse of 'greatness'?

Tippett patently cannot be branded postmodern in any of these senses. However, there may yet be critical purchase to be gained by testing for connections between the terms in more subtle ways. Rather than attempting to assert a relationship of identity between the ideas of 'late Tippett' and 'postmodernism' – that is, rather than forcing one term to map completely

on to the other – we might ask instead what meanings are generated by associating the terms within the same mental frame. Bearing in mind too that postmodernism does not refer to a single, homogeneous cultural movement (any more than modernism ever did), we might posit a parallel between the developments observed in Tippett's late style and roughly contemporaneous tendencies found in figures as diverse as Boulez, Messiaen, Ligeti, Penderecki and Maxwell Davies. In the later work of these composers and others we find evidence of a kind of postmodernization definable not as a rejection of modernism but as a later phase of it: a retraction from some of modernism's previous extremes, amounting to a measured assimilation of previously outlawed codes and channels of meaning from the past. By way of example, one might cite Davies's turn since the later 1970s to such genres as symphony and concerto, accompanied by his talk (albeit a kind of idiolect) of constructs such as 'tonic' and 'dominant' in his music, and a tendency towards greater structural transparency. If this is indeed an equivocal manifestation of postmodernism it might be distinguished from others by placing, as it were, a stress on the 'modern' and a parenthesis around (and possibly hyphen after) the 'post'. Thus '(post-)modern' for these composers means on the one hand maintaining contact with a modernist tradition which by this stage in history is old enough to recognize itself as just that, and on the other hand reflecting a hiatus in (and in effect problematizing) the historically progressive impulse that is part of modernism's paradigm.

That hiatus could be seen as crucial – a source of both consensus and contention that sets many of the terms of the postmodernist debate. On the one hand the tendencies described above – whether explicitly antimodernist, or putatively ongoing modernist – all court the prefix 'post-' because they recognize that the modernist project, even if it has not overtly failed, has none the less needed to entertain a reorientation of its premises. Depending on the individual case, this need could be put down to the exhaustion of certain progressive impetuses within modern art as they reached their extremes; to an awareness of increasing marginalization from wider arenas of communication (in part as a corollary of the pursuit of such extremes); and to an increasing mindfulness – not unrelated to the increasing globalization of culture – of an ever-widening range of sources of cultural production, with their potential for alternative materials and practices. While the last factor – offering for some a way out of the impasse represented by the first two – has featured as a critical element within modern culture at least since the Enlightenment, what arguably makes it distinctive within a postmodern context is its potential as a signifier of inclusiveness.[36]

While these issues appear to take us some way from the original tenor of our discussion, they none the less point to the very cultural circumstances in which Tippett's late works are enmeshed. Moreover, Tippett made it clear on various occasions that, notwithstanding their seemingly autonomous development, his stylistic processes connected in some subterranean way with social developments at large. In the Doty Lectures, for example, his allusions to a gestating style change rub shoulders with other comments implicitly to do with the social mediation of music. At one point he refers to a type of artist (including most notably himself) mandated as 'part of his job' to search within his own psyche (for which read subjectivity) for the counterpart to the turmoil of the 'endless problem of change' in the 'external world'.[37] Internalizing this kind of conflict is risky, he says, at its worst leading to insanity – as in the case of Nietzsche and Hölderlin; but there is also the possibility of 'surviving those elements'. Significantly there then comes a suggestion that while the pathology of the former condition might generate one kind of art (for which we must surely read modernist art), surviving that pathology might generate something other, something which comes *after*:

> As Pasternak, and later Solzhenitsyn, said, the great excitement is that as he put it, 'We have survived, we are here.' Now this would then raise the question . . . of what kind of art might express this survival. It may not come out as *a work of art* at all.[38]

Tippett's thoughts on what might be inferred from this are difficult to disentangle from other, related concerns. However, among his elaborations is a comment that would seem to endorse a move away from the grand narrative of high art:

> That would lead . . . to some other possibility which I'm not sure would mean much to us here. We're not understanding what the new possibilities of the art of music should be. We may only be thinking of it constantly in terms of the concert halls and the grandiose figures. We haven't learned yet how to think of it in terms of social therapy and all sorts of excitements, which, although not producing the work of art, may be producing that great basis upon which the thing is made . . . We have the chance to involve a great many more people in sophistication, in sensibilities, who would in the past have been deprived. If the good things from our enormous technological advances become more widespread, what does that do? Does that merely produce a larger number of Beethoven performances? Or does it produce a lot of possibilities of all sorts of individual ways of making art; pockets of different kinds of music, different types of people? You see it's all open, I hope.[39]

However telegraphically, Tippett presents here an intriguing vision of what could be construed as a postmodern society comprising more diversified, more enfranchised (and also probably more localized) communities of communication, emancipated from the dominance of a rigidified high-art practice. Rather than appearing out of the blue, though, this conception can be seen as a further stage in a recognition of the significance of musical 'others' that was longstanding in Tippett's intellectual and creative consciousness. For example, as early as his 1961 essay 'Towards the condition of music' he prognosticates on a rediscovery of the values of non-Western musical traditions as a consequence of increasing industrialization and globalization – in which process popular music is cast as likely harbinger.[40] None the less, even in the Doty Lectures, Tippett's sights are on a future horizon rather than a transformation of the immediate present; and as if in acknowledgement of a situation not yet authentically attained, his own compositional practice after this time remained firmly within the sphere of autonomous, high art (both his initial aspiration to cast *New Year* as a popular musical and his subsequent reassignment of it to the genre of opera are symptomatic in this respect). Yet a late work such as the Triple Concerto could be seen to prefigure such a set of conditions from *within* that high-art practice (in other words, envisioning a future cultural order from the standpoint of present-day practices) through the heterogeneity of its musical styles – including those with a wider communicative potential.

The inclusion of musical others within the framework of a piece is again nothing new for Tippett. One need only cite the spirituals in *A Child of our Time* (1939–41), the blues in *The Knot Garden* (1966–9) and the Third Symphony, and the mock 'hoe down' as well as the use of electric guitars in *The Ice Break*.[41] Significantly, however, these are all used to register conflict in some way: they escape integration into the dominant musical sound-world of their respective works to the same extent that the collectivities for which they stand are alienated from the dominant bourgeois stratum of society (a pattern continued even as late as *New Year* in the pseudo-rap of Donny's 'skarade'). By contrast, the pluralist elements of the Triple Concerto coexist in a more pacific relationship. Far from representing alienation, the most otherly music of all, the gamelan material, finds fruition in its symbolic position at the centre of the piece, and its motivic content represents a potential source of unification, even as that tendency is resisted by the kinds of procedure we have analysed above.

The Triple Concerto, then, attracts the epithet (post-)modern on two grounds: first owing to the *rapprochement* it stages not only with the composer's own past, but also with the historical stock of musical resources and materials inherited from our culture at large; secondly owing to its

embrace of what is other. However, rather than lapse into an unconsidered celebration of pluralism that might be associated with certain brands of postmodernism, Tippett does not dodge the implications which the resulting diversity of elements has for the notion of the whole. What remains modernist in the Triple Concerto's condition of coming after is the way in which the relation between the musical whole and part is dialectically conceived, such that the part functions in relation to the whole, while at the same time not giving itself up completely to it: the individual moment maintains an autonomy against the larger, closural demands of form. (This situation is reflected, for example, in the interposing of episodes of new material into the unfolding sonata form of the first movement, and in the otherwise inexplicable 'swung' episode for untuned percussion at the start of the second interlude.)

Musical material and its social mediation

From the preceding account we may conclude that the significance of Tippett's late style lies not – as in Beethoven's case – in the turn to some kind of spiritual 'inwardness', but in its intimation of a renewed cultural and social order. If that seems a questionable thing to deduce from what is supposed after all to be a work in an autonomous musical genre, it can be supported in the assertion, barely disguised above, that social relations are somehow reflected, embodied or sedimented in the way the musical material is formed. That is still a fairly bald assertion, and if it is to have a currency greater than the merely metaphorical we shall need to examine how these terms are mediated. In raising the notion of the social mediation of musical material I am of course invoking an agenda of Adorno's; but, however unfaithful, I intend to be pragmatic in what I take from him, and I shall call on other thinkers too.

How, then, can we discern the mediation of the social in the absolute musical form of a work such as Tippett's Triple Concerto? A first step away from the utterly formal being of the music – the status represented by the analytical investigations above – can be taken by contemplating how musical relationships relate to the conditions of truth. This is partly to invoke Adorno's notion of the 'truth content' of a musical work, which, on one level at least, is bound up with its inner consistency. As Max Paddison puts it, this 'corresponds to the traditional philosophical definition of truth as "the identity of the concept with the object of cognition"'; but because autonomous instrumental music 'has no directly identifiable external referent . . . the truth of the work understood in this context is its identity with its own form, the unity and logical consistency of idea and

technical structure'.[42] As we have seen, however, the heterogeneous tendencies of a work such as Tippett's Triple Concerto ensure resistance to any blanket principles of unity and consistency. Such an immanent critique of consistency is, on Adorno's view, a necessary later moment in the dialectical conditions of a work's truth content; and in this context we might also invoke (as Arnold Whittall has done in relation to Tippett's *Byzantium*) Isaiah Berlin's claim, as paraphrased by Noel Annan, that 'truth is not a unity', that 'values collide and often cannot be made to run in parallel. And not only values. Propositions too.'[43]

This assertion is salient here because it portrays pluralism as something other than 'a pragmatic compromise' or a signifier of mere relativism. It rather suggests pluralism as a dynamic chemistry of worldviews in which claims to truth, because bound up with the differing historical and cultural contingencies of those making them,[44] are open to contestation and negotiation. While reason need not be expunged in this process (since it holds potential 'to sort out the conflicting claims of justice, mercy, privation and personal freedom'[45]), the cultural and historical – ultimately social – dynamics which mediate it preclude its operation as an abstract, totalizing principle. And while in reality truth claims may be as much a matter for contestation as negotiation, these pluralist conditions ultimately presuppose communicative interaction between individual subjects (or groups of subjects).[46] What is important in this conception is the inseparability of truth claims – expressed through the medium of a symbolic system (e.g. language, music) – from the socio-cultural situation of the subjects making them.

Moving further along this trajectory away from formalism, I would argue that it is one of the key characteristics of Tippett's Triple Concerto that its own processes embody just such a set of intersubjective dynamics. For the work's interaction of differentiated musical materials is perceived in terms not merely of formal relationships but also of subjective presences. This is because the instrumental forces sing forth as voices, as actants within a context that is inherently one of communication. Tippett ensures that the subjectivities presented are differentiated not only through heterogeneous modes of musical structuring (as analysed above) but also through vivid instrumental characterization. Not least significant here is the plurality of soloists, consciously represented as three individuals rather than a homogeneous ensemble – a principle then extended to the treatment of the orchestra.[47] This yields an image of subjectivities which assert their own positions and engage with the positions of others without seeking forcefully to dislodge or assimilate them – an image, in other words, of subjects coexisting in a mutually critical awareness. This might in turn be read as an analogue for a social order in which differences of

identity are respected rather than marginalized or massaged away: neither a brave new world of happy uniformity, nor an unattainable utopia. I am reminded here of Adorno's statement that 'peace is the state of distinctness without domination, with the distinct participating in each other';[48] and it is fitting that a composer who made practical affirmations of pacifism and wrestled with the conditions of modernity throughout his life should in his late work bring these two ideas into a new convergence.

Mediations of the personal: gay traces

While this musical interplay of distinct subjectivities enacts subjectivity in the abstract, it is further arguable that this vision might have had its roots in the specific subjective life experiences of its composer. Risking perhaps a sizeable conceptual leap, I should like to speculate on the possibility that Tippett might have found a model for the thinkability of 'values [which] collide and . . . cannot be made to run in parallel' (to reinvoke Annan's account of Berlin) through the experience of his sexual orientation. For one corollary of gay experience is a comprehension of two, not necessarily compatible, constructions of desire: that transmitted and legitimated by the representations of a predominantly heterosexual culture; and that gained from an other sexual orientation, which is lived out and legitimated subjectively. If it is reasonable to assume that artworks in some way objectify the subjectivity of their creator, then there is every reason for not censoring discussion of these factors in relation to Tippett's music. I want to argue that the internalized tension between these contradictory constructions of what is natural could have been paradigmatic for Tippett's world view at large and for the channelling of his creative impulses. Some evidence for such a homology was elliptically provided by the composer himself, though this always takes the form of *traces* rather than definitive statements. I shall make these my starting point in the following explorations, before returning to the specific case of the Triple Concerto and Tippett's late period.[49]

The Doty Lectures of 1976 again form a repository in which such traces may be found. In a moment of self-reflection Tippett refers back to a crisis in his personal relations which he underwent in the late 1930s – a crisis which we now know was prompted by the issue of his sexual orientation.[50] Pertinently enough, this mention some forty years later imputes a conflation between qualities of his music (especially his later music) and his own psychological processes. Invoking Ian Kemp's description of his music as being marked by 'polarity' and 'division in two', Tippett clinches a connection between musical material and subjective experience: 'I didn't search for it; I suffered it. I must have known it ever since I can remember, but I've

had to live with it and find out what . . . the function of the thing might be; the "thing" being the fact that you are divided.'[51] And this leads to further autobiographical revelation: 'At one point, I was very troubled in my personal relations and went to a kind of analyst'.[52]

This would be of merely anecdotal significance, and quite tangential to a discussion of the aesthetics of Tippett's late style, were it not for his subsequent comments, which reinforce the idea of a homology between personal, social and compositional dynamics. Tippett recounts how he abandoned his dream therapy before reaching a complete resolution, fearing that he would 'erase some element in [him]self which must be left outside the therapy'; and he continues:

> I know that there must be an element in which the psyche is left open to the wounds . . . Therefore, we come to a point at which . . . there is a possible objectivity in the ambiguity, because I believe that we are in an age of paradox, absolutely and entirely. These paradoxes have lived me, without my being able to analyze them or even tell what they are. Still, I've suffered them. Now, it's out of the violence of this division that I have to search for a [musical] metaphor, though not of union, I think. You accept it, be this as it is. It's an acceptance of this *and* of that as a reality . . .
>
> I'm certain that, if I cleaned away the division in my own psyche, I would clean away some element of apprehension of what our world is.[53]

The 'acceptance of this *and* of that as a reality' is an idea which resonates strongly with the notion of 'values [which] collide and often cannot be made to run in parallel'. Notably, Tippett's comments seem to pertain equally to perceptions of his own subjectivity, to the social divisions of the age, and to the fractured truth content of musical works.

Absent from all this, of course, is any explicit mention of his gay orientation as a factor; indeed his comment about not 'being able to analyze . . . or even tell what [these paradoxes] are' might seem to rule out such an attribution. But two points need to be borne in mind here. First, while Tippett had been long out of the closet in his personal circles, and awareness of his sexual orientation was fairly widespread, he still seemed relatively cautious at this stage of his life about official, public representations of his gayness;[54] hence his comments about his personal crisis of the 1930s are couched somewhat cryptically, though would have been clear enough to those alert to such matters. Secondly, the most significant implication of Tippett's sexual orientation, from the standpoint of the present discussion at least, is less its specific content and more its agency in mediating the composer's perception of himself in relation to society. (This could be seen as another gloss on T. S. Eliot's assertion of the need for the artist to transmute his personal experience into something universal.) Consider, for

example, the following, much earlier, statement by Tippett in his essay 'Too many choices', first published in 1958:

> We are born into such-and-such a society, which has a particular set of dominant values to which it gives absolute status . . . Most people's faculties allow them to grow up in sympathy with the rising or reigning social dynamic. If that be named their choice, then their sacrifice is simply of those values which the reigning social dynamic suppresses . . . They only become aware of the matter through contact with those whose gifts do not permit them to grow up in sympathy with the conventional scale of values.[55]

The minority group to whom Tippett refers in the last sentence in fact consists of 'that handful of men and women whose fate is to be gifted with spontaneous artistic vision'.[56] Yet in the context of the present discussion another reading of the opening lines – one which posits a gay person's critique of what is assumed by mainstream society – begins to look plausible. This is less to infer a gay subtext than to posit a meaningful equivalence, or semantic fluidity, between different kinds of non-identification with the majority worldview (indeed Tippett allows himself such slippage in this essay, drawing parallels, for example, between the situation of Galileo and that of artists in former Soviet Russia). In other words, one kind of 'outsiderness' becomes equivalent to another, and together these hold the potential for insight into social alienation at large. (It is perhaps only thus that Tippett's empathy with a composer such as Shostakovich, or with the plight of minority social groups, might have a pertinence greater than abstract liberal-humanist outrage).[57]

The critical awareness generated by this rupture between self and society could be understood to be transmuted in compositional praxis into what Adorno termed the 'rupture between self and forms' – in other words, 'the split between the expressive needs of composers and the reified characters of the handed-down traditional forms and genres'[58] which leads to a modernist aesthetic under which musical materials are marked by polarity and dislocation. In Tippett's case this is recognizable in the dissonant, discontinuous works of his post-*Priam* period, and especially in a piece such as the Third Symphony whose structural edifice arises out of a process of thoroughgoing negation of the Beethovenian symphonic model.

Self, society and the musical work in late Tippett

As we have observed, however, Tippett's late style displays a different constellation of the social in its musical formation; and, assuming there is

some currency in the preceding argument, this invites the question of whether those shifts might not have been homologous with a relaxing in Tippett's concept of his sexual orientation in relation to its social mediation and representation. At the risk of reinforcing a long-running and not sufficiently critically examined trope of comparison between Britten and Tippett in this regard (in which Britten, portrayed as uptight and closeted about his sexuality, is played off against a more laid-back Tippett), I would suggest that there is some insight to be gained here from briefly considering a connection between the gamelan episodes of the Triple Concerto and Britten's deployment of pseudo-gamelan soundworlds, most notably in his last opera *Death in Venice* (1971–3). That Tippett used the same indigenous scale structures deployed by Britten in that opera almost leads one to wonder indeed whether the former intended some act of homage.[59] But most significant is the different way in which difference is figured in each composer's invocation of gamelanesque elements.

Philip Brett has plausibly argued that Britten's adoption of the oriental and 'exotic' (gamelan music in particular) as a cipher for the inadmissibly erotic in his dramatic works belongs to a historical pattern within Western culture's appropriation of oriental imagery.[60] And, as has been well documented, the oriental soundworld in Britten's opera is used to convey the otherness of the boy Tadzio, whom Aschenbach is eventually compelled to recognize as the object of his desire. Yet despite its permeation into the rest of the opera's fabric Tadzio's music remains a signifier of separateness, of unattainability, and of Aschenbach's alienation from his own sensibilities. By contrast, the gamelan materials of Tippett's Triple Concerto, especially their concentration in and around the slow movement, play an altogether more epiphanic role. Tippett's allusion to the music of a pre-industrial culture (the prolonged F^7 chord of the slow movement being a kind of synthetic 'chord of nature') is a strategy by which to usher diatonic lyricism back in while simultaneously imbuing it with strangeness. This principle also extends to many of the other lush or exotic timbres that characterize the piece, for example the bass oboe and alto flute solos that presage the slow movement's main melody, or the figurations for harp, bass clarinets, solo double basses, glockenspiel and marimba which cradle the sensual second group melody in the first movement (Fig. 16ff.): the concerto is, as it were, peopled by musical actants whose identity is non-normative, yet whose role is anything but peripheral to the totality. If it is justifiable to claim that the biographical fact of Britten's homosexuality registers within works such as *Death in Venice* as a discourse of 'outsiderness', it is no less tenable to posit Tippett's gay identity as a factor in the affirmation of diversity and inclusiveness found in a late work such as the Triple Concerto.

Added to this, we might claim that the regained lyrical impulse found in this and subsequent late pieces represents for Tippett a recovered sense of a more integrated self after the 'howlings . . . and screams' – images of a dissolution of self – heard in *The Knot Garden*.

How far can these generalized images of emancipated subjectivity be linked with contingent biographical factors? In other words, to what extent do these facets of a late style accord with a late phase in the composer's personal processes? In certain respects there is evidence to suggest that Tippett's later life was indeed marked by a greater sense of personal ease, the composer projecting an ever more relaxed public persona. (His inevitable promotion to doyen of the British musical establishment after Britten's death in 1976 might have been a contributing factor here.) Certainly by his last decade Tippett felt at liberty to discuss his sexual orientation in interviews in the mass media,[61] and his autobiography of 1991 offered many candid revelations about his past personal life. Indeed, in the final chapter of that book he corroborates having achieved a resolution of past conflicts, telling of a dream of a house built for him by Bill (Meirion) Bowen in which 'the rooms were full of young, happy people moving about freely'. This 'older man's vision, near the end of his life, of a house that is free and open' is contrasted with the recurring childhood nightmare of another house described in the autobiography's opening chapter: a fortress broached by 'the Biting Lady'; according to Tippett, 'the dream meant that one day I would have to . . . cope with the turbulence inside myself'.[62]

If Tippett charted his lifetime's progress towards personal resolution in the symbolic world of his dreams, we can perhaps trace an analogous journey through the symbolic (and, as we know, often dream-like) world of his operas, specifically in the situation of two of his characters with whom he is known to have identified closely: Dov, the homosexual musician in *The Knot Garden*, and the androgynously named Jo Ann in *New Year*.[63] Noticeably, spatial confinement – and eventual emancipation from it – is an issue in all the cases described: in the houses in Tippett's dreams, in the high-walled garden (metamorphosing into labyrinth and then rose garden) of *The Knot Garden*, and in Jo Ann's room in *New Year* – a self-imposed prison from which she longs to escape. In all these cases, but especially the last, it is tempting to invoke that other metaphor of spatial confinement so pertinent to the gay situation: the closet. It is hard to imagine Tippett writing a line such as Jo Ann's 'they are out and I am in' in the 1980s without being aware of the overtones; moreover her 'never safe from the wound within' resonates with Tippett's account of his own psychological wound given in the Doty Lectures and elsewhere. This is not

to say that *New Year* is a 'coming-out' opera: as ever, the concern would be to draw a universal message from personal experience; but it is neverthe-less also to signal a possible debt which the former owes to the latter. (On this reading, then, the gay person's resolve to exit the closet and face the world with a measure of personal authenticity is seen as only a more acute and more specifiable case of a general situation in which everyone is in some sense queer.) The final stage-image of *New Year* – Jo Ann's exit from the room, the door closing firmly behind her – is indeed a potent one in this light, and far more positive than the 'exit from the inner cage' made only 'for a timid moment' by the characters in *The Knot Garden*. But, pur-suing the biographical line a little further, this is perhaps understandable given the turmoil of Tippett's personal life in the late 1960s, when he was composing the latter opera: it is not inconceivable that Dov's howlings (like a dog) at the impending break-up with his lover Mel in some way reflect the turbulence and tensions in Tippett's declining relationship with Karl Hawker at that time.[64] Conversely, the composition of *New Year*, and with it the story of Jo Ann's freeing of self, was contemporaneous with Tippett's dream of the 'house that is free and open'.[65]

However, we must avoid being too literal-minded in imputing any overly causal relationship between personal, social and creative process. It would be preferable to figure these mediations – between self and society, self and musical work, musical work and society – as a set of mutually rein-forcing cognitive schemata whereby Tippett's sense of identity, his under-standing of his relationship to society, and his intentions towards his creative activity conditioned one another as these mutated over his life-time. As I have attempted to demonstrate, all these elements call for con-sideration in an adequate analysis of the later stylistic shifts of Tippett's output. Corroboration that these homologies were in some way pertinent again comes from his reference in the Doty Lectures to the aporia of attempting to re-create a late-Beethovenian humanism in the modernist era:

> Now there, that element in *my life story* and *our life story* must somehow
> enter in. So the struggle would be, is it possible to make an analog in which
> you could come near, at least in your own terms, with all the ironies that we
> now know, to that intensity of emotion, compassion and intimacy?[66]

Although Tippett demurs from any further explanation of what he means by the terms, he nevertheless makes plain the relevance of biographical factors ('my life story') to this compositional problem, and their equation with cultural-historic factors ('our life story'). But what he also implies in the same discussion is that this particular aesthetic project will be one

appropriate to his last years: 'perhaps analogically, at the end of a long life, I might find my way into that intimacy'.[67]

As to the accuracy, or 'truth', of the social mediations implied by the recaptured lyricism of Tippett's late style, careful interpretation is again called for. That this style period was almost exactly contemporary with a reactionary socio-political regime in Tippett's own country might seem to invalidate any image of increased social harmoniousness read from his late works. But this would be to expect social progress to be uniform and unconflicted. The fact that Tippett was able to be publicly 'out' in this period might be seen as evidence on his part of a society moving towards a greater acceptance of the importance of individual freedoms, in a collective counter-movement to the repressive nature of official government policies. Equally we should bear in mind that Tippett's late period was itself not a homogeneous continuum. Between the lyrical epiphany of the Triple Concerto and the re-enchanted world of *The Rose Lake* lie works such as *The Mask of Time* and the Fifth String Quartet, in which affirmation and irony, lyricism and acerbity go hand in hand. But we should also be careful not to misconstrue artworks as a passive barometer of contemporary social conditions. Tippett himself spoke of the need for his art to run counter to the *Zeitgeist* of any given period[68] – which would mean that we should see his music neither as an unmediated reflection of an existing social order nor, necessarily, as a prognosis for a future one, but as an artefact to hold up critically to our time. Tippett's late period, then, would seem to be concerned with giving us not only a different kind of musical artwork to contemplate, but also different experiences of subjectivity to think *with* as we engage with society's historical movements.

Provided, of course, that we do. Music such as that discussed above can only transcend its status as an aesthetic object if we are awake to the critical potential within it. One justification for the kinds of musicological approach offered here would be exactly to provoke such an attitude.

7   The golden bird and the porcelain bowl: *Byzantium* and the politics of artefacts

What did Tippett mean by 'artefact'?

'Artefact' is a word that hovers problematically around Tippett's last works. The association originates from the composer himself, but he borrows the term from W. B. Yeats. 'In Yeats's jargon', we read in *Those Twentieth Century Blues*, 'an artefact is a work of art that is entirely separated from its creator – where the personal emotion has disappeared into the magnificence of the craft'.[1] And in the eyes of many – Tippett's included – the epitome of such an aesthetic apotheosis, in both construction and subject matter, is Yeats's late poem 'Byzantium' (1930). Hence it is no surprise that when, in the late 1980s, Tippett turned to set the poem he had long loved the same ideal would rank within his own creative criteria: 'My setting, which extends the fairly short poem into a big song lasting about 27 minutes, had to be just such an artefact', he writes.[2] And this is reinforced in the preface to *Byzantium* (1989–90): 'I identified completely with [Yeats's poem's] emphasis on the notion of artefacts, enshrining values that can be set against the impermanence of the everyday world and the complexities of the human beating heart'. There is another cultural-historical connection in this regard, namely T. S. Eliot, who first encouraged Tippett to read Yeats, and in whose essays, notably 'Tradition and the individual talent' (1919), the composer states he 'first met the notion of artefacts'.[3] He probably had in mind comments such as Eliot's claim that 'the more perfect the artist, the more completely separate in him will be the man who suffers and the mind which creates; the more perfectly will the mind digest and transmute the passions which are its material'.[4]

In one sense all this is uncontentious enough: that is, no more or less contentious than the concept of autonomous art itself, which these statements ostensibly promote and which is at the heart of Tippett's mature *œuvre* – the kind of conception which enabled him to say: 'In my maturity, that detachment [of self from work] is complete. The work, once written, belongs to the outside world.'[5] But in other respects this association between artefacts and Tippett's late works does not quite add up. For one thing, why these works especially? If the statement just quoted is valid, then surely the ideal applies to all his mature works and not just the late

ones: the Second Symphony (1956–7) would be just as good an example of an artefact as *Byzantium*. Equally perplexing is Meirion Bowen's comment regarding *The Rose Lake* (1991–3), which seeks to locate this, the composer's last major work, in the same aesthetic territory: 'It's his most reticent piece . . . He's almost saying "I don't exist" . . . Bye-bye. I'm not there. This is the music.'[6] Reticent certainly; but the work's very valedictory qualities seem to me to make it one of Tippett's most touchingly personal statements. (That this may be a merely subjective perception would only testify further to the alleged artefact's breakdown of its ability to enforce its artefactuality.)

These ambiguities lead me to conclude that when Tippett applied the term 'artefact' to a late work such as *Byzantium* it must have held additional, unstated connotations for him. Somewhere, we might surmise, there must be further texts that complete (or at least extend) the jigsaw. The E. William Doty Lectures[7] which Tippett gave at the University of Texas in 1976 were an important forum in which he explored several of the ideas that were to shape his late works; and the talks are no less pertinent to our concerns here than they were to those of the previous chapter. The lectures amplify Tippett's comments on Yeats, as discussed above, as well as bringing Stravinsky into the frame. But most important of all, they show how Tippett's thinking about artefacts is woven into a larger complex of ideas, within which is discernible a concept of musical material in relation to the creative process. However fuzzily formulated, these are genuine aesthetic-theoretical thoughts which also reveal an intuition of the nature of the social and subjective mediations of artistic material, and hint at its associated political ramifications. I shall attempt in what follows to unpack some of these perceptions, and in so doing highlight a contradiction in Tippett's view of artefacts which goes right to the heart of a work like *Byzantium*. Ultimately – as I shall discuss in the second part of this essay – Tippett can be seen to move away from his significant others Yeats and Stravinsky, into territory whose distinctiveness can be highlighted by calling on rather different voices. Such a view broadly endorses that found in Arnold Whittall's study of *Byzantium*.[8] My own contribution to the debate is to chart areas of confluence in the thinking that surrounded Tippett's and Yeats's art; to consider these in the light of political critiques of Yeats's and Stravinsky's positions (particularly of the latter's neoclassicism); to show analytically how the music of *Byzantium* itself puts up resistance to some of the problematic precepts of their aesthetics; and (perhaps an unorthodox final twist) to speculate that the work's peculiarities might gain some illumination when considered alongside ideas from feminist thought – specifically that of Julia Kristeva.

I

Tippett and Yeats: imagination and images

Tippett's concept of music is founded on 'a poetics of the imagination'. This is a notion identified by literary scholars – among them Cairns Craig, who considers its role as part of the ideology of romanticism, and its roots in Coleridge. Under this model 'the imagination not only structured our world, but also revealed the truth about it'.[9] But in the case of Yeats and Eliot, Craig argues, the idea has an ambivalent relationship with an alternative model for poetic communication – one based on memory and association – on which they staked their modernist credentials. Craig points out that the 1960s and 1970s saw a number of studies of Yeats, Eliot, Pound and others, which sought to effect the 'assimilation of the moderns to their romantic predecessors'.[10] Tippett's aesthetics betray a similar equivocation of romantic and modern, as evidenced by an inclination to parcel up romantic-idealist notions in psychological and psychoanalytical language, a process in which he tended to co-opt Yeats and Jung. Even as late as the 1970s, the romantic view of 'the imagination as linked to some transcendent source'[11] still had currency in his thought: the term he uses for it in the Doty Lectures is 'spontaneity', and making reference to Plato he aligns it with a kind of madness, or irrationality.[12] In a characteristic dualism, he argues that a complementary process is also at work in the fashioning of art, namely 'measurement' – a term with an explicitly Yeatsian ring.[13] Measurement, which 'has to do with the nature of skill', is by definition more rational, but is nevertheless 'not only rational' since 'part of the measurement of music' involves measuring its effects on the internal organs.[14] This dialogue – indeed dialectic – between the rational and irrational is fundamental, and its further resonances with Yeats will become clear as we continue exploring it.

Between the initial 'conceptual spark' of spontaneity and the eventual business of measurement, is a mediating stage: 'the accretion of images'.[15] Tippett variably describes this 'accretional process' as being powered by the Jungian collective unconscious, or its Yeatsian counterpart, the 'Great Memory'.[16] This process too has its moment of spontaneity. Tippett's claim in his much earlier essay 'The birth of an opera' that 'the more collective an artistic imaginative experience is going to be, the more the discovery of suitable material is involuntary'[17] has its counterpart in one of Yeats's descriptions of the accretion of images:

> One must allow the images to form with all their associations before one
> criticises ... If you suspend the critical faculty, I have discovered, either as

the result of training, or, if you have the gift, by passing into a slight trance, images pass rapidly before you. If you can suspend also desire, and let them form at their own will, your absorption becomes more complete and they are more clear in colour, more precise in articulation.[18]

Tippett's presentation of this imaginative process as 'accretional' chimes in with the associationism that is essential for Yeats (and indeed for an entire poetic tradition within which Eliot also numbers).[19] Paradoxically, while gestating in the most inner reaches of the subjective imagination, these associations or involuntary accretions are also what underwrite the emerging work's efficacy within the culture which will receive it. In Craig's words: 'The poem, in finding pattern and harmony and revelatory symbol, completes one process of association emerging from the Great Memory through the poet's mind, and, in engaging the reader's mind, re-enters the flow of events that we think of as history'.[20] Images are potent, then, because they galvanize an array of associations; their presence in the poem (re-)activates memories of which the reader may not have been aware – a kind of centrifugal discharge through the historical repository of memories of a culture as whole.[21] Under this conception the artwork, while the self-contained nexus of such images, draws its power from forces beyond itself. The 'revelatory' quality to which Craig refers is also surmised (and slightly qualified) by Tippett:

> If you allow the accretional process to continue to its finality, and follow it, then, with the act of forging and measuring, there's a possibility that out of all that comes a work of art which has within it – I would hesitate to use the word revelation – *apprehensions* beyond other kinds of works of art in which we have a feeling that our apprehensions are concerned almost purely with aesthetics.[22]

The composer is talking here about a (favoured) category of great or sublime art concerned not merely with being savoured for its own sake. In subsequent comments which I will consider presently Tippett implies that the potency of such art lies in the fact that it taps into our full social, historical and cultural being.

But the Great Memory has another, darker, irrational side. For Yeats this tapped into his belief in the occult – the Great Memory as not only a 'passing on from generation to generation', but also the medium through which the memories of the dead are communicated to the living.[23] Tippett did not go this far, of course, but the resonances of his own earlier reference to the Great Memory as a 'demoniac cauldron' should not be ignored.[24] In the Doty Lectures the cauldron again appears as a metaphor for the turmoil of the collective unconscious, which in some way mirrors that of the empirical

world, a world which 'subjects us to an endless problematic of change'.[25] To immerse oneself in the 'cauldron world' (or, as Yeats puts in 'Byzantium', 'That dolphin-torn, that gong tormented sea') carries pathological risks, and Nietzsche and Hölderlin are Tippett's paradigms for those who went under.[26] I would argue that his second period (from *King Priam* onward) is where, metaphorically, he plunges most deeply into this kind of world, empathizing with (or mimetically enacting) the turbulence and contradictions of the historical conditions of modernity within his own psyche. Yeats endorses the need for such internalized warfare in his well-known statement, 'We make out of the quarrel with others, rhetoric, but of the quarrel with ourselves, poetry . . . The other self, the anti-self or the antithetical self, as one may choose to name it, comes but to those who are no longer deceived, whose passion is reality.'[27] The anti-type through which one arrives at such apprehensions of reality is characterized by Yeats as *mask* (a notion he would later incorporate within the arcane systems of *A Vision*): 'I find in an old diary: "I think all happiness depends on the energy to assume the mask of some other life, on a re-birth as something not one's self, something created in a moment perpetually renewed"'.[28] And significantly this mask may have the quality of a *daimon*, which 'comes not as like to like but seeking its own opposite, for man and Daimon feed the hunger in one another's hearts'.[29] Again, it would not be too fanciful to apply these metaphors to the dialectical movements of Tippett's own stylistic changes: in *King Priam* and beyond he begins to wrestle with a dark 'anti-self'; an agon breaks out between his old humanistic side and a form of antihumanism whose archetype bears comparison with the Dionysus of the later Nietzsche (a figure of no small import for Yeats).[30]

Two functions of art

Tippett reflects that such encounters with the daimonic can lead to a kind of artistic material which abjures purity, beauty and closure. He states: 'I am in a very great tradition which is measured by, say, Shakespeare on one side and therefore, I can risk works of art, if they're any good at all, which have non-ends and are not molded into this beautiful thought'.[31] What such artworks risk – a corollary of their resistance to measurement, their courting of the inchoate – is a pathology analogous to that to which their creator exposes himself. In this regard Tippett cites Eliot:

> I'll quote another metaphor of T. S. Eliot's; he called it 'black material', a
> material which he thought was unnameable to total measurement. He uses
> the phrase about Shakespeare's sonnets. He thought the material in the
> sonnets, endlessly argumentative about the ambivalent experience, broke

them into pieces. Eliot said it also of *Hamlet*: that even Shakespeare could not make this black material come within the concept of a completely measured world.[32]

While Tippett recognized the problematics of 'black material', he was clearly willing to entertain a more accepting position towards it – as analysts of his music will be all too aware. Indeed the necessity of black material as the fallout of the artist's encounter with the forces of history is perhaps implicit in his comment of some twenty years earlier, that 'to certain individuals alone, comes . . . the inescapable duty to make conscious the repressed longing locked up in the [collective] inner violence and psychic disarray'.[33]

If black material is the result of engaging in the accretive, 'revelatory' image-making process whereby the artwork is a seismogram of its social and historical circumstances, it has an anti-type in Tippett's thinking which seems to involve removal from the social altogether. Its epitome is the 'porcelain bowl':

> I've said before that I've taken in my hand beautiful, fragile pots or vases of Chinese work, porcelain made in a period as anarchic and almost as horrible as our own, and here (as far as I can see) is no revelatory process at all. But there is an extraordinary value, and we do want to know that this is also a possibility of polarity in our existence.[34]

The porcelain bowl, we might surmise, exemplifies what Tippett understands by an artefact – in both a literal and an extended sense. This is an art which is 'pure', 'wrought' (involving, one assumes, a high degree of 'measurement'); it contrasts with black material by apparently excluding the historical world outside – by disguising its social mediation, by covering all traces of its origins in the turbulence of its creator's imagination. Again there is an intertextual connection with Eliot – this time with lines from 'Burnt Norton', V:

> Only by the form, the pattern,
> Can words or music reach
> The stillness, as a Chinese jar still
> Moves perpetually in its stillness.

In the Doty Lectures, then, Tippett identifies 'two . . . differing sorts of functions of art',[35] for which his poetic exemplars are Shakespeare and Racine:

> Shakespeare's is a rich world in which there are no great pure works of art, but an extraordinary mass of works which are a cauldron and world-wide and reacting. But when you come to Racine, what did he want? He wanted to

exclude everything that couldn't be put within this marvelous poetry. I believe they're both for real, but I think the artist has to know who he is, which he is, and he can't be both.[36]

Although Tippett seems to incline more strongly towards the Shakespearian rather than the Racinian type (in his formulation) he does state 'I feel them both in myself'.[37] This vacillation is most clearly evident in his stance towards Stravinsky – he means here the neoclassical Stravinsky, which is his archetype of the artefactual in music:

My god of present days is really Stravinsky. There's no question about that. Stravinsky held to one thing all his life, that the work of art each time was, so to speak, wrought out of granite. It could be delicate, and so granite is a silly term, but each one of them was separately wrought. He never wanted or tried to produce ambivalent works in any case. Whatever you think of *Oedipus Rex* or any of them, of whatever period, they are just rooted like that. This is to me of tremendous value, so I always want to go towards it; but where I would differ is because of my education in the other process of having antennae that are concerned with the other problems of our society. Stravinsky never did.[38]

This is not the only time in the Doty Lectures in which Tippett expresses an equivocation towards the 'extraordinary' or 'tremendous' value of arte-facts and their would-be abjuration of subjective and social mediation. There is a hint of urgency in this dilemma because he senses a change in his own aesthetic standpoint on the horizon – one in which the artefactual will in some way more strongly feature. (This, as I have described above (chapter 6), is a mutation of aesthetic priorities which invites the notion of a 'late' period in his *œuvre*.) Both intent and ambiguity are evident in his comment that 'I have to measure myself with the Chinese bowl in my hand and say that it's possible that a much greater figure in this turbulent world of our time could produce the bowl. And I know that I am not Francis Bacon; I'm not going to scream forever.'[39] What he seems to be seeking is not the pure artefactuality, as he sees it, of Stravinskian neoclassicism, but some form of synthesis between the two types of art he has identified. And the significance of Yeats's 'Byzantium' now becomes apparent as the alleged archetype of exactly such a synthesis:

The last great person to my mind who put it all in was Yeats. If you read the poem *Byzantium*, you'll see how it was done, wrought and wrestled with. He has a lot of set metaphors and – very Stravinsky-like – a metaphor of being that is the golden nightingale which the Byzantine empress had made with the finesse of smithies and which was so unreal. That takes you straight into *The Nightingale* of Stravinsky. This was some extraordinary value, and Yeats put up against that what he calls the mire and complexity of the blood and

the veins in the body and the sea and the dolphins . . . The furies of complexity he knew, but because he was so much older, he didn't experience them in absolutes by being sent to Siberia or by being removed in Hiroshima. Again, he comes to the final possibility that this golden thing, this music – that the complexities of emotion are the complexity from mind to body – that this might do something for you and calm 'That dolphin-torn, that gong-tormented sea'.[40]

Yeats, Stravinsky and Unity of Being

For Yeats the Byzantium of the late fifth century was simultaneously a historical city, a mythological place and a state of being. His image of the city was informed by the scholarly texts he read and the sites of Byzantine art he visited.[41] In the fifth book of *A Vision* (1925, rev. 1937), 'Dove or swan', Byzantium enters his grand mythologized scheme of history whereby civilizations rise and fall in interlocking gyres. 'Each age', he writes (adumbrating imagery he would deploy in stanza 2 of 'Byzantium'), 'unwinds the thread another age had wound . . . When full moon came round again, amid eastward-moving thought, and brought Byzantine glory, Rome fell; and . . . at the outset of our westward-moving Renaissance Byzantium fell; all things dying each other's life, living each other's death.'[42] And at the zenith of its ascendancy Byzantium epitomized for Yeats a notion at the heart of his values, Unity of Being:

> I think that in early Byzantium, maybe never before or since in recorded history, religious, aesthetic and practical life were one, that architect and artificers – though not, it may be, poets, for language had been the instrument of controversy and must have grown abstract – spoke to the multitude and the few alike. The painter, the mosaic worker, the worker in gold and silver, the illuminator of sacred books, were almost impersonal, almost perhaps without the consciousness of individual design, absorbed in their subject-matter and that the vision of a whole people.[43]

The unification of the sacred and the social, the individual and the multitude is underwritten by the artefactual. 'Marbles of the dancing floor', the gold mosaic and the golden bird 'planted on the star-lit golden bough' – images from Yeats's two Byzantium poems ('Sailing to Byzantium' of 1926, and 'Byzantium' itself) – stand for a permanence and a pure perfection which the poet sets against 'The fury and the mire of human veins'. Throughout 'Byzantium' the opposition between the turbulence of nature and the artifice of culture is reflected in the antinomy of fluidity – 'blood', 'mire', 'sea' – and hardness – 'marble', 'metal'. In the final stanza these images are thrust together in an energetic and arguably

violent synthesis. Here the spirits of the dead, borne on the backs of warm-blooded dolphins, stream towards the eternal city (hence 'death-in-life and life-in-death'). Such antithetical experience is lived by Yeats's 'Daimonic man' – the archetype (associated with phase seventeen of *A Vision*'s 'Great Wheel') who is closest to Unity of Being, whose *mask*, 'simplification through intensity', wrestles with its other, 'dispersal'.[44] 'Byzantium', marshalling a unifying formal and syntactic order over its conflicting and proliferating images, enacts this agon.[45]

Although Tippett might have empathized with Unity of Being from an epistemic standpoint – that is, as a desire for the reconciliation of the spheres of rational, moral and aesthetic knowledge sundered since the Enlightenment – he might have felt more queasy about aspects of the polity implicit in the idea. Craig's argument that '"Byzantium", as focus of aesthetic order, is also a place of political stability, its social world shaped to the rigidity of sculpture' puts an equivocal gloss on the poem's beauty and vision – especially as the argument continues: 'When Yeats expands a theory of society based on activating the irrational commitment of a multitude through images with effective associational impact he is at one with the central strand of Fascist ideology'.[46] Craig refers here to Yeats's conviction – added to 'that first conviction, to that first desire for unity' – that 'Nations, races, and individual men are unified by an image, or bundle of related images'.[47] What embittered the poet in the early decades of the twentieth century was the turn of Irish politics away from its nationalist roots. 'The [Gaelic] League', he quotes Thomas MacDonagh as saying, 'is killing Celtic civilization'.[48] The cultural memory on which his poems depended for their associative imagery was being eroded, and paradoxically, the poet now looked to the imperilled Anglo-Irish aristocracy as the last bastion of a culture suitable for the reception of his work: 'Suggestion is richest to the richest and so art grows unpopular in a democracy like this'.[49] As Craig points out, 'Yeats's regret at the destruction of the Anglo-Irish aristocracy was not to remain a merely elegiac passion but was to fuel his support for the [quasi-fascist] Blueshirts'.[50]

Yeats was not the only artist Tippett admired whose political outlook was so coloured. A similar anti-democratic vein runs through T. S. Eliot's espousal of an 'articulated' or 'graded' society, in which each stratum would possess its own culture, but whose highest level would be an elite whose 'peculiar and essential function' would be to represent 'a more conscious culture and a greater specialisation of culture'.[51] In 1928 Eliot wrote of 'concepts which might have attracted me in fascism', though it is well enough known that his preferred agencies for a centralizing order in his political vision were the monarchy and the church rather than a totalitarian

state. But if Tippett's 'spiritual father' kept some distance from fascism itself, his 'god of present days', Stravinsky, was less reticent. Richard Taruskin provides one of the most searching recent accounts of the darker side of Stravinsky's politics, which was shaped by his counterrevolutionary sentiments and allegiances: not only his anti-Semitism, but also his expressed empathy for Mussolini.[52] In the early 1930s Stravinsky indeed sanctioned a description of himself as the 'dictator of the reaction against the anarchy into which modernism degenerated'.

Significant in all these cases is the fact that political and aesthetic precepts do not remain hermetically closed off from one another. For example, Taruskin asserts that Stravinsky's desire 'to do for modern music what the Duce promised to do for modern Europe . . . was the subtext and the motivation for his "neoclassicism"'.[53] On Taruskin's view, this neoclassicism 'had nothing to do, at first, with stylistic retrospectivism or revivalism, with "returning to Bach", or with vicarious imperial restoration. It had everything to do with a *style dépouillé*, a stripped-down, denuded style, and with the same antihumanism that had already motivated Stravinsky's Eurasianist phase.'[54] This last reference is directed especially towards *Les noces* (*Svadebka*). Taruskin's extended cultural and analytical study traces a dialectic within that work, whereby on the one hand its mobilization of Russian folk and (significantly) pseudo-folk resources represented a counter-hegemonic move against a 'Europeanization' (or 'Romano-Germanization'), while on the other hand those very Russian elements were in turn 'universalized' through formalism and abstraction in order for the piece to make a hegemonic claim of its own. Taruskin's summary description of *Les noces* – as an 'apotheosis under the "universalizing" aegis of abstraction, streamlining, and simplicity'[55] – could apply equally to Yeats's 'Byzantium' and its ethos of 'simplification through intensity'. Like *Les noces*, the poem distils the image of a historically contingent culture into a wrought, crystalline artefact of would-be supratemporal value; and it likewise (and almost exactly contemporaneously) stems from the hand of an artist suffering from post-revolutionary disillusionment.

At bottom these issues concern the politics of romanticism and classicism. Quoting an identical passage from Stravinsky's *Poetics of Music* to which Tippett had also referred in his essay 'Stravinsky and *Les noces*',[56] Taruskin states:

> The Classic and Romantic are opposed in Stravinsky's exposition under the politically charged rubrics of submission and insubordination. The artist must 'submit to the law' . . . because 'Apollo demands it' . . . Apollo vs. Dionysus was first of all music vs. drama, thence stasis vs. flux, beauty vs. frenzy, purity vs. mixture, repose vs. desire, containment vs. expression – all easily decoded as Classicism vs. Romanticism.[57]

As it turns out, these terms come close to those which Tippett uses to describe his 'two . . . differing sorts of functions of art'. Indeed the Doty Lectures' terminology of spontaneity and measurement could be viewed as cognate with a trope of classicism vs romanticism that surfaces a number of times in Tippett's thinking on art and music, particularly modernist art and music. The following examples also employ certain key terms we have noted among other commentators, such as 'abstraction', 'purity', 'form', 'unity':

> Romanticism and classicism are enduring attitudes as well as ways of depicting periods of history . . . This is why I think neo-romanticism and neo-classicism have appeared in modern music simultaneously. Neo-romanticism tends towards expressionism while neo-classicism tends towards abstraction.
>
> I consider the general classicizing [i.e. neoclassicizing] tendency of our day less as evidence of a new classic period, than as a fresh endeavour . . . to constrain and clarify inchoate material. We must both submit to the overwhelming experience and clarify it into a magical unity. In the event, sometimes Dionysus wins, sometimes Apollo.
>
> There is always an aspect of art which throws the emphasis on measurement and relation, rather than on the sensuous . . .
>   We choose purity and we may sacrifice allure. We choose richness, and we may sacrifice form.[58]

Unlike Taruskin, Tippett (on these occasions anyway) is silent regarding the possible political implications of these positions: classicism and romanticism, the Apollonian and Dionysiac, purity and allure – all are broached as wholly aesthetic concerns. That might be one way of dealing with the rather troublesome issues raised by accounts such as Craig's and Taruskin's: to solve the problem of 'the symbiosis of beautiful art and ugly politics'[59] foreground the art and overlook the politics. Yet to hive off the aesthetic from the circumstances of its production – to consume it purely artefactually – would be to reduce it to the merely decorative, perhaps to remove it from the sphere of the human altogether, like Yeats's golden bird. Writ large this becomes a problem fundamental to the aesthetic of autonomous art. On the one hand artworks are not literally autobiographical documents; they hold open the possibility that, to quote from Auden's elegy for Yeats, 'The words of a dead man / Are modified in the guts of the living'.[60] Yet on the other hand (and notwithstanding the real or metaphoric death of the author) where aesthetic formations betray the problematic ideologies of the hand which created them, it is arguably politically culpable to ignore this. Polemics such as Taruskin's may push to extremes, but they are not resolved by simply turning down the intensity.

Perhaps the only authentic answer to these questions is to take to heart their unanswerability. What is compelling in Taruskin's discussion of Stravinsky is that he recommends neither jettisoning a work such as *Les noces* nor marginalizing the ideology legible within it; instead he invites us to register with him the profound ambivalence of the situation (though, even so, his words betray a tendency to aestheticize that very process): 'It is precisely in recognition of the danger in the work's allure, the heart of darkness that lurks behind and conditions its gravely joyous affirmations, that so intensifies reaction'.[61] This makes the point that ambivalence might be a legitimate, perhaps the only possible, response to such complexities. Certainly this is manifested in the pattern of Tippett's influences and affinities: Yeats, Eliot and Stravinsky, as we have seen; also Jung and, I would argue, Nietzsche;[62] as well as Jeffrey Mark, Tippett's friend from his RCM days, who (like Stravinsky) mixed an interest in folk music with an anti-Semitic political agenda.[63] Time and again, it seems, the figures who were important in shaping Tippett's thinking about art were those with problematic political credentials; and while he also revealed a liberal's intuitive resistance to the more repugnant aspects of their ideologies, the very repetition of the pattern leads one to wonder about the significance of this obverse side to their allure.

Signs of such resistance within his attraction are not to be directly found in his comments on the likes of Yeats and Stravinsky, but are rather scattered around other of his observations or revealed in his actual compositional practice. Resistance operates on two main fronts. The first is seen in both a wariness towards the subject-eclipsing tendency of the Apollonian, and an awareness of the politically subversive potential of the Dionysiac. For example, in *New Year* (1986–8) the purged, utopian order of 'Nowhere and Tomorrow' is represented as a nightmare of Apollonian sanitization: Regan, its dominatrix, sings of 'Flying speeding through that sky of dreams' and asserts 'No way to my achieving but by a path of power / No way may feelings stain the shining steel.' Cast in the form of a simplified parable, Tippett's message is similar to Taruskin's warning that 'the "universalizing" aegis of abstraction, streamlining, and simplicity' may be tied up with something politically dicey. Complementing this, in the Doty Lectures Tippett recalls Plato's perception of art as threatening to such an order, as 'dangerous, and dangerous in a political form',[64] because it contained an element of madness, of Dionysiac irrationality ('spontaneity').

The second element of Tippett's resistance is a degree of scepticism towards the order symbolized in the perfection of artefacts, the order of Unity of Being. While, self-evidently, he never abandoned the paradigm of high art, we can glimpse a sensitivity on the horizons of his thinking and

practice towards other possibilities, and towards the cultural and social diversity this would entail. This is one of the areas in which we may detect a shift of ground in Tippett's thinking over the years. For example, in 1941, within the tangled prose of a letter written to Francesca Allinson he posited – 'as a standard for our day' – 'a sort of ladder – the roots in romantic, immediate expression – what [Cecil] Sharp went to find – & the heaven of the ladder will be the classical, artistic, turned, articulated stuff'.[65] Here romanticism and classicism (in this case represented by folk music and art music) function as poles of a cultural continuum (signified by the ladder metaphor) which bears more than a passing resemblance to those models of a stratified yet unified society idealized (roughly contemporaneously) by Eliot and Yeats.[66] But in his modernist period – from *Priam* onwards – and certainly by the time of his late works Tippett's position had altered. He now shows himself open to the notion of a culture emphatically not modelled after the unifying order of art. Unity of Being as an ideal now cedes to plurality of being – to something not unlike a postmodernized society:

> We have the chance to involve a great many more people in sophistication, in sensibilities, who would in the past have been deprived. If the good things from our enormous technological advances become more widespread, what does that do? Does that merely produce a larger number of Beethoven performances? Or does it produce a lot of possibilities of all sorts of individual ways of making art; pockets of different kinds of music, different types of people? You see, it's all open, I hope.[67]

The recognition of plurality, and its corollary, a scepticism towards unity, become shaping forces in Tippett's *Byzantium*; indeed these notions are thematized at length in Whittall's commentary on the work as crucial in defining the 'limitations of affinity' between Tippett and Yeats.[68] But – still more radically – in the penumbra of Tippett's statement is also a sense of the consequences of such a pluralized society: a situation in which the aesthetic practices so central to his own thinking may no longer have pride of place. We might speculate that what makes this thinkable at all for Tippett is that it might in the end be more compatible with his liberal humanist aspirations than present-day social relationships, in which the consumption of 'great art' remains concentrated within the middle classes (whatever the idiosyncratic patterns in the consumption of his own music). And it is perhaps a similarly humanist motivation which drives him to uphold to the end – notwithstanding the simplifying, purgative aspirations of his last works – that moment of unpurged 'spontaneity' against the abstracting, classicizing force of form.

Against Yeats's fantasy of the unified culture of ancient Byzantium (see p. 243, above) comments by Boris de Schloezer, cited by Taruskin, can be illuminatingly juxtaposed:

> Classical culture is fundamentally materialistic and static; herein lies the ever-present danger of its degeneration into fetishism and formalism . . . For the classical mind the world of culture, though manufactured by man, possesses an objective reality equivalent to the world of nature's . . . Its system of values comprises a conglomeration of manufactured objects that tend to assume an autonomous existence, forming a rigid world often hostile to man's emotional life . . . In classical cultures, in which workers and masters labor together, the future is conceived as an accumulation of cultural values, a development and reinforcement of the system whose ultimate aim is perfection in isolation.[69]

To Derrick Puffett's plaint against the later Tippett – 'Why can Tippett not be content with making beautiful objects, the "artefacts" he praises in his autobiography and elsewhere? It was good enough for Stravinsky'[70] – these remarks (together with the other critiques considered here) constitute a robust response. While comments on artefacts in Tippett's autobiography and elsewhere might themselves seem insouciant in such a light, evidence garnered from further sources will, I hope, have shown that the term had more complex and contradictory connotations for the composer. Through encounters with real and symbolic significant others he seems to have intuited that a creative stance which involves a high degree of domination over its materials can elide with sympathy for other kinds of imperiousness. And just as in his Third Symphony (1970–2) Tippett launches a critique of the creator he had previously made his god (i.e. Beethoven), so the many idiosyncrasies of the later *Byzantium* issue from an analogous debate sounded within its material. Albeit less overtly, the work seems to register a similar question: What price Yeats and Stravinsky now?

II

Byzantium: the golden bird

The ambivalence which Tippett's *Byzantium* displays towards Yeats's eponymous poem runs deep. On the one hand the sheer intensity with which the composer renders the text suggests not merely an intention to set the poem but a passionate desire to possess it. On the other hand, having put himself into visionary overdrive he pushes at the boundaries of what is tasteful, sometimes breaking through them into a register close to

parody – as if wanting also to send up the object of his desire. On the cusp of these two states are many moments of literal-minded mimesis in which the gap between imitating and imitated objects is all but eroded: for example, 'great cathedral gong' summons up the sound of tuned gongs; 'glory of the changeless metal' and, later, 'golden smithies of the emperor' a clattering of anvils. But the critical distance between Yeats and Tippett is greatest in the latter's handling of the image of the golden bird, the epitome of the artefactual.

Jahan Ramazani argues that for Yeats the trope of *ekphrasis* – the presentation of an artefact as one's ostensible subject – is usually bound up with meditation on death.[71] In 'Sailing to Byzantium' Yeats celebrates the golden bird as a symbol of translation after death from the physical decay of old age ('An aged man is but a paltry thing, / A tattered coat upon a stick') into 'the artifice of eternity'. In 'Byzantium' itself the bird now takes a central position. Artifice claims superiority over the ephemeral and ceaseless becoming of nature in a tone close to contempt; for the bird

> Can like the cocks of Hades crow,
> Or, by the moon embittered, scorn aloud
> In glory of changeless metal
> Common bird or petal
> And all complexities of mire and blood.

And that is the problem. Existential permanence over nature's cyclic flux of life and death means the rejection of the mortal body in favour of a fetish that is hard, cold, heartless. Although in old age himself at the time of composing *Byzantium*, Tippett seemed to have found this idea a touch ludicrous. His ludic response to Yeats's subtly embedded onomatopoeia – 'Can . . . cocks . . . crow' – is an ornate and disproportionately extended travesty of the bird's song, using invented syllables, 'Cŏ-cŏ-ri-cō' (Fig. 77ff.). As Whittall points out,[72] this is a version of the crow calls from 'Donny's Skarade' in *New Year* (see Fig. 124ff. of the opera); and, I would add, its connotation of the dystopian world of 'Somewhere and Today' could be a further ironic dig at the 'holy city of Byzantium'.

Another important co-ordinate fixed by the golden bird is Stravinsky's *Le rossignol* (*The Nightingale*). As previously cited comments from the Doty Lectures reveal (see pp. 242–3), a link between Yeats's poem and Stravinsky's opera (and/or its subsequent incarnation as the symphonic poem *Chant du rossignol*) was in Tippett's mind many years before starting work on *Byzantium*. Pertinent to our present discussion is Daniel Albright's comment on Stravinsky's version of the Hans Christian Andersen tale (in which real and mechanical birds compete for a Chinese emperor's affections) that it is an exploration of 'the deep equivalence of

the natural and the artificial'; that 'at the center of [Stravinsky's] dramatic imagination is the desire to juxtapose in a single work two competing systems . . . and to subvert these distinctions as best he can'.[73] (This recalls the above-quoted comment of Schloezer: 'for the classical mind the world of culture, though manufactured by man, possesses a reality equivalent to the world of nature's'.)

The music of *Byzantium* takes as dialectical a stance towards the Stravinskian aesthetic as it does towards Yeats. Tippett's piece corroborates his acquaintance with *Le rossignol* at the same as it occupies a different – if no less exotic – aesthetic world. Apart from the general comparability between Stravinsky's glittering score and the opulent soundworld of *Byzantium*, there is a significant specific similarity: between the harmonic background of the song of the mechanical nightingale in the former, and the opening chord of the latter. Both the relevant moments are quoted in Example 7.1, and the harmonies in question are abstracted in Example 7.2(a). What links the two sonorities is their common octatonic derivation: from the three available transpositions of the octatonic scale, illustrated in Example 7.2(c), the two collections draw from the version I have labelled O1. While the collections themselves are not identical, their shared pitch classes, C–E–F♯–E♭–B♭, and their occupation of largely the same registers, form a similarity which seems beyond the bounds of coincidence.

Similarity can throw difference into relief. Stravinsky's texture is elegant, delicate; Tippett's awesome. Stravinsky's sounds create stasis, fix time; Tippett's reverberate through space. Stravinsky's music wants containment: the oboe's pentatonic emulation of the mechanical bird's song is almost entirely encompassed by the octatonic set invoked by the harmonic background (only the pitch class D is aberrant).[74] Tippett's music declares exuberance: the trumpet fanfare which partners the opening collection is only partially mapped by the latter's octatonic source set, and this excess continues in the passionate hypervocality of the ensuing melody for the violins (see Ex. 7.3); not only do we have more material here, but this moves into new octatonic territory – based on version O3 of the scale – containing an anomaly (the pitch E) which will in turn show its own pattern of growth in subsequent varied extensions.

But as significant a difference as any is the fact that the octatonic chord which opens *Byzantium* (hereafter termed the 'Byzantium chord') is not associated with the mechanical or golden bird, but has a more polyvalent meaning. One of its associations is with the more sublime artefact of the cathedral of Saint Sophia. Tippett evokes this space metonymically in his response to Yeats's words 'great cathedral gong' (stanza 1; Fig. 23); here the opening collection returns with the addition of a pulsating synthesizer chord, enhancing and exceeding the octatonic parameters. The

Example 7.1. At (a): Stravinsky, *Chant du rossignol* ('Jeu du rossignol mécanique'). At (b): Tippett, *Byzantium*, opening chord.

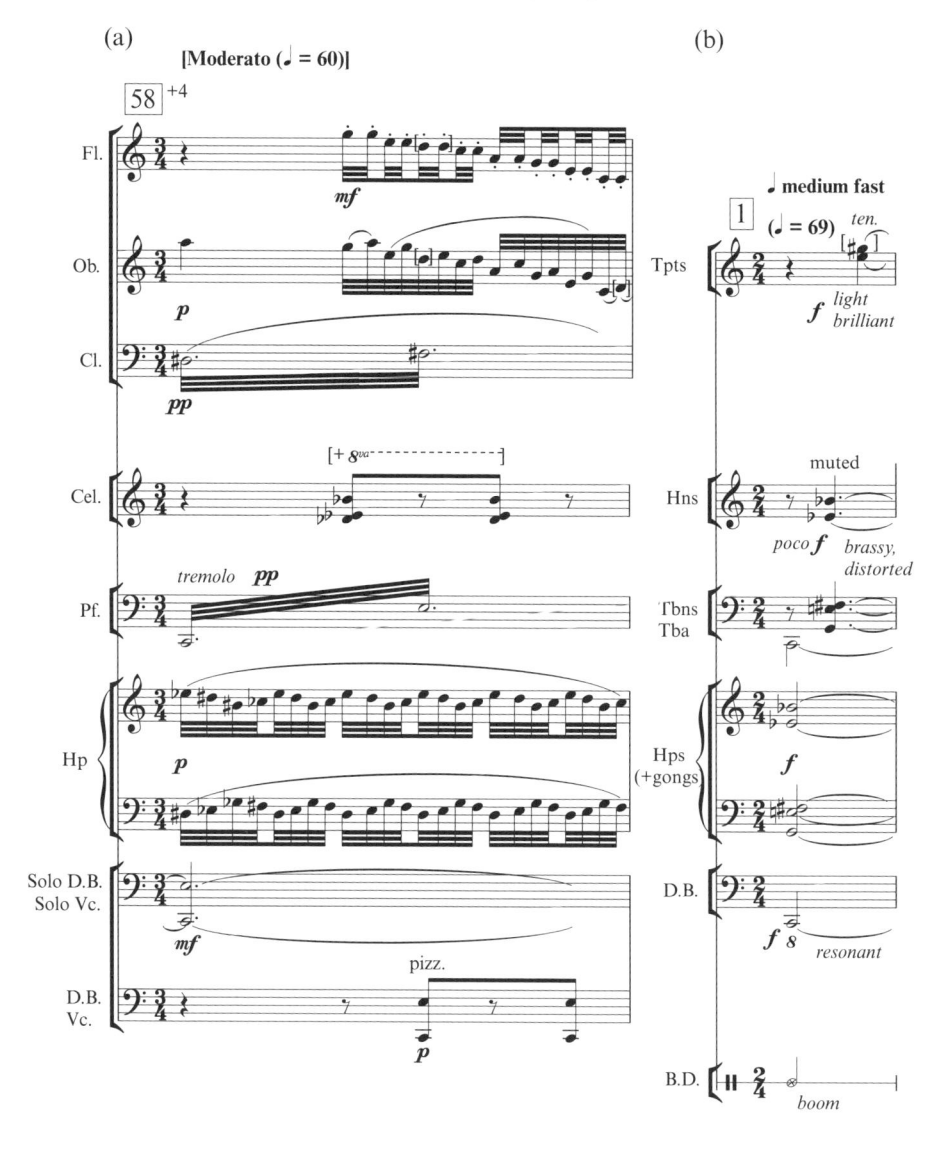

Example 7.2. At (a): 'Nightingale' and 'Byzantium' chords abstracted (cf. Ex. 7.1). At (b): variant of 'Byzantium' chord (e.g., as at close). At (c): three representatives of octatonic scale.

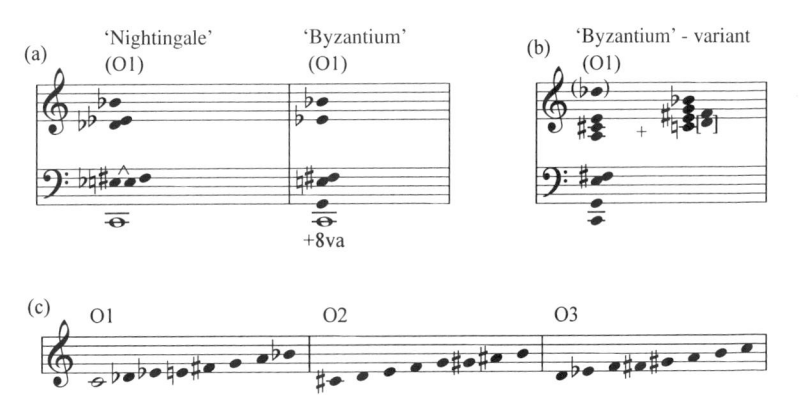

Example 7.3. *Byzantium*: trumpet and violin counterpoints to opening 'Byzantium' chord (cf. Ex. 7.1(b)).

predominant sound of tuned gongs at this point is – as mentioned earlier – a kind of hypermimesis which simultaneously concretizes its referent and sends the imagination transcendentally spinning beyond it. And this indeterminacy, which at the opening allows for a generalized visionary evocation of the city, also makes it possible for the collection to return at the poem's closing lines, 'That dolphin-torn, that gong tormented sea'. (The last chord is a variant of the opening one (see Ex. 7.2(b)), but none the less grounded in the same octatonic source-set – evidence against Paul Driver's characterization of it as 'an undecided welter of sound'.[75]) Thus, if the image of the golden bird forms the literal centre of Yeats's poem (as the subject of the third stanza of five), the sonic image of the Byzantium chord is the metaphorical centre of Tippett's concert aria. In fact both notions of a centre converge in *Byzantium* – as well as the

bathic and sublime modes associated with their respective images – when exactly half way through setting the poem ('Or by the moon embittered'; Fig. 80) Tippett silences his cock-crows with a reinvocation of the Byzantium sonority – one of the piece's most spine-tingling moments.

Structures and imagery

For all that part of Tippett's attraction to 'Byzantium' lay in its 'crystalline intensity', his work abjures the poem's formal precision. Enamoured by that crystalline appearance he transforms the poem's every turn into a redolent musical image of his own making; consequently Yeats's meticulously measured pattern of accumulating internal correspondences is dilated and overwhelmed by the music that colonizes it; and, like Orpheus, Tippett loses the thing he loves. Yet something new and necessarily different arises in its place. Tippett's famous dictum that 'the music of a song destroys the verbal music of a poem utterly',[76] is not sufficient explanation here. In *Byzantium* the disjunction between words and music is to do with the agon of aesthetic premises: an awareness on the composer's part that his own music (unlike, say, Stravinsky's) is not able to render that synthesis of the two modalities of art – let us call them Apollonian and Dionysiac – he so admires in Yeats's poem. In Tippett's *Byzantium* these modalities pay each other their due while enduring an unsettled co-existence. What makes the piece problematic also gives it a critical edge.

I propose to explore this unreconciled relationship by first considering further features tractable by the notion of structure, and then contemplating those aspects of the piece which, while highly meaningful, cannot be 'measured' in the same way. This follows the model of the musical image outlined in chapter 2, as containing an articulate, one might say intellectually formulated, element, as well a component, founded in the sensory, which exceeds it. We will also need to remain sensitive to points of partial mediation between these two elements.

Byzantium certainly provides some evidence of that Apollonian clarification Tippett ascribes to his late works. Extremes of rhythmic and textural complexity are curtailed, and out of this emerge many points of tonal, indeed diatonic lucidity, and an associated vocal and instrumental lyricism. One of the clearest examples is the soprano's rapt melisma on the word 'dome' (Fig. 24ff.; quoted without orchestral figuration in Ex. 7.4(a)). A supporting bass pedal on A reinforces the melody's unambiguous assertion of A major, of which the D♯ in the second bar is merely an inflection; interestingly the only true digression from this pure diatonic field – the melodic sequence G♮–B♭–A–F♯–G–E – delineates an octatonic

Example 7.4. 'A starlit or a moonlit dome disdains'. At (a): soprano's A major melisma (orchestral doublings and accompaniment omitted). At (b): octatonic configurations.

profile instead. Law is further exerted over the melody in the form of a double canon which generates the entire accompanimental texture (bass pedal aside): one voice (lower strings) in literal imitation at the half bar; the other (glockenspiel) in triple augmentation.

Scale forms are one of Tippett's most important resources of musical measurement.[77] And again we can invoke the significance of the octatonic scale (a hallmark not only of *Byzantium* but also of *The Rose Lake*) whose regular alternation of tones and semitones, and its resultant division of the octave into four equal segments, epitomizes measurement. However, whereas Taruskin can show for Stravinsky's *Les noces* that the octatonic scale acts as an overarching organizational principle into which all diatonic surface manifestations are assimilated, no such demonstration is possible for *Byzantium*.[78] In Tippett's piece the octatonic scale might be

used to coax contrary diatonic centres into equilibrium – as in the case of the variant of the Byzantium chord that ends the work, where, in Whittall's words, 'an A major triad (and perhaps an F♯ major triad too) resonates against C major'.[79] But no less often, Tippett's octatonicism serves to displace diatonic configurations rather than absorb them. Indeed 'pseudo-octatonicism' might be a better term, since his octatonic configurations themselves tend to be evasive about their identity.

Events following the 'dome' melody offer a good example of these points, and with it we can also highlight how Tippett's and Yeats's aesthetic premises diverge. In Yeats's line 'A starlit or a moonlit dome disdains /All that man is', the signified of 'dome' is ambiguously both natural – the heavenly canopy ('A starlit . . . dome') – and artefactual – the 'moonlit dome' of Saint Sophia. While the latter might be deemed a celebration of human achievement, its permanent and objective independence from humanity sets it disdainfully above the creatures that created it. These ambivalent sentiments are ordered into a multivalent unity by Yeats's syntax: by the predicative logic of noun-phrase-plus-verb-phrase, which welds the contradictory ideas into a unit that is also concise enough to be savoured as a whole in the mind. In Tippett's setting, however, this syntax is dismembered by his constant desire to contemplate the poem in close-up (moreover, he inflates these lines into a duration – around a minute – well beyond that which the mind can hold in a single immediate present). After the stillness of his 'dome' melody, he responds to the word 'disdains' with a musical image of great turbulence – see Example 7.4(b) – which creates an almost complete cleavage from its precursor. Playing a key role here is form O3 of the octatonic scale (cf. Ex. 7.2(c)) which displaces the previous A major diatonicism: it underpins the soprano's F♯–F♮ leap, the sustained harmonic background in the wind, and the triplet roulades in the rototoms and harp.[80] Even so, Tippett remains temperamentally unable to permit the scale's formal arrangement to dictate terms, and causes the anomalous pitch class G to be as important to the sound as any other element. But the tussle continues as this note becomes a point of leakage into version O2 of the scale – manifest in the rototom figuration on the final beat of the bar at Fig. 26 – only to be abandoned in the next bar as O3 is reinstated.

Tippett does sometimes exploit the octatonic scale's potential for mediating (rather than generating) oppositions – as in his setting of the earlier line from stanza 1, 'Night resonance recedes'. Again the syntax is broken up, with a different musical image for noun phrase and verb, as illustrated in Example 7.5. 'Night resonance' is sung to an angular line, deploying scale form O1 – again with a single anomalous pitch, this time F. Against this the same melody is delivered in canon by the three trombones, each

Example 7.5. 'Night resonance recedes': the octatonic scale as a mediating device.

entering a fifth lower, and thus also bringing versions O3 and O2 of the scale into play. Then, at Fig. 20 the reiterated dyad G–A in the lower strings heralds Tippett's image for 'recedes' – a sustained and fading dyad, B♭–D♭ (recalling the earlier and identical setting of the same verb in the poem's opening line). On this occasion, however, the relationship between the images is not antithetical. Rather, one image melts into the next, and decisive in this process is the scale O1, which at Fig. 20 and after serves as a background presence from which all the musical elements are drawn.

Example 7.6. The cell E–F♮–F♯ as an invariant motif in *Byzantium* (dynamics and expression marks omitted).

Interplay between Dionysiac spontaneity and Apollonian calculation is also manifest in the handling of the work's thematic content. On the one hand there is just as much exuberant proliferation in this domain as in the realm of instrumental colour. On the other hand, Tippett also allows a degree of explicit background motivic invariance that is unusual by his standards. The crucial feature here is the cell E–F♮–F♯ presented by the opening three notes of the soprano's line, quoted in Example 7.6(a). Disregarding for the moment the registral displacement of the F♯, we may observe that initially in this local context the motif extends its implicit chromatic trajectory: the setting of the entire line ('The unpurged images

of day recede') encompasses the additional pitch classes G, G♯, A, B♭, C and D♭. On the work's larger canvas the registral displacement between F and F♯ becomes absolutely salient: the remaining parts of Example 7.6 show how, regardless of whether the order or register of pitch classes is reversed (and hence regardless of whether an augmented or diminished octave is manifest), or of whether the associated E♮ is included or omitted, this figure (indicated with a brace) becomes a distinctive reference point for every stanza of the poem. Tippett has chosen for his chain of objective formal correspondences a figure that is filled with subjective expressive force. Its intervallic properties play a structural role in negating the diatonic spaces of much of the piece while also invoking other, octatonic possibilities; but at the same time these conflicts are perceived as literally embodied, as the voice reaches up or down from one register to the other. This tension finds its apotheosis in the final stanza where the gesture is sung to a wordless melisma (Fig. 153ff.; see Ex. 7.6(k)), and the F♯ is ultimately freed from polarization against chromatically adjacent pitches, as it is prolonged in the voice's passionate rendition of the poem's last line (partly quoted in Ex. 7.6(l)).

As implied above, the significance of structural features of this type is not that they are constitutive of a comprehensive unifying order, but rather that they countervail the centrifugal proliferation of musical invention that is a sure sign of Tippett's continuing commitment to a 'poetics of the imagination'. His fascination with 'Those images that yet / Fresh images beget' creates a different aesthetic currency, predicated on concerns other than unity and measurability. Under this second paradigm, music, from within its own medium as sound, simultaneously reveals a mimetic, non-conceptual affinity for phenomena within the cultural and social world, and makes them 'rich and strange'. It is able to do this because its images – just like Yeats's verbal images – accrue a range of associations through unexpected juxtapositions of elements.

To my mind an archetypal example of this technique can be found at the close of Tippett's *Praeludium for Brass, Bells and Percussion* (1962) – a work whose soundworld anticipates *Byzantium* by nearly thirty years. There the individual sounds of muffled horns, muted trumpet fanfares, a quietly but ominously pounding bass drum, and distantly chiming bells all coalesce into an image of breath and metal suggestive of living and latent human power, unspecified as to whether benevolently or malevolently disposed. While Yeats must present the elements of his images one at a time and forge them together syntactically, the composer can, through the polyphonic possibilities of music, present these in a single moment. Concentrated into an instant, these images trigger a seemingly endless

spillage of signifiers as the linguistic faculty of the conscious mind attempts to get a fix on something which exceeds it. Tippett's Byzantium chord, especially the pulsating version associated with 'great cathedral gong' (Fig. 23), is a yet more pregnant relative of the *Praeludium* chord – a sound of depth whose bell- and gong-laden properties carry connotations of both the foundry and the temple. In a conjunction of the artefactual and natural, metal forged by human handiwork vibrates through the air; brass instruments again infuse the sound with human breath; and each measured decaying stroke asserts the oneness of time and timbre.

Resonance functions as an important mimetic and metaphoric stratum in *Byzantium*. Various of its musical images play with the idea, and thus create a timbral complex around it. In the opening sequence, for example, the Byzantium chord is followed by a diatonic gamelan-like figure (at Figs. 2, 5, 8) that combines chiming glockenspiel and vibraphone, with the 'hard, crackling' sound of xylophone and violas and cellos playing *col legno*. This combination of ringing metallophones and inert wood turns out to be transitional to the ensuing 'dry, crackling', aura-less (and much more dissonant) synthesizer figuration (Whittall's description of a 'continuing tussle with the modern urban jungle' is apposite[81]). Thus Tippett orders his ironizing passage from the mythological to the technological via the pre-industrial. The Byzantium chord and the gamelan figuration together bear a further association – with the brilliant, chirpy motif for piccolos, clarinets and high tuned percussion featured in the interlude prior to the 'Night resonance' episode (Fig. 14ff.). This combination of song and glittering metal seems to evoke the golden bird as part of a sound-picture of Byzantium – though here, stamped with something of the numinous aura of the Byzantium chord, the bird is given its due as something fantastic or fabulous. Again this could be heard as a shift along a sonic continuum, whose next increment comes with the anvils that accompany the reference to the artefactual golden bird in stanza 3 (as well as the 'The golden smithies of the emperor' in stanza 5). Here we again have metallic sounds, but now brittle and hard – an inversion of the ratio of labour to resonance found in the original gong sonorities.

Another crucial sound in *Byzantium* – indeed a constant against the shifting mosaic of images – is of course the soprano voice. As the subject which delivers Tippett's rendition of Yeats's text, this voice-role can be seen as a projection of the former's authorial persona. Equally, its delineation as female cannot be discounted from the array of associations which emanate from it as a sound image. Whittall also signals this associative potential:

> In writing a vocal line intended for a singer with the power and projection of a Jessye Norman, Tippett inevitably creates associations with certain female characters from his other works: *The Knot Garden*'s freedom-fighter [Denise], the Third Symphony's earth mother, even *New Year*'s 'trainee children's doctor' [Jo Ann]. At their most distinctive, Tippett's women can be menacingly visionary, in the mould of *The Midsummer Marriage*'s Madame Sosostris, their music a mixture of rage and sweetness.[82]

What Whittall picks up on is a propensity in Tippett's dramatological thinking to arrange his characters (males included) according to certain gender typologies – constructions that are at least as much cultural as they are universal, natural or essential. The *scena* in movement 15 of *A Child of our Time*, for example, deploys the vocal soloists in a fashion that bears some resemblance to the Freudian narrative of family romance. And Tippett's increasingly detailed designation of his operatic voice types from *King Priam* onwards (e.g. 'lyric dramatic soprano', 'high tenor baritone') suggests a sensitivity towards their cultural connotations. Thus, to rearrange Whittall's ordering a little, Tippett's 'earth mother' roles – e.g. Sosostris, the Nurse (*King Priam*), Nan – are usually sung by mezzos; and these sometimes – as in the case of Helen, and Hannah – shade into a more sexualized version of the 'eternal feminine' (a cultural trope whose roots go back at least as far as Goethe's *Faust*). These are distinct from the more 'aspirational' female visionaries whose desire to be somewhere other than where they are often brings with it more than a hint of alienation from their current situation. This type, usually represented by dramatic sopranos, includes Jenifer, Denise, the Third Symphony soloist, Jo Ann and possibly also Nadia (in this case a lyric soprano). It is arguably under this latter type that *Byzantium*'s soprano also falls, and while Tippett's portrayal of such women is not always untainted by misogyny (especially clear in the more embittered, 'masculinized' variants of the type, such as Hecuba or Regan), he usually represents them positively, as possessed of the power to see their vision through. Indeed, in his identification with these types, we might posit an androgyny assumed within his authorial persona that might also be linked to a critical consciousness of hegemonic models of thought historically and culturally represented as masculine.

The feminine as critical locus

In *Byzantium*, I would argue, the feminine is evident not only through the gender of the singing voice, but also in the determination of musical material and its temporality: this indeed is another index of difference between this work's aesthetic premises and those of Yeats and Stravinsky to

which it ostensibly pays homage. Crucial in this respect is that stratum of the musical image – irreducibly sonic – which remains outside the claims of form and structure. Not everything which Tippett's spontaneous impulses offer to measurement is tractable by it – at least not its conceptual operation: he also refers to 'a method of testing within the body', achieved 'by forcing on the neurological clock . . . a series of electronic shocks that move inside the nervous system. These are artificially stimulated by singing to yourself, by shouting and screaming like Beethoven, and stamping around.'[83] In effect he is talking about a kind of pre-linguistic cognition founded on somatic experience, and this invites comparison with, among other things, Julia Kristeva's psychoanalytic formulation of the *semiotic*.

For Kristeva, the semiotic is 'a psychosomatic modality of the signifying process' which is related to the Freudian drives. Although essential to language – fundamental indeed in the disposition towards its acquisition and continuing utilization – the semiotic is nevertheless 'anterior to sign and syntax'. Hence, while by its nature indefinable in linguistic terms, it is intuitable as a primal energy and motility. Kristeva borrows from Plato the term *chora* to denote an 'extremely provisional' ordering of this energy – 'analogous only to vocal or kinetic rhythm'. Plato is also invoked to endorse representation of the semiotic *chora* as maternal: as a receptacle or space, 'which is everlasting . . . providing a situation for all things that come into being but itself apprehended without the senses'.[84] There is a connection to be made perhaps between this inchoate domain and the 'cauldron world' which Tippett regarded as the font of his spontaneous creative drives. Just as he depicted subsequent stages of his compositional process as bringing these amorphous apprehensions to articulation, so Kristeva describes how language translates the inchoate energies of the semiotic into the articulate realm of the *symbolic*.

On this view, the symbolic modality of language is what enables us to conceptualize the world, to give it structure. The child enters the symbolic at that stage of language acquisition where it grasps the principle of the signifier: the idea that a sound or mark or gesture might stand for something other than itself. Kristeva terms this moment the *thetic*, and characterizes it as a rupture, for it involves the subject separating himself from the object he denotes, and in the process constituting himself. (Paraphrasing Frege, Kristeva writes: 'denotation would be understood as the subject's ability to separate himself from the ecosystem into which he was fused, so that, as a result of this separation, he may designate it'.[85]) Hence the price of our gaining symbolic purchase on the world, and hence also the price of our becoming subjects, is our heterogeneity or alienation from the world.

But, says Kristeva, the practices of the aesthetic makes it possible to experience the re-entry of the semiotic *chora* into the symbolic, and thus for the subject to regain a sense of his/her relation to an extra-linguistic order of being – though the condition of such a breach of the symbolic is that the thetic none the less continues to operate. This possibility is relevant to both Yeats's and Tippett's *Byzantium* not least because Kristeva stresses the effect of rupture on the syntax of poetic language: 'when the semiotic *chora* disturbs the thetic position by redistributing the signifying order, we note that the denoted object and the syntactic relation are disturbed as well. The denoted object proliferates in a series of connoted objects produced by the *transposition* of the semiotic *chora*[,] and the syntactic division ... is disrupted.'[86] The shift from denotation to connotation in both 'Byzantium' and *Byzantium* has been observed in the preceding discussion of images and their associative dimension. A further illustration of Kristeva's point is particularly evident in Yeats's final stanza:

> Astraddle on the dolphin's mire and blood,
> Spirit after spirit! The smithies break the flood,
> The golden smithies of the Emperor!
> Marbles of the dancing floor
> Break bitter furies of complexity,
> Those images that yet
> Fresh images beget,
> That dolphin-torn, that gong tormented sea.

These lines could be seen to describe the irruption of the semiotic *chora* into the symbolic: the motile, sea-born dolphins (with their 'mire and blood') carry the dead towards the city, in a flood which is confronted (or unleashed?) by the fixed, symbolic creations of man. Moreover this process is rehearsed in the poem's syntax. While the verb 'Break' in the fifth line theoretically extends through the last three lines too, its 'governing force' (in Helen Hennessy Vendler's words) 'is spent long before the end of the stanza is reached, and the last three lines stand syntactically as absolutes'.[87] In Tippett's *Byzantium* the situation is even more acute, for, as already noted, Yeats's poetic syntax is further assailed by the composer's tendency to cause practically every grammatical or semantic unit to burgeon into a sonically vibrant or motile musical image of its own. (An extreme form of this rupture between musical and textual organization is the treatment of the final line, which Tippett turns into a miniature set piece.[88]) While these images appear in a sequence dictated by the poem's logic they none the less do not bear an analogous syntagmatic connectivity of their own, tending instead to 'stand ... as absolutes'. The Byzantium

chord, for example, can appear at the beginning of a musical sequence – as at the start of the piece; or in the middle – as at 'Or, by the moon embittered'; or at the end – 'After great cathedral gong'.

This paratactic propensity has a significant effect on the piece as a whole, specifically on its determination of time. For the cumulative result is a neutralization of linear temporality – the temporality which, as Kristeva points out, is 'that of language considered as the enunciation of sentences (noun + verb; topic–comment; beginning–ending)'.[89] This all-pervasive property of *Byzantium* is either its most problematic or its most radical feature – or both. And the critical consciousness to which it arguably points could again, if seen from a Kristevan perspective, be aligned with the feminine. For this amounts to a critique of a temporality that, in Kristeva's words, 'is readily labelled masculine and which is at once both civilizational and obsessional'.[90] I want to propose that the dominating female vocal presence in *Byzantium* finds its counterpart in a temporality that is, if not identical with, then at least akin to, Kristeva's conception of 'women's time' – which in fact is linked to two types of temporality: cyclical and 'monumental'.[91]

Clearly, linearity is far from completely suspended in the foreground of *Byzantium*. The arc-like trajectory of the 'dome' melody or the pounding dotted figure that links stanzas 1 and 2 (Fig. 33ff.) are proof enough of that. And even the quasi-stasis that surrounds the setting of 'trance' in stanza 4 (a compulsive return to the same set of ideas, either transposed or at their original pitch; Fig. 121ff.; Ex. 7.7) involves progress across three musical motifs: an ostinato which crescendos to a pulsating synthesizer chord, followed by a series of descending octave *glissandi* which decrescendos into silence. But what is absent here is any dialectical synthesis between such moments, any middle- or background progression towards a goal. In some ways this could be seen as an inversion of the temporal conditions typical of Stravinsky. In many passages of *Chant du rossignol* and in most of *Les noces*, for example, foreground ostinato-based materials display no immediate goal orientation, yet the overall effect of the succession between such episodes is one of accumulation or kinetic counterstatement. In *Byzantium*, on the other hand, temporal succession is characterized more as concatenation than directed accumulation.

The temporality of *Byzantium* is, then, another index of limited affinity with Yeats's poem. As the latter progresses it continually recapitulates earlier images, but reworks them in the process by subjecting them to an altered syntactic function or changed semantic context. This process finds its climax in the final stanza, which is saturated with references to preceding images, but at the same time heightens them to form the poem's

Example 7.7. 'An agony of trance'.

apogee.[92] Tippett partly emulates this technique: as he treads the poem's path the corresponding musical image of each repeated or varied word or phrase is summoned up again. But this yields no equivalent accretion around the image: the procedure of recall is more mechanistic than organic. True, at the poem's final line Tippett's recapitulation of the opening music, centred around the Byzantium chord, does imbue the ending with a certain climactic intensity, but in contrast to the poem, we end where we began – in a state of no greater and no lesser vibrancy.

The booming Byzantium chord has duration but no forward temporal moment. Rather, it resonates outward through space – a kind of shimmering musical object, around which all the other musical objects in the work are arranged as it were spatially. (This type of relationship is very evident

as the voice first enters: we seem to pan away from the initial scene, as if being shifted to a new location; the two situations are then brought together as the Byzantium chord or its variants subsequently re-enter.) This chthonian sound suggests a further connection with Kristeva's semiotic *chora*, which, as she points out, was represented by Plato himself as pseudo-spatial. She quotes an extract from the *Timaeus*, which says of the *chora*: 'Indefinitely a place; it cannot be destroyed, but provides a ground for all that can come into being'.[93] This notion is suggestive too of a similarly unchanging sound, similarly founded on the idea of resonance, which Tippett uses to evoke the state of pre-creation in *The Mask of Time*: a sonority associated indeed with the very word 'sound'. The determination of temporality by both this sound object and the Byzantium chord bears comparison with what Kristeva designates as 'women's time', for 'female subjectivity would seem to provide a specific measure that essentially retains *repetition* and *eternity* from among the multiple modalities of time known through the history of civilizations'.[94] The Tippett sonorities in question could be described in terms of both the feminine temporalities discussed by Kristeva: on the one hand *cyclic*, in that they recurrently break into present events; on the other hand *monumental*, in that they foster a consciousness of a time that is 'all-encompassing and infinite like imaginary space':[95] a pan-geographic time in which the past is alive in the present.

   Importing Kristeva's profoundly feminist notions into an account of a work by a male composer such as Tippett may be an act no less dubious than positing an imaginative allegiance between them on account of the latter's sexual orientation. Gay does not necessarily equal feminized. Yet what feminist and gay consciousnesses might commonly possess in their different positions is a critical resistance to patriarchically determined models of subjectivity and its construction in history. It is in this sense that temporality has a political dimension. Kristeva points out that 'in its beginnings, the women's movement, as the struggle of suffragists and of existential feminists, aspired to gain a place in linear time as the time and project of history'.[96] This necessary struggle of an earlier generation was followed, Kristeva claims, by a second phase of feminism, partly flowing from the events of May 1968. She writes that 'by demanding recognition of an irreducible identity, without equal in the opposite sex and, as such ... in a certain way non-identical, this feminism situates itself outside the linear time of identities which communicate through projection and revindication'.[97] Little contrivance is needed to locate equivalent – not identical – moments in Tippett's life story, which, notwithstanding the pursuit of ends other than feminist, were coloured both by the feminine and by his

homosexuality. The active Trotskyism of his earlier years, for example, might have taken its significance at least in part from the echoes of his mother's own dialectical engagement in history as a suffragist – in other words as part of the first generation of feminists as described by Kristeva. On the other hand, his repudiation of communism and subsequent turn to pacifism in the war years (which led to the imprisonment that gave his mother cause for greatest pride in her son) could be read as a withdrawal from the teleology of historical events analogous to Kristeva's second phase of feminism – 'situat[ing] itself outside the linear time of identities which communicate through projection and revindication'. This was bound up in Tippett's case with an embrace of an other identity: the acceptance, following his personal crisis and self-analysis of the late 1930s, of his homosexuality. Gender, sexuality, identity, models of time and history all mingle. Those female voice types – the activist Hecuba, the timeless Helen: could they have their origins in the figures of Tippett's own biographical and historical circumstances?

And is it pushing a point to see a possible resonance between a late Tippett work such as *Byzantium* and the consciousness (or 'signifying space'[98]) which Kristeva attributes to a third generation of feminism? Suggestive here is her argument in 'Women's time' that this third generation does not exclude the other two, that they and their associated temporalities may exist in parallel, may even be 'interwoven' with one another. If her definition of the characteristics of this generation and its own temporality is elusive, this is because it attempts to imagine new subjectivities, beyond the limitations of what is known. Among other things, though, it seems to refer back to a notion of time she describes earlier, one 'not in agreement with the idea of an "eternal Europe" and perhaps not even with that of a "modern Europe". Rather, through and with the ensemble of "Europe", which is the repository of memory, this sensibility seeks its own trans-European temporality.'[99] *Byzantium*'s time may not be exactly coterminous with this particular temporality – indeed, ought not to be argued as such, given that this would be an appropriation from feminism of an agenda vital to itself. But we may posit that Tippett, from the standpoint of a dissident masculinity, and drawing on the evocation of a city that straddles occident and orient, here works towards a similar end of envisioning the subjective experience of something beyond the known: a vision in which divergent temporalities are interwoven. Moreover, this vision takes place at a stage in his life and *œuvre* when his sensitivity to other musical and cultural traditions is developed enough to give positive recognition to alternatives to the dominant forms of European musical thought. In *Byzantium* this is registered not by any specious reference to

exotic traditions, but by resistance to received notions of structural organization, and by a mingling of temporalities in which the teleological is no longer uppermost.

Kristeva imagines that under a 'third attitude . . . the very dichotomy man/woman as an opposition between two rival entities may be understood as belonging to *metaphysics*'. Refuting this opposition entails not an 'effacing of difference' or a reconciliation 'between rival groups and thus between the sexes', but an internalizing of that agon into the domain of 'personal and sexual identity itself'.[100] There is something in *Byzantium*'s aesthetic world – Whittall hints at it when he describes the solo soprano persona as an amalgam of 'rage and sweetness'[101] – which overlaps this territory. This singing subject fronts an array of images which decline to efface or reconcile their differences in the interests of a uniformly integrated whole. She (the pronoun is signally inadequate) voices a range of experience that is as heterogeneous as it is passionate. Yeats's words and Tippett's music likewise find no union. Their agon is that between the would-be purgative syntax of the text and the music's libidinal celebration of colour and gesture – a kind of *jouissance*. As against Yeats's city in which spirits (those 'breathless mouths') achieve symbolic transcendence over death, Tippett's Byzantium is a place which celebrates the intensity of living – vivid, turbulent, furious, at times absurd, at times visionary – in which irreconcilability is accepted as a principle of vigour; in which 'all complexities of mire or blood' are not given up for assimilation.

Closing statements

Without doubt, probing the possible adjacencies between Tippett and Kristeva involves a strong measure of speculation. One source of vindication is suggested, however, by the larger discursive cultural web in which both figures are enmeshed. As Julian Johnson points out, for example, Kristeva's dichotomy of the semiotic and symbolic is a reworking of that of the Dionysiac and Apollonian found in the early Nietzsche's *Birth of Tragedy*.[102] The latter nomenclature, as we have explored in the present chapter and elsewhere in this book, is one relevant to, indeed applied by, Tippett himself, not least in his thoughts on the nature of musical material and the forces of creation – the business of 'spontaneity' and 'measurement'. Kristeva's adoption of this dualism involves translating an originally metaphysically founded conception into a psychoanalytic one, and this is also apposite given Tippett's tendency throughout his *œuvre* to traffic somewhat ambiguously between these two modes of thinking. At the root of all these formulations (and others traced during the course of

this book) is the notion of a signifying order disrupted by the consciousness of an existential dimension heterogeneous to it or exceeding it.

What makes Kristeva's particular take on these concerns apposite to *Byzantium* is her relation of them to questions of gender, temporality and subjectivity, and the critical (Kristeva would say revolutionary) orientation that follows from this. If the resonance which *Byzantium* can be shown to establish with her thinking is more in the spirit than the letter, this none the less helps point up a radical dimension in the piece which might otherwise go unnoticed – or indeed be unsought by those for whom Tippett's later works present evidence only of creative decline. And if Tippett's affinities with Kristeva are necessarily limited, I would argue they are significant enough to give a positive definition to the work's negation of aspects of the aesthetics of Yeats and Stravinsky. *Byzantium* does not so much tackle head-on the thorny ideological questions raised by those figures as side-step them by evoking a different critical sensibility of a later time. While we would need to be cautious about positing a postmodern dimension to Tippett's thinking, the kind of connections I have been exploring here suggest that the aesthetic mutations of his late works are not unrelated to certain of the more radical and fruitful avenues of that problematic cultural paradigm.[103]

Of course, none of this means that Tippett frees himself from ideology. While he may have been intuitively aware that the aesthetics of the 'porcelain bowl' have their own difficulties, immersion in the 'cauldron world' is an equally fraught alternative – as Nietzsche's own embrace of the Dionysiac made clear. Moreover, Kristeva herself has drawn criticism for her positive reception of the anti-Semitic writer Louis-Ferdinand Céline.[104] Wherever we stake our claim in the aesthetic or critical landscape there are shadows, it would seem. But Tippett's tactic in his late works – as if in recognition of this state of affairs – was neither to individually fetishize the Apollonian or Dionysiac (or symbolic or semiotic), nor to undertake to reconcile them. It is perhaps not surprising, then, that his musical language continued to bear the stamp of the other aesthetic category he identified, 'black material'. While for some this may be exactly the problem with his late style, I have attempted to demonstrate here that a critical analysis worthy of his *œuvre* needs to be alive to his reasons for engaging the inchoate. Whatever else we make of it, Tippett's is a music that contains a continuing and salutary reminder to face up to contradiction, and to keep our minds and imaginations open.

Notes

1 Tippett and the 'world vision' of modernity

1 Lucien Goldmann, *The Hidden God: A Study of Tragic Vision in the* Pensées *of Pascal and the Tragedies of Racine*, trans. Philip Thody (London: Routledge and Kegan Paul, 1964). The quoted passage appears on p. 15 (though Tippett in fact would have read the text in its original French version, *Le dieu caché*). The book's impact on *King Priam* is discussed by Ian Kemp, in his *Tippett: The Composer and his Music* (London: Eulenburg Books, 1984), 326, 354–8. See also Rowena Pollard and David Clarke, 'Tippett's *King Priam* and "the tragic vision"', in *Tippett Studies*, ed. David Clarke (Cambridge: Cambridge University Press, 1999), 166–85.

2 Goldmann, *The Hidden God*, 17, 20.

3 Michael Tippett, '*The Mask of Time*', in *Tippett on Music*, ed. Meirion Bowen (Oxford: Clarendon Press, 1995), 245–55 (p. 245).

4 Goldmann, *The Hidden God*, 20–1.

5 J. M. Bernstein, *The Fate of Art* (Cambridge: Polity Press, 1992), 5–6. For other glosses on this idea see, for example, Andrew Bowie, *Aesthetics and Subjectivity: From Kant to Nietzsche* (Manchester and New York: Manchester University Press, 1990), 2–8; Robert B. Pippin, *Modernism as a Philosophical Problem* (Oxford and Cambridge, Mass.: Blackwell, 1991), 2–4; and Terry Eagleton, *The Ideology of the Aesthetic* (Oxford and Cambridge, Mass.: Blackwell, 1990), 366–8.

6 Tippett, 'What I believe', in *Music of the Angels: Essays and Sketchbooks*, ed. Meirion Bowen (London: Eulenburg Books, 1980), 49–55 (pp. 52–3); 'Aspects of belief', in *Tippett on Music*, 237–9, 242–4 (p. 242).

7 For more on the periodization of Tippett's *œuvre* see the opening section of chapter 6.

8 Goldmann, *The Hidden God*, 20–1.

9 Julian Johnson, 'The subjects of music: a theoretical and analytical enquiry into the construction of subjectivity in the musical structuring of time', D.Phil. thesis (University of Sussex, 1994), 26.

10 In a letter to Eric Walter White, quoted in White, *Tippett and his Operas* (London: Barrie and Jenkins, 1979), 63; also discussed on p. 39 below.

11 Arnold Whittall, '"Is there a choice at all?": *King Priam* and motives for analysis', in *Tippett Studies*, ed. Clarke, 55–77 (p. 77).

12 Edward Venn also explores this notion in relation to Tippett's essays. See his chapter 'Idealism and ideology in Tippett's writings', in *Tippett: Music and Literature*, ed. Suzanne Robinson (Aldershot, UK, and Burlington, Vt: Ashgate, forthcoming).

13 Johnson, 'The subjects of music', 26.

14 Cf. Goldmann: 'how is the "work" of an author to be defined? Is it everything which he ever wrote, including letters, notes and posthumous publications? Or is it only the works that he himself completed during his lifetime and intended for publication?' (*The Hidden God*, 9).

15 Cambridge orator, 20 February 1964; as quoted in White, *Tippett and his Operas*, 35.

16 Tippett, 'Postscript', in *Moving into Aquarius*, 2nd edn (St Albans: Paladin Books, 1974), 163–7 (p. 167).

17 See Lawrence Kramer, *Classical Music and Postmodern Knowledge* (Berkeley, Calif.: University of California Press, 1995), 21–5.

18 *Ibid.*, 23. Kramer quotes from Mikhail Bakhtin, *The Dialogic Imagination: Four Essays*, ed. Michael Holquist, trans. Caryl Emerson and Michael Holquist (Austin, Tex.: University of Texas Press, 1981), 345–6.

19 See Kramer, *Postmodern Knowledge*, 11–12.

20 See Gary Tomlinson, 'The web of culture: a context for musicology', *19th Century Music* 7/3 (April 1984), 350–62. Tomlinson writes that Geertz in turn adapts the idea from Max Weber (p. 351).

21 See Kramer, *Postmodern Knowledge*, 16–17.

22 Under a strictly chronological ordering the sequence of chapters 5 and 6 – on *The Mask of Time* (1980–2) and the Triple Concerto (1978–9) respectively – ought to have been reversed. However, I have situated my study of *The Mask of Time* immediately after that of *The Vision of Saint Augustine* (1963–5) because both share similar concerns with the theme of the transcendent; similarly my study of the Triple Concerto as a 'late' work places it in the same category as *Byzantium* (1989–90), the subject of the chapter which follows it.

23 Goldmann, *The Hidden God*, 17.

24 Deployed more extensively in chapter 5, below.

2 The significance of the concept 'image' in Tippett's musical thought: a perspective from Jung

1 Michael Tippett, 'Poets in a barren age', in *Moving into Aquarius*, 2nd edn (St Albans: Paladin Books, 1974), 148–56 (pp. 155–6).

2 Philip N. Furbank, *Reflections on the Word 'Image'* (London: Secker and Warburg, 1970).

3 In chapter 7, below, I will consider the notion of image once more, with reference to Yeats.

4 See Tippett, *Those Twentieth Century Blues: An Autobiography* (London: Hutchinson, 1991), 62–3. Other texts by Jung which Tippett is known to have read include: *The Secret of the Golden Flower* (Jung and Richard Wilhelm), *Psychology and Alchemy*, *The Integration of Personality* (reported in *Those Twentieth Century Blues*, 89); *C. G. Jung's Letters* (see 'Postscript', in *Moving into Aquarius*, 163–7 (pp. 166–7)) and *Über die Archetypen des kollektiven*

Unbewusstsein (see 'Sketch for a modern oratorio', in *Music of the Angels: Essays and Sketchbooks*, ed. Meirion Bowen (London: Eulenburg Books, 1980), 127–87 (pp. 131, 178, 180); *Tippett on Music*, ed. Meirion Bowen (Oxford: Clarendon Press, 1995), 117–77 (pp. 121, 168, 170)).

5 Tippett, Introduction to *Moving into Aquarius*, 10–13 (p. 11); Preface to *Tippett on Music*, vii–ix (p. viii).

6 Tippett, 'Contracting-in to abundance', in *Moving into Aquarius*, 19–27 (p. 23). (The passage from which the quotation is taken is omitted in the slightly revised version of the essay, 'The composer and pacifism', in *Tippett on Music*, 282–6.)

7 Tippett, 'Towards the condition of music', in *Music of the Angels*, 17–27 (p. 24); *Tippett on Music*, 7–15 (p. 13).

8 Tippett, 'Drum, flute and zither', in *Moving into Aquarius*, 67–84 (p. 81); *Tippett on Music*, 185–98 (p. 196).

9 Carl Gustav Jung, 'Archetypes of the collective unconscious', in *The Archetypes and the Collective Unconscious*, ed. Herbert Read, Michael Fordham and Gerhard Adler, trans. Richard F. C. Hull, Collected Works 9/1, 2nd edn (London: Routledge and Kegan Paul, 1959), 3–41 (pp. 23–4).

10 Jung, 'Psychology and literature', in *The Spirit in Man, Art and Literature*, trans. Richard F. C. Hull, repr. edn (London: Ark Paperbacks, 1993), 84–105 (p. 105).

11 Jung, 'On the relation of analytical psychology to poetry', in *The Spirit in Man*, 65–83 (p. 75).

12 Jung, 'Psychology and literature', 101–2.

13 Tippett, 'What I believe', in *Music of the Angels*, 49–55 (p. 52); 'Aspects of belief', in *Tippett on Music*, 237–9, 242–4 (p. 239).

14 Tippett, 'Poets in a barren age', 156. *Idem*, 'Towards the condition of music', in *Music of the Angels*, 20; *Tippett on Music*, 9.

15 Jung, *Psychological Types*, ed. Herbert Read, Michael Fordham and Gerhard Adler, trans. Helton G. Baynes, rev. Richard F. C. Hull, Collected Works 6 (London: Routledge and Kegan Paul, 1971), 442.

16 *Ibid.*

17 *Ibid.*, 433.

18 Murray Schafer, 'Michael Tippett', in *British Composers in Interview* (London: Faber and Faber, 1963), 92–102 (p. 97).

19 Jung, *Psychological Types*, 443, 442.

20 Tippett, 'A composer's point of view', in *Moving into Aquarius*, 14–18 (pp. 14–15); *Tippett on Music*, 3–6 (p. 3).

21 The volume is described by David Ayerst as 'one of the most thumbed books on [Tippett's] shelves . . . which [he] first read in 1932 or 1933'. See *Michael Tippett: A Symposium on his 60th Birthday*, ed. Ian Kemp (London: Faber and Faber, 1965), 64–8 (p. 66). See also Tippett, *Those Twentieth Century Blues*, 62.

22 Jung, *Psychological Types*, 443.

23 See *ibid.*, 437.

24 Tippett, 'A composer and his public', in *Moving into Aquarius*, 94–100 (p. 100); *Tippett on Music*, 277–81 (p. 281). The ending of this essay was the model for that of 'Poets in a barren age' which prefaces this chapter.

25 Jung, *Psychological Types*, 445.

26 *Ibid.*, 474.

27 Jung, 'On the relation of analytical psychology to poetry', 75–6.

28 Schafer, *British Composers in Interview*, 97.

29 This description paraphrases various statements quoted above, as well as accounts cited by Richard E. Rodda in 'The genesis of a symphony: Tippett's Symphony No. 3', *Music Review* 39/2 (May 1978), 110–16. See also Tippett, *E. William Doty Lectures in Fine Arts: Second Series 1976* (Austin, Tex.: University of Texas at Austin, 1979), 24–45.

30 Tippett, 'Towards the condition of music', in *Music of the Angels*, 24; *Tippett on Music*, 13.

31 Tippett is also alluding here to ideas in Susanne Langer's *Feeling and Form* (London: Routledge and Kegan Paul, 1953), as a footnote in 'Towards the condition of music' makes clear. Although no particular page reference is given, it would seem that he had a passage such as the following in mind: 'The tonal structures we call "music" bear a close logical similarity to the forms of human feeling – forms of growth and of attenuation, flowing and stowing, conflict and resolution, speed, arrest . . . Such is the pattern, or logical form, of sentience; and the pattern of music is that same form worked out in pure, measured sound and silence. Music is a tonal analogue of emotive life' (*Feeling and Form*, 27).

32 Tippett, 'Towards the condition of music', in *Music of the Angels*, 24; *Tippett on Music*, 13.

33 Tippett, 'Music and the senses' (unpublished essay), 2; quoted in Rodda, 'Genesis of a symphony', 114.

34 See for example Tippett, 'Air from another planet', in *Moving into Aquarius*, 43–9 (*Tippett on Music*, 34–9); idem, 'What I believe'/'Aspects of belief'; idem, 'Towards the condition of music'; and the chapter 'Michael Tippett' in Schafer, *British Composers in Interview*.

35 Tippett, 'Towards the condition of music', in *Music of the Angels*, 24; *Tippett on Music*, 13.

36 Strictly speaking 'aria' is too strong a word, since Tippett has made a point in the opera of paring down all lyrical excess in the interest of forward dramatic movement. Nevertheless, this is one of the moments when he allows his characters breathing space to express their feelings in reaction to the dramatic situation.

37 See pp. 27–9.

38 Jung, 'On the relation of analytical psychology to poetry', 70.

39 See Tippett, 'Air from another planet', in *Moving into Aquarius*, 44; *Tippett on Music*, 35: 'To use platonic language: the Idea can only be expressed by the

Image'. Tippett is not at all specific about his reference here: he may be alluding to Plato's distrust of artistic mimesis voiced in the *Republic*, though the
only named Platonic dialogue to which Tippett refers in any detail in his
writings is the *Phaedrus*.

40 See Tippett, 'The artist's mandate', in *Moving into Aquarius*, 122–9 (pp.
124–5, 128); *Tippett on Music*, 287–93 (pp. 289, 292). The text in question is
Plato's *Phaedrus*.

41 Tippett, 'Air from another planet', in *Moving into Aquarius*, 46; *Tippett on
Music*, 36.

42 Again see 'The artist's mandate', in *Moving into Aquarius*, 123–6; *Tippett on
Music*, 288–90.

43 As recounted for example in Carl Dahlhaus, 'What is developing variation?'
in *Schoenberg and the New Music*, trans. Derrick Puffett and Alfred Clayton
(Cambridge: Cambridge University Press, 1987), 128–33.

44 A similar conceit is also presented earlier in this final section: 'What, what,
what can it be, / that throbs, throbs in every nerve, / beats, beats in the blood
and bone / down through the feet into the earth, / then echoed by the stars?'

45 One suspects that Tippett's use of register is often meant to mirror a topography of the psyche. His emphasis of the bass register in particular seems in
many works intended to evoke – perhaps even stir – the 'primordial depths'
of the unconscious. See also the discussion of archetypes in the next section
of this essay.

46 In, for example, Arnold Whittall, *The Music of Britten and Tippett: Studies in
Themes and Techniques*, 2nd edn (Cambridge: Cambridge University Press,
1990), 5; and *idem*, '*Byzantium*: Tippett, Yeats and the limitations of affinity',
Music and Letters 74/3 (August 1993), 383–98 (pp. 395–7).

47 The exceptions are violin pizzicato chords after Fig. 380, the characteristic
timbre of Andromache's preceding diatribe, evoking her continuing scornful
presence.

48 Ezra Pound, 'Vorticism', in *Gaudier-Brzeska* (London and New York: John
Lane, 1916), 109n. Quoted in Furbank, *Reflections on the Word 'Image'*, 39.

49 See Derrick Puffett, 'Tippett and the retreat from mythology', *The Musical
Times* 136, No. 1823 (January 1995), 6–14 (p. 12).

50 I should stress that 'semiotic' here is used to imply meaning in the broadest,
most neutral sense – in sharp contradistinction from Jung, for whom the
term implied an allegoric representation of something already known, and
from Julia Kristeva, whose usage of the term (invoked in the final section of
chapter 7, below) is paradoxically closer to Jung's notion of the archetypal.

51 Andrew Samuels, Bani Shorter and Fred Plaut, *A Critical Dictionary of
Jungian Analysis* (London and New York: Routledge, 1986), 45–7. An interesting connection is also made here between these dualistic schemata and
recent empirical research on the functioning of the cerebral hemispheres.

52 *Ibid.*, 46.

53 Composer's note to the vocal score.

54 See Schafer, *British Composers in Interview*, 97.

55 Jung, 'The psychology of the child archetype', in *The Archetypes and the Collective Unconscious*, 151–81 (p. 173). As Brooke points out, Jung himself did not arrive at a definitive stance on the relation between psyche and body, shifting between an implicit Cartesian dualism and a more phenomenological position bearing strong parallels with Merleau-Ponty and Heidegger. See Roger Brooke, *Jung and Phenomenology* (London and New York: Routledge, 1991), chapter 5.

56 Thomas Weiskel, *The Romantic Sublime: Studies in the Structure and Psychology of Transcendence* (Baltimore and London: The Johns Hopkins University Press, 1976), 23–4.

57 *Ibid.*, 24.

58 I explore the former possibility in chapter 7, below.

59 In *Music of the Angels*, 37–43 (p. 43); *Tippett on Music*, 16–21 (p. 21).

60 Tippett, 'The artist's mandate', in *Moving into Aquarius*, 128–9; *Tippett on Music*, 292.

61 *Ibid.*, *Moving into Aquarius*, 122; *Tippett on Music*, 287.

62 Jung, *Psychological Types*, 445.

3 Back to Nietzsche? Transformations of the Dionysiac in *The Midsummer Marriage* and *King Priam*

1 Ian Kemp nevertheless offers some important pointers. See his *Tippett: The Composer and his Music* (London: Eulenburg Books, 1984), 323–5.

2 Among an unpublished (and, at the time of writing, incomplete) inventory of books Tippett owned at the time of his death is listed a 1922 edition of Nietzsche, *Schriften 1869–73*, with an inscription by Edward Sackville-West dated 23 March 1926. I am grateful to Meirion Bowen for making this list available to me. More anecdotally, Bowen also reports sighting *Also Sprach Zarathustra* in the original German on Tippett's shelves (personal communication, June 1999).

3 Michael Tippett, '*The Mask of Time*', in *Tippett on Music*, ed. Meirion Bowen (Oxford: Clarendon Press, 1995), 245–55 (p. 245).

4 For example, the third of his four private maxims for composing modern-day opera stresses the need to transmute mythological material 'into an immediate experience of our day'; Tippett, 'The birth of an opera', in *Moving into Aquarius*, 2nd edn (St Albans: Paladin Books, 1974), 50–66 (p. 57); *Tippett on Music*, 198–208 (p. 203). In other words, the supra-temporal has to be considered from the standpoint of our own historical situation.

5 Eric Walter White, *Tippett and his Operas* (London: Barrie and Jenkins, 1979), 63.

6 In a letter dated by White as August 1957. See *ibid.*, 81.

7 Tippett, 'The resonance of Troy: essays and commentaries on *King Priam*', in *Music of the Angels: Essays and Sketchbooks*, ed. Meirion Bowen (London:

Eulenburg Books, 1980), 222–34 (p. 223); *Tippett on Music*, 209–19 (p. 210).

8 See Kemp, *Tippett*, 354–6; also Rowena Pollard and David Clarke, 'Tippett's *King Priam* and "the tragic vision"', in *Tippett Studies*, ed. David Clarke (Cambridge: Cambridge University Press, 1999), 166–85.

9 Tippett, 'Persönliches Bekenntnis', in *Moving into Aquarius*, 117–21 (p. 120); 'Aspects of belief', in *Tippett on Music*, 239–42 (p. 241).

10 Tippett, 'What I believe', in *Music of the Angels*, 49–55 (p. 52); 'Aspects of belief', in *Tippett on Music*, 237–9, 242–4 (p. 239).

11 Tippett, 'Drum, flute and zither', in *Moving into Aquarius*, 67–84 (pp. 80–1); *Tippett on Music*, 185–98 (p. 195).

12 Kemp, *Tippett*, 225.

13 Jane Harrison, *Themis*, 1st edn (Cambridge: Cambridge University Press, 1912), xv.

14 Tippett, 'The birth of an opera', in *Moving into Aquarius*, 50 (this passage omitted from *Tippett on Music*). Cf. Harrison: 'The mystery-god [Dionysus] arises out of those instincts, emotions, desires which attend and express life; but these emotions, desires, instincts, in so far as they are religious, are at the outset rather of a group than of individual consciousness' (*Themis*, ix).

15 See for example, Simon Goldhill, 'Modern critical approaches to Greek tragedy', in *The Cambridge Companion to Greek Tragedy*, ed. P. E. Easterling (Cambridge: Cambridge University Press, 1997), 324–47 (pp. 331–3).

16 Also influential on the group was J. G. Frazer, whose twelve-volume study of comparative myth, *The Golden Bough*, was owned by Tippett and made its mark on the libretto of *The Midsummer Marriage*.

17 Harrison, *Themis*, 2nd edn (Cambridge: Cambridge University Press, 1927), viii.

18 F. M. Cornford, *From Religion to Philosophy* (London: Edwin Arnold, 1912), 111 n. 1; quoted in Michael Silk and J. P. Stern, *Nietzsche and Tragedy* (Cambridge: Cambridge University Press, 1981), 126. See also *ibid.*, 144, for a somewhat more detailed discussion of the links between Harrison, Cornford and Gilbert Murray.

19 Tippett, 'Drum, flute and zither', in *Moving into Aquarius*, 80; *Tippett on Music*, 195.

20 Carl Gustav Jung, 'The Apollinian and the Dionysian', in *Psychological Types*, ed. Herbert Read, Michael Fordham and Gerhard Adler, trans. Richard F. C. Hull and Helton G. Baynes, rev. Richard F. C. Hull, Collected Works 6 (London: Routledge and Kegan Paul, 1971), 136–46. See also Tippett, *Those Twentieth Century Blues: An Autobiography* (London: Hutchinson, 1991), 62.

21 Compare, for example, 'Drum, flute and zither', in *Moving into Aquarius*, 68; *Tippett on Music*, 185–6, and Richard Wagner, *Opera and Drama*, trans. W. Ashton Ellis, repr. edn (Lincoln, Nebr. and London: University of Nebraska Press, 1995), 332–4. See also Tippett, 'The birth of an opera', in *Moving into Aquarius*, 52; *Tippett on Music*, 199; and *Those Twentieth Century Blues*, 38.

22 Tippett, 'The birth of an opera', in *Moving into Aquarius*, 62; *Tippett on Music*, 207.

23 Although I have tended here to highlight the Wagnerian dimension of *The Midsummer Marriage*, my intention is emphatically not to represent it as some kind of twentieth-century English *Gesamtkunstwerk*. Ideally this aspect ought to be considered in relation to the various other elements of the opera's rich aesthetic amalgam, especially its connection with the English masque tradition. Also salient is Tippett's comment regarding *The Midsummer Marriage* that 'there is nothing in the marriage part of it, the comedy, which is not to be found in the schemes of *opera buffa*: recitative, aria, ensemble, and some Verdi and Puccini techniques. And there is nothing in the midsummer part of it which is not to be found in the schemes of music drama: e.g. orchestral music to a natural phenomenon like a sunrise, considered as part of the drama' ('The birth of an opera', in *Moving into Aquarius*, 61; *Tippett on Music*, 206).

24 The connection between Apollo and Athena is discussed by Harrison: see *Themis*, 501–2. Athena's resemblance to Apollo lies in her standing for wisdom and in her characterization through luminosity. In Gilbert Murray's words 'Athena is an ideal . . . the ideal of wisdom, of incessant labour, of almost terrifying purity' (*Five Stages of Greek Religion* (Oxford: Clarendon Press, 1956), 71; also quoted in Camille Paglia, *Sexual Personae: Art and Decadence from Nefertiti to Emily Dickinson* (London: Penguin Books, 1992), 81). This last quality in particular well captures Jenifer's condition at this point in the drama (and also harmonizes with Harrison's suggestion of Athena as representing patriarchy), since she is portrayed as possessed by an inflated *animus*, the male principle of rationality in Jung's analytical psychology. Paglia also draws attention to Athena's 'sexual duality . . . expressed in her masculine armour' (*Sexual Personae*, 83) – and also, incidentally, to the androgyny of Dionysus, equally appropriate here to Mark's corresponding inflated *anima* (*ibid.*, 89–91).

25 In this study, quotations from the librettos of Tippett's first four operas are taken from *The Operas of Michael Tippett*, ed. Nicholas John (London: John Calder, 1985; New York: Riverrun Press Inc., 1985), and are made without page references.

26 Quoted in P. E. Easterling, 'A show for Dionysus', in *The Cambridge Companion to Greek Tragedy*, ed. Easterling (Cambridge: Cambridge University Press, 1997), 36–53 (p. 43).

27 Friedrich Nietzsche, *The Birth of Tragedy*, trans. Francis Golffing (Garden City, NY: Doubleday, 1956), 15. (All subsequent references to *The Birth of Tragedy* are to this edition unless otherwise stated.) The passage cited is from 'A critical backward glance' (§7), which Nietzsche added as a further preface to the second edition in 1886; the passage is itself a quotation from *Thus Spoke Zarathustra* ('Of the higher man', §18).

28 Silk and Stern, *Nietzsche and Tragedy*, 172. The quotation is from Plutarch's

Moralia, in the translation given by W. K. C. Guthrie in his *The Greeks and their Gods* (London: Methuen, 1950), 156.

29 Which is further an allusion to Frazer's *The Golden Bough*.

30 Walter F. Otto, *Dionysus: Myth and Cult*, trans. Robert B. Palmer (Bloomington and Indianapolis: Indiana University Press, 1965), 136.

31 A term Nietzsche borrows from Schopenhauer (discussed below, p. 52).

32 Nietzsche, *The Birth of Tragedy*, 22–3 (§1).

33 See Tippett's introduction to 'The birth of an opera', in *Moving into Aquarius*, 50 (omitted from *Tippett on Music*). See also Nietzsche, *The Birth of Tragedy*, 24 (§2).

34 David Cairns, 'Tippett and *The Midsummer Marriage*', CD liner notes (Lyrita, SRCD.2217, 1995), 8–9.

35 Derrick Puffett, 'Tippett and the retreat from mythology', *The Musical Times* 136, No. 1823 (January 1995), 6–14 (p. 10).

36 Nietzsche, *The Birth of Tragedy*, 27, 56 (§2, §7).

37 *Ibid.*, 31 (§3).

38 *Ibid.*, 21 (§1).

39 *Ibid.*, 20 (§1).

40 *Ibid.*, 36 (§4).

41 *Ibid.*, 146 (§25). It must be said, however, that the formulation of the dualism in *The Birth of Tragedy* is less than totally coherent, an instability due partly to a contradiction in which Nietzsche on the one hand has a mission to emancipate Dionysus (as an attack on prevailing notions of the time of Greek 'serenity'), and on the other hand needs to keep reminding himself that the Dionysiac and Apollonian 'must develop in strict proportion, conformable to the laws of eternal justice' (*ibid.*, 145 (§25)).

42 Discussed in Kemp, *Tippett*, 215.

43 See Tippett, 'The stage', in *Tippett on Music*, 267–74 (p. 270). This echoes Tippett's observation that 'The Rhine is almost a personage of *The Ring*' ('The birth of an opera', in *Moving into Aquarius*, 60; *Tippett on Music*, 205).

44 Nietzsche, *The Birth of Tragedy*, 56 (§8).

45 *Ibid.*, 58 (§8).

46 Nietzsche is silent regarding the mechanism whereby one state is arrived at from the other and how this contradiction can be supported: his description does not seem to assume a synthesis between the two terms, but he nevertheless talks of the 'Apollonian completion of the [spectator's transformed, Dionysiac] state', and of how 'tragedy is an Apollonian embodiment of Dionysiac insights and powers'. *Ibid.*, 56, 56–7 (§8).

47 Even so, Tippett still talks of a 'chorus of young people of the present time sing[ing] themselves into a mantic chorus akin to that of the ancient Greek theatre' ('The birth of an opera', in *Moving into Aquarius*, 61; *Tippett on Music*, 206).

48 Nietzsche, *The Birth of Tragedy*, 57, 52 (§8).

49 The association of Strephon with the natural world was strongly thematized in David Poutney's 1985 English National Opera production of *The Midsummer Marriage*, in which Strephon was presented at numinous moments with the head of a stag – homologous with, if not identical to, the half-man, half-goat condition of the Greek satyr.

50 In *The Birth of Tragedy* music is presented as the quintessentially Dionysiac art. 'In accordance with Schopenhauer's doctrine', Nietzsche writes, 'we interpret music as the immediate language of the will . . . Music incites us to a symbolic intuition of the Dionysiac universality . . . From these facts . . . we deduce that music is capable of giving birth to myth . . . and above all, to the tragic myth, which is a parable of Dionysiac knowledge' (*The Birth of Tragedy*, 101 (§16)).

51 *Ibid.*, 58 (§8). Kemp makes a related point when he says that 'the animals of the Ritual Dances . . . are red in tooth and claw. Tippett's observation of the laws of the countryside is so coldly precise that the dances could have become almost too frightening to contemplate had he not set them at a distance with musical procedures as abstract as anywhere in the opera, and had they not that quality of psychological truth which willy-nilly draws the listener into their aura' (*Tippett*, 257).

52 Meirion Bowen also makes this point in his *Michael Tippett*, 2nd edn (London: Robson Books, 1997), 209. Other Tippett works in which the horns are used in bucolic fashion, or to signify the natural, include his Sonata for Four Horns (1955), Symphony No. 2 (1956–7) (at the end of the slow movement), Symphony No. 3 (1970–2) (beginning of Part II).

53 Tippett's directions regarding the stage picture are a little ambiguous, but given the symmetrical structure of the act, and the final direction, 'the presences are still', it is clear that the characters of the Ritual Dances are already there in the prelude.

54 This material is quoted in the first two bars of Ex. 3.1, but subsequently omitted in the interests of space.

55 See for example pp. 142–3, 145 (§24, §25).

56 The analysis of historical mediations is a complex and non-finite game, however. One could equally invoke Gallic associations, as Ian Kemp has done in his characterization of the passage as 'the English equivalent of Debussy's *Prélude à l'après midi d'un faune*' (*Tippett*, 258). This interpretation is presumably predicated on the common feature of horn sonorities based around the dominant seventh; however, the voice-leading syntax whereby these sonorities are approached and quitted (at, for example, bars 4–11 of Debussy's *Prélude*) can itself be seen as a Wagnerian trait. For that matter, both in its overall shape and in matters of detail such as the neighbour-note figure *a*, the Tippett passage also resembles the sunrise music in Ravel's *Daphnis et Chloë*. Moving closer to home, a similar gesture, also with evocations of myth and the natural world – this time the sea – is found at the opening of Bax's *Tintagel*. But the most immediate connection, in terms of

actual vocabulary (if not of syntax and aesthetics), is with a passage in the trio of the scherzo of Mendelssohn's 'Italian' Symphony, op. 90, which resembles the opening of Tippett's prelude not only in the prominence of horns, but also in an almost identically executed progression from V^7 of E to V^7 of A: compare, for example, the horn parts of *The Midsummer Marriage*, Fig. $145^{+1–3}$, with those of bars 85–8 of the Mendelssohn movement. This may have been an unconscious memory trace, or a more oblique reference to the evocative musical world of the composer of incidental music to *A Midsummer Night's Dream*.

57 Whittall, *The Music of Britten and Tippett: Studies in Themes and Techniques*, 2nd edn (Cambridge: Cambridge University Press, 1990), 140. See also my discussion of another manifestation of the same dualism in D. Clarke, '"Only half rebelling": tonal strategies, folksong and "Englishness" in Tippett's Concerto for Double String Orchestra', in *Tippett Studies*, ed. D. Clarke, 1–26 (pp. 11–17).

58 See, for example, *The Birth of Tragedy*, 77–96 (§12–15).

59 See n. 54, above.

60 Tippett, 'Towards the condition of music', in *Music of the Angels*, 17–27 (pp. 24–5); *Tippett on Music*, 7–15 (p. 13).

61 Gary Tomlinson, *Metaphysical Song: An Essay on Opera* (Princeton: Princeton University Press, 1999), 76–7.

62 *Ibid.*

63 'Michael Tippett', in Murray Schafer, *British Composers in Interview* (London: Faber and Faber, 1963), 97. Tippett, 'Towards the condition of music', in *Music of the Angels*, 21; *Tippett on Music*, 10.

64 Arthur Schopenhauer, *The World as Will and Idea*, repr. abridged edn, ed. David Berman, trans. Jill Berman (London: J. M. Dent, 1998), 59 (§25).

65 *Ibid.*, 87 (supplement to Book 2, 'On the primacy of the will in self-consciousness').

66 *Ibid.*

67 John J. Clarke, *In Search of Jung* (London and New York: Routledge, 1992), 142.

68 Jung, 'The psychology of the child archetype', in *The Archetypes and the Collective Unconscious*, ed. Herbert Read, Michael Fordham and Gerhard Adler, trans. Richard F. C. Hull, Collected Works 9/1, 2nd edn (London: Routledge and Kegan Paul, 1959), 151–81 (p. 173). A longer version of this quotation appears in a similar connection on p. 31 of chapter 2, above.

69 Richard Noll, *The Jung Cult: Origins of a Charismatic Movement* (Princeton: Princeton University Press, 1994), 99–101. Noll argues that this kind of geological metaphor allies Jung with early nineteenth-century German *Naturphilosophie*. Also interesting in this respect is Michael Tanner's characterization of Schopenhauer's will as 'a kind of metaphysical lava', in his introduction to Nietzsche, *The Birth of Tragedy*, ed. Michael Tanner, trans. Shaun Whiteside (London: Penguin Books, 1993), vii–xxx (p. xv).

70 Quoted in J. Clarke, *In Search of Jung*, 33.

71 Noll, *The Jung Cult*, 99. See also J. Clarke's discussion of other critical voices, in *In Search of Jung*, 33–5.

72 Jung, *Psychological Types*, 143.

73 For example, Tippett tells of reading Evelyn Underhill's *Mysticism* (see 'What I believe', 49; 'Aspects of belief', 235); and the while his essay of the early 1950s, 'Moving into Aquarius' (in *Moving into Aquarius*, 35–42; *Tippett on Music*, 25–30) is concerned with the movements of history, the astrological metaphor is not arbitrarily chosen.

74 Tippett, 'Poets in a barren age', in *Moving into Aquarius*, 148–56 (p. 156).

75 See chapter 2, above, for a fuller discussion of this issue.

76 *Wagner on Music and Drama: A Compendium of Richard Wagner's Prose Works*, selected and arranged by Albert Goldman and Evert Spinchorn, trans. H. Ashton Ellis (New York: Da Capo Press, 1981), 185.

77 This notion of the will as it were bifurcating itself so as to communicate (with) itself seems to echo the idealist philosopher F. W. Schelling's conceit of the Absolute dividing itself into the separate domains of the real and ideal (an indication of a further possible expansion of our ideological matrix, inhibited only by limitations of space). For a detailed account of this notion see Ian Biddle, 'Autonomy, ontology and the ideal: music theory and philosophical aesthetics in early nineteenth-century German thought', Ph.D. thesis (University of Newcastle upon Tyne, 1995), 130–3. Isaiah Berlin also refers to Schelling in his tribute to Tippett in Ian Kemp (ed.), *Michael Tippett: A Symposium on his 60th Birthday* (London: Faber and Faber, 1965), 62–3.

78 Her association with the eternal feminine further suggests a connection with Dionysus who was also traditionally figured as feminine; and from her eventual ascent to the Apollonian realm, whose cultural associations are masculine, we might infer a degree of androgyny – which would become explicit in Tippett's later operatic messenger, Astron, from *The Ice Break*. (See Paglia's discussion of the feminine figuration of Dionysus, referred to in n. 24 above.)

79 Cf. Sosostris's line 'I am what has been, is and shall be'.

80 See, for example, Symphony No. 2, ii; Concerto for Orchestra (1962–3), ii; *King Priam*, Act III interlude 2; Symphony No. 3, Fig. 115ff.

81 Schopenhauer, *The World as Will*, 165, 166 (§52).

82 'Background', 'middleground' and 'foreground' are used as relative terms here, and do not in all cases correspond to their orthodox Schenkerian counterparts.

83 A phrase coined by the painter Réquichot, recounted by Roland Barthes: 'The meta-mental is what denies the theological opposition of body and soul'. See Barthes, 'Réquichot and his body', in *The Responsibility of Forms: Critical Essays on Music, Art, and Representation*, trans. Richard Howard (New York: Hill and Wang, 1985), 207–36 (p. 208).

84 The Bergson–Shaw–Tippett connections are described in Kemp, *Tippett*, 232–3.

85 Harrison, *Themis*, 1st edn, viii.

86 Tippett, 'Towards the condition of music', in *Music of the Angels*, 24; *Tippett on Music*, 13.

87 Schopenhauer, *The World as Will*, 169–70 (§52).

88 *Ibid.*, 209 (§61).

89 *Ibid.*, 263, 265 (supplement to Book 4, 'On the metaphysics of sexual love').

90 *Ibid.*, 177 (§54). Tippett would much later in his career (in *The Mask of Time*) invoke Shiva as a god 'dancing our destruction'.

91 Nietzsche, *The Birth of Tragedy*, 96 (§16).

92 Schopenhauer, *The World as Will*, 159 (§51).

93 Nietzsche, *The Birth of Tragedy*, 8 ('Critical backward glance', §4). Cf. also Nietzsche's statement: 'the profound Greek, so uniquely susceptible to the subtlest and deepest suffering, who had penetrated the destructive agencies of both nature and history, solaced himself. Though he had been in danger of craving a Buddhistic denial of the will, he was saved by art, and through art life reclaimed him' (*ibid.*, 50–1 (§7)).

94 *The Birth of Tragedy*, 102 (§16).

95 As Tomlinson puts it: 'Nietzsche's Dionysus sang, at first, with noumenal operatic voice; but this same Dionysus, hardly a moment later, ridiculed noumenalism as a farce of romantic culture' (*Metaphysical Song*, 109).

96 Nietzsche, *The Birth of Tragedy*, 51–2 (§7).

97 See, for example, British Library Add. MS 72037, fol. 8.

98 A conception which reveals the influence of Goldmann – discussed in Pollard and D. Clarke, 'Tippett's *King Priam*', 170–3.

99 Nietzsche, *The Birth of Tragedy*, 52 (§7).

100 *Ibid.*, 26 (§2).

101 Chapter 1 of her *Sexual Personae* (for details see n. 24, above).

102 *Ibid.*, 5–6.

103 *Ibid.*, 2, 3.

104 Hytner's production seems to have been entirely appropriately calculated to highlight Dionysiac content (as well as the opera's Cold War background). Still photographs from the production – which fortuitously illustrate various of the points made about the Dionysiac here and in subsequent paragraphs – can be found in Geraint Lewis (ed.), *Michael Tippett O.M.: A Celebration* (Tunbridge Wells: Baton Press, 1985), 94, 97, 100, 102 and 107.

105 Paglia, *Sexual Personae*, 5.

106 A version of this idea surfaces towards the end of Tippett's next opera, *The Knot Garden*, when the characters together sing 'We sense the magic net / That holds us veined / Each to each to all'. Tippett borrowed the metaphor from Goethe's poem *Magisches Netz* which he already knew in the 1930s; see *Those Twentieth Century Blues*, 81–4.

107 Stravinsky, *Poetics of Music*, as quoted in Tippett, 'Stravinsky and *Les noces*', in *Music of the Angels*, 85–96 (p. 88); *Tippett on Music*, 47–56 (p. 50).

108 An issue explored by Kenneth Gloag in his essay 'Tippett's Second Symphony, Stravinsky and the language of neoclassicism: towards a critical

framework', in *Tippett Studies*, ed. D. Clarke, 78–94. I discuss Tippett's relationship to Stravinsky's neoclassicism further in chapter 7, below.

109 Paul Griffiths discusses the ironization of tonal materials in Stravinsky (see
Griffiths, *Stravinsky* (London: J. M. Dent, 1992), 123) – a point cited in
Gloag, 'Tippett's Second Symphony', 89.

110 Whittall's 'higher consonance' concept; see for example *The Music of Britten
and Tippett*, 5–8.

111 See Tippett, 'Stravinsky and *Les noces*', in *Music of the Angels*, 88; *Tippett on
Music*, 50.

112 Paglia, *Sexual Personae*, 94–5.

113 Kemp, *Tippett*, 365; Bowen, *Michael Tippett*, 1st edn (London: Robson
Books, 1982), 64.

114 This particular polarization does not continue indefinitely. The extremes
find not resolution, but mediation at Fig. 8 (see Ex. 3.6(a)), where the brass
combine in a quasi-linear progression in the middleground, whose initial C$\sharp$
major sonority has elements in common with the previous E collection (C$\sharp$,
D$\sharp$, F$\sharp$ and G$\sharp$) and the E$\flat$ collection (D$\sharp$=E$\flat$, E$\sharp$=F, G$\sharp$=A$\flat$, A$\sharp$=B$\flat$, B$\sharp$=C).
The goal sonority of this progression (Fig. 9) is a kind of dominant of E$\flat$;
however, if at the ending of the prelude this tonality attains a status equal to
or greater than that of the initially predominant E, it does so in a context of
further conflict: pitted against it is now a collection based on C major (itself
perhaps an antagonistic response to the earlier C$\sharp$ collection), resulting in a
further highly dissonant aggregate.

115 Nietzsche, *The Gay Science*, trans. Walter Kaufmann (New York: Vintage
Books, 1974), 168 (§109); *The Will to Power*, ed. Walter Kaufmann, trans.
Walter Kaufmann and R. J. Hollingdale (New York: Vintage Books, 1967),
315 (§584).

116 Tippett, 'The resonance of Troy', in *Music of the Angels*, 234, 225; *Tippett on
Music*, 219, 211.

117 *Ibid.*, in *Music of the Angels*, 234; *Tippett on Music*, 219.

118 Whittall pursues some of the ramifications of this and related sets in his essay
'"Is there a choice at all?": *King Priam* and motives for analysis', in *Tippett
Studies*, ed. D. Clarke, 55–77 (pp. 60–72).

119 Tippett, 'Poets in a barren age', in *Moving into Aquarius*, 148–56 (p. 151).

120 Paglia, *Sexual Personae*, 9.

121 *Ibid.*, 5–6.

122 *Ibid.*, 7.

123 Nietzsche, *The Birth of Tragedy*, 23–4 (§1).

124 Tippett, *E. William Doty Lectures in Fine Arts*, Second Series, 1976 (Austin,
Tex.: University of Texas at Austin, 1979), 57.

125 In a letter to Lady Gregory; see *The Collected Letters of W. B. Yeats*, ed.
Allan Wade (London: Hart-Davis, 1954), 379; as quoted in Patrick
Bridgwater, *Nietzsche in Anglosaxony: A Study of Nietzsche's Impact on
English and American Literature* (Leicester: Leicester University Press, 1972),
68.

126 Otto Bohlmann, *Yeats and Nietzsche: An Exploration of Major Nietzschean Echoes in the Writings of William Butler Yeats* (London: Macmillan, 1982), 190.

127 Tippett asked Eric Walter White in a letter to try and procure him a copy while working on *The Midsummer Marriage*. See White, *Tippett and his Operas*, 58.

128 W. B. Yeats, *A Vision*, repr. edn (London and Basingstoke: Papermac, 1992), 268.

129 Yeats, *Ideas of Good and Evil* (London and Dublin: A. H. Bullen/Maunsel and Co., 1907), 201; as quoted in Bohlmann, *Yeats and Nietzsche*, 15.

130 Which line also resonates with Nietzsche: 'The more [the tree] wants to rise into the heights and the light, the more determinedly do its roots strive earthwards, downwards, into the darkness, into the depths – into evil'; *Thus Spoke Zarathustra*, trans. R. J. Hollingdale, rev. repr. edn (London: Penguin Books, 1969), 69 ('Of the tree on the mountainside').

131 Nietzsche, *Twilight of the Idols*, trans. R. J. Hollingdale (London: Penguin Books, 1990), 54 ('Morality as anti-nature', §3).

132 Nietzsche, *Thus Spoke Zarathustra*, 46 ('Zarathustra's prologue', §5).

133 Tippett, *Those Twentieth Century Blues*, xi.

134 Anthony Clare and Michael Tippett, 'In the psychiatrist's chair', *The Listener* 116, no. 2973 (14 August 1986), 10–11 (p. 11).

135 Terry Eagleton, *The Ideology of the Aesthetic* (Oxford and Cambridge, Mass.: Blackwell, 1990), 368–9.

136 Interesting material on Tippett's relationship with Trotskyism can be found at www.michael-tippett.com; see the page entitled 'Tippett and the Trotskyist movement'.

137 Cairns Craig, in his *Yeats, Eliot, Pound and the Politics of Poetry* (London and Pittsburgh: Croom Helm / University of Pittsburgh Press, 1982), is less equivocal in linking Yeats and Eliot themselves with patterns of fascist thought; see, for example, pp. 196–203, 248. I discuss this point further in chapter 7, below.

138 See for example the account given in Keith Ansell-Pearson, *An Introduction to Nietzsche as Political Thinker* (Cambridge: Cambridge University Press, 1994), 23–34.

139 J. P. Stern, *Nietzsche*, repr. edn (London: Fontana Press, 1985), 84.

140 Ansell-Pearson, for example, recounts how 'in the two decades following [Nietzsche's mental] breakdown, [his philosophy] was taken up with interest and imagination by socialists, anarchists, and feminists' (*Nietzsche as Political Thinker*, 29).

141 Tippett with Bayan Northcott, 'Tippett's Third Symphony', *Music and Musicians* 20/10 (June 1972), 30–2 (p. 30).

142 Whether Nietzsche intended this only metaphorically remains moot. See for example Walter Kaufmann, *Nietzsche: Philosopher, Psychologist, Antichrist*, 4th edn (Princeton: Princeton University Press, 1974), 386–8.

143 See, for example, Nietzsche, *The Gay Science*, 279 (§343).

144 Tippett refers to this concept in 'What I believe', in *Music of the Angels*, 50–1. Interestingly, the relevant passage is omitted in the revised counterpart of this essay, 'Aspects of belief', in *Tippett on Music*.

145 Nietzsche, *The Will to Power*, 14 (§12).

146 Lawrence Lampert, *Nietzsche and Modern Times: A Study of Bacon, Descartes, and Nietzsche* (New Haven and London: Yale University Press, 1993), 415. Much of the following account is indebted to Lampert's analysis.

147 Nietzsche, 'On truth and lying in the extra moral sense'; quoted in Lampert, *Nietzsche and Modern Times*, 416.

148 Nietzsche, *The Will to Power*, 14 (§13).

149 Nietzsche, *The Gay Science*, 168 (§109).

150 *Ibid.*, 169 (§109).

151 Cf. Lampert: 'Nietzsche's whole philosophy [is] . . . to give an account of nature that is in some sense true (while kept under the police supervision of mistrust), and to create the music and poetry that make it possible to live in accord with nature' (*Nietzsche and Modern Times*, 418). Nietzsche's stance, and its explicit attack on Rousseau's concept of the natural, is also broadly that taken up by Paglia.

152 Nietzsche, *Twilight of the Idols,* 49 ('"Reason" in philosophy', §6).

153 *Ibid.*, 121 ('What I owe to the ancients', §5).

154 Stern, *Nietzsche*, 80.

155 Nietzsche, *The Will to Power*, 549–50 (§1067).

156 Stern's critique of Nietzsche also hinges on this point; see his *Nietzsche*, 81–4.

157 Tippett, 'What I believe', in *Music of the Angels*, 52; 'Aspects of belief', 239.

158 This notion is explored at greater length in connection with the *Mask of Time*, in chapter 5, below.

4 Metaphysics in a cold climate: *The Vision of Saint Augustine*

1 Michael Tippett, 'Music of the angels', in *Music of the Angels: Essays and Sketchbooks*, ed. Meirion Bowen (London: Eulenburg Books, 1980), 60–6. The material of this essay and that which precedes it, 'Preface to *The Vision of Saint Augustine*' (*ibid.*, 57–9), a version of Tippett's preface to the score, is reordered and modified as the essay 'St Augustine and his visions', in *Tippett on Music*, ed. Meirion Bowen (Oxford: Clarendon Press, 1995), 228–36.

2 Tippett, 'Too many choices', in *Moving into Aquarius*, 2nd edn (St Albans: Paladin Books, 1974), 130–44; *Tippett on Music*, 294–306. The essay was first published in *The Listener* 59, No. 1503 (16 Jan. 1958), 95–6; 59, No. 1504 (23 Jan. 1958), 151–2.

3 See Arnold Whittall, *The Music of Britten and Tippett*, 2nd edn (Cambridge: Cambridge University Press, 1990), 216.

4 Both versions open with a general acknowledgement of Hammerstein's *Die Musik der Engel: Untersuchungen zur Musikanschauung des Mittelalters* (Bern

and Munich: Frank Verlag, 1962), but are subsequently a little patchy regarding precise referencing. Tippett's description of the *alter ad alterum*, as well as other styles of angel song – e.g. *sine fine* ('they have no rest day nor night') and *una voce* ('with one voice') – cite the original biblical references (see 'Music of the angels', 64–5; 'St Augustine and his visions', 232–3); but it seems likely that the source for this passage was Hammerstein's discussion of those conceits on pp. 17–19 and p. 25 of his book.

5 See Figs. 70^{-2}–74 (trumpets) and 79^{-2}–83 (horns).

6 Compare Tippett 'Music of the angels', 61; 'St Augustine and his visions', 230; with Hammerstein, *Die Musik der Engel*, 20: 'Hier neigt sich der himmlische Lobpreis auf die Erde, der Engelsgesang ragt in die menschliche Heilsgeschichte hinein'.

7 See Hammerstein, *Die Musik der Engel*, 39–41. Tippett also cites *The Wakefield Pageants* and works by G. B. Chambers and Jacques Paul Migne as providing further references to these practices; see 'Music of the angels', 62–3; 'St Augustine and his visions', 230–1.

8 Tippett mentions the *Pistis Sophia* in 'Preface to *The Vision of Saint Augustine*', 59; although Hammerstein is again not acknowledged, the order and arrangement of the syllables cited (exactly as quoted in the main text here) is identical to, if only a subset of, those quoted in *Die Musik der Engel*, 40.

This is not the only occasion on which Hammerstein might be seen to have influenced the textual content of Tippett's work. The quotation from Job, 'Ubi eras quando ponebam fundamenta terrae?' ('Where wert thou when I laid the foundations of the earth?') in Part I of *Augustine* (Fig. 57ff.) is also made by Hammerstein (in Latin as well as the vernacular), significantly in the context of a discussion of the angels' eternal praise of God before the creation of humankind: 'Dieser Lobpreis ist von Anbeginn, vor Erschaffung des Menschen gestiftet: "Wo warst Du, als ich die Erde gründete?"' (*Die Musik der Engel*, 17). Furthermore, the chorus's final 'Attolite portas' in *Augustine* ('Lift up your heads, O ye gates') again invokes an angelic connection, via the association established with these words in *Die Musik der Engel* (this time alluding to the end rather than the beginning of time); Hammerstein quotes the commentary on this text given by Germanius (d. 576) which envisions a procession of angels issuing forth as representatives of Christ triumphant over death: 'Die Prozession der heiligen Engel tritt hervor wie die Macht des über den Tod triumphierenden Christus' (*ibid.*, 49).

9 Gilles Quispel, 'Time and history in patristic Christianity', in *Man and Time: Papers from the Eranos Yearbooks*, ed. Joseph Campbell (London: Routledge and Kegan Paul, 1958), 85–107. The first time Tippett referenced this essay was in 'St Augustine and his visions', in *Tippett on Music*, 228. He does, however, mention it without specifying either author or title in Michael Tippett, *E. William Doty Lectures in Fine Arts*, Second Series, 1976 (Austin, Tex.: University of Texas at Austin, 1979), 35.

10 Most significantly, Quispel quotes in its entirety Augustine's account of the vision of eternity he experienced with his mother, Monica – the very passage which would form the backbone of Tippett's libretto; the first three paragraphs of this account correspond to the baritone soloist's text in the three parts of the piece (see Quispel, 'Time and history', 103–4). Quispel was probably also Tippett's source for the Greek version of the Pauline words which end *The Vision of Saint Augustine* ('οὔπω λογίζομαι κατειληφέναι') and for the other part of this passage, which would become a refrain in the work just as it held enormous significance for Augustine: 'forgetting those things which are behind . . .' ('et praeterita obliviscentes . . .'); see *ibid.*, 107, 100, 106.

   Additionally, the obscure source of one of the few passages in Tippett's libretto belonging neither to the *Confessions* nor to the Bible may have been a footnote in Quispel's paper. This is the passage 'sed facie ad faciem, quod de Moise dictum est, est "os ad os"' ('but face to face, which, as Moses said, is "mouth to mouth"'), which Quispel quotes from Augustine's *De Genesi ad Litteram* (see *ibid.*, 105 n. 35), and which is sung by the chorus between Figs. 187 and 189 of *The Vision of Saint Augustine*.

11 Tippett, 'Too many choices', in *Moving into Aquarius*, 143; *Tippett on Music*, 304–5.

12 BL Add. MS 69422B, fols. 16, 17. Franklin was Tippett's contact at the publishers Routledge and Kegan Paul, with whom he corresponded on matters relating to the impending publication of the first edition of *Moving into Aquarius*; he also seemed to have used the opportunity to sound out ideas on the developing conception of *King Priam*. The letter from which this quotation is taken is undated, but appears in a sequence between others dated 12 August and 13 October 1958. The book to which Tippett refers is probably the one that he requests 'as "pourboire"' in a letter to Franklin written earlier in the year. He refers to 'the book you publish of philosophical "texts"', saying he wants it 'not for the Jung contribution [presumably 'On synchronicity'] – wh I know in its late developed form, but for all the other stuff I don't know, & wld like to browse in' (*ibid.*, fol. 5ᵛ).

13 Tippett makes this point more explicit in the preface to the essay which he added for its publication in *Moving into Aquarius*, probably after he read Quispel. I return to the matter in Part IV of the present essay (see pp. 142–4 below).

14 These were 'to be sought in the city of Rome in the ranks of the national reaction once led by Symmachus, who wished to lay the blame for the sacking of Rome (A.D. 410) upon the Christians' (Quispel, 'Time and history', 96).

15 *Ibid.*, 97.

16 *Ibid.*, 86.

17 *Ibid.*, 87.

18 Saint Augustine, *Confessions*, trans. Henry Chadwick, repr. edn (Oxford: Oxford University Press, 1998), 226 (XI/vii).

19 See *ibid.*, 235, 243 (XI/xx, xxviii).

20 See *ibid.*, 243–4 (XI/xxix). The connection between *distentio* and diaspora is made in Quispel, 'Time and history', 106.

21 See for example Tippett, *Doty Lectures*, 11–13.

22 Tippett, 'Preface to *The Vision of St Augustine*', 57–9 (p. 58); this passage is omitted from the corresponding section of 'St Augustine and his visions'.

23 Quispel, 'Time and history', 93.

24 *Ibid.*, 94–5.

25 Sleeve notes to *The Vision of Saint Augustine* (RCA, SER 5620, 1972); also quoted in Whittall, *The Music of Britten and Tippett*, 214–15. A similar fascination for historical reality is evident in Tippett's revised prefatory notes: 'Augustine was born in AD 354 in the province of Africa on the south side of the Mediterranean. *This gives him a time in history and a place*' ('St Augustine and his visions', 234; emphasis added). And in his later commentary on *The Mask of Time* Tippett repeats this trope, this time drawing a parallel between Augustine and the poet Shelley: 'Just as St Augustine could stand *in an actual place* and have a vision of eternity, so Shelley now can ask himself in *an actual moment and place*: "What do I see of the absolute?"' ('*The Mask of Time*', in *Tippett on Music*, 245–55 (p. 252); emphasis added).

 In one sense Tippett is merely rehearsing Augustine's own sense of the historically and geographically contingent context of his vision of the timeless. As Peter Brown puts it: 'Every incident in [the *Confessions*] . . . is charged with the poignancy of a Chinese landscape – a vivid detail perched against infinite distances: "In the shadow of that day, on which she was to leave the world – a day which You had known, not us, – it so happened, I believe through Your arrangement, by Your hidden ways, that I and my mother stood alone, leaning at a window that looked upon the enclosed garden of the house in which we lodged; it was at Ostia, on the Tiber"' (Peter Brown, *Augustine of Hippo: A Biography* (London: Faber and Faber, 1967), 168).

26 As recounted by Quispel, 'Time and history', 94.

27 'What attracted me was [Quispel's] account of Augustine's theory of visions, which embodies profound psychological insights. Quispel shows that Augustine's subjective notion of time and of visions as products of the memory are consistent with the rest of his thinking, all of it with a strong emphasis on inwardness' (Tippett, 'St Augustine and his visions', 228).

28 Tippett, 'Towards the condition of music', in *Music of the Angels*, 17–27 (pp. 20, 24); *Tippett on Music*, 7–15 (pp. 9–10, 13).

29 See chapter 2, n. 31, above.

30 G. W. F. Hegel, *Aesthetics: Lectures on Fine Art*, trans. T. M. Knox, 2 vols. (Oxford: Clarendon Press, 1975), vol. II, 891.

31 For example August Wilhelm von Schlegel states: 'music occupies the dimension of time, one that is universally experienced by the inner consciousness . . . Music is an image of our restless, mutable, ever-changing life'

(*Vorlesungen über die schöne Literatur und Kunst* (1801)); from an excerpt quoted in *Music and Aesthetics in the Eighteenth and Early-Nineteenth Centuries*, ed. Peter le Huray and James Day (Cambridge: Cambridge University Press, 1981), 266.

32 Tippett, 'Towards the condition of music', in *Music of the Angels*, 24 (emphasis added); *Tippett on Music*, 13.

33 Julian Johnson, 'The subjects of music: a theoretical and analytical enquiry into the construction of subjectivity in the musical structuring of time', D.Phil. thesis (University of Sussex, 1994), 50. Much of the present discussion of these issues is informed by Johnson's lucid account in this thesis, as well as in his 'Music in Hegel's *Aesthetics*: a re-evaluation', *British Journal of Aesthetics* 31/2 (April 1991), 152–62. I have also found valuable Ian Biddle's discussion of Hegel in his 'Autonomy, ontology and the ideal: music theory and philosophical aesthetics in early nineteenth-century German thought', Ph.D. thesis (University of Newcastle upon Tyne, 1995), chapter 5, 'Hegel: music as mediation', 214–80.

34 Hegel, *Aesthetics*, vol. II, 907.

35 *Ibid.*, 914.

36 *Ibid.*, 626.

37 Knox's translation of Hegel's use of this term as 'bar' fails to capture the larger principle at stake – a point also made by Biddle, 'Autonomy', 273 n. 175.

38 Hegel, *Aesthetics*, vol. II, 915.

39 *Ibid.*, 933.

40 See Kevin Korsyn, 'Schenker and Kantian epistemology', *Theoria: Historical Aspects of Music Theory* 3 (1988), 1–58. The account of Kant given here draws on that given on pp. 19–43 of Korsyn's study.

41 Tippett, 'Towards the condition of music', in *Music of the Angels*, 24; *Tippett on Music*, 13.

42 Johnson's discussion of this point (in 'The subjects of music', 54–9) includes as exemplars of this argument Christopher Ballantine, *Music and its Social Meanings* (New York and London: Gordon and Breach, 1984), 32; Wilfrid Mellers, *Beethoven and the Voice of God* (London: Faber and Faber, 1983), 21; Theodor W. Adorno, *Introduction to the Sociology of Music*, trans. E. B. Ashton (New York: Continuum, 1989), 209–10.

   See also the discussion of Adorno's exploration of the relationship between Beethoven and Hegel, in Simon Jarvis, *Adorno: A Critical Introduction* (Cambridge: Polity Press, 1998), 129–31.

43 See Hegel, *Aesthetics*, vol. II, 893.

44 Johnson, 'The subjects of music', 54. This point is also made by Tippett himself: 'In listening to such music we are as though entire again, despite all the insecurity, incoherence, incompleteness and relativity of our everyday life' ('Towards the condition of music', in *Music of the Angels*, 24; *Tippett on Music*, 13).

45 Jonathan D. Kramer, 'New temporalities in music', *Critical Inquiry* 7/3 (Spring 1981), 539–56 (pp. 545, 546). See also *idem, The Time of Music: New Meanings; New Temporalities; New Listening Strategies* (New York and London: Schirmer/Macmillan, 1988), 46–9.

46 Immanuel Kant, *Critique of Pure Reason*, trans. Norman Kemp Smith, repr. edn (Basingstoke: Macmillan, 1992), 154 (B 134).

47 The translation of passages from the *Confessions* set in *The Vision of Saint Augustine* itself is that given in the score.

48 See Augustine, *Confessions*, 235 (XI/xx). Another way of looking at these textual allusions – one which relates again to Augustine's thinking and is also utterly to do with subjectivity – is to see them as traces of the faculty of mind which Augustine calls Memory, explored at length in book X of the *Confessions*. He means this term in a highly extended sense to denote not just remembered contents, but also the mind's power of imagination, its capacity for concepts, its anticipation of the future, its record of an individual's life experiences. As Brian Stock puts it, 'Memory . . . emerges as the point of co-ordination for mental narratives' which 'taken together . . . comprise an intentional discourse of the self' (Brian Stock, *Augustine the Reader: Meditation, Self-Knowledge, and the Ethics of Interpretation* (Cambridge, Mass., and London: Harvard University Press, 1996), 218).

49 Interestingly, the MS of the score reveals that Tippett originally gave these two particular ideas the same tempo designation (see Pencil MS: BL Add. MS 61791, fols. 2 and 5^v).

50 As Kemp points out, Vision II, described here, accounts for about only one of the work's thirty-five minutes (Ian Kemp, *Michael Tippett: The Composer and his Music* (London: Eulenburg Books, 1984), 396).

51 Stockhausen states of moment form: 'A given moment is not merely regarded as the consequence of the previous one and the prelude to the coming one, but as something individual, independent, and centered in itself, capable of existing on its own. An instant does not need to be just a particle of measured duration. This concentration on the present moment – on every present moment – can make a vertical cut, as it were, across horizontal time percep-tion, extending out to a timelessness I call eternity' (Karlheinz Stockhausen, 'Momentform: neue Zusammenhänge zwischen Aufführungsdauer, Werkdauer und Moment', in *Texte zur elektronischen und instrumentalen Musik*, vol. I (Verlag M. DuMont: Schauberg and Cologne, 1963), 189–210 (p. 199); in a translation by Brad Absetz quoted in Kramer, *The Time of Music*, 210).

52 Kemp, *Tippett*, 394.

53 See n. 51, above.

54 This process is described in more detail in Kemp, *Tippett*, 394–6, where all the constituent ostinati are quoted in full.

55 Whittall, *The Music of Britten and Tippett*, 216.

56 See the quotations from Thomas Weiskel, *The Romantic Sublime: Studies in*

the Structure and Psychology of Transcendence (Baltimore and London: The Johns Hopkins University Press, 1976) on pp. 31–2 of chapter 2, above.

57 Such harmonies are what Whittall has in mind when he states in his account of *Augustine* that 'in the absence of triadic harmony, a very wide variety of sustained chords . . . assume the role of generating or cadential sonorities without in any sense fulfilling the larger pivotal function of triads in more traditionally harmonic music' (*The Music of Britten and Tippett*, 217).

58 Adorno, *Aesthetic Theory*, ed. Gretel Adorno and Rolf Tiedemann, trans. Robert Hullot-Kentor (London: Athlone Press, 1997), 143.

59 See the chapter by Tippett in *The Orchestral Composer's Point of View: Essays on Twentieth-Century Music by Those Who Wrote It*, ed. Robert Hines (Norman, Okla.: University of Oklahoma Press, 1970), 203–19; adapted and revised as 'Archetypes of concert music', in *Tippett on Music*, 89–108.

60 This interpretation of Tippett's notional and historical archetype dualism is indebted to Alastair Borthwick's essay 'Tonal elements and their significance in Tippett's Sonata No. 3 for Piano', in *Tippett Studies*, ed. David Clarke (Cambridge: Cambridge University Press, 1999), 117–44.

61 Hegel, *Aesthetics*, vol. II, 932.

62 These words are set in Part III of *The Vision of Saint Augustine*.

63 Perhaps recalling the silver trumpet which accompanies Jenifer's depiction of what she found on ascending the stair in *The Midsummer Marriage*.

64 Interestingly, the final choral phrase, at Fig. 104, is similar in profile and actual pitch content to the flute duo at the end of the very first section of the work ('Impendente'; cf. Fig. 6^{+4-5}; Ex. 4.5). This would suggest the entire 'venimus' passage as a distant relative of the opening, shorn of its bass stratum. Another facet of this is the similarity in spirit if not substance between the former's trumpet/oboe/cor anglais motif, and the latter's celesta motif. Both figures function like a fragmented obbligato (suggesting, very elliptically, the baroque aria as a remote historical archetype); and both draw their formal organization from a principle of absolute thematicism (i.e. with no reliance on implied harmony, tonality or counterpoint).

65 Kemp, *Tippett*, 400, 401.

66 Whittall, *The Music of Britten and Tippett*, 220.

67 *Ibid.*

68 Adorno, *Aesthetic Theory*, 131.

69 Confirmation of this negative relationship between the work and its composer is Tippett's anecdotal admission that even years after completing the work he still did not understand it; see Tippett, *Doty Lectures*, 34.

70 Adorno, *Aesthetic Theory*, 131.

71 'Philosophy and art converge in their truth content . . . The truth content of artworks is not what they mean but rather what decides whether the work in itself is true or false, and only this truth of the work in-itself is commensurable to philosophical interpretation' (*ibid.*, 130).

72 'Today the metaphysics of art revolves around the question of how something spiritual that is made . . . can be true' (*ibid.*, 131).

73 Adorno, *Negative Dialectics*, trans. E. B. Ashton, repr. edn (London:
Routledge, 1996), 385.

74 '[Kant] held on to the metaphysical ideas, and yet he forbade jumping from
thoughts of the absolute which might one day be realized, like eternal peace,
to the conclusion that therefore the absolute exists . . . He disdained the
passage to affirmation' (*ibid.*).

75 I pursue this issue further, in relation to *The Mask of Time*, in chapter 5 below
(pp. 183–7).

76 Indeed he himself comes close to admitting this, as Adorno points out; see
Negative Dialectics, 390.

77 *Ibid.*, 392. I have found Simon Jarvis's discussion of *Negative Dialectics*
helpful in formulating the present account; see Jarvis, *Adorno*, chapter 8,
'Materialism and metaphysics', 191–216 (pp. 207–16).

78 Earlier in his account, Adorno, rehearsing an argument from Hegel, argues
that for reason to 'judge whether it had passed the bounds of possible
experience', it must be able to distinguish itself from its other: yet this paradoxically presupposes a transcendental perspective or Archimedean point
from which it can make such a distinction. Thus in the attempt to construct
itself within a finite sphere, reason ends up negating this putative finitude.
See *Negative Dialectics*, 382–4.

79 *Ibid.*, 392.

80 *Ibid.*, 408, 393.

81 'Despair of the world, a despair that is true, based on facts, and neither
esthetic weltschmerz nor a wrong, reprehensible consciousness, guarantees
to us that the hopelessly missed things exist, though existence at large has
become a universal guilt context' (*ibid.*, 372). 'Grayness could not fill us with
despair if our minds did not harbor the concept of different colors, scattered
traces of which are not absent from the negative whole' (*ibid.*, 377–8).

82 Adorno, *Aesthetic Theory*, 132.

83 *Ibid.*, 135–6.

84 See Adorno, *Negative Dialectics*, 365.

85 The closing lines of *Negative Dialektik*, Part 3/9: 'Nur wenn, was ist, sich
ändern läßt, ist das, was ist, nicht alles', as translated by Jarvis (*Adorno*, 216).
E. B. Ashton's translation reads: 'What is must be changeable if it is not to be
all' (Adorno, *Negative Dialectics*, 398).

86 Tippett, in a passage preceding his 'Preface to *The Vision of Saint Augustine*',
in *Music of the Angels*, 57 (not included in 'St Augustine and his visions').

87 'Stravinsky held to one thing all his life, that the work of art each time was, so
to speak, wrought out of granite . . . This is to me of tremendous value, so I
always want to go towards it; but where I would differ is because of my education in the other process of having antennae that are concerned with the
other problems of our society. Stravinsky never did' (Tippett, *Doty Lectures*,

38). I discuss this view of Stravinsky in relation to Tippett's conception of 'artefacts' in chapter 7, below.

88 'Absolute Music! What the lawgivers mean by this, is perhaps remotest of all from the Absolute in music. "Absolute music" is a form-play without poetic program, in which form is intended to have the leading part. But Form, in itself, is the opposite pole of absolute music, on which was bestowed the divine prerogative of buoyancy, of freedom from the limitations of matter' (Ferruccio Busoni, 'Sketch of a new esthetic of music', in *Three Classics in the Aesthetics of Music*, trans. Theodore Baker (New York: Dover, 1962), 73–102 (p. 78)). See also the discussion in Carl Dahlhaus, *The Idea of Absolute Music*, trans. Roger Lustig (Chicago and London: University of Chicago Press, 1989), 38.

89 Tippett, 'Too many choices', in *Moving into Aquarius*, 132; *Tippett on Music*, 295.

90 Here I paraphrase Tippett's comments in *ibid.*, in *Moving into Aquarius*, 133–5; *Tippett on Music*, 297–8.

91 Tippett, 'Drum, flute and zither', in *Moving into Aquarius*, 67–84 (p. 79); *Tippett on Music*, 185–98 (p. 194).

92 Tippett, 'Too many choices', in *Moving into Aquarius*, 132; *Tippett on Music*, 296.

93 Adorno, *Aesthetic Theory*, 132.

94 Tippett, 'A time to recall', in *Moving into Aquarius*, 101–7 (p. 103). Also 'Persönliches Bekenntnis', in *ibid.*, 117–21 (p. 121); 'Aspects of belief', in *Tippett on Music*, 239–42 (p. 242). (Emphasis added.)

95 Tippett, 'Persönliches Bekenntnis', 121; 'Aspects of belief', 242.

96 Erich Neumann, 'Art and time', in *Man and Time*, ed. Campbell, 3–37 (pp. 29–30); quoted in Tippett, 'The artist's mandate', in *Moving into Aquarius*, 122–9 (pp. 122–3); *Tippett on Music*, 287–93 (p. 287) (quotation corrected).

5 'Shall we...? Affirm!' The ironic and the sublime in *The Mask of Time*

1 The opinions cited are voiced respectively by Arnold Whittall, *The Music of Britten and Tippett: Studies in Themes and Techniques*, 2nd edn (Cambridge: Cambridge University Press, 1990), 299; R. H. Kay, letter to the editor, *Gramophone* 65, No. 770 (July 1987), 147; Geraint Lewis, '"Spring come to you at the farthest in the very end of harvest"', in *Michael Tippett O.M.: A Celebration*, ed. Geraint Lewis (Tunbridge Wells: Baton Press, 1985), 199–212 (p. 210); and Derrick Puffett, 'Tippett and the retreat from mythology', *The Musical Times* 136, No. 1823 (January 1995), 6–14 (p. 7).

2 Composer's Preface; see booklet 1 accompanying CD recording of *The Mask of Time*, conducted by Andrew Davis (EMI, CDS 7 47705 8, 1987), 4.

3 Tippett rejected, for example, the exclusionism implicit in T. S. Eliot's treatment of the spiritual crisis of modernity, which involved privileging Christianity. By contrast, the composer proffered the idea of 'an iconography

that is detached from established religious ritual: for in effect, it needs a new ritual, in which we are all there, fully defined in terms of sex, space, and time' (Michael Tippett, 'What I believe', in *Music of the Angels: Essays and Sketchbooks*, ed. Meirion Bowen (London: Eulenburg Books, 1980), 49–55 (p. 54; see also p. 49); 'Aspects of belief', in *Tippett on Music*, ed. Meirion Bowen (Oxford: Clarendon Press, 1995), 237–44 (p. 243; see also p. 237)). It is already clear in this 1978 postscript to the 1956 essay that Tippett's thoughts are on the gestating *Mask of Time*; and shortly after this statement comes one of his earliest published references to Jacob Bronowski's *The Ascent of Man*, which was an important influence on the work (see 'What I believe', 55; reference omitted in 'Aspects of belief').

4 Annie Dillard, *Pilgrim at Tinker Creek* (London: Pan Books Ltd, 1976), 152. The precise wording used here and in subsequent quotations is that of Dillard's text itself.

5 'The hidden God', a recurring theme in *Pilgrim at Tinker Creek*, is also the title of the book by Lucien Goldmann (originally the French *Le dieu caché*) which informed the conception of *King Priam*; see Lucien Goldmann, *The Hidden God: A Study of Tragic Vision in the* Pensées *of Pascal and the Tragedies of Racine*, trans. Philip Thody (London: Routledge and Kegan Paul, 1964).

6 Dillard, *Pilgrim at Tinker Creek*, 182. The falling mockingbird is an image which recurs throughout the book (see for example pp. 20–1) – as is 'the tree with the lights in it', discussed in n. 33, below.

7 Compare respectively: Triple Concerto for violin, viola, cello and orchestra, Fig. 67ff.; Symphony No. 4, opening; and *The Ice Break*, Fig. 448ff.; with *The Mask of Time*, Figs. 88, 96 and 98.

8 Immanuel Kant, *The Critique of Judgement*, trans. James Creed Meredith (Oxford: Clarendon Press, 1952), part II, 108 (§25/86).

9 Dillard, *Pilgrim at Tinker Creek*, 236.

10 Tippett, *E. William Doty Lectures in Fine Arts*, Second Series 1976 (Austin, Tex.: University of Texas at Austin, 1979), 12.

11 It seems likely that much of the imagery for this movement draws not only from Bronowski's aforementioned *The Ascent of Man*, but also from Loren Eiseley, *The Invisible Pyramid* (New York: Charles Scribner's Sons, 1970), 66–7.

12 A term used by Lucien Lévy-Bruhl and defined by Jung (in a text which we know Tippett read) as denoting 'a peculiar kind of psychological connection with objects, and consist[ing] in the fact that the subject cannot clearly distinguish himself from the object but is bound to it by a direct relationship which amounts to partial *identity* . . . *Participation mystique* is a vestige of this primitive condition' (Carl Gustav Jung, *Psychological Types*, ed. Herbert Read, Michael Fordham and Gerhard Adler, trans. Helton G. Baynes, rev. Richard F. C. Hull, Collected Works 6 (London: Routledge and Kegan Paul, 1971), 456).

13 An important source on which Tippett might have drawn in articulating these sentiments is, again, Eiseley, *The Invisible Pyramid*. See, for example,

ibid., 142–4, and especially Eiseley's observation that 'science, by reason of its detachment, would first of all view nature as might a curious stranger. Finally it would, while giving powers to man, turn upon him also the same gaze that had driven the animal forever into the forest' (p. 144). The sentiments here converge with those cited below from Dewey, Bernstein and Adorno – an important nexus between different intellectual traditions, which offers some justification for their continuing interplay in this chapter and indeed in this book as a whole.

14 J. M. Bernstein, 'Why rescue semblance? Metaphysical experience and the possibility of ethics', in *The Semblance of Subjectivity: Essays in Adorno's Aesthetic Theory*, ed. Tom Huhn and Lambert Zuidervaart (Cambridge, Mass., and London: MIT Press, 1997), 177–212 (pp. 177–8).

15 *Ibid.*, 177.

16 Kant, *Critique of Judgement*, part I, 94 (§25). Edmund Burke, *A Philosophical Enquiry into the Origin of our Ideas of the Sublime and the Beautiful*, ed. J. T. Boulton (London: Routledge and Kegan Paul, 1958), 39.

17 Angela Leighton, *Shelley and the Sublime: An Interpretation of the Major Poems* (Cambridge: Cambridge University Press, 1984), 10. Leighton's source is the reprint edition of Burnet published by Centaur Press (London, 1965).

18 *Ibid.*, 24.

19 *Ibid.*, 40.

20 Indeed Tippett's phrase, 'endless agnosticism' hails from the same discussion in which he makes an early mention of his interest in Shelley's 'The triumph of Life', in connection with the gestating work that would eventually become *The Mask of Time*. See *Doty Lectures*, 61, 62.

21 See *ibid.*, 62.

22 Michael O'Neill, *The Human Mind's Imaginings: Conflict and Achievement in Shelley's Poetry* (Oxford: Clarendon Press, 1989), 179, 184–6.

23 Tippett, 'Poets in a barren age', in *Moving into Aquarius*, 2nd edn (St Albans: Paladin Books, 1974), 148–56 (pp. 150–1); 'Preface to Verses for a symphony', in *ibid.*, 157–9 (pp. 158–9); 'Archetypes of concert music', in *Tippett on Music*, 89–108 (pp. 96, 98).

24 D. C. Muecke, *Irony and the Ironic* (London and New York: Methuen, 1970), 23–5.

25 See, for example, Michael Tippett, *Those Twentieth Century Blues: An Autobiography* (London: Hutchinson, 1991), 247.

26 Walter Benjamin, *Charles Baudelaire: A Lyric Poet in the Era of High Capitalism* (London: Verso, 1976), 176; quoted in Roger Silverstone, *Television and Everyday Life* (London and New York: Routledge, 1994), 24–5.

27 Tippett, '*The Mask of Time*', in *Tippett on Music*, 245–55 (p. 246).

28 Another twentieth-century cultural reference point might be variety performance, whose milieu was the music hall. But this would have been a less than probable historical archetype for Tippett – and indeed for most of his imagined audience for *The Mask of Time*.

29 Raymond Williams, *Television: Technology and Cultural Form* (London: Fontana/Collins, 1974), 86.

30 *Ibid.*, 93.

31 The durations given in this table are taken from the Andrew Davis recording of *The Mask of Time*. While these are of course not absolute, any variation between performances is unlikely to detract significantly from the argument being advanced here.

32 Puffett, 'Tippett and the retreat from mythology', 11.

33 Dillard describes at some length accounts given in Marius von Senden's book *Space and Sight* of the experiences of sight regained by blind patients after cataract surgery. 'A little girl visits a garden. "She is greatly astonished . . . stands speechless in front of the tree, which she only names on taking hold of it, and then as 'the tree with the lights in it'"' (Dillard, *Pilgrim at Tinker Creek*, 38). Dillard becomes fascinated by this possibility of regaining something close to absolute sensory experience of the world (see for example *ibid.*, 42); and indeed this has a fascinating resonance with Kant's account of the sublime, which is achieved, he says, by bracketing out teleological conceptual interpretations of our sense data, and seeing instead 'as the poets do, according to what the impression upon the eye reveals' (Kant, *Critique of Judgement*, part I, 122 (§29)). I return to this aspect of Kant in part III of this essay, below.

34 Ronald Woodley, 'Strategies of irony in Prokofiev's Violin Sonata in F minor Op. 80', in *The Practice of Performance: Studies in Musical Interpretation*, ed. John Rink (Cambridge: Cambridge University Press, 1995), 170–93 (p. 171). As Woodley goes on to point out, in the case of his object of enquiry – Prokofiev's Op. 80 – this is also 'a domain infinitely unattainable' (*ibid.*); and also relevant is Woodley's talk – made, significantly, with reference to Bakhtin (of whom more below) – of 'the necessity to decentre the subject, even if the longer-term strategy of irony is to liberate, transform and re-poeticise that subject at a higher, more "sublime" level' (*ibid.*, 172).

35 Alan M. Weinberg, *Shelley's Italian Experience* (Basingstoke: Macmillan, 1991), 212.

36 See *ibid.*, 217–18.

37 See the comments by O'Neill quoted on p. 153 above. Additionally, Donald Reiman writes: 'Everywhere in "The Triumph" the dark side of human experience is balanced by positive alternatives . . . whereas some mighty men were chained to the Car of Life, "the sacred few", faced by the same obstacles from within and without, had overcome Necessity to become the saving remnant of humanity. In the tale of his own experience Rousseau does not preach the irreconcilability of "power" and "will", only the great difficulty of maintaining one's integrity in a universe in which a vision of the Ideal makes one dissatisfied with the actual' (Donald Reiman, *Shelley's 'The triumph of Life': A Critical Study* (Urbana, Ill.: University of Illinois Press, 1965), 84).

38 Weinberg, *Shelley's Italian Experience*, 205.

39 Michael Tippett, 'Thoughts on word-setting', *Contemporary Music Review* 5 (1989), 29–32 (pp. 30, 31); originally published as the Conclusion to *A History of Song*, ed. Denis Stevens (London: Hutchinson, 1960), 461–6 (pp. 462, 464).

40 Richard Rorty, *Contingency, Irony, and Solidarity* (Cambridge: Cambridge University Press, 1989). See for example pp. 73–4: 'I call people of this sort "ironists" because their realization that anything can be made to look good or bad by being redescribed . . . puts them in the position which Sartre called "meta-stable": never quite able to take themselves seriously because always aware that the terms in which they describe themselves are subject to change, always aware of the contingency and fragility of their final vocabularies, and thus of their selves.'

41 See E. J. Trelawny's account of Shelley's cremation in chapter 12 of his *Recollections of the Last Days of Shelley and Byron* (London: Edward Moxon, 1858); and especially p. 134: 'The only portions that were not consumed were some fragments of bones, the jaw, and the skull, but what surprised us all, was that the heart remained entire'.

42 Tippett adopted a similar principle of ironic double voicing for the hallucinogenic deity Astron in *The Ice Break*.

43 Tippett applies this strategy of metrical ironization at several earlier points, for example in movement 2, in the jocular melismata prompted by the line (invoking Haydn's *Creation*) 'achieved is the glorious work': at moments such as Figs. 43^{+3} and 44^{+3} the previous $\frac{4}{4}$ metre is redivided into (or redescribed as) units of $\frac{3}{16}$.

44 Mikhail Bakhtin, 'Discourse in the novel', in *The Dialogic Imagination: Four Essays*, ed. Michael Holquist, trans. Caryl Emerson and Michael Holquist (Austin, Tex.: University of Texas Press, 1981), 259–42 (pp. 324–5).

45 Kenneth Gloag's valuable analysis of the problematics of the integration of the Negro spirituals in *A Child of our Time* could be seen also as an implicit discussion about the monological or dialogical status of the work. See Gloag, *Tippett: A Child of our Time* (Cambridge: Cambridge University Press, 1999), 71–88.

46 Bakhtin, 'Discourse in the novel', 325, 325–6.

47 I discuss these matters more fully in my essay '"Only half-rebelling": tonal strategies, folksong and "Englishness" in Tippett's Concerto for Double String Orchestra', in *Tippett Studies*, ed. David Clarke (Cambridge: Cambridge University Press, 1999), 1–26.

48 A point discussed at greater length in the following chapter.

49 See for example, Bakhtin, 'Discourse in the novel', 271–3.

50 In this regard a comparative study of the treatment of heteroglossia in Tippett and Mahler might be interesting.

51 Carolyn Abbate, *Unsung Voices: Opera and Musical Narrative in the Nineteenth Century* (Princeton: Princeton University Press, 1991), 11.

52 Edward T. Cone, *The Composer's Voice* (Berkeley and Los Angeles: University of California Press, 1974).

53 Abbate, *Unsung Voices*, 11, 13.

54 See n. 31, above.

55 This redistribution is achieved by stealth. In subsection A/c the chorus sings a wordless *jubilus* which assigns it to neither the poetic ego nor the framing narrative voice. Then in subsection A/d it sounds as an inner projection of the solo tenor voice: when the latter comes to sing of the 'trance which was not slumber, / was so transparent that the scene came through', his delivery stops transfixed on the word 'trance', poising on a sustained A, and the remaining text sinks ever deeper into the choral voices, as if emanating from the protagonist's subconscious.

56 The funereal associations of this music are evident from Tippett's own annotation to the bell part: 'like a distant passing bell' (given in the full score but not the vocal score). A later version of this figure at the beginning of movement 9, also based on the polarization of the pitches B and A♯, is similarly designated 'like a cracked passing bell' (again in the full score only).

57 A theme discussed at length by Leighton; see *Shelley and the Sublime*, 153–75.

58 This definition has intentional resonances with Roman Jakobson's 'poetic function', in which 'equivalence is promoted to the constitutive device of the sequence'. See Roman Jakobson, 'Linguistics and poetics', in *Modern Criticism and Theory: A Reader*, ed. David Lodge, 1st edn (London and New York: Longman, 1988), 32–57 (p. 39).

59 The passage between Figs. 263 and 279 of 'The triumph of Life' quotes music which first appears between Figs. 4 and 8 of Symphony No. 4.

60 *Triumph* (1992), Tippett's instrumental paraphrase of 'The triumph of Life' and other music from *The Mask of Time*, illustrates this point by omission. The piece for band flops precisely because it liquidates the boundary between music and language essential to its signification; the purely musical elements are not thrown into appropriate relief, and the formerly linguistic elements make little sense in purely musical terms.

61 Abbate herself borrows the metaphor from Suzanne Vill – a translation of the latter's term, 'Folie'. See Abbate, *Unsung Voices*, 149; Vill, *Vermittlungsformen verbalisierter und musikalischer Inhalte in der Musik Gustav Mahlers* (Tutzing: Hans Schneider, 1979), 251.

62 The form of the text quoted here is that from Tippett's libretto, which differs slightly from Shelley's original, not least in making an ellipsis after 'might'.

63 The main purpose behind this scheme seems to be the control of pitch content *per se*, rather than to establish the audible hierarchy between pitch centres which the quasi-Schenkerian notation in Ex. 5.2(b) might suggest. For while the putative higher-level motions do sometimes correspond to important moments in the overall texture – for example, the motion to F at Fig. 238 coincides with the goal tone of the chorus's first phrase; and the return to C♯ at Fig. 242 activates the dramatic entry of trumpets and trombones – many of the other formally decisive events of section D do not serve to project the implicit middleground structure of the bass line. As with many ground-bass move-

ments, the bass itself soon cedes its claims on the listener's attention, and becomes significant more for the cross-relationships and non-congruences it establishes with the texture above it than for its own particular attributes.

64 This passage sounds semantically and syntactically odd because Tippett omits the predicate of 'Shape' which follows in Shelley's original, viz.: 'and a Shape / So sate within as one whom years deform'.

65 The bracketed notes at this point in the analysis refer to implied pitches which are occluded, as it were, by the interjections of the tenor soloist: a dramatic analogue of the situation depicted by his words 'The crowd gave way, and I arose aghast'. The posited pitches are in fact confirmed when the material is repeated in the woodwind at Fig. 248ff. (the beginning of the third ground-bass cycle).

66 The quoted text is again the version from Tippett's libretto.

67 Though Tippett's arrangement of the text here involves a cut of some several hundred lines between the cry 'life!' (which in the original is uttered by Rousseau as his voice enters the poem) and this final question.

68 Whittall, *The Music of Britten and Tippett*, 5.

69 See David Clarke, *Language, Form, and Structure in the Music of Michael Tippett*, 2 vols. (New York and London: Garland Publishing, 1989), vol. I, 82.

70 The notion of the perfect fifth and tritone as, respectively, markers of consonance and dissonance resonates in certain respects with Whittall's consideration of the saliency of these intervals (and the binary opposition between them) in Paris's monologue in *King Priam*. See Whittall, '"Is there a choice at all?": *King Priam* and motives for analysis', in *Tippett Studies*, ed. Clarke, 55–77 (pp. 60–71, 75).

71 The alignment of note names between the upper and lower division of each box of Ex. 5.7(b) is intended to make this ambiguity legible.

72 We should not attribute too much significance to this aberration, especially since the chord itself is merely part of the progression between chords D and H, a variant of its more tractable forebear E from the preceding phrase. I would attribute this deviation to Tippett's almost reflex-like tendency to negate any overtly predictable patterning as he composed his material. This, then, is an example of 'black material': material resistant to conceptualization, a kind of analytical anti-matter. (I discuss this notion at greater length in chapter 7, below.)

73 The relationship between chords K and M can be expressed as R_1R_p in Allen Forte's terminology, as shown in Ex. 5.8(b).

74 Or, to borrow an idea from Christopher Mark, metaphorically equivalent. See Christopher Mark, 'Tippett, sequence and metaphor', in *Tippett Studies*, ed. Clarke, 95–116.

75 Or, in Fortean parlance, these two chords, K and C, have an identical interval vector, making them a z-related pair: set classes 6-z25 and 6-z47. (NB: the designation 'z' here has no connection with my own use of Z' to describe Tippett's major-triad-plus-lower-fifth construction.)

76 For example: 'The *narrating voice* . . . is marked by multiple disjunctions with the music surrounding it'; and 'A musical voice sounds unlike the music that constitutes its encircling milieu . . . it is defined not by *what* it narrates, but rather by its audible flight from the continuum that embeds it. That voice need not remain unheard, despite the fact that it is *unsung*' (Abbate, *Unsung Voices*, 19, 29).

77 Tippett, '*The Mask of Time*', in *Tippett on Music*, 246.

78 *Ibid.* As Leighton points out, Shelley himself was caught on the horns of the same dilemma. On the one hand he 'finds in the writings of Locke and Hume a description of the mind's relation to the outside world to accord with his own radical atheism'; yet on the other he 'is perhaps the first consistently unbelieving poet of the sublime' (Leighton, *Shelley and the Sublime*, 1, 24).

79 See for example, J. M. Bernstein's analysis that 'modernity is the separation of spheres, the becoming autonomous of truth, beauty and goodness from one another, and their developing into self-sufficient forms of practice: modern science and technology, private morality and modern legal forms, and modern art. This categorial separation of domains represents the dissolution of the metaphysical totalities of the pre-modern age' (Bernstein, *The Fate of Art* (Cambridge: Polity Press, 1992), 5–6).

80 As Bernstein also points out, it is for this reason that Kant holds a privileged position in Adorno's 'Meditations on metaphysics', the last part of his *Negative Dialectics*. See Bernstein, 'Why rescue semblance?', 187–94.

81 Tippett in his autobiography tells of 'the thrill of opening Kant's *Critique of Pure Reason*' (*Those Twentieth Century Blues*, 16); but there is no primary evidence that this led to any deep acquaintance with the contents.

82 As translated by A. W. Moore in his 'Aspects of the infinite in Kant', *Mind: A Quarterly Review of Philosophy*, 97, No. 386 (April 1988), 205–23 (pp. 208–9).

83 As quoted by Stephan Körner in his *Kant*, repr. edn (London: Penguin, 1990), 136.

84 Immanuel Kant, *Critique of Pure Reason*, trans. Norman Kemp Smith, repr. edn (Basingstoke: Macmillan, 1992), 638 (A 809/B 837).

85 *Ibid.*, 637 (A 807–8/B 835–6).

86 *Ibid.*, 638–9 (A 810/B 838) (emphasis added).

87 In *The Critique of Judgement* Kant asserts that while we can possess a principle (based on the idea of freedom) 'which is capable of determining the idea of the supersensible within us, and . . . also of the supersensible without us', this 'is only possible from a practical [i.e. moral] point of view. This is something of which mere speculative philosophy [i.e. theoretical reason] . . . must despair' (part II, 149 (§30/91)).

88 Kant, *Critique of Pure Reason*, 639 (A 811/B 839).

89 See, for example, *ibid.*, 639–40 (A 811–12/B 839–40).

90 *Ibid.*, 642 (A 815/B 844).

91 Kant, *Critique of Judgement*, part I, 120 (§29). The tension between these two

versions of nature corresponds closely to that expressed by Dillard in the quotation on p. 149–50, above.

92 Unlike his 'concepts of the understanding' which fulfil exactly this function of determining our rational relationship to the phenomenal world.

93 See Kant, *Critique of Judgement*, part II, 122–63 (§27/88–§30/91).

94 *Ibid.*, 120–1 (§26/87).

95 Discussed in the last section of chapter 3, above.

96 George Steiner, *The Death of Tragedy*, repr. edn (London: Faber and Faber, 1995), 8–9.

97 Adorno, focusing on what is aporetic in Kant's account, reminds us that ultimately the latter 'disdained the passage to affirmation'. See Theodor W. Adorno, *Negative Dialectics*, trans. E. B. Ashton, repr. edn (London: Routledge, 1996), 385.

98 *Ibid.*, 377–8.

99 Adorno, *Aesthetic Theory*, ed. Gretel Adorno and Rolf Tiedemann, trans. Robert Hullot-Kentor (London: Athlone Press, 1997), 132.

100 Kant, *Critique of Judgement*, part I, 179 n. 1 (§49). Tippett's source for these words is not altogether clear. Ian Kemp implies the composer came across the inscription by the circuitous route of Thayer's account of Schindler's report of Beethoven copying it from an essay by Schiller; but Kemp adds that Tippett did not at the time know that Beethoven kept these words on his writing desk. (Kant's name and the sublime are, incidentally, also invoked earlier in the relevant passage from Thayer.) See Kemp, *Tippett: The Composer and his Music* (London: Eulenburg Books, 1984), 229, 492 n. 90; and Alexander Thayer, *The Life of Ludwig van Beethoven*, 3 vols. (London: Centaur Press, 1960), vol. II, 167–8.

101 *Critique of Judgement*, part I, 94 (§25).

102 *Ibid.*, 106 (§27).

103 *Ibid.*, 120 (§29).

104 *Ibid.*, 110 (§28).

105 *Ibid.*, 111 (§28).

106 See Steven Z. Levine, 'Seascapes of the sublime: Vernet, Monet, and the oceanic feeling', *New Literary History* 16/2 (Winter 1985), 377–400 (pp. 380–90).

107 *Ibid.*, 397–8.

108 See Meirion Bowen, 'Dare, divining, sound: *The Mask of Time*', in *Michael Tippett O.M.*, ed. Lewis, 215–30 (pp. 229–30).

109 See *ibid.*, 223–4.

110 Kant, *Critique of Judgement*, part I, 122, 121–2 (§29). See also n. 33, above, referring to Dillard's account of present-day empirical findings in this connection.

111 Analogously, the oscillation between the sonorities O and P might be seen as a dramatization of the 'rapidly alternating repulsion and attraction produced by one and the same Object', which is how Kant characterizes the ambivalent

interplay of faculties ('a vibration') in the dynamic sublime. See *Critique of Judgement*, part I, 107 (§27).

112 *Ibid.*, 127 (§29).

113 *Ibid.*, 119, 120 (§29).

114 *Ibid.*, 127 (§29).

115 *Ibid.*, 122 (§29).

116 Paul de Man makes this passage key to his materialist reading of Kant. However, this claims a different materialist dimension than that presented here, one which rests on the argument that 'no mind is involved in the Kantian vision of ocean and heaven', and that Kant's metaphors connote 'an architectonic construct. The heavens are a vault that covers the totality of earthy space as a roof covers a house' (Paul de Man, *Aesthetic Ideology*, ed. Andrzej Warminski (Minneapolis and London: University of Minnesota Press, 1996), 82, 81). I can find no necessary grounds for this latter argument (for example, that the 'horizontal expanse [of the ocean] is like a floor', that 'the walls of heaven . . . close off and delimit the building' (p. 81)). And regarding the former argument, Simon Jarvis points out (in his reading of de Man's reading of Kant) that the notion of materialism as a 'perfected disenchantment' begs the question: 'Is it really only the "eye" and nothing else which "reveals" the ocean "as a clear *mirror* of water"? As "an abyss *threatening* to overwhelm everything"? Are these not themselves already ways of *understanding* the ocean, through a language whose figures and concepts cannot but be contaminated with human experience?' (Simon Jarvis, 'Old idolatry: rethinking "ideology" and "materialism"', in *Between the Psyche and the Polis: Refiguring History in Literature and Theory*, ed. Michael Rossington and Anne Whitehead (Aldershot and Burlington, Vt: Ashgate, 2001), 21–37 (p. 34).

117 Kant, *Critique of Judgement*, part I, 116, 125 (§29).

118 Bernstein, 'Why rescue semblance?' 206–7.

119 Adorno, *Negative Dialectics*, 365.

120 Kant, *Critique of Judgement*, part I, 111 (§28).

121 See, for example, Adorno, *Negative Dialectics*, 393, 404–5; *Aesthetic Theory*, 12, 105–11, 135–6.

122 Kant, *Critique of Judgement*, part I, 128 (§29).

6 The meaning of 'lateness': mediations of work, self and society in Tippett's Triple Concerto

1 Robert F. Jones, 'Tippett's atonal syntax', in *Michael Tippett* O.M.: *A Celebration*, ed. Geraint Lewis (Tunbridge Wells: Baton Press, 1985), 119–42 (p. 128).

2 Ian Kemp, *Michael Tippett: The Composer and his Music* (London: Eulenburg Books, 1984). Kemp divides Tippett's published *œuvre* of the time into four periods: 1934–52, 1952–8, 1958–76, and 1976–. It would not

be a gross violation of Kemp's presentation, however, to interpret this as two main periods – 1934–52 and 1958–76 – between which the period 1952–8 was 'transitional', and after which the period beginning in 1976 was 'late' – both Kemp's own designations.

3 Meirion Bowen, 'String Quartet No. 5', CD liner notes to *Tippett: The 5 String Quartets*, Lindsay Quartet (ASV, CD DCS 231, 1993).

4 Carl Dahlhaus, *Ludwig van Beethoven: Approaches to his Music* (Oxford: Clarendon Press, 1991), 219.

5 Only the minor *Caliban's Song* (1995) followed.

6 *Einfall*, radio talk, prod. Natalie Wheen (BBC Radio 3, 20 February 1995); broadcast prior to the transmission of the previous day's London première of *The Rose Lake*.

7 Published as Sir Michael Tippett, *E. William Doty Lectures in Fine Arts*, Second Series 1976 (Austin, Tex.: University of Texas at Austin, 1979).

8 I also return to them in the following chapter, in connection with another late work, *Byzantium*.

9 See *Doty Lectures*, 34, 1.

10 *Ibid.*, 45.

11 Kemp refers to these words as premonitory of a turn in Tippett's aesthetic values (*Tippett*, 402). Derrick Puffett goes further in quoting them as self-incriminating evidence on Tippett's part for an alleged 'sad decline' in the composer's capabilities after *King Priam* (see Derrick Puffett, 'Tippett and the retreat from mythology', *The Musical Times*, 136, No. 1823 (January 1995), 6–14 (p. 12)).

12 Tippett, *Doty Lectures*, 33, 33–4.

13 Tippett uses the term *Einfall* in his essay 'Archetypes of concert music', in *Tippett on Music*, ed. Meirion Bowen (Oxford: Clarendon Press, 1995), 89–108 (p. 107). Bowen also invokes Tippett's use of it, in the radio broadcast of that title (see n. 6, above). Elsewhere Tippett describes comparable moments of conception and the subsequent prolonged period of 'gestation', specifically with regard to the Second and Third Symphonies: see for example his sleeve notes to Symphony No. 2 (Argo, ZRG 535, 1967); Tippett with Bayan Northcott, 'Tippett's Third Symphony', *Music and Musicians* 20/10 (June 1972), 30–2 (p. 31); Tippett, 'Preface to Verses for a symphony', in *Moving into Aquarius*, 2nd edn (St Albans: Paladin Books, 1974), 157–9 (p. 157) (reproduced in modified form within 'Archetypes of concert music', 95–100 (see pp. 95–6)).

Interestingly, the term *Einfall* also features in Adorno's aesthetics, in which it is used to describe the 'irreducibly subjective' moment in a work's creation, mediated within the form of the work through the 'objective' process of thematic working out (see for example Theodor W. Adorno, *Philosophy of Modern Music*, trans. Anne G. Mitchell and Wesley C. Blomster, paperback edn (London: Sheed and Ward, 1987), 73–4 n. 31). Whereas for Adorno *Einfall* stands for a thematic idea which then enters a process of thematic

development, for Tippett *Einfall* may not be an already formed musical idea at all, and what follows creatively is described by him as a process of *accretion*.

14 Tippett, *Doty Lectures*, 44.

15 *Ibid.*, 45.

16 *Ibid.*, 44.

17 Arnold Whittall makes a similar point when he talks of Tippett's resistance to his earlier resistance to tonality. See his 'Resisting tonality: Tippett, Beethoven and the sarabande', *Music Analysis* 9/3 (October 1990), 267–86 (p. 283).

18 Tippett, *Doty Lectures*, 45.

19 It may be the case that the moment described in the *Doty Lectures* has more than one outcome. Its role as depicted here is in galvanizing an entire style period, but a further specific work which could be traced back to that moment is the String Quartet No. 5 whose slow movement is modelled on the *Heilige Dankgesang* from Beethoven's Op. 132; it is quite conceivable that this was the quartet movement to which Tippett referred (though he does not identify the actual work in question). Peter Wright makes a detailed comparison of these two movements in his 'Decline or renewal in late Tippett? The Fifth String Quartet in perspective', in *Tippett Studies*, ed. David Clarke (Cambridge: Cambridge University Press, 1999), 200–22 (pp. 212–20).

20 My use of the term 'slow movement' is to some extent mnemonic. As described below, the Triple Concerto is in one sense conceived as a single-movement work operating under a kind of cyclic principle; accordingly individual 'movements' have the status more of major sections. However, the relationship between these formal units and their counterparts in a more traditional archetype of the concerto genre is still quite recognizable; hence 'slow movement' is used here as a less ambiguous alternative to, say, 'slow section'.

21 Meirion Bowen, *Michael Tippett*, 2nd edn (London: Robson Books, 1997), 197.

22 A further twist, however, is that in Kemp's different formulation of lateness these features indeed are contributing criteria, adding greater provisionality to this ambivalence.

23 See Michael Tippett, *Those Twentieth Century Blues: An Autobiography* (London: Hutchinson, 1991), 258. Tippett also notes here that he had been lent a copy of recorded gamelan music by Aubrey Russ in the 1930s. It is probable that this informed his invocation of gamelan textures in the first movement of his Sonata No. 1 for Piano (1936–8). According to Mervyn Cooke this represented the first allusion to the gamelan in the work of an English composer; see his *Britten and the Far East: Asian Influences in the Music of Benjamin Britten* (Woodbridge: Boydell Press, 1998), 15.

24 Bowen, *Michael Tippett*, 200, 268 n. 9. The author cites Ex. 320 of the McPhee volume as an instance of the transcriptions to which Tippett

referred; see Colin McPhee, *Music in Bali: A Study in Form and Instrumental Organization in Balinese Orchestral Music*, repr. edn (New York: Da Capo Press, 1976), 337.

25 For an account of the relationship between Britten and McPhee see Cooke, *Britten and the Far East*, chapter 2. As Cooke points out (pp. 25, 27) the source of McPhee's to which Britten turned was not his *Music in Bali*, which was only completed long after the two had lost touch, but his two-piano arrangements, *Balinese Ceremonial Music*, which he and Britten recorded on a 78 r.p.m. set for Schirmer in 1941. Britten's relationship with McPhee is also discussed by Philip Brett in his 'Eros and orientalism in Britten's operas', in *Queering the Pitch*, ed. Philip Brett, Elizabeth Wood and Gary Thomas (London and New York: Routledge, 1994), 235–56 (pp. 237–8).

26 These motifs are drawn in particular from the hemitonic pentatonic subset of the scale, known as *selisir* in its Balinese version. The transposition of the pentatonic scale used by Tippett in the slow-movement melody, B♭–D–E♭–F–A, is exactly that used by Britten in parts of *Death in Venice* and in *The Prince of the Pagodas*; by Poulenc in his Concerto for Two Pianos; and by McPhee in the third piece of his *Balinese Ceremonial Music* (see Cooke, *Britten and the Far East*, 32). However, whereas in these instances the five-note set is centred on B♭, in Tippett's case the centre is F, providing the structurally salient flattened-seventh element, E♭, discussed above.

27 Stephen Collisson, 'Significant gestures to the past: formal processes and visionary moments in Tippett's Triple Concerto', in *Tippett Studies*, ed. Clarke, 145–65.

28 Arnold Whittall, *The Music of Britten and Tippett: Studies in Themes and Techniques*, 2nd edn (Cambridge: Cambridge University Press, 1990), 297.

29 *Songs of Experience: Michael Tippett at Eighty Five*, dir. Mischa Scorer (Antelope West Productions, 1991).

30 This compares with Christopher Mark's discussion of Tippett's 'metaphorical' use of musical materials, which 'stand for' their traditional functions, rather than actually realizing them; see his 'Tippett, sequence and metaphor', in *Tippett Studies*, ed. Clarke, 95–116.

31 This characterization converges in essence with Whittall's view of tonality in Tippett's later music, 'in which tonal extension and tonal contradiction coexist, and there can be no stable synthesis of these divergent tendencies' (Whittall, 'Resisting tonality', 283–4).

32 See, for example, the accretions for piccolos and E♭ clarinets above the cello 'song' at Fig. 66ff. of the slow movement; or the woodwind roulades over the long cello melody in the penultimate section of the fantasia-like finale (Fig. 169ff.). Embryonic versions of these procedures can be found still earlier, for example in *The Midsummer Marriage* (1946–52), at such places as the introduction to Act II (see Ex. 3.1, above).

33 Theodor W. Adorno and Max Horkheimer, *Dialectic of Enlightenment*, trans. John Cumming, repr. 2nd edn (London and New York: Verso, 1992), 32.

34 Alastair Williams, *New Music and the Claims of Modernity* (Aldershot, UK and Brookfield, Vt: Ashgate Publishing, 1997), 7.

35 See Jean-François Lyotard, *The Postmodern Condition: A Report on Knowledge*, trans. Geoff Bennington and Brian Massumi (Manchester: Manchester University Press, 1984), xxiii.

36 This reorientation within the sphere of art might in turn be seen to be par-alleled by developments within political discourses of the latter part of the century – whereby, for example, environmentalism, feminism and the poli-tics of race, ethnicity and sexuality have complicated, even deconstructed, the agenda of a progressive politics based principally on a critique of capital-ism and the class structures engendered by it.

37 Tippett, *Doty Lectures*, 51.

38 *Ibid.*

39 *Ibid.*, 52.

40 Tippett, 'Towards the condition of music', in *Music of the Angels: Essays and Sketchbooks of Michael Tippett*, ed. Meirion Bowen (London: Eulenburg Books, 1980), 17–27 (p. 26; see also p. 24); *Tippett on Music*, 7–15 (pp. 14–15; see also pp. 12–13). For further commentary by Tippett on European music's need to be aware of other global cultures see his 1958 essay 'Too many choices', in *Moving into Aquarius*, 130–44 (pp. 141–2); *Tippett on Music*, 294–306 (pp. 303–4). Moreover, Tippett kept faith with this notion of plurality right up to the end of his life, as is witnessed in his late essay 'Dreaming of things to come', in *Tippett on Music*, 307–9 (here his vision ultimately veers towards the theatre as the forum for such manifestations of pluralism).

41 See also the preceding chapter's discussion of social heteroglossia in relation to *The Mask of Time* (pp. 162–4, above).

42 Max Paddison, *Adorno's Aesthetics of Music* (Cambridge: Cambridge University Press, 1993), 60.

43 Noel Annan, *Our Age: The Generation That Made Post-war Britain*, repr. edn (London: Fontana, 1991), 375. Also quoted by Arnold Whittall in his '*Byzantium*: Tippett, Yeats and the limitations of affinity', *Music and Letters* 74/3 (August 1993), 383–98 (p. 398).

44 See Annan, *Our Age*, 375.

45 *Ibid.*, 377.

46 With these ideas I allude also to the 'theory of communicative action' of Jürgen Habermas – perhaps the most significant of post-Adornian critical theorists of the Frankfurt school. Habermas's theories stem from a recogni-tion of the need to reformulate the 'project of modernity' from within, in order to rescue it; this notion, as well as the period when it began to emerge (the late 1970s), invites interesting parallels with the issues under discussion in this and the previous section. See Jürgen Habermas, *The Theory of Communicative Action*, trans. Thomas McCarthy, 2 vols. (Cambridge: Polity Press, 1984–7). I have found Alastair Williams's discussion of Habermas and

others helpful in considering questions of music's situation after modernity: see Williams, *New Music and the Claims of Modernity*.

47 See Tippett, 'Archetypes of concert music', 101–3.

48 Theodor W. Adorno, 'Subject and object', in *The Essential Frankfurt School Reader*, ed. Andrew Arato and Eike Gebhardt (Oxford: Blackwell, 1978), 497–511 (p. 500).

49 The following account develops issues first raised in my article 'Tippett in and out of *Those Twentieth Century Blues*: the context and significance of an autobiography', *Music and Letters* 74/3 (August 1993), 399–411 (pp. 407–10). Meirion Bowen also takes up the theme of the relationship between Eros and creativity in Tippett (see his *Michael Tippett*, 245–7). This connection includes Bowen's only mention of Adorno, in which the latter is dismissed as representative of critics inclined to make 'specious and glib' parallels between such phenomena. While there are various grounds on which one might take issue with the latter, and while there is certainly much in the Tippettian mind-set that puts up interesting resistances to Adornian ideas, Bowen's characterization of Adorno – as one who used 'short-circuit methods that brush aside nuance and subtlety of reference, linking works of art to sociological or political ideas in the crudest possible way' (p. 247) – is simply factually incorrect. Paradoxically, it is the very sophistication of Adorno's thought – specifically his application of the concept of mediation – that holds out the potential to validate such connections and to evaluate them in a suitably nuanced way – as I hope to indicate below.

50 See Kemp, *Tippett*, 36–7; Tippett, *Those Twentieth Century Blues*, 52–63, 112.

51 Tippett, *Doty Lectures*, 11.

52 *Ibid.*

53 *Ibid.*, 12, 13.

54 For example, while the biography on which Kemp was engaged at the time would include the first authorized public reference to a specific gay romance – with the artist Wilfred Franks – mention of all other gay relationships would be absent or suppressed. Moreover, Tippett explicitly requested his biographer not to use the word 'homosexual' in his monograph (I am indebted to Ian Kemp for this information).

55 Tippett, 'Too many choices', in *Moving into Aquarius*, 138; *Tippett on Music*, 300.

56 *Ibid.*, in *Moving into Aquarius*, 140; *Tippett on Music*, 302.

57 Shostakovich is invoked in this connection in more than one of Tippett's essays; moreover, he and Solzhenitsyn are mentioned a number of times in the Doty Lectures – given shortly after the completion of *The Ice Break*, in which opera the resemblance of the character Lev to a figure such as Solzhenitsyn is barely concealed. These factors would seem to add further support to the argument advanced in part IV of chapter 4, above that the Cold War may well have been determinant in shaping Tippett's historical, personal and creative consciousness in the period of *King Priam* and beyond.

58 Paddison, *Adorno's Aesthetics of Music*, 23.

59 For a discussion of Britten's deployment of Balinese scale forms in *Death in Venice* see Cooke, *Britten and the Far East*, chapter 8; also *idem*, 'Britten and the gamelan: Balinese influences in *Death in Venice*', in *Benjamin Britten: Death in Venice*, ed. Donald Mitchell (Cambridge: Cambridge University Press, 1987), 115–28. Interestingly, the musical example from McPhee's *Music in Bali* which Bowen instances as one of the models for the pseudo-gamelan sounds in the Triple Concerto featured among the gamelan pieces which McPhee transcribed in *Balinese Ceremonial Music* and recorded with Britten many years earlier (see notes 23–4, above).

60 Brett, 'Eros and orientalism'.

61 As, for example, in Tippett's interview with Anthony Clare in the BBC Radio 4 series *In the Psychiatrist's Chair*, first broadcast in August 1986 (transcribed in a much shortened form in *The Listener* 116, No. 2973 (14 August 1986), 10–11); or his interview with Natalie Wheen in the Channel 4 television documentary *Tippett's Time*, dir. Deborah May (Phantom Empire, 1995).

62 Tippett, *Those Twentieth Century Blues*, 277–8, 1–2.

63 For Tippett's identification with Dov see his essay 'Dreams of power, dreams of love', in *Tippett on Music*, 220–7 (pp. 223–4); for his identification with the orphan state of Jo Ann and Donny see Bowen, *Michael Tippett*, 131–2.

64 See Tippett, *Those Twentieth Century Blues*, 227–43, especially pp. 231–3 and 242–3. The relationship with Hawker lasted from 1957 to 1974; Tippett also describes the clandestine beginnings of his relationship with Meirion Bowen in the mid-1960s, which became official after the break-up with Hawker.

65 The dream took place when Tippett was holidaying in Turkey in 1987; the composer also reports how in the same episode he awoke to sounds of the dawn *muezzin* which found their way into the main ensemble in Act II of *New Year*. See *Those Twentieth Century Blues*, 276–8.

66 Tippett, *Doty Lectures*, 45; emphasis added.

67 *Ibid.*, 44.

68 Encapsulated in his now well-known statement, 'Images of vigour for a decadent period, images of calm for one too violent. Images of reconciliation for worlds torn by division' (Tippett, 'Poets in a barren age', in *Moving into Aquarius* 148–56 (p. 156)).

7 The golden bird and the porcelain bowl: *Byzantium* and the politics of artefacts

1 Michael Tippett, *Those Twentieth Century Blues: An Autobiography* (London: Hutchinson, 1991), 274.

2 *Ibid.*

3 *Ibid.*, 271, 274.

4 T. S. Eliot, 'Tradition and the original talent', in *Selected Essays*, 3rd edn (London: Faber and Faber, 1951), 13–22 (p. 18).

5 Tippett, *Those Twentieth Century Blues*, 274.

6 *Einfall*, radio talk, prod. Natalie Wheen (BBC Radio 3, 20 February 1995).

7 Published as Sir Michael Tippett, *E. William Doty Lectures in Fine Arts, Second Series 1976* (Austin, Tex.: University of Texas at Austin, 1979).

8 See Arnold Whittall, '*Byzantium*: Tippett, Yeats and the limitations of affinity', *Music and Letters* 74/3 (August 1993), 383–98.

9 Cairns Craig, *Yeats, Eliot, Pound and the Politics of Poetry* (London and Pittsburgh: Croom Helm/University of Pittsburgh Press, 1982), 27. Craig also refers to Denis Donoghue's *Yeats* (London: Fontana, 1971), 121.

10 *Yeats, Eliot, Pound*, 26.

11 *Ibid.*, 28.

12 Tippett, *Doty Lectures*, 25–7.

13 As in 'Measurement began our might' (Yeats, 'Under Ben Bulben', IV). Tippett incorporates this line in the second movement of *The Mask of Time* (1980–2), and alludes to it in *A Child of our Time* (1939–41) with the line 'Man has measured the heavens with a telescope'.

14 Tippett, *Doty Lectures*, 29–30.

15 *Ibid.*, 10.

16 See for example *ibid.*, 10, 11.

17 Tippett, 'The birth of an opera', in *Moving into Aquarius*, 2nd edn (St Albans: Paladin Books, 1974), 50–66 (p. 55); *Tippett on Music*, ed. Meirion Bowen (Oxford: Clarendon Press, 1995), 198–208 (p. 201).

18 W. B. Yeats, 'Per amica silentia lunae', in *Mythologies*, repr. edn (London: Macmillan, 1962), 319–69 (p. 344).

19 See Craig, *Yeats, Eliot, Pound*, 26–64.

20 *Ibid.*, 183.

21 Pound would intensify this notion by considering the image as vortex. And Yeats, on more than one occasion, construes the Great Memory as a vast sea of images – as for example in the comment that 'our daily thought was certainly but the line of foam at the shallow edge a vast luminous sea . . . and in that sea there were some who swam or sailed, explorers who perhaps knew all its shores' ('Per amica', 346); as well as in the closing line of 'Byzantium' itself: 'That dolphin-torn, that gong tormented sea'.

22 Tippett, *Doty Lectures*, 10.

23 Yeats, 'Per amica', 345. This belief again informs 'Byzantium', and is especially evident in stanza 2: 'For Hades' bobbin bound in mummy-cloth / May unwind the winding path; A mouth that has no moisture and no breath / Breathless mouths may summon'.

24 Tippett, 'A composer and his public', in *Moving into Aquarius*, 94–100 (p. 100); *Tippett on Music*, 277–81 (p. 281). Moreover, some of Tippett's more arcane interests in and around the 1950s were probably fuelled by reading Yeats. The astrological notion of a world month entertained in the essay 'Moving into Aquarius' (in *Moving into Aquarius*, 35–42 (p. 35); *Tippett on Music*, 25–30 (p. 25)) may well be an echo of Yeats's discussion of solar

months and 'the great year' in books III and IV of *A Vision* (repr. edn (London and Basingstoke: Papermac, 1992)). For evidence of further Tippettian esotericism see *Those Twentieth Century Blues*, 215, and British Library additional MS 72037 (*c.* 1955).

25 Tippett, *Doty Lectures*, 51.

26 See for example Tippett, 'Persönliches Bekenntnis', in *Moving into Aquarius*, 117–21 (pp. 119–20); 'Aspects of belief', in *Tippett on Music*, 239–42 (pp. 240–1).

27 Yeats, 'Per amica', 331.

28 *Ibid.*, 334.

29 *Ibid.*, 335.

30 I discuss these matters in chapter 3, above. One might also conjecture whether Yeats's term 'mask' could be one aspect of the 'contemporary ironic ambiguity' which Tippett intends with the title of *The Mask of Time*. (See Tippett, '*The Mask of Time*', in *Tippett on Music*, 245–55 (p. 246).)

31 Tippett, *Doty Lectures*, 20.

32 *Ibid.*, 11. This last reference is probably to Eliot's 1919 essay 'Hamlet', repr. in T. S. Eliot, *Selected Essays*, repr. 3rd edn (London: Faber and Faber, 1976), 141–6. However, I have been unable to locate any reference by Eliot himself to the term 'black material'.

33 Tippett, 'What I believe', in *Music of the Angels: Essays and Sketchbooks*, ed. Meirion Bowen (London: Eulenburg Books, 1980), 49–55 (p. 51); 'Aspects of belief', in *Tippett on Music*, 237–9, 242–4 (p. 241).

34 Tippett, *Doty Lectures*, 10–11.

35 *Ibid.*, 11.

36 *Ibid.*, 19–20.

37 *Ibid.*, 11.

38 *Ibid.*, 38.

39 *Ibid.*, 21.

40 *Ibid.*, 39–40.

41 As outlined by D. J. Gordon and Ian Fletcher in their essay 'Byzantium', in *Yeats: A Collection of Critical Essays*, ed. John Unterecker (Englewood Cliffs, NJ: Prentice-Hall, 1982), 131–8 (pp. 132–5).

42 Yeats, *A Vision*, 270–1.

43 *Ibid.*, 279–80.

44 *Ibid.*, 140–5.

45 The scale and intensity of Yeats's struggle to resolve the poem's disparate ideas into a formal order is evident from studies of his earlier drafts; see for example Jon Stallworthy, *Between the Lines: Yeats's Poetry in the Making* (Oxford: Clarendon Press, 1963), 113–36; and Curtis Bradford, 'Yeats's Byzantium poems: a study of their development', in *Yeats*, ed. Unterecker, 93–130.

46 Craig, *Yeats, Eliot, Pound*, 196.

47 Yeats, *Autobiographies* (London: Macmillan, 1926), 241.

48 Yeats, *Memoirs: Autobiography – First Draft – and Journal* (London: Macmillan, 1972), 178; cited in Craig, *Yeats, Eliot, Pound*, 165.

49 *Memoirs*, 207; cited in Craig, *Yeats, Eliot, Pound*, 164.

50 Craig, *Yeats, Eliot, Pound*, 251.

51 T. S. Eliot, *Notes towards the Definition of Culture* (London: Faber and Faber, 1948), 48.

52 Richard Taruskin, *Defining Russia Musically: Historical and Hermeneutic Essays* (Princeton: Princeton University Press, 1997); see especially chapter 13 (pp. 360–467), 'Stravinsky and the subhuman'. See also *idem*, 'Back to whom? Neoclassicism as ideology', *19th Century Music* 16/3 (Spring 1993), 286–302.

53 Taruskin, *Defining Russia Musically*, 452.

54 *Ibid.*, 465.

55 *Ibid.*

56 See *Music of the Angels*, 85–96 (p. 88); *Tippett on Music*, 47–56 (p. 50).

57 Taruskin, 'Back to whom?' 297–8.

58 Tippett, 'Schoenberg's *Moses and Aaron*', in *Music of the Angels*, 100–8 (p. 100); '*Moses and Aaron*', in *Tippett on Music*, 39–46 (p. 39). *Idem*, 'The birth of an opera', in *Moving into Aquarius*, 64; *Tippett on Music*, 208. *Idem*, 'Too many choices', in *Moving into Aquarius*, 130–44 (pp. 143, 144); *Tippett on Music*, 294–306 (p. 305).

59 Taruskin, *Defining Russia Musically*, 461.

60 Quoted in Jahan Ramazani, *Yeats and the Poetry of Death: Elegy, Self-Elegy, and the Sublime* (New Haven and London: Yale University Press, 1990), 133.

61 Taruskin, *Defining Russia Musically*, 461. Michael Russ describes this view as 'voyeuristic' in his review of Taruskin's book, in *Music and Letters* 80/2 (May 1999), 307–10 (p. 308).

62 See chapter 3, above.

63 In *Those Twentieth Century Blues* (p. 46) Tippett writes: 'Jeff was much more affected by the ideas of Ezra Pound [than by T. S. Eliot] . . . I hadn't before encountered a political theory based on anti-Semitism and I was intrigued. The Jews figured as bankers, and Jeff observed that the banks always had the corner sites – the best sites in town. I found it all naive but fascinating . . . Talking to someone so different from myself . . . about my own ideas and artistic ambitions, provided a lot of stimulation.' Interestingly, Taruskin in his discussion of *Les noces* (see *Defining Russia Musically*, 390, 465) cites passages from an article by Mark in which the latter draws attention to the 'profound gravity and cool inevitable intention' of the folk singer (Jeffrey Mark, 'The fundamental qualities of folk music', *Music and Letters* 10/3 (July 1929), 287–91 (p. 289)). Other of Mark's comments on the alleged impersonality and emotional detachment of folksong renderings have resonances with the present discussion: for example, his claim that 'if the whole mass of so-called art music is . . . an evocation that is definitely subjective and psychological, the purest tradition in folk music, to some extent at least, is an objectification

of biological peculiarities in the culture that produces it . . . Hence it is that little that is personal can find a place' (*ibid.*, 287–8).

64 Tippett, *Doty Lectures*, 27.

65 Quoted in Tippett, *Those Twentieth Century Blues*, 128.

66 I have argued elsewhere that the cultural vision which Tippett describes (and its implied social correlative) is mediated in the structure of his Concerto for Double String Orchestra (1938–9); see my essay '"Only half rebelling": tonal strategies, folksong and "Englishness" in Tippett's Concerto for Double String Orchestra', in *Tippett Studies*, ed. David Clarke (Cambridge: Cambridge University Press, 1999), 1–26 (pp. 25–6). At the time of writing I had not considered the connection made here between Yeats and Eliot, and I suspect Tippett's vision was not identical to theirs in any case; nevertheless, the parallel is at the least suggestive.

67 Tippett, *Doty Lectures*, 52. A longer version of this passage is quoted and dis-cussed in chapter 6, above; see p. 225ff. Tippett also discussed this matter in a television interview with Bernard Levin ('What price Beethoven now?' *The Levin Interviews* (BBC2, 7 June 1980)).

68 See also my discussion in the preceding chapter of musical heterogeneity in Tippett's Triple Concerto (1978–9).

69 Boris de Schloezer (1881–1967), *Scriabin: Artist and Mystic*, trans. Nicolas Slonimsky (Berkeley and Los Angeles: University of California Press, 1987), 280, 284, 287 (quoted in Taruskin, *Defining Russia Musically*, 310–11). I am grateful to Iain Stannard for drawing my attention to this passage.

70 Derrick Puffett, 'Tippett and the retreat from mythology', *The Musical Times* 136, No. 1823 (January 1995), 6–14 (p. 11).

71 Ramazani, *Yeats and the Poetry of Death*, 152–61.

72 Whittall, '*Byzantium*', 391.

73 Daniel Albright, *Stravinsky: The Music Box and the Nightingale* (New York: Gordon and Breach, 1989), 4; quoted in Jonathan Cross, *The Stravinsky Legacy* (Cambridge: Cambridge University Press, 1998), 37.

74 Taruskin also discusses the octatonic properties of the Stravinsky chord and its connection with the pentatonic melody which sits upon it, in his *Stravinsky and the Russian Traditions: A Biography of the Works through Mavra*, 2 vols. (Oxford: Oxford University Press, 1996), vol. II, 1096, 1099.

75 Paul Driver, '*Byzantium* in Chicago', *Tempo* 177 (June 1991), 46–8 (p. 48); also challenged – on different grounds – by Whittall in '*Byzantium*', 395.

76 Tippett, 'Thoughts on word-setting', *Contemporary Music Review* 5 (1989), 29–32 (p. 30); originally published as the Conclusion to *A History of Song*, ed. Denis Stevens (London: Hutchinson, 1960), 461–6 (p. 462).

77 One of the most developed and rigorous explorations of this point has been undertaken by Anthony Pople (in an essay whose importance has so far gone generally unrecognized). Pople argues that Tippett's *Fantasia Concertante* (1953), through its gradual extension and transmutation of diatonic scale forms (or 'gamuts'), presents listeners with a 'rational, learnable, musical

metric (since "Man has measured the heavens with a telescope")' through which to comprehend the idiosyncratic tonal language generated from Corelli's initial diatonic premises. See Pople, 'From pastiche to free composition: R. O. Morris, Tippett, and the development of pitch resources in the *Fantasia Concertante on a Theme of Corelli*', in *Tippett Studies*, ed. Clarke, 27–54 (p. 53).

78 See Taruskin, *Defining Russia Musically*, 431–48, especially the summary analysis on p. 447. (In *Stravinsky and the Russian Traditions* Taruskin provides an even more extended analysis of the interaction of scale types in *Les noces* (see vol. II, 1383–422).) In Tippett's case, the 'Byzantium' chord and others like it in his later *œuvre* continue to embrace some form of upwardly generated root-plus-fifth structure, which countervails any extensive or systematic exploitation of the octatonic scale's symmetrical division of the octave. (Nevertheless, anti-diatonic symmetry is less than entirely absent from Tippett's thinking, as the minor-third based transposition cycles found in the central and final movements of the Third Piano Sonata (1972–3) testify.)

79 Whittall, '*Byzantium*', 395. With this reference I also bring my octatonic interpretation into a kind of equilibrium with Whittall's analysis of the chord as a higher consonance.

80 A subdued and mysterious echo of this image can be found in the music which opens *The Rose Lake*, also based on version O3 of the octatonic scale.

81 Whittall, '*Byzantium*', 391.

82 *Ibid.*, 390.

83 Tippett, *Doty Lectures*, 30.

84 Julia Kristeva, 'Revolution in poetic language', in *The Kristeva Reader*, ed. Toril Moi, repr. edn (Oxford: Blackwell, 1999), 89–136 (pp. 96, 93, 94, 125 n. 12; final quotation cited by Kristeva from F. M. Cornford's translation of the *Timaeus* (Indianapolis: Bobbs-Merrill, *c.* 1959)).

85 Kristeva, 'Revolution in poetic language', 105.

86 *Ibid.*, 108.

87 Helen Hennessy Vendler, *Yeats's* Vision *and the Later Plays* (Cambridge, Mass., and London: Harvard University Press/Oxford University Press, 1963), 117–18; also discussed by Harold Bloom in his *Yeats* (London: Oxford University Press, 1970), 392. See also F. A. C. Wilson, *W. B. Yeats and Tradition* (London: Victor Gollancz, 1958), 242–3.

88 Analysed by Whittall in '*Byzantium*', 386–90.

89 Kristeva, 'Women's time', in *The Kristeva Reader*, ed. Moi, 187–213 (p. 192).

90 *Ibid.*, 193.

91 See *ibid.*, 191–2.

92 Bloom regards the last five lines as 'one of Yeats's remarkable condensations, form[ing] an epitome of the entire poem' (*Yeats*, 392).

93 Quoted in Kristeva, 'Women's time', 211 n. 3; see also 191.

94 *Ibid.*, 191.

95 *Ibid.*
96 *Ibid.*, 193.
97 *Ibid.*, 194.
98 *Ibid.*, 209.
99 *Ibid.*, 193.
100 *Ibid.*, 209.
101 Whittall, '*Byzantium*', 391.
102 Julian Johnson, 'The status of the subject in Mahler's Ninth Symphony', *19th Century Music* 18/2 (Fall 1994), 108–20 (pp. 116–17).
103 Tippett's possible relationship with postmodernism is also considered in chapter 6, above.
104 For a discussion of this point (which includes a refutation of the criticism) see Kelly Oliver, *Reading Kristeva: Unraveling the Double-bind* (Bloomington and Indianapolis: Indiana University Press, 1993), 102–3. See also Kristeva's own account in her 1976 interview with Jacques Henric, 'On Céline: music and the "blunder"', repr. in *Julia Kristeva: Interviews*, ed. Ross Mitchell Guberman (New York: Columbia University Press, 1996), 229–34.

Bibliography

Abbate, Carolyn, *Unsung Voices: Opera and Musical Narrative in the Nineteenth Century* (Princeton: Princeton University Press, 1991).

Abrams, M. H., *The Mirror and the Lamp: Romantic Theory and the Critical Tradition* (Oxford: Oxford University Press, 1953).

Adorno, Theodor W., *Aesthetic Theory*, ed. Gretel Adorno and Rolf Tiedemann, trans. Robert Hullot-Kentor (London: Athlone Press, 1997).

Introduction to the Sociology of Music, trans. E. B. Ashton (New York: Continuum, 1989).

Negative Dialectics, trans. E. B. Ashton, repr. edn (London: Routledge, 1996).

Philosophy of Modern Music, trans. Anne G. Mitchell and Wesley C. Blomster, paperback edn (London: Sheed and Ward, 1987).

'Subject and object', in *The Essential Frankfurt School Reader*, ed. Andrew Arato and Eike Gebhardt (Oxford: Blackwell, 1978), 497–511.

Adorno, Theodor W., and Max Horkheimer, *Dialectic of Enlightenment*, trans. John Cumming, repr. 2nd edn (London and New York: Verso, 1992).

Annan, Noel, *Our Age: The Generation That Made Post-war Britain*, repr. edn (London: Fontana, 1991).

Ansell-Pearson, Keith, *An Introduction to Nietzsche as Political Thinker* (Cambridge: Cambridge University Press, 1994).

Augustine, St, *Confessions*, trans. Henry Chadwick, repr. edn (Oxford: Oxford University Press, 1998).

Bakhtin, Mikhail, 'Discourse in the novel', in *The Dialogic Imagination: Four Essays*, ed. Michael Holquist, trans. Caryl Emerson and Michael Holquist (Austin, Tex.: University of Texas Press, 1981), 259–422.

Ballantine, Christopher, *Music and its Social Meanings* (New York and London: Gordon and Breach, 1984).

Barthes, Roland, 'Réquichot and his body', in *The Responsibility of Forms: Critical Essays on Music, Art, and Representation*, trans. Richard Howard (New York: Hill and Wang, 1985), 207–36.

Bernstein, J. M., *The Fate of Art: Aesthetic Alienation from Kant to Derrida and Adorno* (Cambridge: Polity Press, 1992).

'Why rescue semblance? Metaphysical experience and the possibility of ethics', in *The Semblance of Subjectivity: Essays in Adorno's Aesthetic Theory*, ed. Tom Huhn and Lambert Zuidervaart (Cambridge, Mass., and London: MIT Press, 1997), 177–212.

Biddle, Ian D., 'Autonomy, ontology and the ideal: music theory and philosophical aesthetics in early nineteenth-century German thought', Ph.D. thesis (University of Newcastle upon Tyne, 1995).

Bloom, Harold, *Yeats* (London: Oxford University Press, 1970).

Bohlmann, Otto, *Yeats and Nietzsche: An Exploration of Major Nietzschean Echoes in the Writings of William Butler Yeats* (London: Macmillan, 1982).

Booth, Wayne C., *A Rhetoric of Irony* (Chicago and London: Chicago University Press, 1974).

Borthwick, Alastair, 'Tonal elements and their significance in Tippett's Sonata No. 3 for Piano', in *Tippett Studies*, ed. D. Clarke, 117–44.

Bowen, Meirion, 'Dare, divining, sound: *The Mask of Time*', in *Michael Tippett O.M.*, ed. Lewis, 215–30.

'String Quartet No. 5', CD liner notes to *Tippett: The 5 String Quartets*, Lindsay Quartet (ASV, CD DCS 231, 1993).

Michael Tippett, 1st edn (London: Robson Books, 1982); 2nd edn (London: Robson Books, 1997).

'Tippett's *Byzantium*', *The Musical Times* 132, No. 1783 (September 1991), 438–40.

Bowie, Andrew, *Aesthetics and Subjectivity: From Kant to Nietzsche* (Manchester and New York: Manchester University Press, 1990).

Bradford, Curtis, 'Yeats's Byzantium poems: a study of their development', in *Yeats*, ed. Unterecker, 93–130.

Brett, Philip, 'Eros and orientalism in Britten's operas', in *Queering the Pitch*, ed. Philip Brett, Elizabeth Wood and Gary Thomas (London and New York: Routledge, 1994), 235–56.

Bridgwater, Patrick, *Nietzsche in Anglosaxony: A Study of Nietzsche's Impact on English and American Literature* (Leicester: Leicester University Press, 1972).

Bronowski, Jacob, *The Ascent of Man* (London: BBC, 1973).

Brooke, Roger, *Jung and Phenomenology* (London and New York: Routledge 1991).

Brown, Peter, *Augustine of Hippo: A Biography* (London: Faber and Faber, 1967).

Burke, Edmund, *A Philosophical Enquiry into the Origin of our Ideas of the Sublime and the Beautiful*, ed. J. T. Boulton (London: Routledge and Kegan Paul, 1958).

Busoni, Ferruccio, 'Sketch of a new esthetic of music', in *Three Classics in the Aesthetics of Music*, trans. Theodore Baker (New York: Dover, 1962), 73–102.

Cairns, David, 'Tippett and *The Midsummer Marriage*', CD liner notes (Lyrita, SRCD.2217, 1995).

Campbell, Joseph (ed.), *Man and Time: Papers from the Eranos Yearbooks* (London: Routledge and Kegan Paul, 1958).

Chadwick, Henry, *Augustine* (Oxford and New York: Oxford University Press, 1986).

Chatman, Seymour, *Story and Discourse: Narrative Structure in Fiction and Film* (Ithaca and London: Cornell University Press, 1978).

Chua, Daniel K. L., *The 'Galitzin' Quartets of Beethoven* (Princeton: Princeton University Press, 1995).

Clarke, David, *Language, Form, and Structure in the Music of Michael Tippett*, 2 vols. (New York and London: Garland Publishing, 1989).

'"Only half rebelling": tonal strategies, folksong and "Englishness" in Tippett's Concerto for Double String Orchestra', in *Tippett Studies*, ed. D. Clarke, 1–26.

'Tippett in and out of *Those Twentieth Century Blues*: the context and significance of an autobiography', *Music and Letters* 74/3 (August 1993), 399–411.

Clarke, David (ed.), *Tippett Studies* (Cambridge: Cambridge University Press, 1999).

Clarke, John J., *In Search of Jung* (London and New York: Routledge, 1992).

Clayton, Jay and Eric Rothstein, *Influence and Intertextuality in Literary History* (Madison, Wisc.: University of Wisconsin Press, 1991).

Collisson, Stephen, 'Significant gestures to the past: formal processes and visionary moments in Tippett's Triple Concerto', in *Tippett Studies*, ed. D. Clarke, 145–65.

Cone, Edward T., *The Composer's Voice* (Berkeley and Los Angeles: University of California Press, 1974).

Cooke, Mervyn, *Britten and the Far East: Asian Influences in the Music of Benjamin Britten* (Woodbridge: Boydell Press, 1998).

'Britten and the gamelan: Balinese influences in *Death in Venice*', in *Benjamin Britten:* Death in Venice, ed. Donald Mitchell (Cambridge: Cambridge University Press, 1987), 115–28.

Cornford, F. M., *From Religion to Philosophy* (London: Edwin Arnold, 1912).

Coupe, Laurence, *Myth* (London and New York: Routledge, 1997).

Craig, Cairns, *Yeats, Eliot, Pound and the Politics of Poetry* (London and Pittsburgh: Croom Helm/University of Pittsburgh Press, 1982).

Cross, Jonathan, *The Stravinsky Legacy* (Cambridge: Cambridge University Press, 1998).

Crowther, Paul, *The Kantian Sublime: From Morality to Art* (Oxford: Clarendon Press, 1989).

Dahlhaus, Carl, *The Idea of Absolute Music*, trans. Roger Lustig (Chicago and London: University of Chicago Press, 1989).

Ludwig van Beethoven: Approaches to his Music, trans. Mary Whittall (Oxford: Clarendon Press, 1991).

Schoenberg and the New Music, trans. Derrick Puffett and Alfred Clayton (Cambridge: Cambridge University Press, 1987).

Daverio, John, *Nineteenth-Century Music and the German Romantic Ideology* (New York: Schirmer Books, 1993).

David, Hugh, *On Queer Street: A Social History of British Homosexuality* (London: HarperCollins, 1997).

Davies, Tony, *Humanism* (London and New York: Routledge, 1997).

Day, Aidan, *Romanticism* (London: Routledge, 1996).

De Man, Paul, *Aesthetic Ideology*, ed. Andrzej Warminski (Minneapolis and London: University of Minnesota Press, 1996).

'Shelley disfigured: "The triumph of Life"', in *Percy Bysshe Shelley*, ed. Harold Bloom (New York: Chelsea House, 1985), 121–44.

Dentith, Simon, *Bakhtinian Thought: An Introductory Reader* (London and New York: Routledge, 1995).

Detienne, Marcel, *Dionysos Slain*, trans. Mireille Muellner and Leonard Muellner (Baltimore and London: The Johns Hopkins University Press, 1979).

Dews, Peter, *Logics of Disintegration: Post-structuralist Thought and the Claims of Critical Theory* (London and New York: Verso, 1987).

Dillard, Annie, *Pilgrim at Tinker Creek* (London: Pan Books Ltd, 1976).

Driver, Paul, '*Byzantium* in Chicago', *Tempo* No. 177 (June 1991), 46–8.

Eagleton, Terry, *The Ideology of the Aesthetic* (Oxford and Cambridge, Mass.: Blackwell, 1990).

Easterling, P. E., 'A show for Dionysus', in *The Cambridge Companion to Greek Tragedy*, ed. Easterling, 36–53.

Easterling, P. E. (ed.), *The Cambridge Companion to Greek Tragedy* (Cambridge: Cambridge University Press, 1997).

Eiseley, Loren, *The Invisible Pyramid* (New York: Charles Scribner's Sons, 1970).

Eliot, T. S., 'Hamlet', in *Selected Essays*, 141–6.
  Notes towards the Definition of Culture (London: Faber and Faber, 1948).
  Selected Essays, repr. 3rd edn (London: Faber and Faber, 1976).
  'Tradition and the original talent', in *Selected Essays*, 13–22.

Epstein, Steven, 'Gay politics, ethnic identity: the limits of social constructionism', in *Forms of Desire: Sexual Orientation and the Social Constructionist Controversy*, ed. Edward Stein (New York and London: Routledge, 1992), 239–93.

Foucault, Michel, *The Will to Knowledge: The History of Sexuality: Vol. I*, trans. Robert Hurley, repr. edn (London: Penguin Books, 1990).

Freund, Elizabeth, *The Return of the Reader: Reader–Response Criticism* (London and New York: Methuen, 1987).

Furbank, Philip F., *Reflections on the Word 'Image'* (London: Secker and Warburg, 1970).

Garber, Frederick (ed.), *Romantic Irony* (Budapest: Akadémiai Kiadó, 1988).

Gloag, Kenneth, *Tippett: A Child of our Time* (Cambridge: Cambridge University Press, 1999).
  'Tippett's Second Symphony, Stravinsky and the language of neoclassicism: towards a critical framework', in *Tippett Studies*, ed. D. Clarke, 78–94.

Glover, Jonathan, *I: The Philosophy and Psychology of Personal Identity*, repr. edn (London: Penguin, 1991).

Goldhill, Simon, 'Modern critical approaches to Greek tragedy', in *The Cambridge Companion to Greek Tragedy*, ed. Easterling, 324–47.

Goldman, Albert and Evert Spinchorn (eds.), *Wagner on Music and Drama: A Compendium of Richard Wagner's Prose Works*, trans. H. Ashton Ellis (New York: Da Capo Press, 1981).

Goldmann, Lucien, *The Hidden God: A Study of Tragic Vision in the* Pensées *of Pascal and the Tragedies of Racine*, trans. Philip Thody (London: Routledge and Kegan Paul, 1964).

Gordon, D. J. and Ian Fletcher, 'Byzantium', in *Yeats*, ed. Unterecker, 131–8.

Graves, Robert, *The Greek Myths*, Vol. II, rev. repr. edn (Harmondsworth: Penguin, 1977).

Green, Lucy, *Music, Gender, Education* (Cambridge: Cambridge University Press, 1997).

Griffiths, Paul, *Stravinsky* (London: J. M. Dent and Sons Ltd, 1992).

Guthrie, W. K. C., *The Greeks and their Gods* (London: Methuen, 1950).

Habermas, Jürgen, *The Theory of Communicative Action*, trans. Thomas McCarthy, 2 vols. (Cambridge: Polity Press, 1984–7).

Haines, Simon, *Shelley's Poetry: The Divided Self* (Basingstoke: Macmillan, 1997).

Hammerstein, Reinhold, *Die Musik der Engel: Untersuchungen zur Musikanschauung des Mittelalters* (Bern and Munich: Frank Verlag, 1962).

Handwerk, Gary J., *Irony and Ethics in Narrative: From Schlegel to Lacan* (New Haven and London: Yale University Press, 1985).

Hanhardt, John G. (ed.), *Video Culture: A Critical Investigation* (Rochester, NY: Visual Studies Workshop Press, 1986).

Hark, Helmut (ed.), *Lexikon Jungscher Grundbegriffe*, 3rd edn (Solothurn and Düsseldorf: Walter-Verlag, 1994).

Harrison, Jane, *Themis*, 1st edn (Cambridge: Cambridge University Press, 1912); 2nd edn (Cambridge: Cambridge University Press, 1927).

Hegel, G. W. F., *Aesthetics: Lectures on Fine Art*, trans. T. M. Knox, 2 vols. (Oxford: Clarendon Press, 1975).

Henn, T. R., *The Lonely Tower: Studies in the Poetry of W. B. Yeats*, 2nd edn (London and New York: Methuen, 1965).

Hines, Robert (ed.), *The Orchestral Composer's Point of View: Essays on Twentieth-Century Music by Those Who Wrote It* (Norman, Okla: University of Oklahoma Press, 1970).

Homans, Peter, *Jung in Context: Modernity and the Making of a Psychology*, 2nd edn (Chicago and London: University of Chicago Press, 1995).

Homer, *The Iliad*, trans. R. V. Rieu, repr. edn (Harmondsworth: Penguin, 1981).

Hopcke, Robert H., *Jung, Jungians and Homosexuality* (Boston and London: Shambhala Publications Inc., 1989).

  A Guided Tour of the Collected Works *of C. G. Jung* (Boston and Shaftesbury: Shambhala Publications Inc., 1989).

Jakobson, Roman, 'Linguistics and poetics', in *Modern Criticism and Theory: A Reader*, ed. David Lodge, 1st edn (London and New York: Longman, 1988), 32–57.

Jarvis, Simon, *Adorno: A Critical Introduction* (Cambridge: Polity Press, 1998).

  'Old idolatry: rethinking "ideology" and "materialism"', in *Between the Psyche and the Polis: Refiguring History in Literature and Theory*, ed. Michael Rossington and Anne Whitehead (Aldershot and Burlington, Vt: Ashgate, 2001), 21–37.

John, Nicholas (ed.), *The Operas of Michael Tippett* (London: John Calder, 1985; New York: Riverrun Press Inc., 1985).

Johnson, Julian, 'Music in Hegel's *Aesthetics*: a re-evaluation', *British Journal of Aesthetics* 31/2 (April 1991), 152–62.

  'The status of the subject in Mahler's Ninth Symphony', *19th Century Music* 18/2 (Fall 1994), 108–20.

  'The subjects of music: a theoretical and analytical enquiry into the construction of subjectivity in the musical structuring of time', D.Phil. thesis (University of Sussex, 1994).

Jones, Robert F., 'Tippett's atonal syntax', in *Michael Tippett* O.M., ed. Lewis, 119–42.

Jung, Carl Gustav, *The Archetypes and the Collective Unconscious*, ed. Herbert Read, Michael Fordham and Gerhard Adler, trans. Richard F. C. Hull, Collected Works 9/1, 2nd edn (London: Routledge and Kegan Paul, 1959).

  'Archetypes of the collective unconscious', in *The Archetypes and the Collective Unconscious*, 3–41.

  'On the relation of analytical psychology to poetry', in *The Spirit in Man, Art and Literature*, trans. Hull, 65–83.

  Psychological Types, ed. Herbert Read, Michael Fordham and Gerhard Adler, trans. Helton G. Baynes, rev. Richard F. C. Hull, Collected Works 6 (London: Routledge and Kegan Paul, 1971).

  'The psychology of the child archetype', in *The Archetypes and the Collective Unconscious*, 151–81.

  'Psychology and literature', in *The Spirit in Man, Art and Literature*, trans. Hull, 84–105.

  The Spirit in Man, Art and Literature, trans. Richard F. C. Hull, repr. edn (London: Ark Paperbacks, 1993).

Kant, Immanuel, *The Critique of Judgement*, trans. James Creed Meredith (Oxford: Clarendon Press, 1952).

  Critique of Pure Reason, trans. Norman Kemp Smith, repr. edn (Basingstoke: Macmillan, 1992).

Kaufmann, Walter, *Nietzsche: Philosopher, Psychologist, Antichrist*, 4th edn (Princeton: Princeton University Press, 1974).

Kay, R. H., letter to the editor, *Gramophone* 65, No. 770 (July 1987), 147.

Kemp, Ian, *Michael Tippett: The Composer and his Music* (London: Eulenburg Books, 1984).

Kemp, Ian (ed.), *Michael Tippett: A Symposium on his 60th Birthday* (London: Faber and Faber, 1965).

Kirwan, Christopher, *Augustine* (London and New York: Routledge, 1989).

Köhler, Joachim, *Nietzsche and Wagner: A Lesson in Subjugation*, trans. Ronald Taylor (New Haven and London: Yale University Press, 1998).

Körner, Stephan, *Kant*, repr. edn (London: Penguin, 1990).

Korsyn, Kevin, 'Schenker and Kantian epistemology', *Theoria: Historical Aspects of Music Theory* 3 (1988), 1–58.

Kramer, Jonathan D., 'New temporalities in music', *Critical Inquiry* 7/3 (Spring 1981), 539–56.

  The Time of Music: New Meanings; New Temporalities; New Listening Strategies (New York and London: Schirmer/Macmillan, 1988).

Kramer, Lawrence, *Classical Music and Postmodern Knowledge* (Berkeley: University of California Press, 1995).

  Music as Cultural Practice, 1800–1900 (Berkeley: University of California Press, 1990).

Kristeva, Julia, 'Revolution in poetic language', in *The Kristeva Reader*, ed. Moi, 89–136.

  'Women's time', in *The Kristeva Reader*, ed. Moi, 187–213.

Kristeva, Julia with Jacques Henric, 'On Céline: music and the "blunder"', in *Julia Kristeva: Interviews*, ed. Ross Mitchell Guberman (New York: Columbia University Press, 1996), 229–34.

Lampert, Laurence, *Nietzsche and Modern Times: A Study of Bacon, Descartes, and Nietzsche* (New Haven and London: Yale University Press, 1993).

Langer, Susanne, *Feeling and Form* (London: Routledge and Kegan Paul, 1953).

Le Huray, Peter and James Day, *Music and Aesthetics in the Eighteenth and Early-Nineteenth Centuries*, 1st edn (Cambridge: Cambridge University Press, 1981).

Leggett, B. J., *Early Stevens: The Nietzschean Intertext* (Durham, NC and London: Duke University Press, 1992).

Leighton, Angela, *Shelley and the Sublime: An Interpretation of the Major Poems* (Cambridge: Cambridge University Press, 1984).

Levine, Steven Z., 'Seascapes of the sublime: Vernet, Monet, and the oceanic feeling', *New Literary History* 16/2 (Winter 1985), 377–400.

Lewis, Geraint (ed.), *Michael Tippett o.m.: A Celebration* (Tunbridge Wells: Baton Press, 1985).

Lidov, David, 'Mind and body in music', *Semiotica* 66/1 (1987), 69–97.

Lodge, David, *After Bakhtin: Essays on Fiction and Criticism* (London and New York: Routledge, 1990).

Lukacs, John, *A New History of the Cold War*, 3rd edn (Garden City, NY: Anchor Books, 1966).

Mark, Christopher, 'Tippett, sequence and metaphor', in *Tippett Studies*, ed. D. Clarke, 95–116.

Mark, Jeffrey, 'The fundamental qualities of folk music', *Music and Letters* 10/3 (July 1929), 287–91.

McCauley, Martin, *Russia, America and the Cold War, 1949–1991* (London and New York: Longman, 1998).

McPhee, Colin, *Music in Bali: A Study in Form and Instrumental Organization in Balinese Orchestral Music*, repr. edn (New York: Da Capo Press, 1976).

Mellers, Wilfrid, *Beethoven and the Voice of God* (London: Faber and Faber, 1983).

Messing, Scott, *Neoclassicism in Music: From the Genesis of the Concept through the Schoenberg/Stravinsky Polemic*, repr. edn (Rochester, NY: University of Rochester Press, 1996).

Moi, Toril (ed.), *The Kristeva Reader*, repr. edn (Oxford: Blackwell, 1999).

Monk, Samuel H., *The Sublime: A Study of Critical Theories in XVIII-Century England* (New York: MLA, 1935).

Moore, A. W., 'Aspects of the infinite in Kant', *Mind: A Quarterly Review of Philosophy* 97, No. 386 (April 1988), 205–23.

Morris, Pam, *The Bakhtin Reader: Selected Writings of Bakhtin, Medvedev and Voloshinov* (London: Edward Arnold, 1994).

Muecke, D. C., *The Compass of Irony* (London: Methuen, 1969).

  Irony and the Ironic, 2nd edn (London and New York: Methuen, 1982).

Murray, Gilbert, *Five Stages of Greek Religion* (Oxford: Clarendon Press, 1956).

Neumann, Erich, 'Art and time', in *Man and Time*, ed. Campbell, 3–37.

Nietzsche, Friedrich, *The Birth of Tragedy* and *The Genealogy of Morals*, trans. Francis Golffing (Garden City, NY: Doubleday, 1956).

  The Gay Science, trans. Walter Kaufmann (New York: Vintage Books, 1974).

  Thus Spake Zarathustra, trans. R. J. Hollingdale, rev. repr. edn (London: Penguin Books, 1969).

  Twilight of the Idols, trans. R. J. Hollingdale (London: Penguin Books, 1990).

  The Will to Power, ed. Walter Kaufmann, trans. Walter Kaufmann and R. J. Hollingdale (New York: Vintage Books, 1967).

Noll, Richard, *The Jung Cult: Origins of a Charismatic Movement* (Princeton: Princeton University Press, 1994).

Oliver, Kelly, *Reading Kristeva: Unraveling the Double-Bind* (Bloomington and Indianapolis: Indiana University Press, 1993).

O'Neill, Michael, *The Human Mind's Imaginings: Conflict and Achievement in Shelley's Poetry* (Oxford: Clarendon Press, 1989).

Orage, A. R., *Friedrich Nietzsche: The Dionysian Spirit of the Age* (London: T. N. Foulis, 1906).

Ornstein, Ruby, s.v. 'Indonesia, Bali, Music', in *The New Grove Dictionary of Music and Musicians*, ed. Stanley Sadie, vol. IX, 179–87.

Otto, Rudolf, *The Idea of The Holy*, trans. John W. Harvey, 2nd edn (London: Oxford University Press, 1950).

Otto, Walter F., *Dionysus: Myth and Cult*, trans. Robert B. Palmer (Bloomington and Indianapolis: Indiana University Press, 1965).

Paddison, Max, *Adorno's Aesthetics of Music* (Cambridge: Cambridge University Press, 1993).

Paglia, Camille, *Sexual Personae: Art and Decadence from Nefertiti to Emily Dickinson* (London: Penguin Books, 1992).

Philipson, Morris H., *Outline of a Jungian Aesthetics*, 2nd edn (Boston: Sigo Press, 1994).

Pippin, Robert B., *Modernism as a Philosophical Problem* (Oxford and Cambridge, Mass.: Blackwell, 1991).

Pollard, Rowena, 'From ancient epic to twentieth-century opera: the reinvention of Greek Tragedy in Tippett's *King Priam*', M.Litt. thesis (University of Newcastle upon Tyne, 1995).

Pollard, Rowena, and David Clarke, 'Tippett's *King Priam* and "the tragic vision"', in *Tippett Studies*, ed. D. Clarke, 166–85.

Pople, Anthony, 'From pastiche to free composition: R. O. Morris, Tippett, and the development of pitch resources in the *Fantasia Concertante on a Theme of Corelli*', in *Tippett Studies*, ed. D. Clarke, 27–54.

Pound, Ezra, *Gaudier-Brzeska: A Memoir* (London and New York: John Lane, 1916).

Puffett, Derrick, 'Tippett and the retreat from mythology', *The Musical Times* 136, No. 1823 (January 1995), 6–14.

Quispel, Gilles, 'Time and history in patristic Christianity', in *Man and Time*, ed. Campbell, 85–107.

Ramazani, Jahan, *Yeats and the Poetry of Death: Elegy, Self-Elegy, and the Sublime* (New Haven and London: Yale University Press, 1990).

Reiman, Donald, *Shelley's 'The Triumph of Life': A Critical Study* (Urbana, Ill.: University of Illinois Press, 1965).

Rieger, Branimir M. (ed.), *Dionysus in Literature: Essays on Literary Madness* (Bowling Green: Bowling Green State University Popular Press, 1994).

Robinson, Suzanne, 'The pattern from the palimpsest: the influence of T. S. Eliot on Michael Tippett', Ph.D. thesis (University of Melbourne, 1990).

Rodda, Richard E., 'The genesis of a symphony: Tippett's Symphony No. 3', *Music Review* 39/2 (May 1978), 110–16.

Rorty, Richard, *Contingency, Irony, and Solidarity* (Cambridge: Cambridge University Press, 1989).

Russ, Michael, review of Taruskin, *Defining Russia Musically*, *Music and Letters* 80/2 (May 1999), 307–10.

Samuels, Andrew, *Jung and the Post-Jungians* (London, Boston and Henley: Routledge and Kegan Paul, 1985).

Samuels, Andrew, Bani Shorter and Fred Plaut, *A Critical Dictionary of Jungian Analysis* (London and New York: Routledge, 1986).

Schafer, Murray, 'Michael Tippett', in *British Composers in Interview* (London: Faber and Faber, 1963), 92–102.

Schopenhauer, Arthur, *The World as Will and Idea*, ed. David Berman, trans. Jill Berman, repr. abridged edn (London: J. M. Dent, 1998).

Scorer, Mischa (dir.), *Songs of Experience: Michael Tippett at Eighty Five*, film (Antelope West Productions, 1991).

Scruton, Roger, *Kant* (Oxford and New York: Oxford University Press, 1982).

Selby, Keith and Ron Cowdery, *How to Study Television* (Basingstoke: Macmillan Press, 1995).

Shelburne, Walter A., *Mythos and Logos in the Thought of Carl Jung: The Theory of the Collective Unconscious in Scientific Perspective* (Albany, NY: State University of New York Press, 1988).

Silk, Michael and J. P. Stern, *Nietzsche on Tragedy* (Cambridge: Cambridge University Press, 1981).

Silverstone, Roger, *Television and Everyday Life* (London and New York: Routledge, 1994).

Sinfield, Alan, *Gay and After* (London: Serpent's Tail, 1998).

Singer, Peter, *Hegel* (Oxford and New York: Oxford University Press, 1983).
    Marx (Oxford: Oxford University Press, 1980).

Sorrell, Neil, *A Guide to the Gamelan* (London and Boston: Faber and Faber, 1990).

Stallworthy, Jon, *Between the Lines: Yeats's Poetry in the Making* (Oxford:
    Clarendon Press, 1963).

Steiner, George, *The Death of Tragedy*, repr. edn (London: Faber and Faber, 1995).

Stern, J. P., *Nietzsche*, repr. edn (London: Fontana Press, 1985).

Stock, A. G., *W. B. Yeats: His Poetry and Thought* (Cambridge: Cambridge
    University Press, 1961).

Stock, Brian, *Augustine the Reader: Meditation, Self-Knowledge, and the Ethics of
    Interpretation* (Cambridge, Mass. and London: Harvard University Press,
    1996).

Stockhausen, Karlheinz, 'Momentform: neue Zusammenhänge zwischen
    Aufführungsdauer, Werkdauer und Moment', in *Texte zur elektronischen und
    instrumentalen Musik*, vol. I (Schauberg and Cologne: Verlag M. DuMont,
    1963), 189–210.

Subotnik, Rose Rosengard, *Developing Variations: Style and Ideology in Western
    Music* (Minneapolis and Oxford: University of Minnesota Press, 1991).

Tanner, Michael, Introduction to Friedrich Nietzsche, *The Birth of Tragedy*, ed.
    Michael Tanner, trans. Shaun Whiteside (London: Penguin Books, 1993),
    vii–xxx.

Taruskin, Richard, 'Back to whom? Neoclassicism as ideology', *19th Century
    Music* 16/3 (Spring 1993), 286–302.
    Defining Russia Musically: Historical and Hermeneutic Essays (Princeton:
    Princeton University Press, 1997).
    Stravinsky and the Russian Traditions: A Biography of the Works through Mavra,
    2 vols. (Oxford: Oxford University Press, 1996).

Thayer, Alexander, *The Life of Ludwig van Beethoven*, 3 vols. (London: Centaur
    Press, 1960).

Theil, Gordon, *Michael Tippett: A Bio-Bibliography* (New York: Greenwood Press,
    1989).

Tippett, Michael, 'Air from another planet', in *Moving into Aquarius*, 43–9;
    Tippett on Music, 34–9.
    'Archetypes of concert music', in *Tippett on Music*, 89–108.
    'The artist's mandate', in *Moving into Aquarius*, 122–9; *Tippett on Music*,
    287–93.
    'The birth of an opera', in *Moving into Aquarius*, 50–66; *Tippett on Music*,
    198–208.
    'A composer and his public', in *Moving into Aquarius*, 94–100; *Tippett on Music*,
    277–81.
    'A composer's point of view', in *Moving into Aquarius*, 14–18; *Tippett on Music*,
    3–6.

'Contracting-in to abundance', in *Moving into Aquarius*, 19–27; 'The composer and pacifism', in *Tippett on Music*, 282–6.

'Dreaming on things to come ...', in *Tippett on Music*, 307–9.

'Dreams of power, dreams of love', in *Tippett on Music*, 220–7.

'Drum, flute and zither', in *Moving into Aquarius*, 67–84; *Tippett on Music*, 185–98.

E. William Doty Lectures in Fine Arts, Second Series 1976 (Austin, Tex.: University of Texas at Austin, 1979).

'*The Mask of Time*', in *Tippett on Music*, 245–55.

Moving into Aquarius, 2nd edn (St Albans: Paladin Books, 1974).

'Moving into Aquarius', in *Moving into Aquarius*, 35–42; *Tippett on Music*, 25–30.

Music of the Angels: Essays and Sketchbooks, ed. Meirion Bowen (London: Eulenburg Books, 1980).

'Music of the angels', in *Music of the Angels*, 57–66; 'St Augustine and his visions', in *Tippett on Music*, 228–36.

'Music and the senses' (unpublished essay, 1972).

'Persönliches Bekenntnis', in *Moving into Aquarius*, 117–21; 'Aspects of belief', in *Tippett on Music*, 239–42.

'Poets in a barren age', in *Moving into Aquarius*, 148–56.

'Postscript', in *Moving into Aquarius*, 163–7.

'Preface to Verses for a symphony', in *Moving into Aquarius*, 157–9 (reproduced in modified form within 'Archetypes of concert music', in *Tippett on Music*, 95–100).

'The resonance of Troy: essays and commentaries on *King Priam*', in *Music of the Angels*, 222–34; *Tippett on Music*, 209–19.

'Schoenberg's *Moses and Aaron*', in *Music of the Angels*, 100–8; '*Moses and Aaron*', in *Tippett on Music*, 39–46.

sleeve notes to Symphony No. 2 (Argo, ZRG 535, 1967).

sleeve notes to *The Vision of Saint Augustine* (RCA SER 5620, 1972).

'The stage', in *Tippett on Music*, 267–74.

'Stravinsky and *Les noces*', in *Music of the Angels*, 85–96; *Tippett on Music*, 47–56.

Those Twentieth Century Blues: An Autobiography (London: Hutchinson, 1991).

'Thoughts on word-setting', *Contemporary Music Review* 5 (1989), 29–32; originally published as the Conclusion to *A History of Song*, ed. Denis Stevens (London: Hutchinson, 1960), 461–6.

'A time to recall', in *Moving into Aquarius*, 101–7.

Tippett on Music, ed. Meirion Bowen (Oxford: Clarendon Press, 1995).

'Too many choices', in *Moving into Aquarius*, 130–44; *Tippett on Music*, 294–306.

'Towards the condition of music', in *Music of the Angels*, 17–27; *Tippett on Music*, 7–15.

'What I believe', in *Music of the Angels*, 49–55; 'Aspects of belief', in *Tippett on Music*, 237–9, 242–4.

Tippett, Michael, with Anthony Clare, 'In the psychiatrist's chair', *The Listener* 116, No. 2973 (14 August 1986), 10–11.

Tippett, Michael, with Bayan Northcott, 'Tippett's Third Symphony', *Music and Musicians* 20/10 (June 1972), 30–2.

Tippett, Michael, (and others) with Natalie Wheen, '*Einfall*', radio broadcast (BBC Radio 3, 20 February 1995).

Tomlinson, Gary, *Metaphysical Song: An Essay on Opera* (Princeton: Princeton University Press, 1999).

'The web of culture: a context for musicology', *19th Century Music* 7/3 (April 1984), 350–62.

Trelawny, E. J., *Recollections of the Last Days of Shelley and Byron* (London: Edward Moxon, 1858).

Turetzky, Philip, *Time* (London and New York: Routledge, 1998).

Unterecker, John (ed.), *Yeats: A Collection of Critical Essays* (Englewood Cliffs, NJ: Prentice-Hall, 1982).

Vendler, Helen Hennessy, *Yeats's Vision and the Later Plays* (Cambridge, Mass., and London: Harvard University Press/Oxford University Press, 1963).

Venn, Edward, 'Idealism and ideology in Tippett's writings', in *Tippett: Music and Literature*, ed. Suzanne Robinson (Aldershot, UK and Burlington, Vt: Ashgate, forthcoming).

Wagner, Richard, *Opera and Drama*, trans. W. Ashton Ellis, repr. edn (Lincoln, Nebr. and London: University of Nebraska Press, 1995).

Webster, Brenda S., *Yeats: A Psychoanalytic Study* (London and Basingstoke: Macmillan, 1974).

Weinberg, Alan M., *Shelley's Italian Experience* (Basingstoke: Macmillan, 1991).

Weiskel, Thomas, *The Romantic Sublime: Studies in the Structure and Psychology of Transcendence* (Baltimore and London: The Johns Hopkins University Press, 1976).

White, Eric Walter, *Tippett and his Operas* (London: Barrie and Jenkins, 1979).

Whittall, Arnold, 'Analytic voices: the musical narratives of Carolyn Abbate', *Music Analysis* 11/1 (March 1992), 95–107.

'*Byzantium*: Tippett, Yeats and the limitations of affinity', *Music and Letters* 74/3 (August 1993), 383–98.

'"Is there a choice at all?": *King Priam* and motives for analysis', in *Tippett Studies*, ed. D. Clarke, 55–77.

The Music of Britten and Tippett: Studies in Themes and Techniques, 2nd edn (Cambridge: Cambridge University Press, 1990).

'Resisting tonality: Tippett, Beethoven and the sarabande', *Music Analysis* 9/3 (October 1990), 267–86.

Williams, Alastair, *New Music and the Claims of Modernity* (Aldershot, UK and Brookfield, Vt: Ashgate, 1997).

Williams, Raymond, *Television: Technology and Cultural Form* (London: Fontana/Collins, 1974).

Woodley, Ronald, 'Strategies of irony in Prokofiev's Violin Sonata in F minor Op. 80', in *The Practice of Performance: Studies in Musical Interpretation*, ed. John Rink (Cambridge: Cambridge University Press, 1995), 170–93.

Wright, Peter, 'Decline or renewal in late Tippett? The Fifth String Quartet in perspective', in *Tippett Studies*, ed. D. Clarke, 200–22.

Yeats, W. B., *Autobiographies* (London: Macmillan, 1926).

    The Collected Letters of W. B. Yeats, ed. Allan Wade (London: Hart-Davis, 1954).

    Ideas of Good and Evil (London and Dublin: A. H. Bullen/Maunsel and Co., 1907).

    'Per amica silentia lunae', in *Mythologies*, repr. edn (London: Macmillan, 1962), 319–69.

    A Vision, repr. edn (London and Basingstoke: Papermac, 1992).

Index